Time
And
Relative
Dissertations
In
Space

Manchester University Press

D0061123

Time
And
Relative
Dissertations
In
Space

Critical perspectives on *Doctor Who*

edited by
David Butler

Manchester University Press
Manchester and New York

distributed exclusively in the USA by Palgrave

Copyright © Manchester University Press 2007

While copyright in the volume as a whole is vested in Manchester University Press, copyright in individual chapters belongs to their respective authors, and no chapter may be reproduced wholly or in part without the express permission in writing of both author and publisher.

Published by Manchester University Press
Oxford Road, Manchester M13 9NR, UK
and Room 400, 175 Fifth Avenue, New York, NY 10010, USA
www.manchesteruniversitypress.co.uk

Distributed exclusively in the USA by
Palgrave, 175 Fifth Avenue, New York,
NY 10010, USA

Distributed exclusively in Canada by
UBC Press, University of British Columbia, 2029 West Mall,
Vancouver, BC, Canada V6T 1Z2

British Library Cataloguing-in-Publication Data
A catalogue record for this book is available from the British Library

Library of Congress Cataloging-in-Publication Data applied for

ISBN   978 0 7190 7681 7   *hardback*

ISBN   978 0 7190 7682 4   *paperback*

First published 2007

16 15 14 13 12 11 10 09 08 07   10 9 8 7 6 5 4 3 2 1

Typeset in 10.5/12.5pt Minion
by Graphicraft Limited, Hong Kong
Printed in Great Britain
by Antony Rowe Ltd, Chippenham, Wiltshire

To Janet for sharing these adventures with me the first time round and buying 'The Deadly Assassin' in 1991 to start the journey all over again . . . . . . and the Whalley Range Time Team (Ben, Dan, Pete, Rob and Seb) – splendid fellows all of them.

'As we learn about each other so we learn about ourselves.'
(The Doctor, 'The Edge of Destruction', 1964)

Contents

List of figures

All images © BBC Worldwide

Note on titles, terms and structure

Any book that considers the early years of *Doctor Who* is faced with a contentious issue: what to call the first three stories? It is not until 1966 and 'The Savages' that the constituent parts of a *Doctor Who* story are referred to as 'Episode 1', 'Episode 2' and 'Episode 3', etc. (This format shifts to 'Part One', 'Part Two' and so on in December 1973 with the beginning of 'The Time Warrior'). For the majority of the programme's first three years, however, each episode would have its own title. So, the original four-part story, which began in November 1963, is made up of the following episodes: 'An Unearthly Child', 'The Cave of Skulls', 'The Forest of Fear' and 'The Firemaker'. But the 'umbrella' title for the first three stories is not agreed on. The first story has been referred to variously by its working title of 'The Tribe of Gum' and '100,000 BC'. For the sake of clarity, I have chosen to go with the titles used by the BBC for the respective VHS and DVD releases of these stories. So the first story is referred to as 'An Unearthly Child', the second as 'The Daleks' and the third as 'The Edge of Destruction'. References to 'An Unearthly Child' will specify whether they are discussing the first episode or the story as a whole.

References to archival documents from the BBC Written Archives at Caversham are noted as BBC WAC then the file number containing the document.

Throughout the collection, 'science fiction' is abbreviated regularly to 'SF'.

Details of films and programmes discussed at length in the chapters are included at the end of the book rather than in lists following each chapter as many of these lists would repeat the same data.

Acknowledgements

This project began in June 2003 following encouraging conversations with Matthew Frost and Christoph Lindner. Once in progress, the collection started life as a conference, held on 1 July 2004. I'm grateful to colleagues at the University of Manchester for their support in running the conference, especially Christine Grimshaw, Samantha Colling, Timothy Rogers, Viv Gardner, Karl Spencer and the Research and Graduate Support Unit for funding to enable us to invite international speakers. Above all, I want to thank all those delegates – speakers and non-speakers alike – who contributed to the conference and helped to make it such an enjoyable and (I hope) stimulating day. In particular, the help and support of Stephen Griffiths and Ian Potter in chairing the panels ensured the day flowed as smoothly as possible – even if we did over-run! Following the conference, the harsh task of selecting papers to go forward into the collection began – and it's not been an easy one. The limits of space and the need to balance topic areas have meant that several strong papers could not be included and I can only apologise to the writers in question.

Along the way, I have been extremely grateful at various times for the support of Peter Anghelides, Mark Ayres, Paul Cornell, Steven Duckworth, Simon Forward, Lincoln Geraghty, Peter Gregg, Lea Hays, Shaun Lyon and Joey Reynolds for spreading the word, Kate Orman, Nick Seidler and John Curtis (Earthbound Timelords and guardians of the fine online resource for academic work on *Doctor Who* at http://homepages.bw.edu/~jcurtis/home. htm), Darrell Patterson and Robert Shearman. Several of the chapters, including my own, could not have been completed without the generous assistance of Jeff Walden and the staff of the BBC Written Archives Centre at Caversham. The structure of the collection has also benefited greatly from the constructive suggestions of Catherine Johnson. I am also thankful to the School of Arts, Histories and Cultures' research support committee for funds to complete the book and to Matthew Frost, Jonathan Bevan, Alison Kelly and everyone at MUP.

All of the contributors to this volume have brought great patience and commitment to the project and it really has been a privilege to work with them. It is unfair to pick out any names but during the lengthy editing of the collection, which seemed at times like it had been cast into a recursion trap, I took great heart from the advice and encouragement of David Berezan, Emily Brick, Rajinder Dudrah, Maggie Gale, Vicky Lowe, Paul Magrs, Andy Murray, Andrew Pixley, Ian Potter, David Rafer, Dave Rolinson, Dale Smith, Simon Smith and James Thompson, all of whom have helped to lift the spirits when the slog was on.

I can't conclude this section without thanking all my students who have tolerated their tutor's love for *Doctor Who*. In particular, the 'Falstaff and Gandalf' class of 2003 and 'Art of Film' classes of 2004 and 2005 have been an inspiration in allowing me to try out my thoughts on the programme. In return, the ideas and suggestions of Jonathan Anelli, Abigail Anketell-Jones, Mark Astley, Martin Behrman, Stuart Brown, Stuart Burns, Ross Darlow, David Dickinson, Sapphire Goss, Matt Jones, Ally Khalid, Carys Lavin, William Newell, Lizzie Nurse, David Roocroft, Amy Ruffell and Sarah Spears have all enriched my work.

Last but never least, I must thank my family – who've been forced to watch an indecent amount of *Doctor Who* over the years but have done so with great humour (usually!). My Mum only has herself to blame for making me a stunning ninth birthday card in the shape of the K-1 Robot. My Gran, however, didn't care for *Doctor Who* at all – until the new series when she confessed that Billie Piper was great, even though 'I don't like all that space stuff'. If my Gran can revise her opinion of *Doctor Who* there's hope for academia and so this book is for her.

Introduction

David Butler

It's the last Saturday of September 2005 and, somewhere in the south of Wales, the owner of a battered, blue police telephone box (a disguised time machine that's bigger on the inside than the outside) is fighting the forces of evil and conformity. The mysterious alien known as the Doctor, time's champion and lover of adventure, is at work, just in time for broadcast on television early next year.

That's not quite how this book was supposed to begin.

The first draft of this Introduction was written in late 2004 as the long-awaited new series of *Doctor Who* was in production at BBC Wales, still half a year from its initial broadcast on 26 March 2005. The very first *thought* of this Introduction was in June 2003, five months before the original series of *Doctor Who* (1963–89) was to celebrate the fortieth anniversary of *its* first broadcast on Saturday 23 November 1963. Barring a one-off TV Movie in 1996, the show had been out of regular production for nearly fifteen years. The chances of new televised *Doctor Who* in the near future seemed slim.

The aim for this book, then, was for a collection of essays looking back on the original series of *Doctor Who* and its vibrant afterlife as a long-running series of comic strips, books, CDs, internet dramas . . . as a phenomenon of popular culture. In this respect, the book would be similar to Christoph Lindner's edited collection on James Bond (2003), which was due for publication later in the year.

And then . . . regeneration. In late September 2003, Lorraine Heggessey, then controller of BBC 1, announced that *Doctor Who* was returning. The media response was sudden and extensive – 'the most eagerly anticipated comeback in television history' proclaimed the front page of the *Daily Telegraph* (26 September) – but why?

As is usual with academic texts on popular culture I was already preparing my defence and justification for a book on *Doctor Who*. Why compile a collection of essays on a television programme that had been out of regular production since late 1989? Was this collection just a thinly-veiled attempt to legitimate my (and my fellow contributors') own fandom? In short, did *Doctor Who* merit detailed discussion as an 'important' cultural artefact? Surely, as Thomas Sutcliffe asked in his review of the first episode of the 2005 series, this programme was just a 'tea-time serial that had the production values of a wonky supermarket trolley and [wouldn't] raise a flicker of recognition from anyone under the age 35. Could it all possibly be worth it?' (Sutcliffe, 2005: 21).

Sutcliffe's summary of the popular perception, or memory, of the original series of *Doctor Who* raises interesting questions for Television Studies in terms of what is considered 'quality' and the status of genre or children's television (a 'tea-time serial') in relation to the canon and academic discussion in general. The academic study of genre television has benefited greatly in recent years from the attention of writers such as James Chapman (2002), Jonathan Bignell and Stephen Lacey (2005), Catherine Johnson (2005), John R. Cook and Peter Wright (2005) and Helen Wheatley (2006) but, for many, the 'cheapness' of *Doctor Who* and its status as a children's programme (I'll return to the programme's demographic later) might automatically preclude it from any discussion of quality television. How can we justify studying a programme with 'wobbly sets' and 'clunky' special effects? There's a disappointing emphasis on surface visuals here at the expense of an interest in, say, imagination, ambition and story, qualities that the best episodes of *Doctor Who* have excelled in (although there are plenty of *Doctor Who* episodes lacking in the very same qualities). Film Studies has already been here of course – as far back as 1951, André Bazin lamented people's preconceptions about the cinema's relationship to theatre and consequently how cinema should 'look':

> The cinema must be more lavish than the theatre. Every actor must be a somebody and any hint of poverty or meanness in the everyday surrounding contributes, so they say, to a flop [. . .] It is an inferiority complex in the presence of an older and more literary art, for which the cinema proceeds to overcompensate by the 'superiority' of its technique – which in turn is mistaken for an aesthetic superiority. (Bazin, 2005: 87)

Television and Television Studies has had to fight hard to overcome its own 'inferiority complex' or, if not suffering from such a complex itself, the prejudices of others toward the subject area, whether those prejudices come from within academia or beyond. 'It's just television': disposable ephemera playing in the background of our homes. But it's precisely the presence of television in our daily and domestic lives that makes it an important subject of study. We neglect an understanding of the ideas and concepts, images and sounds that we allow into our homes through television at our peril.

And to dismiss a 'tea-time' serial as being of no consequence is, to follow such an assumption through to its logical conclusion, to demonstrate a lack of care and concern for the stories and ideas that children consume. As Margery Hourihan states in her study of the hero figure in children's literature:

> Stories are important in all cultures. People have always used stories [. . .] to explain the behaviour of the physical universe and to describe human nature and society. They are the most potent means by which perceptions, values and attitudes are transmitted from one generation to the next. All teachers know the power of stories as educational tools. They are vivid, enjoyable, easily under-stood, memorable and compelling. They appeal to people of all ages, but for children who have not yet achieved the ability to reason abstractly they provide images to think with. (Hourihan, 1997: 1)

If nothing else, *Doctor Who* merits study as the source of a considerable body of stories 'told' to several generations of children in Britain and beyond. The qualities the Doctor relies on to overcome his enemies and the nature of the monsters and challenges he encounters are important messages being transmitted to developing minds. What traits are portrayed as virtues? What traits are coded as villainous and flawed? As Richard Jenkyns surmises in a brief overview of British children's literature in the wake of the success of J.K. Rowling and Philip Pullman:

> The triumph of *His Dark Materials* may tell us as much about the present time as *Eagle* tells us about England in the 1950s. Indeed, a popular children's book can be worth as much to the cultural historian as half a dozen sociological treatises. If you want to understand the spirit of an age, cherchez l'enfant. (Jenkyns, 2005: 43)

In his excellent book on fantasy film and social alienation, *Framing Monsters* (2005), Joshua David Bellin warns against the naïve perception of fantasy as being divorced from reality and therefore having no social relevancy, respons-ibility or function. Bellin is a fan of the genre, with his favourite film being the original *King Kong* (1933) (for Bellin, the 'greatest fantasy film of all' [2005: 24]), but he is also conscious of the film's troubling function as a vehicle for 'a pervasive and urgent early-twentieth-century cultural project to define and defend whiteness, a project that ritualistically found its fulfilment in the conjuring to life, and condemning to death, of a fantasised scapegoat: the black ravisher of white womanhood' (2005: 24). Bellin's project is thus to demonstrate that fantasy films are anything but 'pure' and that it is 'those cultural places that seem most benign or innocuous that must be most closely scrutinised for their part in harbouring widespread, malignant social attitudes' (2005: 2).

I mention Bellin's work not as the basis for launching an attack on 'malig-nant social attitudes' contained within *Doctor Who* (although this collection is far from uncritical of the programme) but to highlight the need to acknowledge the show's social function and that its stories, whether they have condemned or harboured malignant attitudes, are seldom innocent and free from social relevancy – regardless of authorial intent. The perception of what is a socially malignant attitude, of course, varies from viewer to viewer, and *Doctor Who* has accrued considerably differing responses and interpretations during the course of its lengthy run. Two reactions to the 2005 series are of particular interest here. *Doctor Who*'s return in 2005 was a remarkable popular and critical success (awards for most popular television drama, actor [Christopher Eccleston] and actress [Billie Piper] at the October 2005 National Television Awards were followed by three BAFTAs in May 2006, including best series) but not everyone liked what they saw. After the broadcast of the new series' first episode, 'Rose', the following messages were posted on a UK website:

> Is nothing sacred? The poison from the BBC continues to drip feed into our homes. I was one of the generation terrified to death by the Cybermen and the Daleks, I was hoping to pass on my enthusiasm for the sci-fi series to my two dear ones, aged 8 and 12 respectively. But lo and behold, the BBC uses any opportunity to force multi-culturalism down our throats. Now we have a Dr. Who assistant who has a black boyfriend. This is multi-cultural propaganda at its most pernicious. Hartnell, Troughton and Pertwee must be turning in their graves. (Mickey, 2005)

> I can't stand this country much more. Every day I get sickened by the sights that I am forced to see. Our town is getting more like Baghdad and Calcutta all the time. Not even in the privacy of my home can my family watch what goes for 'entertainment' these days without getting fed filth, perversion and multi-culturalism. Tonight my kids wanted to watch Dr. Who. Me and Clare are careful what we allow them to watch and we turned on to watch that mincing Graham Norton presenting some pornographic dancing displays [. . .] Then, if worse was to come it arrived in the form of a BBC steaming pile of rubbish with Dr. Who being involved in some kind of multi-racial family in some squalid part of London. This country is going to the dogs. (McCaskill, 2005)

Both of the above responses were posted to the British National Party's (BNP) online discussion forum within hours of the episode's broadcast. Yet, a matter of weeks later, the new series of *Doctor Who* was receiving just as heated a reaction from the opposing end of the political spectrum in response to its third episode, 'The Unquiet Dead' (broadcast 9 April 2005), set in Victorian Cardiff and featuring a race of aliens who deceive the Doctor into allowing them entry to Earth:

> 'The Unquiet Dead' is a story, made at a point in time when the big electoral issue is whether the British should put up with foreigners at all or treat them

like scrounging gypsies, about a bunch of REFUGEES – about a bunch of
ASYLUM-SEEKERS – who ask the Doctor for his help and then turn out to be
EVIL ALIENS WHO JUST WANT TO SWARM YOUR COUNTRY NYHAH
HAH HAAAAAH WE WILL RAPE YOUR WOMEN AND DEFILE YOUR
CORPSES.

   This is a programme that teaches children never to trust people who look a
bit weird, especially not if they're asking for sanctuary from a war that nearly
wiped them out, because they're obviously criminals playing on our bleeding-
heart compassion and will always stab us in the back. This is offensive, poisonous,
xenophobic shit. (Miles, 2005)

This review, posted to his own website by the writer Lawrence Miles (author
of some of the most formally radical *Doctor Who* novels), generated considerable discussion in the *Doctor Who* fan community. Although Miles
would praise later episodes (specifically 'Aliens of London') for their wit and
humanism and has since withdrawn his original review, acknowledging that
any anti-asylum seeker subtext in the episode was not intentional, his review
is still of great interest here. What interests me most is not whether *Doctor
Who* is really 'multi-cultural propaganda' or 'poisonous, xenophobic shit'
(although the opposing views here demonstrate the difficulty in applying any
one 'meaning' to a long-running programme such as *Doctor Who* with so
many producers, writers, script editors, directors and production contexts
[in short, 'authors']) but what the responses of Mickey, Pete McCaskill and
Lawrence Miles have in common. All three convey a strong concern for the
effect of *Doctor Who* on children – not in terms of the criticisms of *Doctor
Who* familiar to the original series' run (i.e. violence and horror) but more in
terms of the programme's ability to shape children's worldviews and values
(respect – or lack of respect – for 'others'). There's also a sense of each
response feeling betrayed by the programme and that the Doctor could and
should be a heroic figure embodying values one would hope to find expressed
by British society as a whole. The Doctor and his relationship to national
identity (whatever that might be) are of concern and the writers expect better
of him. In other words, for these viewers and many others, the Doctor *matters*.

   How did the programme get to this stage? This collection does not focus
on the new series but addresses instead the original twenty-six-year run of
Doctor Who and its survival throughout the 1990s in other forms of media
prior to the programme's return to television in 2005. The first extended
academic study of *Doctor Who* was Manuel Alvarado and John Tulloch's
The Unfolding Text, published in 1983, but much has happened to the show
since then. When *The Unfolding Text* was written *Doctor Who* was building
up to its twentieth-anniversary celebrations, had just enjoyed a season of
improved audience ratings and seemed secure in its status as a scheduling
fixture. *The Unfolding Text* closed with the programme looking forward to the

years ahead. As anyone familiar with the history of *Doctor Who* now knows, however, those years would be troubled and the programme was entering one of its most turbulent periods (for some, this period of decline had already begun earlier than 1983), leading to an eighteen-month hiatus in 1985, dwindling ratings and an unofficial 'cancellation' following the last episode of 'Survival' in December 1989, just as the programme was experiencing a creative renaissance. BBC statements suggested that *Doctor Who* was merely resting and had not been axed. As one of the most familiar statements regarding the programme's limbo status during the early and mid-1990s put it:

> There is no question of *Doctor Who* being abandoned. It is still an important programme and when the time is right it should return. However, the show's popularity over the years has waned in the UK, with an average audience of 4 million. A decision was taken to rest the programme for an extended period so that when it returns it will be seen as a fresh, inventive and vibrant addition to the schedule – rather than a battle-weary Time Lord languishing in the back-waters of audience popularity. *Doctor Who* is too valuable a property for us to relaunch until we are absolutely confident of it as a major success once again. (in Segal and Russell, 2000: 6)

If the programme was felt to be 'languishing in the back-waters of audience popularity' one might have expected it to fade from audience memory the longer it ceased to be in regular production after the 1989 season. *Doctor Who* would go the way of other childhood favourites and be packed away with fondness by some and embarrassment by others. Except that didn't happen. A one-off US co-produced TV movie was released in 1996 but there were two other incidents during the 1990s and early 2000s that I'd suggest were more revealing of a growing awareness of *Doctor Who*'s cultural importance.

In 1996, the BBC held its sixtieth anniversary celebrations with the 'Auntie Awards' to find the 'all-time' favourite BBC programmes and performers in various categories. The shortlist of programmes was drawn up by BBC programme-makers but the final votes were cast by the British public. Despite having been out of regular production for seven years, *Doctor Who* won in the category of favourite popular drama programme, beating then current ratings giants such as *EastEnders* (1985–) and *Casualty* (1986–). This result was more than a little embarrassing for the BBC and several cynical explanations for the victory by on-looking commentators suggested that *Doctor Who* had only won because hardcore fans had organised a mass phone-in to ensure their favourite programme would win. Whether this was true or not (I phoned in spontaneously with my vote for *Doctor Who* and can honestly report that there was nobody in a Cyberman costume standing behind me with a plastic blaster gun at my head in case I blurted out '*All Creatures Great and Small*' in a fit of madness) the significant point was missed: that despite its tremendous ratings success, a programme such as *EastEnders* could not generate quite the same warmth and affection among its viewers to encourage enough of them to care about voting for it, whereas *Doctor Who* could.

A more objective and less easily dismissed acknowledgement of *Doctor Who*'s status as a programme of quality and significance (in spite – or maybe in part because – of its perceived 'wonky' production values) was the British Film Institute's 2000 survey to establish the one hundred greatest British television programmes of all time. The BFI poll was made up of the votes of over 1,600 individuals involved with the television industry (programme makers, executives, writers, critics, academics) and the results were revealing.[1] *Doctor Who* came first in the children's television section and third in the overall poll for the greatest programme regardless of category, behind *Fawlty Towers* (1975, 1979) and 'Cathy Come Home' (1966) from *The Wednesday Play* (1964–70). This result seemed to suggest there was something more at work here than mere nostalgia for a childhood favourite. Several years later in early 2003, the *Guardian* ran a piece on 'The new breed of television' (McLean, Catterall and Raeside 2003), which profiled figures in the vanguard of British television, including the acclaimed writer Stephen Poliakoff. Asked to name his 'favourite TV ever', Poliakoff cited the first series of *Doctor Who*. This shift in the acknowledgement of *Doctor Who* as quality television seemed complete following the 2005 series, spearheaded by the writer Russell T. Davies. Writing for *Prospect* in his 'Smallscreen' column, David Herman offered an overview of the previous ten years of British television and noted that there had been a decline and general 'dumbing down' of programme content with some notable exceptions, including *Doctor Who*:

> The dumbing down, though, has been uneven. There is plenty of intelligent programming: political analysis by Andrew Marr [. . .] *The West Wing* and *Scrubs*; cricket coverage on Channel 4; *The South Bank Show* and Melvyn Bragg's series on [. . .] Christianity; *Doctor Who* and documentary series like Adam Curtis' *Pandora's Box* [. . .] *The Power of Nightmares*; BBC 4's output [. . .] This is impressive – as good as anything put out ten years ago. It doesn't mean, however, that television has not dumbed down. (Herman, 2005: 85)

If *Doctor Who* is to be considered a piece of 'quality' television and welcomed into the canon of important programmes (as it has been via Matt Hills' entry for the show in Glen Creeber's *Fifty Key Television Programmes* [2004]), what are the particular qualities it possesses?

As Alan McKee's essay in this collection notes, *Doctor Who* fans love to argue about what aspects and eras of the programme are the best, and the contributors to this book are no different. (The last thing this book seeks to do is impose a conformity onto interpretations of *Doctor Who* and one of the delights for me in editing the collection has been encountering a diverse range of opinions on what makes 'good' *Doctor Who*: it is this openness to diversity and change that is one of the great strengths of the programme.) At the risk of abusing my editorial privilege, however, I'd like to suggest some of the reasons why I think *Doctor Who* is a remarkable programme meriting study and analysis.

What makes *Doctor Who* particularly notable, and has perhaps enabled it to last so long, is its blurring of boundaries. *Doctor Who* has defied easy classification but one of its greatest gifts has been to the imagination by transforming the ordinary into the extraordinary, the earthly into something *un*earthly – be that a telephone box, a sink plunger, a shop dummy or a nearby quarry. As children, *Doctor Who* encouraged us to reinvest the everyday with a sense of wonder (or terror). I'm guided here by Tolkien's essay 'On Fairy Stories' in which he addresses the value of fantasy in our lives. For Tolkien, one of the most profound effects of fantasy and fairy stories is the way we are encouraged to look again at the familiar world with renewed respect and wonder. Rather than taking the world around us for granted we should learn to see it again as something filled with possibility:

> We should meet the centaur and the dragon, and then perhaps suddenly behold, like the ancient shepherds, sheep and dogs, and horses – and wolves. (Tolkien, 2001: 57)

Doctor Who has the potential to function in a similar way. By taking recognisable objects and locations (forced upon it by a low budget) but giving them a twist of the uncanny or the bizarre, *Doctor Who* encouraged us to re-view the ordinary and not take surface impressions for granted. This is not necessarily a running away from the world but can be a means of re-engaging with it. I'd caution (as Bellin does) against a facile interpretation of fantasy or science fiction as being nothing more than harmless escapism with no meaningful relation to the 'real' world. Tolkien warns against confusing the 'flight of the deserter with the escape of the prisoner' (2001: 61). I can only speak from personal experience here, and hope that the reader is willing to indulge me, but as a young child attempting to come to terms with his parents' separation and divorce, *Doctor Who* provided me with the perfect metaphor to make sense of the changes to my known world. As my parents separated in 1984, Peter Davison's kind and gentle Fifth Doctor regenerated into Colin Baker's brash and abrasive Sixth Doctor. At first I felt betrayed – who was this strange new man who'd replaced my hero? How dare he! In time, of course, I came to accept that, underneath the surface changes, this new Doctor was still the same hero as before and just as deserving of my support as his predecessor – people change, was the lesson, but that didn't necessarily mean they stopped caring about us underneath.

Regeneration, then, became a metaphor for divorce and step-fathers – not a denial and running away from the world, to a safe place where the Doctor always wins (he doesn't), but a means of coming to terms with and accepting it. I am not, of course, claiming that *Doctor Who* has this effect for all its viewers (children or otherwise) but the programme's *potential* to stimulate metaphorical thinking is substantial.

Doctor Who has also endured through its ability to blur generic boundaries. The programme has shifted between science fiction, horror, mystery, costume drama, comedy, pantomime and the fantastic (sometimes within a single story) but at its core is the generic dominant of adventure. As I argue later, the prevailing perception of *Doctor Who* may be as a science fiction programme but it has thrived most when it has resisted indulging the science fiction impulse too much (particularly in its 'launch' episodes, 'An Unearthly Child' and 'Rose'). Mystery, imagination and adventure propel the best *Doctor Who* narratives forward. As Robert Louis Stevenson observed of the Arabian Nights, 'Adventure, on the most naked terms, furnishes forth the entertainment and is found enough' (Stevenson, 2002: 160).

The most important blurring of boundaries in *Doctor Who*, however, is the boundary between children's drama and adult drama. The finest *Doctor Who* stories offer storytelling and elements that appeal, respectively or not, to young children, teenagers and adults, all in the same episode. One of the most astute observations about the reasons for *Doctor Who*'s success is from Tom Baker, the Fourth Doctor, and his identification of the programme's ability to cut across generational divides:

> *Doctor Who* is watched at several levels on an average household. The smallest child terrified behind a sofa or under a cushion, and the next one up laughing at him, and the elder one saying 'Shh! I want to listen!', and the parents saying 'Isn't this enjoyable?'! (*More Than Thirty Years in the TARDIS*, 1994)

This appeal to a family audience has been one of the most-quoted triumphs of the 2005 series of *Doctor Who*. Toward the end of the series' run, David Lister, in his 'The week in arts' column for *The Independent*, reported that television executives were already celebrating *Doctor Who*'s resurrection of family evening viewing:

> The successful return of *Doctor Who*, which notches up the 10th episode in the current series tonight, is being hailed as the catalyst for a more unlikely return, the return of family viewing [. . .] Television executives have long told us that families don't watch together any more [. . .] family viewing (and consequently family programming) [was] declared obsolete. Even the writer of the current *Doctor Who*, Russell T Davies, was worried. He told one newspaper this week: 'I lived in fear that the family audience had disappeared. A demographics expert told me that it did not exist because children have television sets in their

bedrooms and are embarrassed to be watching the same programmes as their parents. We could have been dead in the water. I was ready for *Doctor Who* to fail'. It didn't, and one happy result is that programmers are thinking once more about what constitutes family viewing. (Lister, 2005: 41)

By the end of the new series' run, with Christopher Eccleston's Ninth Doctor regenerated into a tenth incarnation played by David Tennant, the perception of *Doctor Who*'s recovery of the family audience was widespread. Greg Dyke, former Director-General of the BBC, in a piece titled 'Doctor Who's greatest triumph – the return of TV for all the family', was fulsome in his praise and noted that the programme had demonstrated 'that it is still possible to use a family drama series to build a Saturday night schedule' (Dyke, 2005: 14). More succinct was the series overview provided by Charlie Brooker, in his often caustic 'Screen burn' column for *The Guardian*: 'Best. BBC. Family. Drama. Series. Ever' (Brooker, 2005). By bringing children, teenagers and adults together, layering the stories so that there is something for everybody within an episode (when it is at its very best), *Doctor Who* offers the possibility of the great television dramatist Dennis Potter's dream of a collective experience of television, a television culture that brings audiences together rather than dividing them into focus-group-defined separation. There is something hopeful, even utopian, in this bringing together of young and old and it's here that much of the fondness for *Doctor Who* is nurtured and its longevity assured.

How, then, do you begin to tell the story of *Doctor Who*? You could chart the fortunes of the programme alongside those of the BBC as a whole. *Doctor Who* begins in 1963 as a key part of Sydney Newman's mission to develop popular but intelligent programming at the BBC and, indeed, gave the BBC one of its first major popular successes: the popularity of the Daleks (discussed at length by Jonathan Bignell later) and their related merchandising frenzy ('Dalek mania') were crucial in the development of the corporation's merchandising division (what would become, in time, BBC Enterprises then BBC Worldwide). Into the 1970s and, by 1977, Melvyn Bragg could step out of the doors of the TARDIS and announce in a documentary that *Doctor Who* was a 'national institution'.[2] By now *Doctor Who* was a vital component in BBC 1's domination of the Saturday evening schedules, providing a bridge to the family programming of shows such as *The Generation Game* (1971–81, 1990–2002) and *The Two Ronnies* (1971–86), which, in turn, would lead into *Parkinson* (1971–82, 1998–) and *Match of the Day* (1964–): an overall package of viewing that would provide the BBC with one of its greatest periods of sustained ratings success. Even in its absence from the television schedules after 1989, *Doctor Who* could still be invoked as a metaphor for the state of the BBC. In his attack on the then current BBC Director-General,

John Birt, and his doctrine of producer choice at the Edinburgh Television Festival in August 1993, Dennis Potter would summon up the name of the Doctor's arch-enemies in branding Birt a 'croak-voiced Dalek' and a threat to public-service broadcasting. If the Doctor represented a creative and maverick spirit then the Daleks represented homogenous and conformist thinking and were an effective metaphor for Potter's perception of the Birtist era (1992–2000) as lacking in creativity. The US co-produced TV Movie from 1996 can be seen as an attempt at launching a global franchise and an indicator of the changing television marketplace with the increased need to develop brands that can cross into foreign territories. The return of *Doctor Who* in 2005, produced by BBC Wales (and thus reflecting the corporation's stated aim to move away from too many London-centric productions), as a popular piece of intelligent programming for all the family is a much-needed success story for a BBC whose charter and future, at the time of writing, are under consideration by the government. In short, to tell the story of the changing fortunes of *Doctor Who*, good and bad, is to tell the story of the changing fortunes of the BBC.

This book does not attempt to be the definitive collection of essays on *Doctor Who* – an entirely different set of essays could be compiled and be just as valid, if not more so. *Doctor Who* has been done great service through the archival research of writers such as Andrew Pixley, David J. Howe, Mark Stammers and Stephen James Walker. This book cannot improve on such work and thus does not offer a comprehensive history of the programme: such histories exist already.[3] Within fandom, analysis and debate have thrived for over twenty years through fanzines, the programme's long-running official magazine and, latterly, the online fan community. It may well be that many of the ideas and observations expressed in this collection have already been long-since discussed by fandom but, as anyone who has attempted to write an academic essay on *Doctor Who* knows, out-of-print fanzine articles or discontinued Internet discussion threads are often difficult – if not impossible – to track down and, rightly or wrongly, can be perceived as lacking the necessary academic authority to form the backbone of an essay's or dissertation's bibliography. Since *The Unfolding Text*, published scholarly work on *Doctor Who* has tended to centre on studies of fandom (e.g. Tulloch and Jenkins, 1995) rather than the programme itself, with only occasional articles to break the mould (e.g. Cull, 2001). Since this collection was first proposed, the work of Piers Britton and Simon Barker (2003) on set and costume design has been an extremely welcome and refreshing expansion of the academic discourse on *Doctor Who*. It is my hope that this collection continues in that spirit to bring together a wide-ranging set of essays, from both practitioners and academics, on core aspects of *Doctor Who* and its production and reception that will provide future writers with a more easily accessible body of work, as well as stimulating and paving the way for further critical discussion of the programme.

The collection is divided into four parts, each (as readers in the know will have noticed) titled in the style of a story from the various eras of *Doctor Who*. Part I, 'An earthly programme', considers the origins and initial directions of the series in its early years. One of the recurrent themes in this section is the far from consistent use of genre in the programme. Drawing on the work of Tzvetan Todorov and Darko Suvin, my paper challenges the popular perception of the programme as science fiction by arguing that *Doctor Who* has been able to appeal to a wider audience through embracing the fantastic: the uncertain, hesitant space between the real and unreal. Jonathan Bignell makes extensive use of archival sources to provide a detailed study of the programme's first period of major popular appeal, the Dalek mania of the mid-1960s, and the complex role of children both within the programme's diegesis and watching the programme at home. Both Daniel O'Mahony and Matthew Kilburn address *Doctor Who*'s historical adventures. The programme's initial mandate was to switch between stories set in the future, the past and 'sideways' (in alternate realities). The purely historical stories fell by the wayside in the mid-1960s and Matthew Kilburn concentrates on the last, 'The Highlanders', providing a parallel case study of the *Doctor Who* production team's approach to dramatising history alongside that of Peter Watkins' drama-documentary set in the same historical period, *Culloden* (1964). Conversely, Daniel O'Mahony focuses on the so-called pseudo-historical – those stories in which history is 'invaded by a science-fictional presence' other than the Doctor – and argues that far from being a series of adventures in space and time, *Doctor Who* is, in fact, a series of adventures in genre and the distinction between science fiction tales, historicals and pseudo-historicals is a false one.

Part II, 'The subtext of death', addresses the narrative themes and structures of the programme and begins with two contrasting pieces by Tat Wood and Alec Charles that discuss the activities of the Doctor and his companions in the socio-historical context of the programme's production. Whereas Charles reads the Doctor, and by extension the programme (in its original run), as being consistent with traits and tropes recognisable from Imperialist adventure-fiction, Wood proposes a different reading of the First Doctor (William Hartnell) that problematises him as both observer and observed rather than imposing his own beliefs onto those he meets. David Rafer looks elsewhere for patterns shaping the nature of the various incarnations of the Doctor and his paper explores in detail the mythic structures and identities at work in the Doctor's changing characterisation. Fiona Moore and Alan Stevens then conclude the section by shifting attention to the Doctor's arch-enemies with an extensive study of the Dalek stories from the programme's original run. For Moore and Stevens, the distinctive feature of the Dalek stories is the way they articulate differing approaches to the concept of human evil through their use of the Faust archetype.

Part III, 'The seeds of television production', concentrates on the look and sound of the actual programme and the production factors that shaped its audio-visual realisation. Ian Potter considers how the nature of studio recording in the 1960s contributed to the 'rhythm' of *Doctor Who*, in terms of the minimal resources available for video editing, and its approach to spectacle, which would determine the kind of stories the programme could tell effectively. Dave Rolinson's paper moves forward in time and focuses instead on the 1980s in order to discuss the programme's complicated web of authorship during an era whose failings have typically been laid at the door of one individual: the producer, John Nathan-Turner. Rolinson demonstrates how a range of factors beyond Nathan-Turner's control impacted on the programme throughout his tenure and that a broader understanding of the discourses of authorship is necessary to fully appreciate the strengths and weaknesses of this uneven phase in *Doctor Who*'s history. The final two chapters in this section are dedicated to one of the genuinely innovative aspects of the programme's audio-visual style: its use of music and sound design. Kevin Donnelly provides an overview of the evolution of the programme's music, which can be divided into four distinct periods ranging from the pre-synthesiser electronica and musique concrète of the 1960s to the use of freelance composers and predominantly synthesiser-based music in the late 1980s. Louis Niebur then focuses on the work of Brian Hodgson, one of the key figures at the BBC Radiophonic Workshop, and a collection of stories from the late 1960s in which Hodgson blurred the distinction between sound effects and music to create an effective audio-visual unease.

Part IV, 'The parting of the critics', is devoted to questions of value and canon formation. Andy Murray provides a study of Robert Holmes, *Doctor Who*'s most prolific writer (and, at one time, script editor), and argues that Holmes' contributions to the programme merit him being considered its finest writer. Building on his existing work on value judgements in *Doctor Who*, Alan McKee selects 'City of Death' as a candidate for an extended piece of textual analysis in order to argue its status as the 'best' televised *Doctor Who* story. The section then broadens its scope to consider *Doctor Who* stories beyond the televised adventures and the programme's survival throughout the 1990s as a series of, principally, original novels and, latterly, audio adventures on CD. The programme has thrived in other media as well, notably comic strips and online drama, but these varying narrative strands have often played havoc with attempts to create a coherent continuity for the programme. Lance Parkin provides a thoughtful consideration of the value of continuity and a meaningful canon to *Doctor Who*, acknowledging both its strengths and its restraints on the writer. Dale Smith and Matt Hills focus on the Virgin novels and Big Finish audios respectively, discussing how they have both been bound to the television programme and also sought to expand its televisual limitations. The collection as a whole then finishes with Paul Magrs' self-reflexive Afterword on his relationship to *Doctor Who* and how the programme has affected his own writing, whether academic or fictional. Magrs' piece brings the collection to a moving and fitting end, serving as a testimony to the programme's enduring ability to inspire young, creative minds as well as cautioning against becoming so absorbed by *Doctor Who* that one loses one's own personal voice – the Doctor would approve!

Notes

1   A full breakdown of the top 100 and accompanying notes is available online at www.bfi.org.uk/features/tv/100/index.html (accessed 25 September 2005).
2   This documentary, 'Whose Doctor Who', was first broadcast on 3 April 1977 on BBC 2 as part of *The Lively Arts* strand and is included as an extra on the 2003 BBC Worldwide DVD release of 'The Talons of Weng-Chiang' (BBCDVD 1152).
3   See, for example, Howe et al. (2005) and Howe and Walker (2003).

References

Bazin, André. [1951] 2005. *What is Cinema? Volume One.* Trans. Hugh Gray. Berkeley: University of California Press, pp. 76–94, 'Theatre and cinema – part one'.

Bellin, Joshua David. 2005. *Framing Monsters: Fantasy Film and Social Alienation.* Carbondale: Southern Illinois University Press.

Bignell, Jonathan and Stephen Lacey (eds). 2005. *Popular Television Drama: Critical Perspectives.* Manchester: Manchester University Press.

Britton, Piers D. and Simon J. Barker. 2003. *Reading Between Designs: Visual Imagery and the Generation of Meaning in The Avengers, The Prisoner and Doctor Who.* Austin: University of Texas Press.

Brooker, Charlie. 2005. 'Spot of brother'. *The Guardian*, 11 June. www.guardian.co.uk/arts/screenburn/ (accessed 18 June 2005).

Chapman, James. 2002. *Saints and Avengers: British Adventure Series of the 1960s.* London and New York: I.B. Tauris.

Cook, John R. and Peter Wright (eds). 2005. *British Science Fiction Television: A Hitchhiker's Guide.* London: I.B. Tauris.

Cull, Nicholas J. 2001. 'Bigger on the inside: *Doctor Who* as British cultural history'. In Graham Roberts and Philip M. Taylor (eds). *The Historian, Television and Television History.* Luton: University of Luton Press, pp. 95–111.

Dyke, Greg. 2005. 'Doctor Who's greatest triumph – the return of TV for all the family'. *The Independent: Media Weekly*, 20 June, p. 14.

Herman, David. 2005. 'Smallscreen'. *Prospect*, No. 115, October, p. 85.

Hills, Matt. 2004. '*Doctor Who*'. In Glen Creeber (ed.). *Fifty Key Television Programmes.* London: Arnold, pp. 75–9.

Hourihan, Margery. 1997. *Deconstructing the Hero: Literary Theory and Children's Literature*. London and New York: Routledge.

Howe, David J. and Stephen James Walker. 2003. *The Television Companion: The Unofficial and Unauthorised Guide to Doctor Who*. Tolworth, Surrey: Telos.

Howe, David J., Stephen James Walker and Mark Stammers. 2005. *The Handbook: The Unofficial and Unauthorised Guide to the Production of Doctor Who*. Tolworth, Surrey: Telos.

Jenkyns, Richard. 2005. 'Cherchez l'enfant'. *Prospect*, No. 115, October, pp. 38–43.

Johnson, Catherine. 2005. *Telefantasy*. London: BFI.

Lindner, Christoph (ed). 2003. *The James Bond Phenomenon: A Critical Reader*. Manchester: Manchester University Press.

Lister, David. 2005. 'The fantasy world of television executives'. *The Independent*, 28 May, p. 41.

McCaskill, Pete. 2005. 'We are British – get us out of here!' Posted on 26 March to www.bnp.org.uk/democracy/lettersmain.php (accessed 28 October 2005).

McLean, Gareth, Ali Catterall and Julia Raeside. 2003. 'The new breed of television'. *The Guardian*, 8 February.

Mickey. 2005. 'Dr. Who tragedy'. Posted on 26 March to www.bnp.org.uk/democracy/lettersmain.php (accessed 28 October 2005).

Miles, Lawrence. 2005. 'Doctor Who, season X-1, "The unquiet dead"'. www.beasthouse.fsnet.co.uk/who03.htm (accessed 16 April 2005 [the original review has now been removed but excerpts can be found on the Internet via Google]).

More Than Thirty Years in the TARDIS (1994) Produced and directed by Kevin Davies. Music by Mark Ayres. 87 mins. BBC Enterprises. BBC Video BBCV 5403.

Segal, Philip with Gary Russell. 2000. *Doctor Who: Regeneration*. London: Harper-Collins Entertainment.

Stevenson, Robert Louis. [1887] 2002. *Memories and Portraits*. Honolulu: University Press of the Pacific.

Sutcliffe, Thomas. 2005. 'The weekend's television: That's just the way to Who it'. *The Independent Review*, 28 March, p. 21.

Tolkien, J.R.R. [1947] 2001. *Tree and Leaf*. London: HarperCollins, pp. 3–81, 'On fairy-stories'.

Tulloch, John and Manuel Alvarado. 1983. *Doctor Who: The Unfolding Text*. London and Basingstoke: Macmillan.

Tulloch, John and Henry Jenkins. 1995. *Science Fiction Audiences: Watching Doctor Who and Star Trek*. London: Routledge.

Wheatley, Helen. 2006. *Gothic Television*. Manchester: Manchester University Press.

Part I

An earthly programme:
origins and directions

Chapter 1

How to pilot a TARDIS: audiences, science fiction and the fantastic in *Doctor Who*

David Butler

Towards the end of their study of audience responses to the 1995 film based on *Judge Dredd*, Martin Barker and Kate Brooks discuss the 'gross power' of what they call 'folk theories of the media' (Barker and Brooks, 1998: 302–3). These persistent folk theories take the form of statements and claims that fuel the construction of myths, and *Doctor Who* has accrued more than its fair share of them, many of which are generated within its own fandom. Whether it's notions of gothic horror in the mid-1970s; a format that can apparently go anywhere and tell any kind of story; an all-powerful alien race intent on conquering the universe but with an inability to storm a well-defended staircase or the claim that the programme is a national institution, there is much about *Doctor Who* that is taken for granted and not all of these folk theories have been advantageous.

One of the most oft-stated phrases about *Doctor Who*, as Matt Hills notes in his entry for the show in *Fifty Key Television Programmes* (2004: 75), is its status as 'the longest-running science fiction programme in the world'. It's a statement that, as fans, we can make with pride but it's also a label that has created problems for the programme, particularly during the 1980s and 1990s as dominant trends in mainstream science fiction changed. In *Reading Between Designs* (2003: 136), Piers Britton and Simon Barker observe that the success of science fiction (SF) blockbusters meant that *Doctor Who* was under pressure to 'live up to new standards of hyperrealism' and that it was only in its final seasons as a returning programme that the makers realised it couldn't compete with big-budget SF and perhaps didn't need to try: there were other stories worth telling.

If that's so, then was this lesson truly learnt? A BBC statement on the future of *Doctor Who*, released in May 2000, suggested that the answer was 'no'. *Doctor Who* was perceived as science fiction and science fiction therefore meant *The Phantom Menace* (1999), *Terminator 2* (1991), *Independence Day* (1996) and *The Matrix* (1999), and that's what audiences wanted:

Audience expectations for the effects in science fiction programmes are far higher
than they once were. New technology and special effects to match people's expectations are expensive and we do not believe it is appropriate to continue
with the programme as a low budget enterprise. (in Segal and Russell, 2000: 157)

The perception of *Doctor Who* as science fiction, and the related perception
of science fiction as requiring big-budget spectacle, became one of the major
stumbling blocks in efforts to resurrect *Doctor Who* throughout the 1990s.
The time wasn't right for the Doctor to return because audiences wanted
science fiction with lavish effects and blockbuster-standard set pieces. But is
that really the best way to 'hook' an audience on *Doctor Who*? We've got
several models to consider but I want to focus here on two of the most wildly
contrasting: the original episode from 23 November 1963, 'An Unearthly
Child', and the attempted re-launch from 1996, a television movie co-
produced by BBC Worldwide and Universal TV, broadcast in the US by Fox
Television. Although sharing several core icons (the distinctive theme tune;
the Doctor's time machine, the TARDIS, stuck in the shape of a British
police telephone box and the Doctor himself) these two episodes are from
quite different genres and neither of them can be classified as thorough
science fiction. One of the greatest strengths of *Doctor Who* is its lack of
genre purity, its refusal to be confined to any one category, and I want to
argue here, through an incorporation of audience responses to the two
'pilot' episodes, that a strict adherence to science fiction and spectacle is
not the key to the programme's success or, indeed, its essence. In particular,
in light of the work of Tzvetan Todorov on the fantastic and Darko Suvin
on science fiction, *Doctor Who*'s status as the longest-running SF series in
the world becomes distinctly unstable.

Origins: we are not writing science fiction!

The latter-day certainty over *Doctor Who*'s categorisation as science fiction
is far removed from the press releases and internal discussions surrounding
the programme's initial launch, way back in November 1963. As far as the
official line tended to go, *Doctor Who* was categorically *not* science fiction.
One of the pivotal figures in the development of the programme was Cecil
Edwin 'Bunny' Webber, a writer based in the BBC's Script Department.[1]
In a paper from 15 May 1963, describing the approach to the stories ahead,
Webber was clear:

We are interested in human beings reacting to strange circumstances. This is not
space travel or science-fiction: avoid the limitation of such labels, and make free
use of any style of category that happens to suit a story. (BBC WAC T5/647/1)

And later in the same document:

We are not writing science-fiction. We shall provide scientific explanations too, sometimes, but we shall not bend over backwards to do so, if we decide to achieve credibility by other means. Neither are we writing fantasy: the events have got to be credible to the three ordinary people who are our main characters [. . .] Granted the startling situations, we should try to add meaning; to convey what it means to be these ordinary human beings in other times, or in far space, or in unusual physical states. (BBC WAC T5/647/1)

Following directly on from this section, Webber then discussed the nature of 'Dr Who's "Machine"'. Here again, there was clear unease over the programme appearing to be science fiction. The appearance of the Doctor's time machine, Webber acknowledged, was going to be problematic in terms of the programme's relationship to genre:

We are in danger of either Science Fiction or Fairytale labelling. If it is a trans-parent plastic bubble we are with all the lowgrade space fiction of cartoon strip and soap-opera. If we scotch this by positing something humdrum, say, passing through some common object in (the) street such as a night-watchman's shelter to arrive inside a marvellous contrivance of quivering electronics then we simply have a version of the dear old Magic Door. (BBC WAC T5/647/1)

In spite of Webber's concern over using some 'common object' as the exterior of the machine, the production team, as we know, opted for exactly this approach and the night-watchman's shelter was traded in for a police tele-phone box. But once more, the anxiety over explicit science fiction icono-graphy was prominent. By 30 July, the official promotional material for the programme (which was also used in November of the same year, with some amendments) stated that *Doctor Who* 'cannot accurately be described as either space travel of (sic) science fiction' (BBC WAC T5/647/1). Yet although in apparent denial, Webber himself referred to what would become *Doctor Who* as 'science fiction' on more than one occasion. Following a meeting on the 26 March 1963, chaired by the then Head of the Script Department, Donald Wilson, Webber produced an outline titled, brazenly, 'Science Fiction', for a 'loyalty programme' running at least fifty-two weeks and made up of various linked SF serials (BBC WAC T5/647/1). More telling was a revised version of Webber's 15 May outline for the programme (which had stressed 'we are not writing science-fiction'), distributed the very next day and now referring to *Doctor Who* as an 'Exciting Adventure–Science Fiction Drama Series for Children's Saturday Viewing' (BBC WAC T5/647/1). From its earliest discus-sions, then, *Doctor Who* was a programme with an identity crisis, but this crisis would result in a genuine strength.

The source of this confused identity can be traced to two reports com-missioned by the BBC on the merits of science fiction and its potential for mainstream programming: the first completed by Donald Bull and Alice

Frick in April 1962 and the second, a follow-up report, produced by Frick and John Braybon on 25 July in the same year. The reports make for fascinating reading: they are a glimpse into the perception of science fiction before it would become clouded by popular franchises such as *Star Trek* and *Star Wars*, both of which, for better or worse, would go a long way to establishing what science fiction 'should' look like and what kind of stories it should and could tell in the minds of mainstream audiences and television executives alike, as the BBC memo from May 2000 confirms. These two reports, based on a study of *literary* as opposed to screen SF, would have a huge influence on the development of *Doctor Who*.

The conclusion of each report was bleak. Their implication was that the British public were not yet ready for a mainstream science fiction show or, perhaps more accurately, that the science fiction writing community was yet to produce a story that could reach out to a wider, mainstream audience. Surveying a range of predominantly American SF literature, as well as British exponents such as Fred Hoyle and C.S. Lewis, the April report concluded that 'there is a wide gulf between SF as it exists, and the present tastes and needs of the TV audience, and this can only be bridged by writers deeply immersed in the TV discipline' (BBC WAC T5/647/1). To be blunt, the report advised that:

> In its major manifestation, the imaginative short story with philosophic over-tones, it is too remote, projected too far away from common humanity in the here-and-now, to evoke interest in the common audience [. . .] Our conclusion therefore is that we cannot recommend any existing SF stories for TV adaptation. (BBC WAC T5/647/1)

The concern throughout both reports was whether a large audience could relate to science fiction and accept SF scenarios and characters. Conceptual science fiction, what Frick and Bull, quoting Kingsley Amis, called the 'idea as hero', was deemed lacking in wide appeal but the later July report was also sceptical about the reliance on spectacle and the presence of obvious SF iconography. This 'ironmongery', whether it was tin robots, bug-eyed monsters, spaceships or elaborate planet landscapes, would result, cautioned Braybon and Frick, in a 'psychological blockage' where the audience would always be thinking, however impressive the monster, ' "My goodness, there's a man in there and isn't he playing the part well" ' (BBC WAC T5/647/1).

In discounting excessive iconography as well as conceptual SF (in other words, what Rick Altman would refer to as the semantic and syntactic elements of a genre), these reports didn't seem to leave any credible options.[2] Although praising the work of Ray Bradbury, Isaac Asimov and James Blish's *A Case of Conscience* (1958), the April report admitted that American writers would prove unavailable to the BBC. That left British talent but Frick and

Bull were not overly impressed. They considered C.S. Lewis 'clumsy and old-fashioned' with a 'sense of condescension in his tone, and his special religious preoccupations are boring and platitudinous'. Arthur C. Clarke was a 'modest writer' but 'able to concoct a good story, and a master of the ironmongery department' whereas Charles Eric Maine was 'too much a fantasist'. The report's assessment of Maine's work is revealing in its dismissal of his obsession 'with the Time theme, time-travel, fourth dimensions and so on – and we consider this indigestible stuff for the audience'. Although *Doctor Who* would appear to defy Bull and Frick's opinion of the 'Time theme' ('have you ever wondered what it's like to be wanderers in the fourth dimension?'), the programme would seldom deal at length with the implications and ethics of time travel ('The Aztecs' [1964], 'Mawdryn Undead' [1983] and 'Father's Day' [2005] being notable exceptions) and the TARDIS, in general, would indeed become Webber's 'dear old Magic Door', a means of transporting the characters to their next adventure rather than a locus for discussing the quandaries of time. Two British SF writers *were* identified as offering the best potential for adaptation: Fred Hoyle and John Wyndham. Only one of Wyndham's books was deemed usable, *The Midwich Cuckoos* (1957), but the report considered him the best exponent of 'Threat and Disaster SF', which was the strand of science fiction they felt most suitable for a broad audience. Once again, the report was prophetic of the form *Doctor Who* would ultimately take as invasion stories slowly began to proliferate in the programme (peaking in the Troughton and Pertwee eras) following the picaresque wanderlust of its first year. But although the April report felt the time was not yet right for televised SF, it remained 'morally certain' that television writers would 'answer the challenge and fill the need'. By the time of the July report, the tone was more hopeful with an SF serial or series now considered a 'possibility' and two scenarios offering the most potential because 'they ask the audience to suspend disbelief scientifically and technologically on one fact only, after which all developments follow a logical pattern': telepathy and time travel.

The reports' emphases on the need to engage with a broad audience and to offer human interest in the drama, their warnings about the dangers of too much spectacle, as well as an overall caution that the general public weren't ready for science fiction, would all feed directly into the look and structure of the first episode of *Doctor Who* and be crucial in shaping its distinctive tone.

'This is absurd' or 'This is amazing'?

'An Unearthly Child' is concerned with drawing an audience into its world but it's difficult to make the same claim for the TV Movie. To illustrate that point, there's no better way than contrasting the opening moments of both episodes. Everything in the opening sequence from 'An Unearthly Child' is constructed around the tension between the familiar and the unfamiliar, or making the known strange. The episode doesn't begin by establishing a naturalistic and mundane world before disrupting that ordinariness with the introduction of the extraordinary and impossible (as, for example, in Spielberg's *War of the Worlds* [2005]) and neither does it begin with something obviously unreal. Instead, 'An Unearthly Child' develops something that is much more difficult to maintain in mainstream film and television: an uncertainty between what is real and unreal.

That uncertain tone is established through Waris Hussein's thoughtful and sensitive direction and is present from the episode's very first, extraordinary shot: a travelling shot as the camera moves through a dark and foggy street, past a policeman searching for something or someone, enters a junkyard via a door which opens, seemingly, of its own volition before coming to rest its gaze on a police telephone box, emanating an electronic hum. The camera moves in on the box's notice-board and then dissolves to a notice-board in a busy school corridor. It's an iconic moment – the first appearance, although we don't know it yet, of the TARDIS – but this opening shot is important in setting the tonal quality for the episode to come. Rather than beginning at the school (as the original synopsis for the first story specified) it creates an eerie prologue and a sense of something, the contents of the phone box humming strangely, waiting in the darkness. But it's also a shot that breaks one of the fundamental tools of storytelling in classical cinema: continuity editing. In this style, shot follows shot in a logical and linear sequence that is designed to orientate the spectator and aid their understanding of the narrative. Among the basic editing patterns is the shot/reverse-shot sequence, usually employed to clarify, for example, who is talking to whom (one shot, showing the talker, is followed by a reverse shot showing who is being talked at). But in the opening sequence to 'An Unearthly Child', Hussein dispenses with a reverse shot. (This is partly because he has to: as Ian Potter's excellent chapter on the restrictions of video editing in early 1960s BBC television production discusses in greater detail, a reverse shot would require financial resources not readily available to most directors [a second camera positioned in the correct area, a more complete set that wouldn't reveal the studio floor in a reverse shot and, above all, time to achieve all this].) For over a minute we get a sustained exploratory shot, snaking around the junkyard. Which prompts the question: who is doing this exploring?

What we've got here is a point-of-view shot – a fact confirmed when the junkyard door creaks open to allow us/the camera/the mysterious owner of this gaze entry – but whose gaze? Who is doing the looking here? Are we looking through Susan's eyes, as she wanders back through the fog hoping to avoid being noticed on her way home? Or are we the Doctor? Or perhaps we're somebody or something else, aware of this alien presence hiding on Earth. Whatever the identity of this gazer, they have special properties: the policeman walks right up to us/the camera and doesn't notice us – at which point we might be thinking we're a disembodied gaze, i.e. we're not really there. But then the door opens for us, acknowledging our presence in the diegesis. It's a perfect shot to open the episode with as it shifts between being unreal and real, absent and present: a visual correlate of the anxiety expressed in Webber's outlines for the programme and whether or not it was science fiction.

The withheld reverse shot is, of course, a popular technique in horror and supernatural cinema. Kubrick uses it to memorable effect in *The Shining* (1980): as the camera tracks down the hotel corridors after Danny we both want and don't want to see who might be following him – we want to be reassured that it's nothing malevolent but what if it is? What if it's the twins? Tarkovsky is one of its finest exponents; consider the slow, invasive point-of-view shot drifting over Kelvin's resting body in *Solaris* (1972) right up to his face, only for Tarkovsky to finally reveal the owner of the gaze as being in a spatially impossible location and thus confirm their alien/uncanny nature. Hussein offers something more troubling in 'An Unearthly Child' because no owner of the opening shot's gaze is revealed – the episode begins with an unanswered question (if you don't count the question posed in the programme's very title). Slavoj Žižek has discussed the function of this device at length in relation to the films of Hitchcock (Žižek, 2001: 31–9). For Žižek, Hitchcock is at his most unnerving when the spectator becomes aware that 'there is no possible subject within the space of diegetic reality who can occupy the point of view of this shot' (2001: 36). The result is an impossible subjectivity, which lends the preceding objectivity a 'flavour of unspeakable, monstrous evil' (2001: 36). Although that might be overstating it a bit for 'An Unearthly Child', nonetheless, the principle of unease holds and, right from the start, Hussein succeeds in creating an effective uncertainty about the nature of what we're seeing.

That uncertainty is heightened massively through the episode's astonishing music and sound design. Kevin Donnelly and Louis Niebur discuss the work of the BBC Radiophonic Workshop elsewhere in this collection but it can't be overstated just how utterly strange these sounds would have been at the time to a mainstream audience in a pre-synthesiser age. Although we might know the secrets of these sounds now (all oscillators, wobbulators and fragments of found and recorded sound slowed down, speeded up or looped round and round), their nature and origin were bewildering then and remain a source of fascination today. But in all the deserved attention given to Delia Derbyshire's outstanding realisation of Ron Grainer's *Doctor Who* theme and Brian Hodgson's equally striking special sound, it's all too easy to neglect the important contribution of Norman Kay's acoustic music score. The nature of early 1960s television production in Britain is crucial here – Kay's score could not be timed to specific moments in the action but had to be composed and recorded in advance, as a series of appropriate mood pieces, and then played back in-studio. The result of this approach is that there is a looser relationship between what is heard and what is seen, which adds to the episode's tone of mystery.

John Debney's full-bodied score for the TV Movie is very much in the tradition of the classical model of Hollywood film music, with actions and emotions constantly being emphasised through the music and synchronised to perfection – splendid for a rip-roaring adventure but often overbearing and obvious in its effects (the signifying function of the music leaves little to the imagination and there is copious 'mickey mousing'). Kay's small-scale score (confined, largely, to bass clarinet, harp and timpani with the occasional use of muted horns) echoes the work of one of the first composers to challenge the classical model of film music: Bernard Herrmann. Herrmann's signature features (a preference for short, repeated phrases; the absence of extended melody; the use of distinctive instrumentation rather than a reliance on the large-scale orchestra) are all at work in Kay's moody and rumbling score. Contrast the music for 'An Unearthly Child' with Herrmann's small-group scores for *The Twilight Zone* (1959–64), especially an episode such as 'Living Doll' (1963), and there is a striking similarity (indeed, 'An Unearthly Child' would not be out of place in *The Twilight Zone*, unlike the majority of later *Doctor Who*). Herrmann's approach to film and television music would make him the perfect model for early *Doctor Who*. As Royal Brown notes, Herrmann's rejection of melody robs the listener of recognisable, predictable and rational patterns with which to make sense of what is going on (Brown, 1994: 154) and leaves them, as Kay does, in a more uncertain and irrational musical landscape.

The title music and opening credits, created by Bernard Lodge, are far from being generic SF titles: no star-fields as the *Doctor Who* titles would later become but swirling clouds and abstract, symmetrical patterns, a pulsing, animated Rorschach test. The next indication that something is not quite right with this familiar world is the junkyard gate opening by itself, but the first emphasised moment is the electronic hum generated by the police box. It's a classic example of what the film sound theorist and composer Michel Chion calls *audiovisual dissonance* (Chion, 1994: 37–9). This dissonance between the visual and audio information prompts metaphoric thinking: what is the connection between these two elements? Even at the level of sound, the familiar is made strange. The most famous example, of course, is Brian Hodgson's creation of the sound of the TARDIS dematerialising, produced (in part) by Hodgson scraping a key along a piano string, recording the sound then distorting it to construct monstrous engines out of the most familiar of elements, blurring the distinction between organic and electronic.[3]

This making strange of the familiar is one of the key features of the literary fantastic as identified by Tzvetan Todorov (1975). As Rosemary Jackson notes, addressing the psychoanalytical implications of Todorov's work, fantastic narratives:

> pull the reader from the apparent familiarity and security of the known and everyday world into something more strange, into a world whose improbabilities are closer to the realm normally associated with the marvellous. The narrator is no clearer than the protagonist about what is going on, nor about interpretation; the status of what is being seen and recorded as 'real' is constantly in question. (Jackson, 1981: 34)

Mainstream film and television is not predisposed to such a questioning approach. Classical Hollywood cinema, as David Bordwell, Janet Staiger and Kristin Thompson (1985) have observed, is 'excessively obvious' and its visual, narrative and audio codes are geared towards *clarifying* what is going on. The answer to the question of whether the events in *Doctor Who*'s 1963 launch episode could really happen or not is held back for as long as possible – and isn't properly resolved until the next episode. There is a constant pull towards avoiding specific details and maintaining the mystery that is fundamental to the programme (and is evident in its very title). We know that this decision was being made right down to the broadcast of the pilot episode: the unbroadcast pilot (available on DVD) reveals a very different tone and one which would have taken the programme to a more obviously secondary and marvellous world (Susan's 'I was born in the forty-ninth century' is changed, in the broadcast version, to a less-specific 'another time another world').[4] The emphasis, as John Tulloch and Manuel Alvarado argue (1983: 13–35), is on mystery and maintaining the audience's credulity by not revealing *too* much. When the programme was re-launched in 1996, however, there was a clear shift in focus with mystery no longer a priority. The TV Movie begins (and continues) with a barrage of information that is bewildering for the mainstream audience and perplexing (if not infuriating) for the dedicated fan audience (inasmuch that it often gets *Doctor Who* mythology wrong) – therefore alienating both. This information dissipates much of the potential mystery in the programme (the Doctor's nature is revealed – he's a Time Lord from the planet Gallifrey with multiple lives, elements that were only introduced into the original series over a matter of years: regeneration in 1966, the Time Lords in 1969, Gallifrey in 1973) and it also runs the risk of repelling those members of the audience who are put off by obviously unreal narratives.

The TV Movie, then, moves away from Todorov's definition of the fantastic and more towards what he terms the *marvellous* – that is, a narrative set in a clearly secondary world (Time Lords, Gallifrey, Daleks and Skaro). It further aligns itself with the marvellous through its opening voice over by the Doctor. The Doctor's 'it was on the planet Skaro . . .' functions in exactly the same way as the classic fairytale phrase 'Once upon a time . . .'. The effect, argues Rosemary Jackson, is one of a voice:

> positioned with absolute confidence and certainty towards events. It has complete knowledge of *completed* events, its version of history is not questioned and the tale seems to deny the process of its own telling – it is merely reproducing established 'true' versions of what happened. (Jackson, 1981: 33)

For Jackson, the marvellous ultimately results in formulaic patterns, most usually in the standard closing expression of 'and they all lived happily ever after'. And there is much about the TV Movie that is formulaic – many of the idiosyncrasies of the original *Doctor Who* are replaced with standardised tropes and terms (I am not, of course, implying that the original series was free from standardisation: far from it. Individual writers [e.g. Terry Nation] and extended periods of the programme's production [e.g. the run of 'base under siege' stories in the Troughton era] would also be open to the charge.) For the TV Movie, the Doctor's chameleon circuit (enabling the TARDIS to change its shape to blend in with its surroundings) is renamed a cloaking device, bringing it into line with *Star Trek* (1966–9) terminology. The Doctor's biological origins, always a mystery, are now revealed as half-human and, perhaps most conventionally, he is given a (heterosexual) romantic interest, something that the original series never attempted in any depth. The Doctor operates here as a more traditional hero figure (far more than William Hartnell's Doctor in 'An Unearthly Child' or even Christopher Eccleston's Doctor in 'Rose' [2005]) and the story has little room for complexity in its straightforward Manichaean struggle between the Doctor and the Master. Where the 1963 episode takes familiar genres and icons and makes them strange (the classroom, the telephone box, the opening moments with the policeman referencing *Dixon of Dock Green* [1955–76]), the 1996 TV Movie goes out of its way to *explain Doctor Who*'s strangeness through familiar models (incorporating elements of mise-en-scène and terms from *The X Files* [1993–2002], *Terminator 2*, *ER* [1994–], *Star Trek* and so on), right down to the music as the uncanny electronic theme tune is transformed into a generic piece of orchestral bombast. The TV Movie seems to be at pains to clarify what is going on almost out of fear that the audiences will switch off if everything is not explained to them. The mystery of the TARDIS, which is the central mystery established at the beginning of the 1963 episode (why is this police box making such an otherworldly noise?), is revealed in the opening credits before the episode has even begun as we see the police box barrelling through the space–time vortex and, shortly afterwards, cut to the interior of the time machine. The special effects may be impressive but the effect on the imagination is less so. The audience is not given the opportunity to wonder about the *nature* of this police box.

What is crucially missing is the hesitancy that Todorov argues is an essential feature of the literary fantastic:

> The text must oblige the reader to consider the world of the characters as a world of living persons and to hesitate between a natural and supernatural explanation of the events described. Second, this hesitation may also be experienced by a character; thus the reader's role is entrusted to a character [. . .] the hesitation is represented, it becomes one of the themes of the work. (Todorov in Jackson, 1981: 28)

This is certainly true of the 1963 episode, as the two schoolteachers, Ian (William Russell) and Barbara (Jacqueline Hill), demonstrate when they stumble into the TARDIS and discover that it is bigger on the inside and full of alien technology. It is Ian in particular, established as the rational science teacher, who struggles to come to terms with the seemingly impossible ('It's absurd!' 'It's an illusion, it must be!' 'But I *want* to understand!').[5] But contrast that with the reaction to the TARDIS of the TV Movie Doctor's human companion, the cardiologist Grace Holloway (Daphne Ashbrook), when she first steps into the time machine:

Grace:	This looks pretty low-tech.
The Doctor:	Low-tech? Grace, this is a Type 40 TARDIS – able to take you to any planet in the Universe and to any date in that planet's existence: Temporal physics.
Grace:	(*Matter-of-factly*) Oh. You mean like inter-dimensional transference. That would explain the spatial displacement we experienced as we passed over the threshold.
The Doctor:	(*Somewhat disappointed*) Yes if you like.

Grace's response may be read as an ironic and knowing reversal of the female companion's expected reaction in *Doctor Who*, but it's damaging in terms of establishing credible characterisation and audience acceptance of *Doctor Who*'s extraordinary features. The glib reaction to the TARDIS' mind-boggling nature removes the sense of wonder but also deprives the audience of a character through which their own hesitancy at *Doctor Who*'s narrative can be expressed.

Grace's response downplays the estrangement experienced by Ian and Barbara in the original episode: she automatically makes sense of and rationalises the ship's fantastic properties. In this respect the TV Movie offers a less than convincing moment of cognition that is not developed enough to fulfil Darko Suvin's definition of science fiction as revolving around the dialectic between cognition and estrangement.

For Suvin (1979), science fiction required the presence of a novum, or 'new thing'. This novum could be technological or alien but its function would be to estrange the reader from their familiar world. The extent to which the text seeks to explain and make sense of the novum (the process of cognition) is what determines its status as science fiction. 'Hard' science fiction would engage in a more extensive and plausible process of cognition; estrangement on its own, as Carl Freedman has observed, could be anything from fantasy to Brecht (Freedman, 2000: 13–23). In this sense, *Star Wars* (1977) might *look* like science fiction (it has the semantic components) but its light sabres and X-Wing fighters could just as easily be understood as magic swords or flying carpets: it doesn't really estrange us and the one element which *is* given extensive discussion, the mystical Force, reveals George Lucas' leanings towards myth rather than genuine SF. Although explanations would come in later episodes of *Doctor Who* (and the next story's co-director, Richard Martin, was so concerned that the properties of the TARDIS '<u>must</u> [. . .] be understood by the audience before the adventures of its occupants are given credence' that he went to the trouble of sending the production team some 'phoney science' to explain how the time machine functioned [BBC WAC T5/648/1]), 'An Unearthly Child' doesn't really allow Ian that moment of cognition – he can't accept what he's experiencing and the Doctor doesn't even bother to give him a convincing explanation.

There is a marked difference in the reactions of characters from the respective episodes to their discovery of the TARDIS' true properties. In the TV Movie each of those reactions is played for comic effect: Chang Lee's, that of the cop on the motor bike (who rides his motor bike at speed into the TARDIS and then back out again in horror) and Grace's. The contrast in mise-en-scène is also startling: in 'An Unearthly Child' there is a violent cut from the gloom of the junkyard to the brightness of the TARDIS interior (as well as a sudden shift in sound design with a wave of electronic noise), the estrangement being further emphasised by a close-up on Barbara's face as she runs towards the camera (lending the moment a strong sense of kinesis) and stops in her tracks as she and we attempt to make sense of her new surroundings.[6] The first thing we see on discovering the interior of the TARDIS is not the extraordinary contents of the time machine but the disbelieving reaction of an ordinary human being struggling to understand what they're experiencing (Figure 1). In the TV Movie the contrast in lighting between exterior and interior is less distinctive (it's dark in both) and we don't even see Grace's initial reaction as she's walking in long-shot, dwarfed by the TARDIS console room. We hear her say 'this is amazing' but visually we're used to amazing sets in contemporary science fiction and fantasy film or television, and Grace doesn't seem overly amazed (Figure 2). The moment of

Figure 1 Barbara enters the TARDIS in 'An Unearthly Child' (1963)

Figure 2 Grace enters the TARDIS in the TV Movie (1996)

wonder is lost and quickly undermined by the dialogue to come. The sets may indeed be more impressive in the TV Movie but it is 'An Unearthly Child' that maximises the potential of the TARDIS interior for dramatic effect and creates a far more memorable encounter.

The use of the close-up on Barbara underlines her estrangement by taking us into her personal, subjective space and experience. It's worth recalling here the words of Béla Balász on the virtues and properties of the facial close-up as they are particularly apt for this crucial moment in *Doctor Who*:

> Facing an isolated face takes us out of space, our consciousness of space is cut out and we find ourselves in another dimension: that of physiognomy [. . .] A face can speak with the subtlest shades of meaning without appearing unnatural and arousing the distaste of the spectators. In this silent monologue the solitary human soul can find a tongue more candid and uninhibited than in any spoken soliloquy. (Balász, 1999: 306–7)

Barbara's entry into the TARDIS is the first genuine moment in the episode where the spectator is openly confronted with a non-naturalistic element rather than hesitancy between the real and unreal, but the use of the close-up here ensures that we are still rooted in the human response.[7]

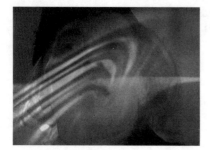

Figure 3 Time travel in 'An Unearthly Child' (1963)

The shift in emphasis between the corresponding scene in 'An Unearthly Child' and the TV Movie, the human companion's first reaction on stepping inside the TARDIS, couldn't be more marked. With no dialogue, 'An Unearthly Child' focuses on human drama and a believable reaction whereas the TV Movie opts to emphasise the lavish set, almost as if it is proud of its furnishings (and perhaps wanting to reassure its viewers: 'Look, we've got money! We're not like that old show with the wobbly sets!'), but in doing so neglects credible characterisation and human emotion. In this sense, 'An Unearthly Child' is more in keeping with the approach to science fiction and portrayal of space travel in Andrei Tarkovsky's *Solaris* (1972) than the objectivity of Stanley Kubrick in *2001* (1968). Tarkovsky might seem an unlikely soul-mate here but his depiction of space travel mirrors that of Waris Hussein (Figure 3). Hussein was specifically asked not to show the ship taking off (for budgetary reasons) but the result is that the camera focuses on the effect of the process on the characters. Similarly, Tarkovsky rejected model shots for the space-travel sequence in *Solaris*, feeling that these elements were a 'distraction' and presented space travel instead as subjective, human experience (Tarkovsky, 1986: 199). The method that both Tarkovsky and Hussein adopt is, again, the close-up on the performer's face. We're not exactly sure *what* is happening, especially in the time-travel sequence in 'An Unearthly Child', but we are fully aware of its traumatic effect on the travellers and are thus encouraged to be more involved in the drama. This is not to say that 'An Unearthly Child' is really an intense voyage into man's spirit and his struggle with material and technological gain, as Tarkovsky would want it, but that, as with Tarkovsky, its emphasis is on human reaction rather than science fiction iconography.

The episode closes with a shot of the police box now in a completely different location – a barren wasteland. We don't know how the police box got there. We don't even know where 'there' is. And then the shadow of a figure is cast across the landscape, their identity unknown.

Audience research

The final section of this chapter centres on audience research I conducted in May 2004 and 2005. My research follows models established by Martin Barker in his work with Kate Brooks on *Judge Dredd* and his current major study of audience responses to *The Return of the King* (2003). My main interest here was the audience's perception and understanding of genre and also the qualities that they found enjoyable in *Doctor Who*. Were the familiar structures and improved production values of the TV Movie essential to the enjoyment of a modern-day audience? Were, as the BBC statement in May 2000 implied, audience expectations of special effects so high that 'An Un-earthly Child' would function as nothing more than a fascinating historical curio? Did the audience perceive these programmes as being predominantly science fiction? The research comprised questionnaire data from 97 forms completed by students following a double-bill screening of 'An Unearthly Child' and the TV Movie. The students' ages ranged from 18 to 31 and the 97 samples were predominantly female (only 27 being male). Again, the vast majority were unfamiliar with *Doctor Who*, 41 having never seen an episode before the screening and only 5 stating they had seen the programme frequently. The students were required to complete the first section of the questionnaire on 'An Unearthly Child' immediately after the 1963 episode, then a section on the TV Movie and a final comparative section on the two episodes after the 1996 instalment had finished. The respondents were asked to comment on the generic status of the two episodes as well as the characters that most interested them and which of the episodes they had enjoyed more and would be more interested in continuing to watch.

The overwhelming preference (78 out of 97 respondents) was for the 1963 episode. With one exception, none of the respondents rated it at less than 'reasonably enjoyable' (45 rating it as 'very enjoyable') whereas the highest cluster of ratings (34) for the TV Movie was 'hardly enjoyable' (a further 12 extending the scale to 'painful' or a similar adjective). The vast majority of respondents were curious to see the next episode of 'An Unearthly Child' but, again, the majority of respondents (55 out of 97) stated that they were not at all interested in seeing what happened after the TV Movie. Although 12 respondents found the TV Movie 'extremely enjoyable' it also drew a considerable amount of vitriol.

Reasons cited for the TV Movie being 'hardly enjoyable' were its clichéd plot, overfamiliar set pieces and a lack of believable or interesting characters. Negative comments were made about its music, which was felt to be over-bearing, sentimental and telling the audience what to feel ('what did they do to the theme?!' queried one female respondent, a sentiment echoed by a male respondent from Germany who'd never seen the programme before but loved the original version of the title music; the TV Movie 'music was <u>atrocious</u>: *Baywatch* come *Power Rangers*', wrote another male respondent). There was also a widespread feeling that the special effects were underwhelming even though they were more expensive than anything in the 1963 episode. 'Naff CGI', 'cheesy', 'dated' and too excessive – these were all comments made about the TV Movie's visual effects. The feelings of many were summed up by one response on the visual effects in the TV Movie as being 'not so special to succeed' whereas in 'An Unearthly Child' they were 'important in their simplicity, they leave the audience space to dream'.

One male respondent who had never seen an episode of *Doctor Who* before commented:

> [The TV Movie] was more of a mindless, action movie, complete with guns, girls and fast cars [. . .] I honestly failed to connect with a single character [. . .] The mood of ['An Unearthly Child'] was strange; we watched the mundane environment we have all experienced upset by a bizarre and unusual scenario – compelling. It was based around routine life, rather than a Hollywood vision of a fictional, fast-track lifestyle.

As that reaction suggests, the perceived 'Hollywood-ness' of the TV Movie was a recurring criticism and corresponds with similar findings in Martin Barker and Kate Brooks' study of responses to *Judge Dredd* (1998: 77–9). A number of respondents commented on the 'Americanisation' of the *Doctor Who* format, even if they had never seen another episode of the programme prior to 'An Unearthly Child'. Among these responses, there was a strong sense of protectiveness towards British culture and distaste for what they felt was cultural theft. At the same time, for a minority, these glossy production values were precisely the reason why they preferred the TV Movie to 'An Unearthly Child'. Out of the 97 respondents, 18 preferred the TV Movie, with reasons for this preference ranging from its emphasis on action and suspense to it being more modern and thus having a recognisable aesthetic. One female respondent, who preferred the TV Movie but found both episodes 'ridiculous', noted that for her it was easier to identify with the TV Movie as:

> It was more modern and was set in my country with younger characters playing leads I connected [with] more easily [. . .] [I preferred] the young Doctor in the movie because he was younger and appeared more vulnerable, which was more like me.

Yet, this correspondent also acknowledged that in the TV Movie 'all the fancy tricks seemed pretty dumb and overdone'. Similarly, for a male respondent, 'the modern-ness of the episode created a more realistic atmosphere to relate to, plus the inside of the TARDIS was cooler'.

The preference for 'An Unearthly Child' centred on its moody atmosphere, its sense of mystery and, for most respondents, its more believable characters and dialogue. As one female respondent commented, 'there was no barrage of information which we're expected to believe so much so quickly'. For another female respondent, 'An Unearthly Child' was 'just better – less insulting and obvious – bit of mystery and embedded the story in real England [. . .] the excellent "real life" characters and scene-setting made the fantasy easier to believe'.

Asked to identify their favourite and most interesting characters from each episode, the responses to 'An Unearthly Child' were largely split between the Doctor and his granddaughter, Susan (Carole Ann Ford). There was a fascination for many with the Doctor and the sense that there was 'more about him than meets the eye'. Several respondents stated that the appeal of the character was in his tendency to deviousness, one respondent liking his 'punk' attitude and another male respondent from Italy, who had never heard of *Doctor Who*, admitting that 'I shared with him a subtle desire of punishing with a bit of sadism the annoying and bourgeois curiosity of the teachers'. But a significant number of respondents chose Ian Chesterton as their favourite character (several identifying his comedy tumble when the TARDIS dematerialises as being what sold the character to them), one female respondent stating that his appeal was that he was 'most like a typical everyday guy, unwilling to accept what is before him and desperate for an explanation'. In this sense, Ian functions exactly as the hesitant character Todorov argues is essential for nurturing the fantastic in the text and on the part of the reader/spectator.

Although the Doctor was the most interesting character for the majority of respondents due to his enigmatic nature, Susan also rated extremely highly. The appeal of Susan was largely given as being her dilemma in being 'torn' between two worlds. Respondents found her emotional struggle between her loyalties to her family (the Doctor) and, as one male respondent phrased it, 'her own developing interests/attachments to the real world' a recognisable and sympathetic portrait of adolescence and the journey into adulthood.[8]

The characterisation in 'An Unearthly Child' gave the vast majority of respondents readily identifiable characters and dilemmas. By contrast, 21 respondents rated *none* of the TV Movie characters as meriting interest (as one female respondent put it: 'no character engaged or interested me in the least') and a further 10 selected minor characters such as the Morgue attendant, the Security Guard, the Snake or Bruce's wife. 'An Unearthly Child' also created mystery and enigma, while the TV Movie, created a sense of confusion. This state was underlined when the respondents were asked to identify up to three genres that they felt were most evident in the respective episodes. Given 12 categories or genres to choose from (epic, good versus evil, mystery, SF, fantasy, fairytale, myth/legend, action, romance, adventure, thriller, children's drama), the results were revealing. There was a strong clustering for 'An Unearthly Child' around the triad of mystery (80), fantasy (60) and science fiction (76), with mystery just edging science fiction out as the most frequently cited generic category.[9] This relative balance between fantasy, science fiction and mystery would seem to confirm the status of 'An Unearthly Child' as a fantastic text – respondents hovering between the rational (science fiction) and the irrational (fantasy) with mystery the generic dominant and a mark of the fantastic's requisite hesitancy.

The TV Movie responses, conversely, were scattered across a far wider range of categories (indeed, the film scored in each of the available genres) with good versus evil (67) being easily the most-cited genre, followed by action (50), science fiction (37) and a strong rating for romance (33). Several respondents commented on what they felt was the confused nature of the TV Movie, a sense of trying to appeal to too many people and be too many things without establishing its own distinct identity. For one female respondent, who had never seen *Doctor Who* before, the TV Movie was:

> Like every bad Hollywood blockbuster rolled into one – there was everything: horror/fantasy/suspense/comedy/adventure/romance. But the mood was generally very very cheesy and predictable (highlight = magic dust at the end!).

Other responses were less forgiving: one male respondent, who had rarely seen *Doctor Who* but rated the 1963 episode as 'very enjoyable', commented that the TV Movie plot made no sense 'at all' and the episode as a whole was 'probably the worst ninety minutes of TV I've ever seen. Like standing on a rake. And then being set on fire. And then being eaten by a bear. On Christmas Day'.

Conclusion

It's important to take a number of mitigating factors into consideration here. For instance, as a 'niche' sector, i.e. students on a film history course at university, some of the respondents might have felt they were 'supposed' or 'expected' to be critical of the commercial nature of the TV Movie; there may also be some latent anti-Americanism coming to the fore. However, there are enough consistencies and trends across the results to find them revealing. What the results demonstrate above all is a clear preference for interesting characters, mood and believability over an emphasis on effects and unoriginal set pieces. For all its creakiness, 'An Unearthly Child' *still* 'works' as an effective first episode – it still has a remarkable ability to intrigue and 'hook' a modern audience.[10] Although a number of respondents stated that they had enjoyed the TV Movie, a large proportion of these responses added qualifying statements along the lines of 'it was so bad it was hilarious'. As one female respondent put it (rating the 1996 episode as 'extremely enjoyable' for 'pure comedy value' even though 'none of the characters inspired any kind of interest because it was all given to us on a plate'), 'An Unearthly Child' was 'a lot more stimulating and interesting but the TV Movie just made me chuckle'. Although 'very curious' to find out more about the mystery of Susan and the Doctor in 'An Unearthly Child', the TV Movie was 'quite enough for now' and she had no interest in seeing where Paul McGann's Eighth Doctor might go next.[11]

Russell T. Davies' comments in 1999, interviewed by *Doctor Who Magazine*, suggested his approach to the series would move away from the TV Movie and perceptions of telefantasy in the 1990s that deemed it essential to have spectacular effects:

> I think that if the moment the opening titles are over, you go into a Scene One that's set on a purple planet with three moons, and some man in a cloak making a villainous death threat [. . .] then the audience would just switch off in their millions. That's just an instinct, but I think you should set all that high flown end-of-the-world stuff in a very real world of pubs and mortgages and people. (in Gillatt, 1999: 10)

This 'very real world' is not entirely unlike that encountered in the original episode. In more ways than one, 'An Unearthly Child' offers a glimmer of *Doctor Who* in 2005, a *Doctor Who* that the original series was seldom able to be. As Ian and Barbara spy on their pupil, Susan, entering a run-down junkyard, they speculate as to what she might be doing in there alone on a dark winter's evening. Ian suggests, matter-of-factly, that she might be meeting a boy and Barbara responds that she almost wishes that were the case: 'it would be so normal'. It's only a throw-away comment but it still manages to surprise given what we know of the programme that *Doctor Who* would become. The possibility of a surreptitious romantic encounter between two teenagers is not familiar *Doctor Who* territory (as Alec Charles observes elsewhere in this collection), but for a fleeting moment, right at its outset, *Doctor Who* allows its characters the possibility of impossible mystery and adventure *alongside* the everyday mysteries and adventures of growing up and leaving home, before Daleks and bases under siege would become the priority for much of the 1960s. It's a possibility that the 2005 series has explored at length and to considerable success.

As with Webber's outline, the promotional material for the 2005 series avoided the term science fiction and chose instead to emphasise the programme's human qualities: 'Wherever they go, whoever they meet, every story will come back to Earth. For all the danger and tension, this is a fundamentally optimistic series [. . .] Prepare for brand-new, spellbinding adventures in the human race'. Alien worlds have been conspicuous by their absence from the first series of the revitalised *Doctor Who*, a conscious decision by

Davies (and one which the second series will address), but this cautiousness has been rewarded with a greater prize: a loyal, mainstream family audience as opposed to a niche audience of 'cult' television. Davies has, in many ways, brought the new series back to basics and its original mission statement.

If the TV Movie presents *Doctor Who* as a traditional struggle between good and evil, 'An Unearthly Child' emerges as a genuine piece of the fantastic, shaped by the nature and constraints of 1960s British television production. The programme can provide, and has provided, moments of 'hard' science fiction or the pure uncanny (strange events made explicable as the result of unconscious but natural forces [Jackson, 1981: 24–5]). Ultimately, *Doctor Who* will tend to resolve itself as an example of the marvellous, but the longer it holds off that resolution, through the uncertainty of the fantastic, the better are its chances of hooking a mainstream audience. Once the series has done that then the TARDIS can whisk audiences away to wherever it pleases, whether that's the roof of the world and the caravan of Marco Polo, the ice tombs of Telos or the leisure hives of Argolis. But to get them to go on that journey, the programme perhaps needs to make them hesitate over what is real and what is not and create an uncertainty about whether what we are seeing/hearing could actually happen. Rather than the 'longest-running science fiction series in the world', I'd suggest that *Doctor Who*'s future as a returning programme might be better ensured with another phrase: *Doctor Who* – the 'fantastic long-running series'.

Notes

1   Other driving forces in the genesis of *Doctor Who* at the BBC were the Head of the Script Department, Donald Wilson, newly appointed Head of Drama, Sydney Newman, and staff producer/director Rex Tucker. At a meeting on 26 March 1963, Wilson brought together Webber, John Braybon and Alice Frick to discuss possible topics for a science fiction drama. Several options were put forward and these were further whittled down in April by Newman before Webber would put together his 'General Notes on Background and Approach' to *Doctor Who* in May 1963.

2   The semantic properties of a genre are its visual icons and central themes, whereas a study of its syntactic properties would consider *how* these icons and themes interact with each other. See Altman (1999: 216–26) for a semantic/syntactic approach to film genre.

3   For many *Doctor Who* fans, the sound of the TARDIS dematerialising is best described in prose as either 'vworp vworp' (the *Doctor Who Magazine* comic strip) or Terrance Dicks' seminal 'wheezing groaning' sound from numerous Target novelisations. Describing this wonderful sound should be a challenge and a joy for any writer and the ongoing series of *Doctor Who* novels has seen some vivid interpretations. In December 2003 I was giving a lecture on the use of

sound to create a sense of the supernatural and fantastic in film/television and it provided a good opportunity to conduct some audience research. I was curious how somebody who'd never heard the TARDIS before would make sense of it and asked the audience to listen and write a short description of what they were about to hear. The responses ranged from the functional and perfunctory (lots of 'space ship taking off' and laser battles) to much more creative accounts. Out of the 38 responses, 17 identified both organic and electronic/industrial elements within the sound. Elephants and strange creatures being shot at in caves were popular but my favourites were Emma's 'a huge monster is coming out of a big pit and roaring like an elephant. They shoot it with lasers, which form a wall around it, a web, whirling up and carrying the creature off into space. It spins off, higher and higher' and Lizzie Nurse's doomed 'mutant lion – put into space pod and shot along long tunnel – gradually getting faster – turning into individual particles'. Somewhat disappointingly, and proving that ignorance really is bliss, those who did recognise the sound tended to write a blunt 'the TARDIS in *Doctor Who* setting off'.

4   The question of authorship in 'An Unearthly Child' is not so straightforward. Several key elements in the broadcast version of the story were influenced by Sydney Newman's handwritten comments on viewing the unbroadcast pilot. This document (Newman's copy of the script on which he'd written) is held in the BBC Written Archives Centre at Caversham (BBC WAC T5/647/1). Key suggestions were 'on cop – more mysterious', 'they (the teachers) don't act as if he's locked her in box' and 'must be a decided change in sound or music between outside and inside (the TARDIS)'. It was Newman who demanded that Hussein and Lambert remount the episode, which resulted in the broadcast 'An Unearthly Child'. Important changes are made (see n. 6 below) but the majority of the mise-en-scène remains intact, including the opening travelling shot.

5   This emphasis on the need for hesitancy and believable character reaction to extraordinary situations is on display in much of the early *Doctor Who*. Ian is still struggling to come to terms with the journey through time well into the second episode and in the following story, 'The Daleks', Barbara and Ian are visibly disturbed by their first visit to an alien world, Skaro. But not everyone involved with the production of *Doctor Who* shared this awareness of the need to maintain credible characterisation in the face of the fantastic. Terry Nation's scripts for 'The Daleks' received stern criticism from Christopher Barry, the story's co-director. In a letter to the programme's story editor, David Whitaker, dated 18 October 1963, Barry expressed his frustration that Nation was 'continually having them [the main characters] accept a situation in a most undramatic manner, and therefore losing a lot of potential value' (BBC WAC T5/648/1). In this and an earlier letter to Whitaker (11 October 1963), Barry systematically went through Nation's scripts, highlighting moments where characters should demonstrate 'much greater reaction', commenting that there should be 'more fear' from Ian and Barbara on several occasions, especially during their conversation when they discover that they are no longer on Earth.

6   Again, Sydney Newman's handwritten recommendations on viewing the unbroad-
     cast pilot episode are worth acknowledging here. Newman advised that there was
     a need to 'see their faces' and that 'entrance not good' (BBC WAC T5/647/1).
     It's difficult to be certain, but it seems likely that Newman is referring here
     to Barbara and Ian's entrance into the TARDIS (Newman's comments are in
     sequence with the events in the episode and the above two suggestions are
     made after 'when [TARDIS] door opens – must have [. . .] pause to really hear
     music'). These suggestions are relevant – the video release of the unbroadcast
     pilot contains three alternate takes of Barbara's entrance and none of them is
     the shot of her running into a facial close-up. In each of these rejected takes,
     Barbara is seen running into medium-shot (from the waist up) and the results
     don't have anything like the dramatic power of the close-up in the broadcast
     version. Newman's contribution then to the authorship of this important moment
     should not be discounted.

7   In the 2005 series both Keith Boak (director of the first episode, 'Rose') and
     Euros Lyn (director of the second episode, 'The End of the World') follow Waris
     Hussein's lead. Rose's first entrance to the TARDIS makes use of a remarkably
     similar shot composition to Barbara's first entrance: rather than a shot of the
     striking new TARDIS set, the first thing we see is a close-up of Rose's bewildered
     reaction. Similarly, for Rose's first journey into the far future, Euros Lyn
     demonstrates thoughtful attention to the scene's dramatic potential: rather than
     rushing to impress us with the spectacle of a future world, the first thing we see
     is Rose's excited face as she peers out wondrously from the TARDIS. The 2005
     series knows how to use spectacle ('The End of the World' features an array of
     effects shots, by The Mill, previously unheard of in a piece of episodic British
     television) but, more importantly, it also knows not to rely on spectacle at the
     expense of human drama.

8   This strong identification with Susan (36 selecting her as their favourite character
     with 45 favouring the Doctor) is fascinating given the sorry lack of development
     for her character in almost every ensuing episode of the programme, up to her
     departure. As the respondents' reactions confirm, the character had considerable
     dramatic potential and appeal but this was allowed to stagnate following 'An
     Unearthly Child'. It's notable that Russell T. Davies has gone out of his way to
     ensure that the new series of Doctor Who does not repeat this almost systematic
     neglect of the young female companion's character development (honourable
     [partial] exceptions in the original series include Leela and Ace).

9   Asked 'which of the following expressions comes closest to capturing the kind
     of story "An Unearthly Child"/the TV Movie was for you' the full results were
     as follows (each respondent was allowed to select up to three generic categories;
     number of selections is given in brackets): 'An Unearthly Child' – epic (3), good
     versus evil (2), mystery (80), science fiction (76), fantasy (60), fairytale (0), myth/
     legend (1), action (1), romance (0), adventure (34), thriller (1), children's drama
     (8), other (0). The TV Movie – epic (4), good versus evil (67), mystery (6),
     science fiction (37), fantasy (19), fairytale (1), myth/legend (1), action (50),
     romance (33), adventure (31), thriller (6), children's drama (6), other (1 –
     melodrama).

This section of the questionnaire was augmented from that used by Martin Barker et al. in the ongoing global research project into audience responses to *The Return of the King*, preliminary findings of which are available online at www.lordoftheringsresearch.net (accessed 31 August 2005).

10 Viewing figures alone do not tell the full story of these episodes' contrasting levels of success. On its first broadcast in 1963, the ratings for 'An Unearthly Child' indicated that it was watched by 4.4 million viewers in Britain, a modest figure for the time but perhaps understandable given that the new programme was an unknown property. These figures improved over the following episodes and by the end of the second story, 'The Daleks', ratings had exceeded 10 million. When the TV Movie was broadcast in 1996 it performed well in Britain at just over 9 million: a strong figure given the increasingly fractured viewing habits of British audiences. (By 2005, 10 million would be considered an outstanding result for a primetime show and the heavily promoted new series of *Doctor Who* opened with such a figure. The average viewing figure for the new series settled at just under 8 million – still an extremely impressive result, and *Doctor Who* was unbeaten by all other UK channels in its time slot throughout its thirteen-episode run.) The TV Movie was an 'event' broadcast, going out over a Bank Holiday weekend, and how many of those 9 million viewers would have remained loyal to it is difficult to say. The findings of this research (and the slight falling away of the 2005 series' audience following its launch episode) suggest that it would have struggled to hold on to such a figure without significant changes in its format and approach. The chances of the show being extended, however, were doomed following its disappointing performance in the United States (hampered by competition from a pivotal episode of the popular sitcom, *Roseanne*) and BBC Worldwide's US co-funders withdrew their support, leaving Paul McGann's Doctor in limbo.

11 Asked whether they would be most likely to want to watch the following instalment of 'An Unearthly Child' or the TV Movie (a trick question as the TV Movie doesn't have one), the respondents gave interesting answers. Several of those who had enjoyed the TV Movie *more* expressed no interest in wanting to see how it might develop and shifted their interest to 'An Unearthly Child'. The results: 'An Unearthly Child' (84), the TV Movie (5), neither (2), blank (6).

References

Altman, Rick. 1999. *Film/Genre*. London: British Film Institute.

BBC WAC T5/647/1, '*Doctor Who*, General A'.

BBC WAC T5/648/1, '*Doctor Who*, General B'.

Balász, Béla. [1945] 1999. 'The face of man'. In Leo Braudy and Marshall Cohen (eds). *Film Theory and Criticism: Introductory Readings*, 5th edn. New York: Oxford University Press, pp. 306–11.

Barker, Martin and Kate Brooks. 1998. *Knowing Audiences: Judge Dredd, Its Friends, Fans and Foes*. Luton: University of Luton Press.

Bordwell, David, Janet Staiger and Kristin Thompson. 1985. *The Classical Hollywood Cinema: Film Style and Mode of Production to 1960*. London: Routledge.

Britton, Piers D. and Simon J. Barker. 2003. *Reading Between Designs: Visual Imagery and the Generation of Meaning in The Avengers, The Prisoner and Doctor Who.* Austin: University of Texas Press.

Brown, Royal S. 1994. *Overtones and Undertones: Reading Film Music.* Berkeley and Los Angeles: University of California Press.

Chion, Michel. 1994. *Audio-Vision: Sound on Screen.* Trans. Claudia Gorbman. New York: Columbia University Press.

Freedman, Carl. 2000. *Critical Theory and Science Fiction.* Hanover: Wesleyan University Press.

Gillatt, Gary. 1999. 'We're gonna be bigger than Star Wars!' *Doctor Who Magazine,* No. 279, pp. 8–12.

Hills, Matt. 2004. '*Doctor Who*'. In Glen Creeber (ed.). *Fifty Key Television Programmes.* London: Arnold, pp. 75–9.

Jackson, Rosemary. 1981. *Fantasy: The Literature of Subversion.* London: Routledge.

Segal, Philip with Gary Russell. 2000. *Doctor Who: Regeneration.* London: HarperCollins Entertainment.

Suvin, Darko. 1979. *Metamorphoses of Science Fiction.* New Haven: Yale University Press.

Tarkovsky, Andrei. 1986. *Sculpting in Time.* Trans. Kitty Hunter-Blair. Austin: University of Texas Press.

Todorov, Tzvetan. 1975. *The Fantastic: A Structural Approach to a Literary Genre.* Trans. Richard Howard. Ithaca, NY: Cornell University Press.

Tulloch, John and Manuel Alvarado. 1983. *Doctor Who: The Unfolding Text.* London and Basingstoke: Macmillan.

Žižek, Slavoj. 2001. *The Fright of Real Tears: Krzysztof Kieślowski Between Theory and Post-Theory.* London: British Film Institute.

Chapter 2

The child as addressee, viewer and consumer in mid-1960s *Doctor Who*

Jonathan Bignell

This chapter draws on archival research, analysis of programmes and theoretical approaches to childhood and children's culture.[1] It discusses three aspects of the mid-1960s Dalek serials using these methodologies. First, it presents an analysis of the design of the programme format for children watching with their parents, and locates the assumptions about children as addressees that this involved. This issue is connected to conceptions of Public Service Broadcasting, the capabilities and interests of children, and relationships with other programme forms. Second, the chapter shows how the figure of Susan Foreman in particular, but also other humanoid characters and the monstrous Daleks, offer patterns of identification and disidentification which construct the place of the child as a valued proto-adult, but also an alien creature. Finally, the chapter discusses the invocation of children as consumers of *Doctor Who*-related merchandise, especially products relating to Daleks, and how the domestic consumption of television and merchandise remodulates the two other parts of the argument.

Addressing the audience

Doctor Who was conceived, scheduled and advertised to address mixed adult and child audiences. British Public Service Broadcasting has aimed to provide educative or improving programmes as well as entertaining ones, and to offer a range of different programme types at different levels of accessibility (Scannell, 1990). *Doctor Who* claimed all of these qualities, through its historical and scientific content, its focus on adventure, mystery and exploration, and its address to mixed family audiences of different age groups, sexes and social classes. However, *Doctor Who* was not produced for solely altruistic and paternalistic motives. The BBC Head of Television Drama Sydney Newman created the programme because of his concern with ratings, in a slot poised between different audience constituencies. Newman (*Radio Times*, 1983: unpaginated) described the target audience:

I wanted to bridge the gap on a Saturday between the afternoon's sports coverage, which attracted a huge adult audience, and *Juke Box Jury*, which had a very large teenage following. It was never intended to be simply a children's programme, but something that would appeal to people who were in a rather child-like frame of mind!

Juke Box Jury (1959–67) was a light-hearted panel game in which celebrities were invited to listen to a newly released record and predict whether it would be a 'hit' or a 'miss'. Its primary audience was teenagers, of a similar age to the Doctor's first companion, Susan Foreman (Carole Ann Ford). The audience for BBC sports coverage was mainly adult men. It was known that children were already viewing programmes in the early Saturday evening slot, such as the BBC's literary adaptations of classic literature that formerly occupied the place in the schedule that *Doctor Who* would take. So as Newman explained, the task of the programme that would become *Doctor Who* was to gather these different audience constituencies together at a transitional point in the BBC schedule. *Doctor Who* was being planned in relation to BBC output in other genres, and moreover in the context of the BBC's rivalry with the commercial ITV channel over ratings and public profile.

These institutional imperatives shaped the decisions made about the format of *Doctor Who*: its characters, kinds of storyline, serial structure and its tone or mode of address to the viewer. In March 1963, BBC staff writer Bunny Webber wrote a long memo (BBC WAC T5/647/1) arguing that the central characters in the new series could not be children because child viewers were thought to dislike characters younger than themselves.[2] But Newman was keen to provide a figure of identification for children, hence the central role of the Doctor's teenage companion Susan. An older woman should be included and an older man, Webber proposed, because adult viewers would also be watching and because the adult characters could embody the scientific and historical knowledge that storylines would dramatise. This argument led to the specification of the Doctor (William Hartnell) as an irascible old man, and the roles of Barbara Wright (Jacqueline Hill) and Ian Chesterton (William Russell), who were history and science teachers respectively. BBC Audience Research Reports provide a glimpse of how well the format succeeded in bringing the BBC a large audience composed of family groups, who could use *Doctor Who* as part of collective familial home life at weekend teatime, and enjoy it both for its own aesthetic qualities and for its role in mediating relationships between adults and children. In an Audience Research Report (BBC WAC T5/1243/1) dated 22 July 1965, on episode six of the Dalek adventure 'The Chase' (1965), a 'Housewife' reported that her children 'sit fixed before the television as though hypnotised'. A grandmother recounted: 'I don't like it but if my grandchildren are here it gives me a peaceful half hour or so as they sit enthralled', and a 'Salesman' reported 'I wouldn't miss it for anything and nor would the children'. The function of *Doctor Who* was to offer pleasures to both children and adults, and ways of using the programme in family viewing contexts that suited the needs and desires of different audiences. As the quotations from viewers show, *Doctor Who* was sometimes enjoyed by adults and children simultaneously, or adults used it as a kind of child-minder to give themselves a break, or children adopted the programme as something that was 'their property' and gave them control over domestic space and the choice of what to watch. It is worth remembering that in the mid-1960s households would have only one television set, usually positioned in the main living room. Negotiations and arguments over which programmes to watch, and an expectation that most programming would be watched collectively by all the members of a family, clearly affected the design of *Doctor Who*'s programme format and the ways it was experienced by actual viewers.

Despite the deeply felt concern of members of its production team that *Doctor Who* should educate and inform children (and also adults) about history and authentic scientific subjects, the programme was always intended to be exciting. The form of the series was specifically designed to engage audiences with the question of what would happen next, through the division of stories into multi-part serials, with cliffhanger turning points concluding the storylines of each episode, and teaser sequences introducing the next serial at the end of each final episode in a story. These cliffhangers usually took the form of a plot development that imperilled the main charac-ters, in the manner of an adventure serial for children, but the pleasure of setting up a crisis in the expectation of its resolution next week is only one aspect of television's broader promise of excitement and entertainment. According to John Hartley (1992: 17), broadcasters:

> appeal to the playful, imaginative, fantasy, irresponsible aspects of adult beha-viour. They seek the common personal ground that unites diverse and often directly antagonistic groupings in a given population. What better, then, than a fictional version of everyone's supposed childlike tendencies which might be understood as predating such social groupings?

The Doctor and his companions' adventures in time, space and dimension were planned from the start to provide open-ended possibilities of mystery, fantasy and imagination that the serial form could develop week to week, alongside coherent and naturalistic characterisation and the incorporation into storylines of historical and scientific plausibility. This mix of fact and fiction with fantasy and naturalism offered pleasures to both child and adult audiences, and most significantly, each different component could have an appeal that overlapped between child and adult viewers and brought them together in shared experiences of engagement with the programme. Despite the assumption that children were the main target audience for *Doctor Who*, the childlike pleasures of watching it were available to adults too, and Audience Research Reports provide evidence that adults did adopt a mode of viewing that enabled them to share viewing pleasures with their children, at least some of the time.

For the audience of the 1960s, television science fiction would have been seen largely as a genre for children. Science fiction in the cinema, going back to the film serials of the 1930s and 1940s, was a comparatively low-budget, low-quality form. There had been considerable anxiety and moral panic about the science fiction and horror comics imported from America in the 1950s onwards, which were thought to be both trashy and damaging to children (see, for example Wertham, 1954). Although this negative evaluation of television science fiction had been challenged by the mid-evening serial *Quatermass and the Pit* (1958–9) and the anthologies *Out of this World* (1962) and *Out of the Unknown* (1965–71), both science fiction and fantasy on television (*The Prisoner* [1967–8], for example) were subject to widespread criticism for their supposed implausibility or sensationalism, partly because of their association with American media culture and pulp paperback publishing. With the knowledge that the audience for *Doctor Who* contained a significant number of child viewers, the production team needed to imagine the potential reactions of children to what they saw in the programme, and the possible effects it could have on them. Some aspects of this issue were governed by official BBC policy and legal regulation: since *Doctor Who* was screened before the 9.00pm watershed it would never be possible to show explicit physical violence or sexual scenes or to use offensive language. More subtly, however, the producers had to make finely judged decisions about how frightening some scenes in *Doctor Who* could be. As is the case with all television for children, this meant that adults had to imagine themselves in the position of vulnerable child viewers, as well as exercising their adult professional judgement about the most exciting ways to dramatise thrilling moments in a script. So the imperative to make *Doctor Who* 'quality television' (see Bignell, 2005) could entail a conflict between the responsible attitude to the audience (especially children) that was consistently claimed by the BBC, and the desire to make programmes that had a powerful and memorable effect on the audience.

When the producer Verity Lambert made notes on the draft scripts that the screenwriter Terry Nation had sent in for 'The Chase', for example (BBC WAC T5/1241/1), she commented about episode one: 'I think that the mire beast should be a mere suggestion of tentacles. I do not think that, at any time, we should see the whole thing'. Her primary reason was that 'if it works as well as it should, it will be too horrifying'. Here, Lambert expected that making this scene well would conflict with the expectation that *Doctor Who* should never damage children emotionally (as some commercial products for children, especially US comics, were thought to do). Similarly, in episode two, she noted:

> I think Terry has gone too far in making the Aridians unpleasant looking. It does not serve any purpose in the script. It seems to me that this is just presenting unpleasantness for the sake of unpleasantness and I feel very strongly about this particular thing. If we want to dehumanise them, we must find some less revolting way to do so.

The dramatic objective was to dehumanise the Aridian characters, which Lambert thought was a valid way of giving meaning to the story. But she believed that Nation's realisation of this objective was opportunistic and irresponsible. This concern was sometimes corroborated by Audience Research Reports. In a report (BBC WAC T5/1248/1) on 'Destruction of Time', the final episode of 'The Daleks' Master Plan' (1966), members of the audience panel commented that although they particularly enjoyed the rapid ageing of the Doctor's companion in this story (achieved through make-up effects and time-delay recording), they thought this was too scary for children, especially when the character disintegrated into dust. However, Verity Lambert commented in the *Radio Times Doctor Who 20th Anniversary Special* (1983: unpaginated), referring to parents' complaints that *Doctor Who* was too frightening: 'But I believe children love being scared, provided they are in safe, protected circumstances, and not simply dumped on their own in front of the television'. She imagined the programme to be viewed by a family audience of both parents and children, and *Doctor Who* encouraged this familial culture in its own format by the inclusion of adult and child characters. The programme negotiated its address to the audience partly by imagining the needs and competencies of children within the context of a family viewing situation, and by offering ways of viewing that could be shared by children and adults.

Children, adults and monsters

Doctor Who is about growing up, not only in the programmes themselves but also in the ways that audiences learnt to watch them. For example, 'The Dalek Invasion of Earth' (1964) was the last story in which Carole Ann Ford appeared as Susan Foreman. In the final episode, Susan makes a transition from being an independent and mischievous teenager, yet still somewhat childlike and vulnerable, into being a more mature woman who decides to stay with the human resistance leader David Campbell after the Doctor discovers them in an embrace as he returns to the TARDIS. The Doctor concludes, 'I've been taking care of you and you've been taking care of me.

[. . .] You're still my grandchild and always will be, but now you're a woman too'. The Doctor's concern is for her to find her adult identity in a hetero-sexual couple, thus exiling her from the rootless picaresque ensemble of char-acters in the series, and establishing her in one place and time. The Doctor locks her out of the TARDIS and it dematerialises, leaving Susan to drop the key to its door on the ground and move off with her new companion. The camera shot emphasises this by tilting down to a close-up on the falling key, then tilting up again to see Susan walking away with her arm around her lover. In a reversal of the British tradition that people become independent at 18 and gain 'the key to the door', Susan's independence from the Doctor consists in her losing the key to her surrogate home. She is passed from one man to another, from grandfather to lover, and she begins to establish an independent life. The representation of home and the demands of grow-ing up away from it are consistent in *Doctor Who* because of the presence of the TARDIS as the place of homelike safety and familiarity, and the pseudo-parental relationship between the Doctor and the companions. One of the ways that the programme could address its audience of both children and adults was by building storylines that dealt with the mutually defining roles of child and adult, and with overlaps or slippages between those roles.

Despite the significance of more public spaces like the playground or the classroom in providing frameworks for children's experience of television, the home is the space where most of their interaction with the medium takes place. It is also the site where children's sense of their own identity (as individuals framed in gender, race and class categories, for example) is first formed. The sense of self not only consists in establishing what that self is in its own right, but also how it is defined against other people and things which it is not, such as adult masculine and feminine roles, and in relation to the outside world. The experience of childhood as a process of identity-formation involves shifting, moment to moment, from one role or sense of self to another, and negotiating the boundaries between self and other. Television plays a part in this, because it is embedded in day-to-day house-hold experience, and because it brings visions of the outside into the space of the home. The home is criss-crossed by different uses of television by parents and children, and the television functions as a parental delegate, substitute and babysitter, and as a representative of public space beyond the home. *Doctor Who* not only takes part in the general function of television as a homely medium that links the domestic space to the world beyond, but also has specific characteristics that reflect on the dualism of familiar and alien.

As a programme that featured off-world adventure, yet contained this in a stable format, *Doctor Who* mediated between the unfamiliar and the homely. *Doctor Who* gained homely familiarity because it was a long-running series, broadcast for most of the year and persisting in the schedules at a regular viewing time. Despite the regenerations of the Doctor as new actors arrived to take on the role, and the changes in the companions and the opponents that the hero team faced, the format remained very stable. This was because of *Doctor Who*'s use not only of continuing characters and repeated narrative forms such as the quest or the journey, but also of consistent visual strategies. For periods of months or years, the setting of the TARDIS remained the same, and the design and costume choices for the main characters established the programme's familiarity. Against the background of familiarity and repetition, storylines were able to represent alien settings and monstrous antagonists, introduce horrifying or shocking moments, incorporate suspense and defer resolution to storyline enigmas.

The 1960s Dalek stories represent the Daleks themselves as somewhat childlike, and therefore as both familiar but also uncanny. The Daleks share the powerful drives to get what they want that children experience, and like children they are often incapable of adopting the social codes of politeness, deferral of satisfaction and empathy with others that adult life, and especially family life, require. They are outsiders who are stigmatised as different, and who stigmatise others who are different from them. As creatures who are differentiated from the adult main characters in *Doctor Who* (as well as other humanoids and youthful companions) they can also represent the otherness that children may feel as beings who are not yet privileged to take part in adult life and its social and sexual roles. So although the Daleks exhibit many human adult characteristics, such as a generally rational approach to problems, competence with technology and advanced knowledge, and interest in political control and the administration of societies, their uncanny and alien properties in particular may predispose child viewers to identify with them. Since the Daleks are always defeated by the humanoid heroes, *Doctor Who* demonstrates the ultimate failure of their strategies, so they are certainly not role models for children in any obvious sense. But their brash self-confidence, physical power and determination may have many attractions for children, whose role it is to be relatively powerless, physically undeveloped and uncertain. Furthermore, the Daleks' capitulation to the liberal humanist values demonstrated to succeed in the narratives of *Doctor Who* stories as a whole does not stop them from being attractive figures of identification for children at particular moments within those narratives. It is well known that children played at being Daleks throughout their 1960s heyday and thereafter, and this adoption of a Dalek role by children was made possible by some of the visually arresting ways in which they were represented in the episodes.

Television scholarship has defined the medium as one in which a distracted domestic viewer glances at relatively simple image compositions with low density of visual information, where sound predominates over image (see, for example, Ellis, 1982). But television science fiction and fantasy can both use and surpass the restriction to dialogue and intimate, small-scale storytelling that this characterisation of the medium suggests. Terry Nation's early Dalek scripts took advantage of the knowledge that Mervyn Pinfield, Doctor Who's associate producer, had gained in using Inlay and feedback, for example. Within technical and budgetary constraints, the visual revelation of monsters and their embedding within the domestic reception of popular television is crucial to their meaning. Nation's storyline for 'The Daleks' (1963–4) (BBC WAC T5/647/1) described them as hideous, legless, machine-like creatures with no human features, a lens on a flexible shaft replacing eyes, and arms with mechanical grips and strange weapons. The Daleks were intended to be uncannily monstrous, drawing on science fiction's popular forms, especially in visual media. While 'The Daleks' contained motifs and narrative structures that linked it to literary science fiction, it was also conceived as an opportunity for a specifically visual revelation of alien and thrilling creatures and physical action, in the tradition of low-budget US cinema and comics.

Images of science fiction settings, creatures and technologies, as well as punctual narrative moments which foreground spectacular effects, are aesthetic components that are crucial to Doctor Who. The Dalek stories make use of the intimacy of multi-character, multi-camera performance 'as if live' in the restricted space of the television studio, but also provide opportunities for spectacle, thus connecting the serial with both conventional television's naturalistic characters and interior settings, and cinematic science fiction. Doctor Who's production team aimed for the visual emphasis that cinema was reputed to do better than television, yet also the sense of immediacy and closeness to the action that distinguished television from cinema. This combination of spectacle and intimacy can lead to contrasting ways of experiencing Doctor Who stories. There may be moments that seem shocking or disturbing to the extent that their meaning is not contained and controlled by the onward movement of narrative or the removal of the threat apparently posed. For example, the final shot of episode one of 'The Daleks', where Barbara is menaced by an as yet unknown creature, cannot be contextualised by an explanation or by her rescue because it is the last shot of the episode. This moment was certainly one that many viewers (not only children) found both exciting and disturbing (see Bignell and O'Day, 2004: 87–8). Alternatively, the introduction of a visual moment that arrests the narrative and is potentially spectacular or disturbing can lose its effect if it is too easily assimilated into the audience's knowledge and expectations of the programme. This was the case for adult viewers of some Dalek stories when the repetition of narrative motifs (such as Susan getting lost and apparently threatened by an alien creature) had become established as regular storyline features (see Bignell and O'Day, 2004: 93–8). Clearly, the viewer's competence in evaluating the significance of such a moment in relation to his or her strategies for interpreting television, and *Doctor Who* narratives in particular, is the determining factor here.

Defences against the argument that monster stories are too scary for children draw on the concept of media literacy, which concerns children's knowledge of media codes and conventions, genre, narrative and production processes (see Hodge and Tripp, 1986, for example). This approach emphasises the acquisition of viewing skills and the drive for rational control by the child over media interactions, arguing for the possibility of children's role as active agents rather than victims of television. David Buckingham (1996) focuses on the other hand on children's and parents' emotional responses to television. What Buckingham discovers is that watching scary television and talking about it are important means for children to understand themselves and others. This involves gaining and deploying media literacy. Children sometimes seek out disturbing programmes in order to test their own maturity at coping with troubling emotions. This coping is achieved partly by gaining the understanding of modality (the conventions of narrative and genre specific to a medium) which will allow them to repudiate and manage these emotions, and the awareness of modality is itself a characteristic of adults' relationships with media texts. By including the relatively vulnerable and/or childlike figures of the Doctor, Susan, Barbara and Ian, *Doctor Who* could offer identifications for children where the characters could alternately embody the child's wish to exercise adult rationality and control, and also the child's own sense of vulnerability and powerlessness. The *Radio Times* of 21 November 1963 carried the feature 'DR. WHO' to announce the new series, which explained that Doctor Who 'has a grand-daughter Susan, a strange amalgam of teenage normality and uncanny intelligence'. Susan was designed to be both normal and alien, both a figure for aspirational identification and also a vulnerable child like the child viewer. The TARDIS crew's opponents such as the Daleks could also represent both the dictatorial and technological adult world, and children's own desire for mastery, power and freedom of action. The duality of the Daleks' meanings, as both monstrously different from the child and yet also figures for children's identification, was strongly supported by their visibility beyond the television episodes, and especially in merchandise and publicity.

Dalek mania: alien and familiar

Television science fiction not only draws on other texts (such as the similarities between 'The Daleks' and H.G. Wells's story *The Time Machine*), but also creates them, and this affects the ways that programmes' meanings are shaped and how they are remembered. Spin-off texts and merchandising change the meaning of the programme. The BBC was initially slow to capitalise on Dalek merchandising, turning down an offer by entrepreneur Walter Tuckwell to sell licences for products because the Daleks would not last long in *Doctor Who* storylines. But when the BBC realised what a success it had on its hands, it fuelled the 'Dalek mania' that swept Britain in the mid-1960s. The publication of *Doctor Who* novels and annuals began at Christmas 1964, and badges, Dalek costumes, comics, toy Daleks and sweet cigarettes with collector cards were produced. These activities raised and maintained *Doctor Who*'s profile, but also supported the BBC's brand identity, gained income for the BBC from merchandising agreements, and promoted viewer inter- action with and loyalty to the programme. Strategies for interaction with a programme brand had already been developed for children's programming very successfully by the BBC, for example in the opportunities for interaction with *Blue Peter* (1958–) through writing letters to the programme, making toys or foods, or taking part in charity appeals. Though *Blue Peter* also had commercial merchandising spin-offs such as annuals, the promotion for *Doctor Who* had much closer connections with the toy and media industries.

The effect of these merchandising and publicity efforts was that although the Daleks were established by the television text as threatening, scary and alien, they also became extremely familiar and homely because of the mer- chandising and publicity generated around them. Daleks could be seen 'in real life' on the streets of Birmingham in December 1964, and they fea- tured in the *Daily Mail* Boys and Girls Exhibition in late December and early January 1964–5, for example. Press coverage, toys and comics brought the Daleks into the familiar and usually safe space of the home, and this embedding into viewers' lives complicates their meaning beyond how they are represented in the television episodes. Inasmuch as they concretise and express social meanings for children, toys are totemic objects around which children's difference from adults can be organised, and which can represent aspects of the child himself or herself, or aspects of the world around the child that he or she can manipulate during play.[3] Playing with a toy Dalek extends the possible meanings of the creatures outlined above, either as rep- resentations of the child's own desires or as representations of those forces outside him or her with which the child has to negotiate.

Memorable moments in Dalek stories are given form by social interaction and their placing in viewers' lived experience. Here are two examples of memories of 'The Dalek Invasion of Earth' (1964), both of which refer to the end of episode one. In a characteristic use of the cliffhanger in which a Dalek is revealed at the end of an episode, in this case the creature unexpectedly emerges from the waters of the Thames, moving directly towards the camera: 'My earliest memory of *Doctor Who* is my terror at the sight of the Dalek's head coming out of the water. Its eye bobbing up and down, and its other arms, one of which my brother told me was a weapon' (quoted in Mulkern,

1988: 19). This was contributed by Esther Flyte of Kendal, and draws attention to three points. First, the memory is one of uncanniness and terror, as the monstrous Dalek appears in the midst of a familiar setting. Second, the fact that this woman was watching with her brother in the room shows the extent to which commentary and explanation was significant to young viewers' experience since they normally watched with other children or adults. Third, the memory is specifically visual. It is not a memory of a narrative sequence or plot development, but of a spectacular visual revelation. Another memory of the same episode was described by James Robertson of Swansea (in Mulkern, 1988: 19–20):

> The return of the Daleks was looked forward to with great excitement by me, and my friends. I can remember everyone cutting out pictures from the paper and *The Radio Times* and playing Daleks after school. Then on that Saturday afternoon, about five of us went round to my friend's house and we all watched in silence as the episode was shown [. . .] the ending when the Dalek appeared out of the Thames had us all cheering.

Collective play and gathering supporting media materials shaped the meaning of one striking image from the story, so the revelation of the monster became both pleasurable and shocking, and its possible scariness was tamed by being expected and watched collectively. The emergence of *Doctor Who* as a 'cult' programme and the growth of Dalek-related merchandise was significantly dependent on the visual aesthetic developed in the televisual form of the episodic serial, and its collective and domestic viewing context that included other texts and products as well.

Children's television, toys and play are not separate from the discourses of culture as a whole. Children's media culture is produced not by children, but for them, and thus encodes the pressures and contradictions of adult culture (see Bignell, 2002). As Dan Fleming (1996: 147) has shown, the manifestations of children's culture 'take as their jumping-off point the bleakest features of a post-liberal reality: social disintegration, the isolation of groups defined by their own ritualised difference from each other, an *anomie* that justifies the existence of militaristic saviours, *ninja* experts and awesome technological solutions'. For Fleming, the objects, products and practices within children's media 'belong in a system of meanings with the potential to tell stories which transcend that bleakness, while nevertheless recognising it. Such recognition is vital to the effective object relations that play depends on if it is to be an antidote to bewilderment'. The hopelessness of individual action, the uncertainties of social role and the ever-present threats of violence and environmental degradation which both adult and child audiences felt about contemporary society are present in *Doctor Who* in a coded form. These problems are both granted spectacular power as threats, but also symbolically tamed both within the story and by the narrative structure of the serials themselves, where repeated tropes of capture, pursuit and techno-logical danger are given reassuring and sometimes spectacular resolutions. The uncanny, monstrous and other are brought into the domestic viewing experience by the programme text, but are also tamed by the text and by that viewing context. Part of that context is the peripheral culture of toys, play and consumption related to the programme and selected features of its imagery, characters and themes. In the case of *Doctor Who*, it was possible in the mid-1960s (and also today) to watch the programme while playing with toy Daleks, gazing at images of Daleks and talking about them with fellow viewers, for example. For the children who were a key audience for the programme, they were addressees, viewers and consumers whose experience of it had multiple points of connection with ways of understanding themselves and the domestic and public worlds in which they lived; worlds in which television was itself a crucial participant.

Acknowledgements

I gratefully acknowledge the assistance of the BBC Written Archives Centre in granting access to original documents on *Doctor Who*. This chapter is one of the publications arising from the research project 'Cultures of British Television Drama, 1960–82' funded by the Arts and Humanities Research Board, and I am grateful for their support for that initiative.

Notes

1   Some of the research presented here is discussed in the context of Terry Nation's writing for *Doctor Who* in Bignell and O'Day (2004).
2   References to BBC Written Archives Centre files are shown in the text as BBC WAC followed by the file number. The titles of files are given in the References.
3   For discussion of toys in relation to children's development of identity, especially in terms of gender and aggression, see Bignell, 1996, 2000, 2003.

References

BBC WAC T5/647/1, '*Doctor Who*, General A'.
BBC WAC T5/1241/1, '*Doctor Who* The Chase'.
BBC WAC T5/1243/1, '*Doctor Who* The Chase'.
BBC WAC T5/1248/1, '*Doctor Who* and the Daleks' Master Plan'.
Bignell, Jonathan. 1996. 'The meanings of war toys and war games'. In Ian Stewart and Susan L. Carruthers (eds). *War, Culture and the Media: Representations of the Military in 20th Century Britain*. Trowbridge: Flicks Books, pp. 165–84.

Bignell, Jonathan. 2000. '"Get ready for action!": reading Action Man toys'. In Tony Watkins and Dudley Jones (eds). *'A Necessary Fantasy?': The Heroic Figure in Children's Popular Culture*. New York and London: Garland, pp. 231–50.

Bignell, Jonathan. 2002. 'Writing the child in media theory'. *Yearbook of English Studies*, No. 32, pp. 127–39.

Bignell, Jonathan. 2003. 'Where is Action Man's penis?: determinations of gender and the bodies of toys'. In Naomi Segal, Lib Taylor and Roger Cook (eds). *Indeterminate Bodies*. Basingstoke: Palgrave Macmillan, pp. 36–47.

Bignell, Jonathan. 2005. 'Space for "quality": negotiating with the Daleks'. In Jonathan Bignell and Stephen Lacey (eds). *Popular Television Drama: Critical Perspectives*. Manchester: Manchester University Press, pp. 76–92.

Bignell, Jonathan and Andrew O'Day. 2004. *Terry Nation*. Manchester: Manchester University Press.

Buckingham, David. 1996. *Moving Images: Understanding Children's Emotional Responses to Television*. Manchester: Manchester University Press.

Ellis, John. 1982. *Visible Fictions: Cinema, Television, Video*. London: Routledge.

Fleming, Dan. 1996. *Powerplay: Toys as Popular Culture*. Manchester: Manchester University Press.

Hartley, John. 1992. *Teleology: Studies in Television*. London: Routledge.

Hodge, Robert and David Tripp. 1986. *Children and Television: A Semiotic Approach*. Cambridge: Polity.

Mulkern, Patrick. 1988. 'The Dalek invasion of Earth'. *Doctor Who Magazine*, No. 141, pp. 18–22.

Radio Times, 21 November 1963.

Radio Times Doctor Who 20th Anniversary Special, 19–26 November 1983.

Scannell, Paddy. 1990. 'Public service broadcasting; the history of a concept'. In Andrew Goodwin and Garry Whannel (eds). *Understanding Television*. London: Routledge, pp. 11–29.

Wertham, Fredric. 1954. *Seduction of the Innocent*. New York: Rinehart.

Chapter 3

'Now how is that wolf able to impersonate a grandmother?' History, pseudo-history and genre in *Doctor Who*

Daniel O'Mahony

Doctor Who fans don't stake their territory by genre. In fan discourse, the series is subdivided along fault lines of performance (e.g. split into *eras* named for the leading actor or producer of the time) or fractures of production and broadcast (e.g. separating the 'adventure in space and time' into *seasons*). This isn't to say that comparisons of stories by content and form don't exist, but typically they haven't coalesced into specific categories. There's one exception to this general rule: the *historical*.

In this chapter, I argue that this distinction, while rooted in the production of *Doctor Who*, is unhelpful and that the changing character of the historicals reflects the nature of the programme itself. History in *Doctor Who* is treated largely as a genre and the essay will demonstrate this with specific reference to both 'pure historicals' and the hybrid 'pseudo-historical' whose emergence is central to the way that history is and has been portrayed in the series.

The historical, like many genres, like many types, is resistant to definition. History, in a series at least nominally about time travel, is a tricky concept to pin down. The best starting point for the fan definition is probably Marvel Comics' 1986 *Doctor Who Magazine Summer Special*, which takes 'historicals' as its theme (while contemporary specials from the same publisher focused on more concrete topics – 'merchandise' or 'Jon Pertwee' or 'designers'). The Marvel special is itself an important part of the ongoing discourse as it focused, for the first time in a professional publication, on a subset of stories that were at this time usually derided or ignored by fandom. From the 1990s, this situation was partially reversed as the historicals were more frequently championed over their 'science fiction' (SF) contemporaries. Even so, the initial assumptions remain intact: historicals are still singled out as aberrant and oppositional to the core values of the series. By contrast, when 'science fiction' is discussed, it is as a default or invisible value. In this scheme, if science fiction is the thesis of *Doctor Who* then historicals are its antithesis.

There are two articles by Gary Russell in the *Summer Special* that bring the definitions into focus. 'Observing history' (1986a) describes 'pure historical' stories that mainly take place within the William Hartnell 'era', with the only subsequent examples being 'The Highlanders' (1966–7) – at the cusp of Patrick Troughton's tenure as the Doctor – and 'Black Orchid' (1982). In these stories the Doctor, his companions and the TARDIS are the only science-fictional intrusion into a narrative that otherwise features only historical elements (or fictional events that can be plausibly passed off as historically contextual). History itself is a topic for debate within the story but typically it can't be changed or potential change is at least undesirable. The lead characters' priorities are at odds with the narrative. Their motive is mutual survival (the characters are forcibly separated from the TARDIS or from one another in almost every example of the 'pure historical') by extricating themselves from the various local intrigues that occupy the supporting cast.

By contrast, there are the 'pseudo-historicals', which aren't separated from the main body of *Doctor Who* to the same extent but are still identifiable as a genre, subgenre or para-genre. 'Making history' (Russell, 1986b) surveys these and comes up with a more nebulous body of serials than 'Observing history', beginning with 'The Time Meddler' (1965). In these stories, the historical period has either been invaded by a science-fictional presence before the Doctor shows up (as in 'The Time Meddler') or turns out to be a fabrication mocked up by the villains for their own dubious purposes (as in 'The War Games' [1969]). History is now up for grabs. Although lip-service is still paid to the idea that it can't be changed, the stakes are such that the Doctor makes it his business to resolve the situation. Sometimes this is because of exceptional circumstances (most explicitly in 'Pyramids of Mars' [1975]); on other occasions it isn't rationalised at all – the Terileptils in 'The Visitation' (1982) aren't temporal invaders and should therefore be as historical as the Great Fire of London (they are in fact invaders from another genre). The Doctor's intervention is the driving force of the story. A characteristic difference from the 'pure historicals' is that the Doctor has become the central heroic figure, displacing the collective set of 'time travellers' in the early years of the programme. In short, the plot of a pseudo-historical operates in much the same way as the dozens of *Doctor Who* stories that take place in other worlds, in the future or in the present. These stories occupy the borderlands between the 'historical' and science fiction adventures; they resemble history but they speak the default language of SF.

The phrase 'pseudo-historical' is an invention of fan discourse, though one that fed back to the perception of *Doctor Who*'s producers before 1982, in time for 'Black Orchid' to be promoted as a break with tradition. Fandom began to coalesce into its modern form in the mid-1970s, by which time the pure historical was a long-dormant genre and needed to be accommodated into contemporary perspectives on the series – but the distinction does have a solid basis in production fact. The format for *Doctor Who* was first discussed at the BBC Script Department on Tuesday 26 March 1963. When the subject of a time machine was raised, department head Donald Wilson 'suggested if this were used, it should be a machine not only for going forward and backward in time, but into space, and into all kinds of matter' (Howe et al., 1994: 167). Immediately this set the parameters for a format with distinctions, a time travel series that, unlike subsequent programmes such as *Quantum Leap* (1989–93) or *Crime Traveller* (1997), wouldn't be exclusively concerned with 'the past'.

Behind-the-scenes documentation reveals a generic separation of early *Doctor Who* stories: 'past', 'future' and 'sideways'. All three labels quickly fell into disuse as the series developed. Their last sighting in BBC paperwork is on Tuesday 14 April 1964 in a memo drawn up by story editor David Whitaker for producer Verity Lambert, which outlined the shape of *Doctor Who*'s second series (Howe et al., 1994: 250–2).

Three things are suggestive here. First, Whitaker and Lambert were *Doctor Who*'s original production team, who had experimented and laid ground rules that later teams could build upon – but with no guarantee that those teams would follow their examples (Whitaker left the series in autumn 1964 with Lambert departing the following spring). Second, the terms 'past' and 'future', which until then had been designated to stories without obvious bias, no longer share an equal billing. There are five proposed 'future' serials (twenty-six episodes altogether) – as compared to four 'past' ones (forming twenty episodes) – all given potential settings (e.g. 'Spanish Armada', 'Egyptian', etc.). This is clearly for practical reasons – the past did after all offer ready-made dramatic scenarios as well as pre-existing props and costumes with which television producers such as the BBC were already familiar – but at the same time it suggests a conscious separation of the requirements of the two types. By now *Doctor Who* had been running for almost five months and was readily associated in the public (and media) consciousness with the Daleks. They hadn't provided its most popular serial – roughly the same number of viewers had tuned in for 'Marco Polo' (1964) – but they were certainly more marketable and more tangible. (Curiously, 'Marco Polo' was suggested for adaptation as both a comic serial and a feature film, the latter proposed by Walt Disney Productions, but these went unrealised and there was little other interest in merchandising the historicals in the 1960s [Howe et al., 1992: 152, 127].) Terry Nation, the Daleks' creator, had been commissioned for an Indian Mutiny story titled 'The Red Fort' prior to their first appearance but he was soon switched to the hurriedly written 'future' serial 'The Keys of Marinus' (1964). The 'past' was becoming a less attractive option and once

Lambert and Whitaker had gone, later production teams would seek to consolidate what they perceived as *Doctor Who*'s generic strengths.

The third point hinges on interpretation. Labels like 'past' and 'future' were practical definitions for a practical purpose; they aren't necessarily any more helpful than illustrative fan-words like 'historical'. They contain certain assumptions and evasions about the nature of the stories in question. The familiar SF storytelling devices that underpin the pseudo-historicals, rendering them more legible to modern fans, weren't in place in the series from the outset but developed over time – and that development is more complex than fans have assumed.

Is 'The Time Meddler' the first pseudo-historical? Using the definition outlined earlier, it would seem to be. In the third instalment of the immediately preceding serial, 'The Chase' (1965), the Daleks terrorise the crew of the *Mary Celeste* into abandoning ship, but this is an almost disposable sequence taking up roughly half the episode. Its proximity to 'The Time Meddler' suggests the production team were grasping for a new idiom or innovation within a series that had been running for over eighteen months and was now familiar and *old*.

The aim of 'The Time Meddler' wasn't to upset the audience's expectations of what could be done with *Doctor Who*'s format. In fact, audience research from the period found some casual viewers became lost in the confusion of anachronistic signs such as the juxtaposition of gramophones and Saxons. The story was actually intended to introduce to the programme a staple trope of adventure fiction: the villain who 'doubles' for the protagonist in abilities but has opposing values or methods. Here, it's a time traveller disguised as a monk who proves to be of the Doctor's own people with a TARDIS of his own. Unusually he's a figure of fun as much as an outright villain, but this is understandable as the series had already established the Daleks as relentlessly evil antagonists (who became 'doubles' for the Doctor both through sheer force of popularity and by unveiling their own time machine in 'The Chase'). The Monk has no companions, suggesting that the emphasis of the series has shifted from the adventures of a group of time travellers to one where the Doctor (the only character now remaining from the original regular lineup) is now clearly identified as the programme's lead. His intentions are to change history (for the better, he imagines, though this is never challenged). This forces the Doctor from being an observer into an active defender of history – the moment when the genre expectations of the 'future' stories leak through to the 'past'. It's conceivable that 'The Time Meddler' could have been set in the future or on another planet. By choosing to place it in English history – on the most iconic date of that history – Dennis Spooner was fulfilling a genre function. The Monk could well have been interfering in the history of Vortis or Xeros but for the audience nothing would be at stake. It would take some time before *Doctor Who* repeated this trick again but this is the point where *Doctor Who*-as-history becomes subservient to *Doctor Who*-as-genre.

'The Time Meddler' was the culmination of Spooner's reimagining of the series, not the start of the process. Two of the five full-blown pure historicals before 'The Time Meddler' (leaving the problematic first serial 'An Unearthly Child' [1963] aside for the moment) were scripted by Spooner and both show signs of slippage away from a conception of pure history and towards popular storytelling styles (a process I'll refer to as 'genre-creep'). 'The Reign of Terror' (1964) was an espionage story set in France in 1794, drawing for inspiration on fiction such as Baroness Orczy's *Scarlet Pimpernel* novels and the freshly popular James Bond film series. Its conclusion is the unhistorical revelation of Napoleon Bonaparte as the prime mover in the conspiracy that has turned the plot. Napoleon's involvement is purely to create a dramatic pay-off when the audience (and the characters) recognise him. This historical is pure in the fan sense because the sinister Lemaitre is an English spy – and not, say, the Master – while the suggestion for Nero's unhistorical burning of Rome in Spooner's next story, the 'experimental' comedy 'The Romans' (1965), comes from the Doctor rather than some other time traveller – but they aren't *classical*.

For fans, the pure historical is held up as an example of what *Doctor Who* was like, for good or ill, before it fell away from the initial instincts of its creators (which only appear uniform in hindsight). They are therefore both a genre and a set of virtues invested in that genre. But these virtues – which could be summarised as high-minded storytelling, educational content and historical fidelity – are vanishing qualities in, for example, 'The Smugglers' (1966) or are diluted as in 'The Reign of Terror'. The virtues imagined by modern fandom are in fact mainly found in the two 1964 serials by John Lucarotti – 'Marco Polo' and 'The Aztecs' – which I'll refer to as *classical* historicals (there is also 'The Crusade' [1965] by David Whitaker, who edited the two Lucarotti stories, but which is consciously theatrical in its origins). Lucarotti also wrote a third serial – 'The Massacre of St. Bartholomew's Eve' (1966) – but this was conceived amid behind-the-scenes wrangling, rewritten heavily by story editor Donald Tosh and effectively repudiated by Lucarotti in his novelisation of 1987, which reshaped the basic materials into a new plot and added further historical detail. It shares with the earlier Lucarotti scripts a general earnestness that's absent from Spooner's work but any imputation of classicism is challenged by Tosh's later comment: 'I knew quite a lot about the St. Bartholomew's Massacre and so when John delivered his scripts I looked through them and found that historically there were a lot of things wrong with them' (Evans, 1992: 12).

The plots of 'Marco Polo' and 'The Aztecs' both develop along 'pure' lines: they are variations on the complications that unfold as the travellers try to

escape from Marco Polo's caravan and from the Aztec civilisation respectively. Both stories are pocked with historical detail, of varying degrees of
relevance to the unfolding story but pertinent to *Doctor Who*'s early (elusive)
educational brief. Lucarotti later specified the example of the use of a wheel
in 'The Aztecs'. The Doctor's construction of a crude wheel-and-pulley device
enables him to escape and the programme to impart the historical detail that
wheels were unknown to the Aztecs for practical purposes. Less relevant to
the immediate exigencies of plot is the long sequence in 'Marco Polo' where
Ping-Cho recites a poem about the *hashshashins*; this kind of longueur is
virtually absent from any other story and further confirms in fan minds
the essential difference of historicals from the remainder of the programme
(though in the context of the comparatively new series of 1964, no such
distinction could be made). Like Marco Polo's animated map, this is a dis-
tancing device in a story that makes compromises with its popular fiction
status purely because the alternative would be to make *Doctor Who* as a kind
of time-travelogue with the Doctor and his companions as framing narrators.
Marco Polo himself is classically distant; the unhistorical villain Tegana is
visceral and more familiar.

'Marco Polo' presents a more profound historical problem than genre-
creep. Its historical palimpsest is *Il Milione* (c.1298), the account Polo gave of
his travels to Rustichello da Pisa while they shared a Genoese prison cell. This
account may not be true – it contains a number of odd omissions – and Polo
himself does not appear in the detailed documentation of the Yuan Dynasty.
Il Milione is suspected of being – in modern terms – a work of fiction based
partly on accounts of Persian merchants with Polo inserted as the kind of
narrative figleaf that the Doctor avoids becoming in Lucarotti's story (for
further discussion of this point, see Wood, 2003). Lucarotti's entire narrative
line, on which he hangs historical detail and his own fiction, may itself be
fictional. On the other hand, the prospect of a story set during the Venetian–
Genoese conflict that led to Polo's imprisonment – which could be at least as
historically interesting as anything dramatised on screen – seems never to
have been a possibility. Why? The likely answer is because the *Doctor Who*
historical ultimately demands a pre-viewed familiarity on the part of the
audience in order to tell the story.

Polo's account, while it may not be true, had the advantage of being
generally familiar to the viewing audience and of fulfilling a certain view of
history as the accumulation of 'great men' doing 'great things'. Polo would
be followed by Robespierre, Napoleon, Nero, Richard Coeur de Leon (interestingly not portrayed as the unambiguous hero of English popular myth)
and Wyatt Earp (a more obvious historical fake than Polo). While some fans
consider the setting of 'The Massacre of St. Bartholomew's Eve' to be obscure,
it fits with the British educational tradition of celebrating Catherine de Medici's

contemporary rival Elizabeth I. None of this, of course, is unique to *Doctor Who* but from here it would only be a short step to the likes of 'The Visitation' and 'The King's Demons' (1983), in which the history is, in the words of the satirical *1066 and All That* (1930), 'what you can remember'.

Aside from Barbara's guiding foreknowledge of Cortez, 'The Aztecs' side-steps the problem of 'great men' – the featured characters are all fictional, the history is cultural – but is potentially more troubling. It's the keystone story where the Doctor first states that history can't be changed and this idea is explored dramatically in the fiction. Barbara, mistaken for the reincarnation of the priest Yetaxa, attempts to use her political power to end human sacrifice in the belief that this might prevent the later destruction of Aztec civilisation by the *conquistadors*. She is opposed both by the Doctor and by Tlotoxl, the High Priest of Sacrifice. Separated from preconceptions about 'pure historicals', 'The Aztecs' can easily be read as a science fiction story about a time traveller's failure to change the course of history. This is couched entirely in the human drama, rather than as technobabble or special effects, which goes some way to disguising its science fictionality in a series whose fandom tends to see SF as icons (e.g. the spaceship of 'The Sensorites' [1964], the alien landscapes of 'The Keys of Marinus', etc.). Lucarotti would repeat the theme in 'The Massacre of St Bartholomew's Eve', where the Doctor's inability to interfere in history means he must abandon the Huguenot girl Anne to die in the slaughter. Anne had been considered as a new regular character but the production team decided that removing her from history would transgress the series' established rules – rules that were implicitly science fictional, rules that would be ignored by later producers (Evans, 1992: 13).

Also known as '100,000 BC', 'An Unearthly Child', the very first serial, is set in prehistory and is similarly as much SF as historical. Its setting and characters are based on anthropological and archaeological speculation (partly through omission, as it was decided early in the serial's development that the tribespeople should be able to speak despite evidence to the contrary). The very idea of 'prehistory' removes the layers of historical familiarity that allows fans to read 'The Aztecs' as 'pure historical'. It suggests that the problem – one that *Doctor Who* on television was never really equipped to deal with – is that history is not simply what is past but the way knowledge about that past is arranged. History is a construct of the present. Viewed through the prism of popular fiction, it can become genre.

Lucarotti was consciously writing in a fictional tradition, as he drew on his own previous work including a Canadian radio serial about Marco Polo. In general, the 'classical historical' has obvious roots in the 'classic serials' vein of BBC drama, aimed at a family audience. This was an institutional genre, a BBC genre, and still palpably Reithian in its mission to 'educate, inform and entertain'. If history in *Doctor Who* is a form of genre, then the nature of the 'historical' can only be understood in terms of the evolution of the series itself. Rather than being an aberration to be ignored or celebrated, the pure historical is an expression of the way the series treated genre in its early years. The classicism of 'Marco Polo' is only a specific version of the way many early stories are framed; the travellers' problems escaping from history, for instance, are common to most stories in the first year. Genre-creep in 'The Time Meddler' or the openly satirical 'The Myth Makers' (1965) was no less apparent in serials like 'The Daleks' Master Plan' (1965–6) or 'The Ark' (1966), which were also striving for a new idiom to adapt to changing expectations and changing producers. Where 'The Myth Makers' interrogates (or at least pokes fun at) the idea of 'history' as constructed in a popular television series, later teams would simply abandon the 'pure historical' altogether, or at least see genre hybridisation as the way to approach series set in the past. The juxtaposition of visually striking SF iconography (mainly monsters) and easy-to-realise historical settings would be a signature for *Doctor Who* that few other programmes could comfortably replicate.

By the 1970s, *Doctor Who* was confidently embracing pastiche and genre-play. Fans easily recognise the literary or legendary provenance of, for example, 'The Brain of Morbius' (1976) or 'The Horns of Nimon' (1979–80), and the emerging full-blown pseudo-historicals are simply another expression of this. Robert Holmes' 'The Time Warrior' (1973–4) is a good example of history-as-genre while the same author's 'The Talons of Weng-Chiang' (1977) inverts this to present genre-as-history. In 'The Time Warrior' the newly introduced companion Sarah Jane Smith has been transported to thirteenth-century England without realising it; she rationalises that she's on a film set (old news to the author of the metafictional 'Carnival of Monsters' [1973]) and – more interesting in genre terms – that the people she meets are part of a medieval pageant. Effectively both explanations are true. By contrast, 'The Talons of Weng-Chiang' is set in a late nineteenth century that never was, constructed out of pieces of contemporary popular fiction like *Fu Manchu* (faithfully pastiched, with derogatory attitudes towards the Chinese retained intact) or nostalgic 1970s TV reconstructions such as *The Good Old Days* (1953–83). These two stories are not of a piece simply because they both feature intrusions of time-travelling villains into historical settings; they have the complex similarities and dissimilarities of a common genre.

These stories depict a mix of familiarity and incongruity. Their versions of history are histories of the common imagination, constructs set in worlds that the audience is likely to recognise from their personal education and other fiction. Into this come the elements of incongruity that turn uncharacterised fiction into *Doctor Who*. The materialisation of the TARDIS into a recognised landscape, the instant when the pastiche is intruded upon and fruitfully spoiled, can be equally potent when that landscape is a pre-historic wilderness, the hold of a spacecraft or a backstreet of never-never Victoriana.

Though 1980s scriptwriter Christopher Bailey didn't write historicals for *Doctor Who* ('The Children of Seth', his proposed serial set in ancient Byzantium, was never made), his description of how the series operated by the early 1980s has a bearing on the way the series' pseudo-historicals work:

> [I]f it was a *Doctor Who* version of Little Red Riding Hood [...] they'd [...] say, 'Now how is that wolf able to impersonate a grandmother?' [...] And then somebody would say, 'Well of course, it's the mind-transfer fibrulator on the wall' [...] Things get explained too much – or not really explained at all. (Tulloch and Alvarado, 1983: 256–7)

For Bailey this attitude is sloppy and he has stated his dislike of elements of the produced version of his script 'Kinda' (1982) where a colonialist theme is represented by dressing certain characters in British Raj-style uniforms and pith helmets (Cook, 2003: 15). Yet it also describes the relationship within *Doctor Who* between pageant/pastiche and pseudo-science which is perhaps the key to understanding pseudo-historicals. The earliest stories saw the Doctor accompanied by Ian and Barbara, respectively teachers of science and history, consciously representing two separate strands of culture. The period of the classical historical ends when the materials of both strands are treated the same way, to the point where it's no longer possible to see the join, when in fact the Doctor becomes a Renaissance Man, equally comfortable with science and the humanities, when pseudo-science and pseudo-history become interchangeable.

The use of familiar historical elements to generate back-plot or theme occurs in many stories that are far removed from any genuine history. 'The Androids of Tara' (1978) is a romantic adventure story inspired by Anthony Hope's *The Prisoner of Zenda* (1894). Set on another planet (which looks like Kent, for obvious reasons), it revolves around a villainous count's plot to seize the local throne for himself and the Doctor's counter-plotting using android doubles. There is SF gadgetry, which is mostly camouflaged (ostensibly as technology is the province of the peasantry and therefore – to the aristocratic inhabitants of the story – vulgar). There are androids but also natural duplications (the plot turns on the coincidence that the Doctor's companion Romana is an exact double of Princess Strella). There is (briefly) a monster, which is just an animal. In an earlier period this might well have been performed 'straight', as a Ruritarian fantasy without any SF complications, without Bailey's mind-transfer fibrulator on the wall. It wouldn't be a 'pure historical' by any obvious definition of the term but it would fit comfortably alongside 'The Smugglers' and 'The Highlanders', stories from the fag-end of the run of pure historicals, which never pretend to be anything more than period romps inspired by the popular fiction of Robert Louis Stevenson or Russell Thorndyke.

For sections of a new generation of *Doctor Who* writers, the series' treatment of history has become problematic. The historical pageantry of a story like 'The Androids of Tara' becomes the source of mockery in Stephen Marley's novel *Managra* (1995). This is set in the thirty-third century when the whole of Europe has become an enormous patchwork theme park named Europa. The physical recreations of the different periods are populated with *reprises* (clones) of historical figures such as Byron and Casanova, along with fictional characters (cloned from actors strongly identified with these roles). Cross-fertilisation between fake histories is forbidden by an equally fake airborne Vatican but the whole edifice proves to be the pastiche creation of an obscure Jacobean playwright. The story is both a critique and a celebration of genre-play; the reader is supposed to enjoy the clash of symbols.

The post-television forms of *Doctor Who* have seen a partial re-emergence of the pure historicals, not least because the creators are often fans-turned-gamekeepers with their own varying takes on fan discourse. Authors with a penchant for history such as Mark Gatiss and David A. McIntee are often still telling stories comfortably within the adventure tradition of 'The Smugglers', albeit with classical historical research stressed as a priority. Lance Parkin's *Just War* (1996) complicates its historical plot with the revelation that a companion of a previous Doctor let slip anachronistic details with the result that history might be changed. It plays with the expectation that this will be a pseudo-historical or counterfactual, and indeed it is but not one that would be readily identified as such by conventional fan discourse. Other recent examples similarly slip in time paradoxes to leaven the 'pure' plots, notably the audio plays 'The Marian Conspiracy' and 'The Fires of Vulcan' (both 2000), both of which revolve around the personal threat to the Doctor posed by untamed history. These are monster-free, space-travel-free 'pure historicals' but the Doctor and his companions are still agents in history and the priorities of the story are those of pseudo-historicals. They demand a reason for the Doctor's involvement and for his commanding the centre stage.

More challenging than these are recent novels that have begun to take seriously the critique that Marley posed mischievously in *Managra*. Mags L. Halliday's *History 101* (2002) seizes on the notion of history-as-a-construct in a conscious challenge to the usual historical assumptions of *Doctor Who*. The Absolute, an observer-agent from outside normal space-time, becomes bogged down by the multiple perspectives around the Spanish Civil War. It attempts to impose an arbitrary history, collapsing the complexity of the events. George Orwell (whose novel *Nineteen Eighty-Four* [1949] links totalitarianism with the mediation and editing of history) appears as a character under his real name Eric Blair and gets detourned by the Absolute. The clue that alerts the Doctor to this state of affairs is a display of a neutered version of Picasso's *Guernica* (1937), which the Absolute's interference has rendered meaningless.

History 101 also includes the character of Sabbath, who first appeared in Lawrence Miles' *The Adventuress of Henrietta Street* (2001). As with the Monk in 'The Time Meddler', he is introduced as an antagonist, as a narrative 'double'. The difference here is that Sabbath has a keener grasp of the nature of history than the Doctor. While *History 101* at times struggles to accommodate its argument in a conventional *Doctor Who* framework, *The Adventuress of Henrietta Street* abandons the series' traditional storytelling limitations altogether. Aside from the conventional third-person prologue and epilogue (both headed 'fiction') the novel is written in the form of a history book, wringing pertinent detail (both real and invented) out of fictional sources. The distinction between 'pure history' and 'pseudo-history' evaporates completely. There is nothing to differentiate between the reported activities of genuine individuals and the fictional eruptions of the apelike *babewyns* into late eighteenth-century London. These monsters are at once incongruous and – because they are filtered entirely through historical and contemporary perceptions – very familiar.

Even so, this is still a genre game. *The Adventuress of Henrietta Street* is clearly indebted to current popular historical biographies as well as novels such as Thomas Pynchon's *Mason & Dixon* (1997). The first sentence of the first 'fiction' section playfully tells us: 'This is true'. The emergence of time travel as a fictional theme in the 1780s becomes a plot point and a minor character is jokingly given the name 'Dr Who'. History here is important, distinct from fiction, but the story doesn't have the 'classical' virtues one could impute from 'Marco Polo'.

Though in pre-publicity Miles claimed that *The Adventuress of Henrietta Street* belonged properly to *Doctor Who*'s earliest traditions and Halliday argued that *History 101* was a break from those traditions, these two novels can be read together as a potential new subgenre within *Doctor Who* (Darlington, 2001: 6; Darlington, 2002: 31). The coarsening of Sabbath's character in later books by other hands suggests that they are likely to remain one-offs: author-led explorations of history rather than a general trend encouraged by the producers and editors of the series. Nevertheless the potential exists for *Doctor Who* to re-engage with history on a deeper level than genre-play. The flawed classicism of 'Marco Polo' probably can't be recaptured in the twenty-first century without resorting to pastiche but these novels represent a new development. Neither 'pure' nor recognisably 'pseudo', they are a new wave of historicals waiting to break.

References

Cook, Benjamin. 2003. 'Moments of pleasure: interview with Christopher Bailey'. *Doctor Who Magazine*, No. 327, pp. 12–17.

Darlington, David. 2001. 'Coming up . . . *The Adventuress of Henrietta Street*'. *Doctor Who Magazine*, No. 310, p. 6.

Darlington, David. 2002. 'Coming up . . . *History 101*'. *Doctor Who Magazine*, No. 319, p. 31.

Evans, Andrew. 1992. 'Script editing Who: interview with Donald Tosh'. *Doctor Who Magazine*. No. 191, pp. 10–13.

Halliday, Mags L. 2002. *Doctor Who: History 101*. London: BBC.

Hope, Anthony. [1894] 1994. *The Prisoner of Zenda*. London: Penguin.

Howe, David J., Mark Stammers and Stephen James Walker. 1992. *Doctor Who: The Sixties*. London: Virgin.

Howe, David J., Mark Stammers and Stephen James Walker. 1994. *Doctor Who: The Handbook: The First Doctor*. London: Virgin.

Marley, Stephen. 1995. *Doctor Who – The Missing Adventures: Managra*. London: Virgin.

Miles, Lawrence. 2001. *Doctor Who: The Adventuress of Henrietta Street*. London: BBC.

Parkin, Lance. 1996. *Doctor Who – The New Adventures: Just War*. London: Virgin.

Russell, Gary. 1986a. 'Observing history'. *Doctor Who Magazine Summer Special*.

Russell, Gary. 1986b. 'Making history'. *Doctor Who Magazine Summer Special*.

Tulloch, John and Manuel Alvarado. 1983. *Doctor Who: The Unfolding Text*. London and Basingstoke: Macmillan.

Wood, Tat. 2003. 'Whom do they meet at the Roof of the World?' *Spaceball Ricochet*.

Discography

Doctor Who: 'The Marian Conspiracy' (2000) Produced by Jason Haigh-Ellery and Gary Russell. Directed by Gary Russell. Written by Jacqueline Rayner. Music by Alistair Lock. 110 mins (4 episodes). Big Finish Productions.

Doctor Who: 'The Fires of Vulcan' (2000) Produced by Jason Haigh-Ellery and Gary Russell. Directed by Gary Russell. Written by Steve Lyons. Music by Alistair Lock. 104 mins (4 episodes). Big Finish Productions.

Chapter 4

Bargains of necessity?
Doctor Who, Culloden and fictionalising history at the BBC in the 1960s

Matthew Kilburn

Doctor Who (1963–89) and *Culloden* (1964), Peter Watkins's filmed inter-pretation of the battle of Culloden in 1746 and its aftermath, were both projects originated by members of staff within the BBC in the early 1960s. A comparison between *Doctor Who* and *Culloden* might seem at first to be an unlikely one. One was a teatime drama serial intended for an audience whose average age was expected to be fourteen, and the other was a reconstruction of a historical event, using methods which were self-consciously experimental, and which distanced itself from the conventions of televised drama. They were commissioned by different departments in the BBC, and where the development of *Culloden* reflected the demands of a director committed to the pursuit of his own singular, authored vision, *Doctor Who* accepted, however much it sometimes protested, the compromises of production by committee within the hierarchical structures of a public-sector broadcaster. *Culloden* was broadcast as a freestanding documentary, although conceived as a forerunner of a series, seemingly irregular, of reconstructions of historical events; *Doctor Who* was a weekly serial which sought to engender viewer loyalty through familiarity of scheduling and format. However, both *Culloden* and *Doctor Who* were motivated by a desire to challenge conventional cul-tural assumptions. *Culloden* sought to portray a battle from a (subsequently romanticised) rebellion against the British government, using a style of reportage that British television viewers in 1964 would have associated with television news reporting of the Vietnam War. *Doctor Who*'s settings were initially divided between the futuristic and the historical with the intention that its predominantly youthful audience should be shown that both techno-logical innovation and the past events which had shaped their world were the province of ordinary people as well as members of the pantheon of great men and women celebrated by, for example, the Ladybird history books of L. Du Garde Peach, and to some extent by the adaptations from the English literary canon which populated weekend teatimes before *Doctor Who*.

In their different ways both *Doctor Who* and *Culloden* were products of a working environment at the BBC shaped by the corporation's quest to sustain its role in the cultural life of the United Kingdom in a transformed broadcasting environment. Television had replaced radio as the dominant medium, and the BBC's monopoly had been ended by the introduction of ITV from 1955. Director-General Hugh Greene intended that the BBC should be best placed, in words borrowed from the American broadcaster Ed Murrow, to 'hold a mirror to what was going on in contemporary society' (Briggs, 1995: 317) and reflect it to this new context. To achieve this end, the BBC had to prove the impossibility of its ITV rivals fulfilling this task, compromised as they were by the demands of their industrial shareholders and advertisers. At the same time the BBC was to attract innovative talent from the ITV contractors across all forms of output. BBC executives were keen to attract their own innovators as well.

Doctor Who and *Culloden* can be perceived, simplistically, as products of these two trends within the BBC of the early 1960s. From at least May 1963 Sydney Newman, Head of the Drama Group at BBC Television, had taken a leading role in the shaping of the proposed Saturday afternoon science fiction serial which became *Doctor Who*, and as such is regarded, at least, as one of the principal creators of the series. He had been 'poached' from ABC Television (the ITV contractor for the North of England and the Midlands at weekends from 1956 to 1968) during 1962, if not to refashion BBC television drama entirely in the 'kitchen sink' image of ABC's *Armchair Theatre* (1956–72), then certainly to invest BBC productions with Newman's 'agitational contemporaneity' (Sendall, 1982: 338). Several creative personnel of the early years of *Doctor Who* had either worked at ABC with Newman or had begun their careers at other ITV companies before joining the BBC. In contrast Peter Watkins, director of *Culloden*, came into the BBC from independent amateur filmmaking, outside the broadcasting hierarchy entirely. However, both programmes were governed by the decisions of the same group of executives, including Donald Baverstock, who in 1963 and 1964 held the post of Chief of Programmes, BBC 1; Huw Wheldon, who as Head of Documentaries and Music, Television, recruited Peter Watkins, was by 1965 Managing Director, Television, and as such also had an input, albeit a distant one, into the development of *Doctor Who*. They also drew from the same pool of television expertise, probably smaller than it is today: for example, both Watkins's BBC films, *Culloden* and *The War Game* (1965), had fight scenes co-ordinated by Derek Ware, a regular contributor to *Doctor Who*.

Historical dramatisation was part of the way in which the BBC presented itself as distinct from the 'contemporary' ITV. *Doctor Who*, through its early historical serials, and *Culloden* were both attempts to find new ways of presenting history to a television audience and thus fulfilling the BBC's duty as a national broadcaster by interpreting the collective past to the viewer. Almost every historical story saw the Doctor and his companions encountering a society which had an influence on the nature of British identity. *Culloden* was more overtly politically sensitive for the BBC than *Doctor Who*; but *Doctor Who*'s historical stories presented their own difficulties, both in terms of how the programme should dramatise history, and how the placement of historical stories was perceived by viewers and by BBC senior staff.

For the purposes of this chapter, the *Doctor Who* 'historicals' are defined as any serial transmitted between November 1963 and January 1967 which was set in Earth's past. This includes 'The Time Meddler' (1965), which although including the science fiction element of another time traveller, the Monk, independent of the Doctor and his companions, was classified as a historical story within the production office and justified as a story about the background to the Norman invasion of 1066. The one exception is the Ancient Egyptian section of 'The Daleks' Master Plan' (1965), where the setting is substantially a backdrop for the Daleks to carry out exterminations and be humiliated once more by the Doctor.

The last of *Doctor Who*'s historical stories was 'The Highlanders', broadcast in four parts in December 1966 and January 1967. 'The Highlanders' demonstrates that the historical serials were still fulfilling their function within the programme's format even when the educative brief of the series was being undermined during a period when it sought consolidation rather than the experimentation which the initial division into scientific and historical stories had encouraged. 'The Highlanders' deserves special comparison with Peter Watkins's *Culloden* because both are interpretations of the same historical event. 'The Highlanders' was the end product of a period when *Doctor Who* gradually moved away from its initial challenge to what had been established in the 1950s as suitable for early evening children's viewing, and was incorporated into a cosy, unthreatening BBC worldview. *Culloden*, meanwhile, was intended to initiate a series of documentary reconstructions of historical junctures which would challenge viewers' understanding of the nation, but its methods and message threatened the BBC's institutional relationships. Both Peter Watkins and *Doctor Who* can be portrayed as victims of their institutional position within a BBC which was expected by government and large interest groups to provide reassurance rather than revolution.

Establishing the 'historical'

The division between 'science fiction' and 'history' in its first few seasons is one of the commonplaces of writing about the early years of *Doctor Who*. The assumption that *Doctor Who* was created to meet a demand for these types of story would be misleading. The concept of serials set in the past, which showed the regular characters experiencing well-known historic events, arose from Sydney Newman's reaction to the draft format document for *Doctor Who* written in May 1963. Newman called for 'drama based upon and stemming from factual material and scientific phenomena and actual social history of past and future' (Howe et al., 1994: 177). This observation became an injunction. The 'General Notes on Background and Approach' drawn up in May 1963 envisaged stories located in 'real environments based on the best factual information of situations in time, in space and in any material state we can realise in practical terms' (Howe et al., 1994: 180). The document argued that *Doctor Who* was 'neither fantasy nor space travel nor science fiction' (Howe et al., 1994: 179) and pledged that 'each story will have a strong informational core based on fact' (Howe et al., 1994: 179).

Doctor Who's portrayal of history was to be neither nostalgic nor reverential. Sydney Newman was committed to *Doctor Who* being a beacon for progress, and emphasised the need for the time travellers to experience 'social' history. The 'General Notes' called for 'unusual exciting backgrounds, or ordinary backgrounds seen unusually' (Howe et al., 1994: 180). In the first serial, 'An Unearthly Child', the attitude of the travellers to the culture of the Palaeolithic tribe among which they find themselves is as much the concern of the script as the effect of their circumstances upon the regular characters. Correspondence from those connected with the serial suggests that the authenticity of the production was taken very seriously; yet the uncertain placing of that authenticity between scholarly study of the prehistoric (or such as was available to the production office) and dramatic credibility potentially compromised the serial. 'Dealing with cavemen, it's obviously ludicrous', was Waris Hussein's comment forty-one years later, citing the dramatic limitations of making 'a suspense story out of people grunting' (Cook, 2004: 13).

Hussein's observation reveals two assumptions: that *Doctor Who* was always going to be a 'suspense story'; and that Palaeolithic society was inarticulate. In a memorandum of September 1963, David Whitaker had ruled that stories set in the past had to be as full of 'excitement and action' as those set in the 'future'; but he acknowledged that the historical stories were proving more difficult in this regard. The serial provoked a detailed critique from two postgraduate students of archaeology, Barbara Johnson and Tony Priddy, who wrote on 30 November 1963 to 'the Director of Children's Television' to take the second episode to task (BBC WAC T5/649/1). Johnson and Priddy's letter was a list of technical observations about the distinction between the upper Palaeolithic and Neolithic ages, the scanty evidence for a patriarchal tribal system during the Palaeolithic, the variation of mean temperature within two generations, and the fully articulated condition of the skeleton found in the Cave of Skulls. Many of the factual statements in Whitaker's reply to

Johnson and Priddy have been questioned (Barnes, 2003: 31), but his letter was robust, arguing, for example, in the case of the 'social point about the tribal system being patriarchal, the evidence is certainly slender, but it is not an unfortunate means of presenting a dramatic plot, it does not quarrel too violently, I fancy, with fact, since there are no definite facts to the contrary' (BBC WAC T5/649/1, 10 December 1963). The question of whether the pre-historic tribe in the serial should talk had exercised the production team, writer Anthony Coburn having particularly pressed the case. Whitaker's fall-back position of 'dramatic licence' was reached swiftly. The grind of making *Doctor Who* would always depend on winning such generosity from the audience. For the historical stories, this confirmed that (at least under Lambert and Whitaker) interpretation would be led by what could be realised in the studio within the confines of an adventure serial.

Whitaker sought to find action in his scripts, but to Donald Baverstock, his efforts to do so were not successful. Baverstock found both 'An Unearthly Child' and 'The Daleks' (1963–4) too verbose, and considered the innocence of the Doctor and Susan, supposedly exiles from an advanced civilization, implausible. Looking ahead to the seven-part 'Marco Polo' (1964) serial, he argued that:

> Any ordinary man of the mid-twentieth century returning to, say, the Marco Polo age could hardly help making assertions all the time which would sound to the fourteenth century Chinese or Venetians like mad ludicrous prophecies. Likewise, the characters of the past and the future should also have appeared more strikingly and differently ingenious – the one more often reminding us of lost simple knowledge; the other of credible skills and capacities that can be conceived likely in the future. (BBC WAC T5/647/1, 31 December 1963)

Baverstock's solution to the challenge was to step away from it – 'to centre the dramatic movements much more on historical and scientific hokum' (BBC WAC T5/647/1, 31 December 1963). *Doctor Who* was endorsed, but Newman's hopes for a serial that would dramatise social history and scientific discoveries for a teatime audience were discouraged by Baverstock in favour of entertaining them with broad strokes.

Background and interpretation of history in *Culloden*

Doctor Who sought to familiarise its viewers with historical events and situations. Peter Watkins's intentions for *Culloden* were comparable, but from the outset were self-consciously polemical. On his Internet site he describes his motivation in these terms:

> This was the 1960s, and the US army was 'pacifying' the Vietnam highlands. I wanted to draw a parallel between these events and what had happened in

our own UK Highlands two centuries earlier, including because our knowledge of what took place after 'Culloden' was basically limited to an exotic
image of 'Bonnie Prince Charlie' on the label of a Drambuie whiskey bottle.
(Watkins, 2000)

Watkins's film was intended as a pilot for a new strand using non-
professional performers along the lines of Watkins's amateur work. He had
been making films since the mid-1950s and had come to the notice of broadcasters after his film *The Forgotten Faces* (1960), a reconstruction of the
Hungarian rising of 1956, won an amateur Oscar. These films would recreate
events from current affairs or history, in Watkins's words 'minute by minute',
under precise and close control of the director, mimicking the documentary
form. Watkins sought 'to offer a way of countering the effects of soap-opera
historical reconstructions and TV news broadcasts, by sharing with the public an alternative exploration and presentation of history – especially their *own*
history – be it past or present' (Watkins, 2000). His agenda bore comparison
to that which Sydney Newman had pursued when Head of Drama at ABC
Television: 'It's my role, when trying to reach a mass audience, to exclude
from my programme all Shakespeare, all the classics, all costume drama'
(Wiseman, 1962). While Newman's anxiety was that his ITV audience wouldn't
have the specialised knowledge to understand an overtly literary play, Watkins
in contrast wanted to explain the gaps in his BBC audience's knowledge by
forcefully manipulating images and sound.

Watkins had first planned a film about the consequences of the battle of
Culloden in the wake of the publication of John Prebble's book *Culloden* in
1961. Prebble attributed the depopulation of the Highlands directly to the
defeat of the Jacobite army, and rejected the conventional narrative of the
battle as a conflict between royal houses: 'the pretensions of princes quickly
become anachronisms, but the suffering they bring to ordinary people is
sadly familiar, whatever the century' (Prebble, 1996: xv). Prebble's book was
perhaps the more influential because he was not an academic; as a journalist
and dramatist he knew the power of both emotive storytelling and thorough
research. Watkins was actively developing the film as early as April 1962, when
he received a letter from W.A. Thorburn of the Scottish United Services
Museum, in reply to one from Watkins asking advice on military uniforms
and practice. By the time the film was commissioned for BBC 1 in early 1964,
Watkins was arguing for a project on a large scale, accurately reflecting the
quantity of participants in the events depicted.

Peter Watkins identified potentially sympathetic experts; not only W.A.
Thorburn, but John Prebble himself, clan historians R.W. and Jean Munro,
and Iain Cameron Taylor of the National Trust for Scotland. His BBC library
slips remain on file: they include the relevant volume of the *Oxford History of
England* for the period, *The Whig Supremacy* by Basil Williams (1939, revised

1962), Robert Laird Mackie's *A Short History of Scotland* (1929, revised 1962), Charles Petrie's *The Jacobite Movement* (1932, third edition 1959) and books on regimental uniform and highland dress (BBC WAC T32/515/1). The authoritative texts on the political history of the period were thus revised versions of books published two or three decades before Watkins started work; this could be viewed as representing complacency in academic eighteenth-century studies, which may be congruent with Watkins's wish to challenge what seemed to be deeply entrenched preconceptions about the Jacobite rising of 1746. None of Watkins's experts held a university post, which again puts Watkins's historical sensibility at a distance from the establishment, although it is worth remembering that the university sector was still small in the early 1960s.

Research and the *Doctor Who* historicals

All versions of the *Doctor Who* writers' guide in use between 1963 and 1966 urged that the writers base their work upon the latest historical and scientific research. The only *Doctor Who* historical for which a reading list survives is 'The Myth Makers' (1965), as part of a document entitled 'Historical Facts Surrounding the Trojan War' (BBC WAC T5/647/1, April 1965). It is almost certainly compiled by the story's writer, Donald Cotton, and lists volumes 2 and 3 of the *Cambridge Ancient History*, volume 22 of the *Encyclopaedia Britannica*, a *History of Greece, to 322 B.C.*, by M.G.L. Hammond (1959), and several other scholarly or general works dealing with early Greek civilisation. Cotton then remarks upon the non-Homeric sources for the war, many of which include names which appear in the *Iliad*, thereby justifying the inclusion of an episode from mythology and romance in *Doctor Who*'s historical strand. He recommended one particular book, *Homer and the Monuments* by H.L. Lorimer, as of potential interest to the designer.

Some documentary evidence survives for design research. Producer Verity Lambert sent a list of books used by Barry Newbery when designing the sets for 'Marco Polo' to Anthony J. Ireland, a teacher in Norwich (BBC WAC T5/647/2, 16 April 1964); these were mainly broad surveys of architecture and garden design, but included Sir Aurel Stein's archaeological study *Ruins of Desert Cathay* (1912), appropriate for the desert trek that makes up a considerable proportion of the serial's travelogue. When preparing to direct 'The Romans' (1965), Christopher Barry wrote to Professor A.M. Collini of the Museo Della Civita Romana in Rome requesting photographs or post-cards of the museum's models of first-century Rome (BBC WAC T5/1235/1, 29 October 1964). There were practical constraints on the application of this kind of research. The production of *Doctor Who* had to negotiate between 'accuracy' and what was thought proper for or expected by its audience. It's stated on the commentary track for the DVD release of 'The Aztecs' (1964) that the costume designer for that story had to compromise between authentic Aztec costume, too immodest for a teatime audience, and what was deemed acceptable for the programme. Tony Snell's research in Tombstone proved of little use to Barry Newbery, whose sets for 'The Gunfighters' (1966), Daniel O'Mahony (2004: 76) has observed, drew 'on audience expectations as much as' and probably much more than 'authenticity'.

This balance was explored practically in *Culloden* by Peter Watkins, who would kick the legs of his cameraman's tripod in order to simulate the effects of the vibrations of cannon shot striking the battlefield, but rejected the site of the battle of Culloden itself as a location for his film on the grounds that 'for me, there was not one jot of "feel" of the original at all at Culloden' (BBC WAC T32/515/2, 26 June 1964). Watkins was an individual filmmaker expressing strongly held personal views about his particular historical juncture; *Doctor Who* was made by a group of people who inevitably held conflicting interpretations of the vague brief to be educational from their superior.

For most *Doctor Who* writers their imagination was more valuable than research in libraries. There is enough in John Lucarotti's depiction of the Aztecs' social structure to suggest that he may have read George C. Vaillant's *The Aztecs of Mexico*, published by Penguin in the UK in 1950, but if so he simplified what he learned to serve an audience of children and tired weekending adults. Alan Barnes has argued convincingly that the foundation of Anthony Coburn's research for 'An Unearthly Child' was actually a novel, William Golding's *The Inheritors* (Barnes, 2003: 30). Dennis Spooner claimed that 'The Romans' was heavily influenced by *Carry On Cleo*:

> We had the same researcher, and the 'Carry On . . .' films were never very serious with their research [. . .] Gertan Klauber was in both; that wasn't a coincidence – that's where it all came from! (Tulloch and Alvarado, 1983: 157)

The contrast with Cotton's approach is marked. In the 1980s *Doctor Who* fan critics would group Spooner's 'The Romans' together with 'The Myth Makers' and 'The Gunfighters' as comic stories, probably contributing to the decision of publishers W.H. Allen to commission Cotton to novelise Spooner's story. The unfavourable reviews revealed the difference between Cotton's and Spooner's priorities. Spooner's stories were more lighthearted and tended to exploit rather than challenge audience expectations based upon perceptions of history rooted in popular culture. 'The Reign of Terror' establishes a shaky parallel between the Revolutionary France of 1793 and Nazi-occupied Germany of the early 1940s, with its story of an underground network smuggling British agents and government opponents out of the country, under the noses of a government whose values are presented as alien. Napoleon is brought on, ahistorically, in the final episode as an aside, to inform the viewer of what happened 'next', brushing aside the regimes that immediately followed that of Robespierre. 'The Romans', after having the Doctor indirectly inspire the Great Fire of 64 AD, concludes the section of the story involving the non-regulars by showing Nero's servant Tavius holding a cross hung around his neck, collapsing the time between the reign of Nero and the triumph of Christianity three centuries later, as well as playing up to connections that the audience might make between 'The Romans' and near-contemporary cinema such as *Quo Vadis* (1951), *The Robe* (1953) and *Ben Hur* (1959), which all intermixed the struggles of early Christianity and the hardships of life under Roman emperors of the Julio-Claudian line. Cotton's *Doctor Who* serials, meanwhile, play with form to subvert audience expectations: Greek heroes become country gentleman soldiers going through the motions of a stagnant war, while the legendary figures of the American west are exposed as petty villains.

Historical reconstruction in *Culloden*

Culloden was widely recognised in the wake of its broadcast as having challenged the established self-image of nations and nationhood within the United Kingdom. Much of the criticism came from Scotland. A columnist in the *Inverness Courier* of 18 December 1964 thought that the film was 'a gross insult to the Highland people and an equally gross perversion of Highland history' (BBC WAC T32/1164/1), a charge thoroughly denied by Watkins in his response to the paper. Much later, Watkins remarked to John Cook that many of those who appreciated *Culloden* failed to realise that it was engaging contemporary notions of national identity and history; thus up to a point it failed (Cook, 2003).

Watkins's belief in historical reconstruction that involved both passive and active participating publics challenged structural relationships within the BBC and between the BBC and interest groups with which it had effective partnerships. The arguments the BBC had with Equity over the use of non-professionals in *Culloden* were based around whether Watkins had violated an accord between the BBC and the actors' union reached by a standing joint committee of both parties in 1954, and reiterated by a meeting between the BBC and Equity in the wake of *Culloden*, that 'the BBC did not use amateurs when suitable professionals were reasonably available' (BBC WAC T32/515/1, 19 July 1965).

The battle lines of the defending armies at *Culloden* proved well fortified; Equity was to help ensure that historical personalities remained interpreted on television within accepted dramatic conventions and by paid professionals. Watkins's historical reconstruction argued its case to a mass audience by placing people who were ordinarily part of that audience, and notionally representative of that audience, in the roles of historical characters. Thus, the BBC, who normally employed professionals on behalf of the community, was instead overrun by self-nominated representatives from the general public, an *ad hoc* community re-enacting, under an opinionated director, a turning point in British national history.

The *Doctor Who* historicals and the Sunday serial

Doctor Who featured audience identification figures played by actors and was scheduled in a time slot traditionally associated with viewing exclusively for children (which would have made it appear less threatening than a mid-evening broadcast such as *Culloden*). However, although there were no contemporary serials until very close to the end of its third series, *Doctor Who* was established with an eye to dramatising contemporary issues. A memorandum from November 1963 gives the proposed sixth serial as set in Britain in 400 AD, 'when the Romans are just about to retire from the island. The Romans leave behind them an authority which intends to carry on their civilisation but this is opposed by a group of people who see profit in destruction and disorder. This latter group are excellent allies for invading Saxons, completely opposed to anything Roman' (BBC WAC T5/647/1). The subject evokes anxieties about Britain's decolonisation process in the 1960s. It suggested that *Doctor Who* stood for a classical civilised society, perhaps not too far removed either from the parallels between imperial Britain and ancient Rome favoured by British elites in the eighteenth and nineteenth centuries, or from the welfare state technocracy of the post-war generation, run by a professional class similar to the BBC. *Doctor Who* also stood for 'ordinary people' pursuing their daily lives – which might happen to be that of an emissary of Kublai Khan in thirteenth-century Cathay, a widow in fifteenth-century Mexico, or tradesmen getting by in revolutionary France.

The problem of communicating ideas through adventure stories remained. Audience reports tended towards championing the series as escapist, undemanding fare. Mrs B.M. Strachan of Merthyr Tydfil told the BBC's Audience Research Department in March 1964 that 'from the comments of many children I do not think it will retain its popularity with the new Marco Polo episode, the unknown future of the Daleks, etc. being more interesting to the children' (BBC WAC T5/647/2, 29 March 1964).

In August 1964 Whitaker would tell an aspiring contributor to the series, Patricia Ammesley, that she was wrong to think that the child audience were only interested in the science fiction stories, but he also revealed that 'This is fortunate because we only regard the historical stories as necessary make-weights between the futuristic science fiction ones' (BBC WAC T5/649/1, 21 August 1964). Perhaps it was the increasing confidence of the production office that they could deliver futuristic adventure stories on £2,300 or so a week that ensured that there were fewer historicals in the second season, as much as any perception that these were less popular and that the public was looking for Daleks or other extraterrestrials.

The dichotomous structure of the series developed from the need to concentrate on serial formats that worked and would hold audiences. From the viewpoint of Donald Baverstock, *Doctor Who* was 'the Saturday afternoon serial': a format that allowed otherwise disconnected serials to appear under the same banner with the hope of deterring viewers from deserting after a popular segment. *Doctor Who* was probably expected to enjoy a comparable budget to the Sunday serial, transferred from the children's department to the Drama Group in 1963. The Saturday and Sunday serials were seen as having a close relationship. *Doctor Who* shared its press launch in November 1963 with the Sunday afternoon dramatisation of Robert Louis Stevenson's *Kidnapped*.

The *Doctor Who* historical could potentially be used to deflect criticism that the variety of children's programmes had been stifled by a monolithic science fiction serial. The Doctor's voyages into the past were biased away from the seventeenth- and eighteenth-century locales of the teatime literary canon of *Lorna Doone*, *The Old Curiosity Shop*, *Kidnapped*, *Catriona*, *Martin Chuzzlewit* and *Rupert of Hentzau*, all of which were screened on Sundays in 1963 or 1964. Sydney Newman expressed a wish to escape from literary adaptations: 'for Sunday serials they should consider dramatised biographies of great men, for example, Bell of the telephone, Louis Pasteur, Braille etc.' (BBC WAC T16/62/3, 17 July 1964). This suggestion was not taken up, but is revealing of Newman's continuing desire that the family serials should both be improving and break away from literary archetypes.

In the event, the literary serial survived on Sundays, and the format of *Doctor Who*'s historicals respected it. Only 'The Reign of Terror', of the serials in the first year of production, entered familiar literary territory. In 1964 incoming story editor Dennis Spooner explained to viewer Roderick Adams that the setting of *Doctor Who*'s historical stories had to respect the periods in which the Sunday adaptations were set, and thus a policy had been agreed to avoid stories set after 1600 (BBC WAC T5/649/1, 16 October 1964). This argument was deployed again by Spooner later in the production of the 1964–5 season, to justify his rejection of a storyline by John Lucarotti about the Indian Mutiny, despite the idea having first been commissioned from Terry Nation by David Whitaker in September 1963 (BBC WAC RCONT 18, John Lucarotti, 25 June 1965). The effect was to stop *Doctor Who* from challenging literary interpretations of history and instead to become dependent on them; a trend embraced by the programme's fourth story editor, Gerry Davis, when commissioning and eventually co-writing the last historical story, 'The Highlanders'.

Genesis of 'The Highlanders'

'The Highlanders' was made by a *Doctor Who* production office seemingly impatient with historical settings and determined to concentrate on the future as a destination for their time and space travellers. Innes Lloyd asserted to Rex Tucker, director of 'The Gunfighters', that: 'it has been proved before that if you put him next to historical characters [...] it does in some way diminish the feeling the audience has of him as a science fiction figure' (BBC WAC T5/1249/1, 10 May 1966). Gerry Davis claimed to see more potential in the historicals, albeit with qualifications. Nearly twenty-five years after commissioning 'The Highlanders', he wrote that 'At the time I was looking for historical stories that were based on identifiable areas of fiction [...] if you could get close to some of the established classics like *Kidnapped*, people might be familiar with it' (Davis, 1991). Despite this, an informational core as envisaged by the series format document remains present. The provisional title for the serial, 'Culloden', recalls not only Peter Watkins's documentary, but also the book by John Prebble which acted as one of Watkins's sources. According to Prebble, 936 of the 3,470 Jacobite prisoners shared the fate narrowly escaped by those imprisoned on the *Annabelle* in the serial, and were transported abroad to serve as indentured labourers in the colonies (Prebble, 1996: 233). The sentiments of the *Annabelle*'s deposed skipper, Willie Mackay, echo those of Prebble, for whom the highlanders shipped abroad to the plantations suffered the worst fate of all the captured Jacobites: 'Better a quick and honourable death at the end of a rope' ('The Highlanders' episode three, 31 December 1966). In the final episode (7 January 1967), the Doctor mentions sleepily that the highlanders will be able to return from exile after seven years; this is a reference to the Act of Grace of 1752, by which those who had risen in support of the Stuart cause in 1745 and 1746 were pardoned by the Hanoverian British state.

Gerry Davis wrote that he thought that historical characters should remain in the background in *Doctor Who* stories, 'influencing events but never getting involved' (Davis, 1991). 'The Highlanders' is about ordinary people caught up in events rather than about the main protagonists. Davis was justified in arguing this style of storytelling as a break from *Doctor Who*'s established tradition. The 'General Notes', as quoted by David Whitaker, rationalised the characters' influence on historical characters thus: 'We cannot tell Nelson how to win at the Battle of the Nile because no viewer would accept such a hypothesis. However, we can influence one Captain on board a minor ship in Napoleon's Armada' (BBC WAC T5/649/1, 1 May 1964). In fact, the first two seasons saw the Doctor interacting with and influencing historical characters, such as Marco Polo, Nero and Richard the Lionheart, as well as coming into close proximity with Robespierre.

Interfering in history

David Whitaker had stated, in a letter to a viewer, that 'Doctor Who is an observer' (BBC WAC T5/649/1, 1 May 1964). Whitaker doubtless had in mind 'The Aztecs', then in studio, where the history teacher Barbara Wright (with science teacher Ian Chesterton representing both halves of the series' dual authority as interpreter of the 'historic' past and 'scientific' future) is frustrated in her desire to end the Aztec custom of human sacrifice:

Barbara: If I could start the destruction of everything that is evil here, then everything that is good would survive when Cortes lands.
The Doctor: You can't rewrite history! Not one line!

Barbara eventually learns her lesson, and reminds the Doctor, and the audience, of it in the subsequent historical story, Dennis Spooner's 'The Reign of Terror' (1964), where she recognises that she can't stop the guillotining. Spooner would later allow himself more latitude with the house doctrine on the involvement of the Doctor and company with historical events, allowing the Doctor inadvertently to give Nero the idea for starting the Great Fire of Rome ('The Romans', 1965). He made amends with 'The Time Meddler' (1965), at the close of the second season, where the Doctor's responsible attitude to historical events is contrasted with the Monk's enjoyment of their instigation. The Doctor even had expository dialogue early in the serial which narrated the recorded course of events to the viewer. Yet the implication is that the Doctor's earlier argument to Barbara has been mistaken; the Doctor is an observer because he chooses to be, just as, outside the fiction of the Doctor's travels, the writers chose not to have the Doctor influence any real historical figures.

By contrast, in 'The Highlanders' the Doctor not only facilitates the escape of the captive Jacobites from the *Annabelle*, he takes one of them, Jamie, with him. The Doctor, as written by Gerry Davis and played by Patrick Troughton, was now exhibiting a happy-go-lucky interventionism and carrying his moral burden more lightly. Furthermore, Davis provides 'The Highlanders' with a happy ending. Lieutenant Algernon ffinch arrests Solicitor Grey and takes him off for trial, telling him 'There's only one end for slave-traders, solicitor!' It's unlikely that moonlighting solicitors were actively shipping prisoners off to the colonies illicitly so soon after the battle of Culloden; and they did not need to when transportation, with lucrative official contracts, was to become government policy.

'The Highlanders' sidesteps a concern explored earlier in 'The Massacre of St Bartholomew's Eve' (1966) that the historical situations in which the travellers found themselves could demand moral decisions which from a twentieth-century standpoint might be found reprehensible. 'The Highlanders' showed cruelty defeated and the villains anachronistically found out. 'The Massacre of St Bartholomew's Eve' seeks to establish that the Doctor's victories in historical situations would be limited. His companion Steven pronounces the Doctor to be responsible for the death of a young sixteenth-century French protestant, Anne Chaplet. The Doctor's dismissal of Steven's anxieties about Anne's safety earlier in the episode seems played as deliberate and it is difficult at first for the viewer to dissent from Steven's interpretation of events. The Doctor justifies his actions:

> History sometimes gives us a terrible shock. That is because we don't quite fully understand. Why should we? After all, we're all too small to realise its final pattern. Therefore, don't try and judge it from where you stand. I was right to do as I did. Yes, that I firmly believe. I dare not change the course of history.

The final sentence refers back to the Doctor's argument with Barbara in 'The Aztecs', but writer Donald Tosh's more considered treatment of the Doctor's engagement with human history was the unsurprising outcome of the amendments to Whitaker's doctrine of non-interference introduced in Dennis Spooner's second and third historical serials.

Watkins had several misapprehensions which his historical advisers endeavoured to correct, the principal one being that the government army was exclusively 'English'. This occasionally slipped into the finished production even though Watkins early made the point that there were more Scotsmen ranged against Prince Charles Edward than in the ranks of his army. In contrast 'The Highlanders' enthusiastically depicts the Jacobite army – whose cause is never properly explained – as the Scots, and their opponents as the English.

'The Highlanders' and *Culloden*

The similarities between 'The Highlanders' and *Culloden* seem more remarkable than those shared with its supposed model *Kidnapped*. We move from the battlefield, to Inverness, and then deal with the fates of the prisoners. Both anecdotal and documentary evidence suggests that Elwyn Jones had very little to do with the finished product. However, given that the provisional title for the *Doctor Who* serial was 'Culloden' it may initially have been conceived as a pastiche of the Watkins documentary. Elwyn Jones had been Head of the Drama-Documentary Unit within the old Drama Department before Sydney Newman arrived in 1963, whereupon the unit disappeared. In obtaining a commission for *Culloden* Watkins had driven his tanks on to what had been Jones's field.

A more helpful parallel is that the reaction to both *Culloden* and *Doctor Who*, from outside and within the BBC, showed that there was sustained interest in the presentation of history on television. John Crockett, who directed 'The Aztecs' for *Doctor Who*, submitted a list of potential periods or historical crises worthy of dramatisation to Verity Lambert. Watkins had drawn up such a list himself. Period drama was common on BBC television in 1964. In addition to the emergence of the BBC 2 classic serial, in some cases later repeated on BBC 1, BBC 2 embarked on original sequences of plays, such as the three plays by Ken Taylor on the history of religious thought in Europe, *The Heretics* (BBC 2, 3 May 1964–17 May 1964), set in the twelfth, sixteenth and twentieth centuries, and four plays by Ted Willis, *The Four Seasons of Rosie Carr* (BBC 1, 4 July 1964–25 July 1964), taking a working-class woman from her poverty-stricken childhood in 1907, to 'this strange and altered England which is called the Welfare State' (Willis, 1964). Willis noted in the *Radio Times* that the Rosie Carr series was endorsed by Sydney Newman, and perhaps indicates the sort of history that Newman hoped the TARDIS travellers would encounter.

The end of the *Doctor Who* historical

It was perhaps these mid- and late-evening non-juvenile dramas that helped create the context for the end of the *Doctor Who* historical. If the historical stories served as a touchstone of familiarity for the BBC's financial planners, then as *Doctor Who* progressed this need became less pronounced as it became clear what could be realised on the budget and what could not. The decision made by Innes Lloyd and Gerry Davis in 1966 to introduce stories set on contemporary or near-contemporary Earth, a simple but dramatic reinterpretation of the initial format's requirement for 'usual situations seen unusually', enabled the balance of the series to change from future/past to future/contemporary. Science fiction elements in period settings were now featured – as in 'The Evil of the Daleks' (1967) and 'The Abominable Snowmen' (1967) – which treated such mingling as just something the series did and not, as did 'The Time Meddler', as a commentary on the series' responsible attitude to history.

Lloyd was also moving to defend *Doctor Who* by altering the elements in its dichotomous structure. In the months before Lloyd's arrival at *Doctor Who*, there had been criticism that the programme lacked a character to represent the contemporary viewer following the departure of Ian and Barbara at the conclusion of 'The Chase' (1965). According to the BBC Audience Research Report on the first two episodes of the succeeding story, 'The Time Meddler', some viewers did not identify with 'the new young man', Steven, on the grounds that he was from the future and not from twentieth-century London (BBC WAC T5/2529/1). Five months later Gerald Savory, Head of Serials, rebuked *Doctor Who*'s producer John Wiles: 'May I once again emphasise that the part of Stephen [sic] must be firmly rooted in the present [. . .] This means that he must show no surprise at anything modern nor at events such as a cricket match' (BBC WAC T5/1246/1, 31 December 1965). Savory was probably referring to the TARDIS's materialisation during a test match during episode eight of 'The Daleks' Master Plan', where neither the Doctor, Steven nor the equally futuristic Sara Kingdom recognised the game or even that they were on Earth. Savory's memo was copied to Lloyd, and it is suggestive that the first serial to be made that was commissioned by Lloyd was the assertively modern 'The War Machines' (1966).

'The War Machines' furnished the Doctor with two contemporary assistants, Ben and Polly, meeting Savory's anxiety, but also showed that the attractions of the 'future' stories – both speculation (global computer network) and threat (computer at heart of said network wants to subjugate humanity) – could be realised in the present day and thus further overcome perceived problems with audience identification. Additionally, Lloyd had to secure *Doctor Who* from the threat of another BBC 1 Saturday early evening serial, aimed at the pre- and early teens audience. *Quick Before They Catch Us* (1966) was described in 2003 as 'a mod mystery series for older kids' whose three young adult leads 'patrolled the mean streets of Carnaby and bedsit land' (McGown and Docherty, 2003: 34). *Quick Before They Catch Us* did not reach a second series, and its commissioning history has not been researched; but its twenty-episode run between May and October 1966 suggested the mood of the moment at the serials department, and *Doctor Who* was success-fully refashioned to take advantage of that mood.

Thus, after 'The Highlanders', the historicals disappeared, and with them much of *Doctor Who*'s original personality. Attempts were made by Lloyd and Davis early in their tenure to boost the 'informational core' – there are elements of 'The War Machines' and 'The Tenth Planet' (1966) in particular that bear witness to this, as well as 'The Highlanders'. However, under pressure from the requirement to tell 'strong, simple stories' which would aggressively engage the viewers' attention, the dominance of the 'informational core' was compromised (Howe et al., 1994: 305). The legacy of the historical stories was most immediately a negative one; the response to them recorded by the Audience Research Department suggested that viewers regarded them as too challenging, or incongruous within a science fiction series. 'The Smugglers' and 'The Highlanders' were perhaps too close to the subject matter of the Sunday evening serials. *Doctor Who* had moved from a series which surprised teatime audiences with the unfamiliar, to being a series which presented them with a science fiction based familiarity where the historicals seemed lost. The new model of science fiction stories introduced under Lloyd and Davis, the so-called 'base under siege' strand, combined futuristic settings with recognisable power structures; no longer would viewers have to accustom themselves to fifteenth-century Aztec society, or indeed the complex power structures of the Earth empire of the year 5000 ('The Daleks' Master Plan', 1965). The lesson learned was that the audience of *Doctor Who* liked to be entertained rather than stretched, and it would be several years before a producer came into the office who again recognized *Doctor Who*'s potential for social commentary.

The vicissitudes of the *Doctor Who* historicals stemmed from their position as the product of a studio system; the vision behind the programme was always subordinate to the corporate needs of the BBC. Peter Watkins appears to have left because the BBC fell short of his expectations as the champions of a pluralist democractic society. The BBC preferred directors who worked as professionals within the closed elite of the BBC, rather than pursuing the agenda sought by Watkins, which would have bridged the divide between professional and non-professional, the rulers and the ruled.

Perhaps ironically, *Doctor Who* abandoned the historical story just as its department within Drama Group, Serials, found a successful model for period drama in *The Forsyte Saga* (1967). This seemed to confirm that popular historical drama was best approached as adaptation. *Doctor Who*'s development seems to have owed little or nothing to *The Forsyte Saga*; it is difficult to envisage *Doctor Who* undertaking a family saga or an historical critique of merchant capitalism in the late 1960s. In contrast, and in keeping with the aforementioned practice of building stories around recognisable hierarchies, Innes Lloyd encouraged his directors to approach actors who had appeared in the ATV boardroom dramas, *The Plane Makers* (1963–5) and *The Power Game* (1965–9), leading to the appearance of Peter Barkworth in 'The Ice Warriors' (1967).

By the time that the 'pseudo-historical' had become part of *Doctor Who*'s stylistic repertoire in the mid-1970s, historical drama on television had moved further, literary adaptations sharing the limelight with biographical dramas that drew from specific biographical texts. The first of these was perhaps Donald Wilson's *The First Churchills* (1969), relying on the eighteenth-century apologia written by Sarah, duchess of Marlborough; but probably the best-known exponent of the genre was ATV's *Edward the Seventh* (1975). *Doctor Who*'s period serials of the 1970s had the trappings of historical costume drama but had few claims to be familiarising the audience with the period. A discussion of experiments late in the run of the original series, such as a story where the period trappings alone were to suffice for the drama ('Black Orchid', 1982) and, later, 'The Mark of the Rani' (1985) and 'Remembrance of the Daleks' (1988), which blended the programme's science fiction mythology with historical information and commentary, would say more about the problems of maintaining *Doctor Who* as an ongoing series on BBC 1 in the 1980s than it would provide insight into the programme's

1960s context or about the presentation of history on British television in the 1980s.

References

BBC WAC T5/647/1, '*Doctor Who*, General A'.
BBC WAC T5/647/2, '*Doctor Who*, General A'.
BBC WAC T5/649/1, '*Doctor Who*, Viewers' Letters'.
BBC WAC T5/1246/1, '*Doctor Who*, Series V episodes 1–2'.
BBC WAC T5/1249/1, '*Doctor Who*, Series Z'.
BBC WAC T5/2529/1, '*Doctor Who*, Series S episodes 1–4'.
BBC WAC T5/1235/1, '*Doctor Who*, Series M episode 2'.
BBC WAC T16/62/3, 'TV Policy Drama 1959–64'.
BBC WAC T32/515/1, '*Culloden*, General Correspondence'.
BBC WAC T32/515/2, '*Culloden*, General Correspondence'.
BBC WAC T32/1164/1, 'TV Talks *Culloden*, General Correspondence'.
BBC WAC RCONT 18, 'John Lucarotti'.
Barnes, Alan. 2003. 'The fact of fiction: 100,000 BC'. *Doctor Who Magazine*, No. 337, pp. 26–33.
Briggs, Asa. 1995. *The History of Broadcasting in the United Kingdom*, Vol. 5, *Competition*. Oxford: Oxford University Press.
Cook, John. 2003. Commentary. *Culloden* [DVD]. London: British Film Institute.
Cook, Benjamin. 2004. 'Making history: interview with Waris Hussein'. *Doctor Who Magazine*, No. 344, pp. 12–17.
Davis, Gerry. 1991. 'Introduction to "The Highlanders" photonovel'. *DWB*, No. 89.
Howe, David J., Mark Stammers and Stephen James Walker. 1994. *Doctor Who – The Handbook: The First Doctor*. London: Virgin Publishing.
Lambert, Verity, William Russell and Carole Ann Ford. 2002. Commentary. *Doctor Who*: 'The Aztecs' [DVD]. London: BBC Worldwide.
McGown, Alistair and Mark Docherty. 2003. *The Hill and Beyond: Children's Television Drama – An Encyclopedia*. London: British Film Institute.
O'Mahony, Daniel. 2004. 'I fought the law'. *Doctor Who Magazine Special Edition: The Complete First Doctor*, p. 76.
Prebble, John. [1961] 1996. *Culloden*. Rev. edn with new introduction. London: Penguin.
Sendall, Bernard. 1982. *Independent Television in Britain. Volume 1: Origin and Foundation, 1946–62*. London: Macmillan.
Tulloch, John and Manuel Alvarado. 1983. *Doctor Who: The Unfolding Text*. London and Basingstoke: Macmillan.
Watkins, Peter. 2000. 'Culloden'. www.mnsi.net/~pwatkins/culloden.htm (accessed 23 January 2005).
Willis, Ted. 1964. *Radio Times*, 2 July.
Wiseman, T. 1962. 'Keeper of the public's drama'. *Time and Tide*, 7 June.

Part II

The subtext of death:
narratives, themes and structures

Chapter 5

The empire of the senses: narrative form and point-of-view in *Doctor Who*

Tat Wood

For a series which ran from the era of 405-line monochrome to digital paint-box effects, and from turret-mounted lenses on Orthicon cameras in Lime Grove studio to hand-held ENG-style cameras in stories made entirely on location, the narrative style and mode of address in *Doctor Who* is remarkably consistent. This is curious enough, but when one considers that many if not most of the people making the series were young and ambitious (from Verity Lambert and Waris Hussein onwards), and that the effects and pop-cultural references that such a series needs required so much innovative work, it is weird. There may be noticeable differences in budget and the pace of editing between a story made in 1964 and 1984, but these are trivial. For all that individual directors (such as Douglas Camfield, Michael Ferguson, David Maloney and Graeme Harper) may have looked to the cinema for their visual style, or copied US cop shows here and there, as a whole *Doctor Who* seems to have hit on its ideal form very quickly, and stuck with it. (Prior to 1970 there are only a few trims and technical changes, and barely any after 1974's debut of the Outside Broadcast VT camera. The major shift is making whole stories in one go, rather than an episode per week. Most people don't know this, and can't tell any difference.) But where did this 'baseline' form draw its influences from? In this chapter, I contend that the form of address in the series, the 'default' style of narrative, is a consequence of how the BBC made non-fiction in the years leading up to 1963.

With the BBC's Written Archive being so gleefully plundered by fans and academics alike, there is a well-rehearsed creation-myth for the series. The tale is told of how ABC's Head of Drama, Sydney Newman, came to the BBC, saw and conquered; how *Quatermass* (1953–9) and *Pathfinders* (1960–1) begat *Doctor Who* (sort of) and how a time machine was wrought from a blown-up photo of fruit-packaging (for the walls of the TARDIS interior), plus a piano and an old door-key (for the sound effect). The BBC was reinventing itself, we are told, and needed an exciting, educational

science-and-history show, pedagogy with fights and chases, to go between
Juke Box Jury (1959–67) and *Dixon of Dock Green* (1955–76). The space age
and the era of the satire boom led to a nostalgic yearning for the great age
of imperial certainties and the virtues of exploration for its own sake.

I'd like to propose another story.

Unlike conventionally 'authored' pieces, *Doctor Who* has generally eschewed
a conventional narrator. In those cases where someone has intervened between
the viewer and the story to offer a point-of-view (POV), this has been a piece
of local 'colour', such as Marco Polo's journal ('Marco Polo' [1964]), the
woodcuts depicting the *Bartholemée* ('The Massacre' [1966]) or 'The Ballad
of the Last Chance Saloon' ('The Gunfighters' [1966]). Such narrative gim-
micks are part of how we expect a story set in the period in question (1285,
1572 and 1888 respectively) to be told. Interventions between a supposedly
real 'event' and the viewers belong with the genre of story being told. Even
when Tom Baker's voice recites from a *Maltese Falcon*-style scroll at the start
of 'The Deadly Assassin' (1976), the 'oddness' of this is intentionally foregrounded. (As the core of that story is the subjective battle of the Doctor in
the 'Dreamscape' of the APC Net, a transition accompanied, as with the
'mind-duel' in 'The Brain of Morbius' [1976], with a clip of the title sequence,
we're intended to think of this as the Doctor's consciousness 'narrating'
throughout the story.) The Doctor is not usually narrating, but *some* agency
is deciding whose face we can see in a whodunnit, or the precise sequence of
events in a cliffhanger. In a story such as 'The Keys of Marinus' (1964) both
the 'correct' version of events in Morphoton (Barbara's 'subjective' POV
being 'true' and the 'objective' one an hallucination) and withholding the
identity of the person who frames Ian for Eprim's death are options the
programme selects for us. A possible 'internal' explanation of this is offered
in 'The Trial of a Time Lord' (1986), in which the Matrix shows not just the
Doctor's sense data but a synthesis of all subjective accounts from within the
TARDIS's (presumably telepathic) 'collection field'.

No such 'explanation' was offered in the early 1960s because none was
necessary. In each new environment visited by our heroes, the style of address,
the appropriateness or otherwise of the formal properties of narrative, was
part of the setting, along with the incidental music or set design. If one
story had electronica and *musique concrète* and also had a subjective shot
of something approaching Barbara with a sink-plunger outstretched before
it ('The Daleks' [1963–4]) that was all part of how that planet and that
story worked.

In effect, *Doctor Who* had authority. Whilst no one character, not even
the eponymous Doctor, was the 'focal point' of the story, we were seeing
what happened to the TARDIS crew as though this were the most important

element (although this is not universally true, especially in the more assured phase of Donald Tosh's story editorship, 1965–6). When an important piece of 'background' is told to the crew, it is told to us; the viewers are not shown events in the distant past unless they have a direct bearing on the protagonists and their adventure. Even a gap of 140 million years between Eldrad's execution and Sarah finding the remains (in 'The Hand of Fear' [1976]) is shown as cause-and-effect. A whole one-episode story, 'Mission to the Unknown' (1965), is shown to set up the events of a longer story four weeks later in screen time ('The Daleks' Master Plan' [1965–66]) with a six-thousand-year 'detour' back to the Trojan Wars to explain why Steven is injured and who this new girl on the ship is ('The Myth Makers' [1965]).

Even though the Doctor has installed a 'Time-Space Visualiser' aboard his vessel, it is empirical, first-hand observation which is deemed important. The story where this contraption is unveiled, 'The Chase' (1965), begins with a vision of the TARDIS as – to all intents and purposes – a weekend with the folks.[1] Ian is reading a book of space adventures, Barbara is sewing for Vicki and the Doctor is tinkering. And when he shows off his new acquisition, the 'family' gathers around the set to watch big moments in history, 'live'.[2] Eventually, this tendency is made a signature of the programme's ideological bent, by setting the Doctor's first-handedness against the remote observation of the Time Lords. The means by which they catch him is a box of telepathic signals he sends to them, which he later submits is the 'direct, first-hand' account, an eye-witness testimony to the crimes of the War Lords ('The War Games' [1969]).

For the viewers, the TARDIS crew performed a multitude of functions, but the conventional 'identification' portfolio was originally pretty low in the mix. None of the original crew was an uncomplicated 'representative' or 'ideal'. Ian, the closest to it, has plot function as dispenser of everyday science tips and (somewhat improbably for the average comprehensive teacher) being effective in a fight. What he and his friends do, however, is to allow us to see them seeing things. Vivian Sobchack (1987: 141–3) has usefully described the progress of most monster/disaster/space films as being from montage to mise-en-scène. The 'money shot' is not so much seeing Godzilla, but seeing Godzilla *in* Tokyo, in a surrounding that gives it a sense of scale and of his potential to cause damage (and Susan Sontag's comments on the appeal of this sort of spectacle are just as valid, although London is never *quite* destroyed [2004: 40–7]). So when we have, through the magic of state-of-the-art, 1963-style Inlay shots, a picture with the Dalek city on the left of the screen and the TARDIS crew on the right, all subsequent shots of Dalekopolis 'read' as being of a place (and close-ups are used to establish where in the city each part of the story is happening). The cast members function as yardsticks, figures in a landscape. And in this regard *Doctor Who* is different from

Quatermass (which got its *frisson* from England-made-strange, yes, but the end of the first story was the only occasion in which this 'motion' is concluded with a shot of an alien in London, discounting the Martian energy projection *over* London at the end of *Quatermass and the Pit*) but very close to a whole tradition of BBC Television.[3]

The television era and the birth of jet travel coincided neatly. It would have been possible for the BBC to adopt the 'travelogue' approach, or, in the case of wildlife films, the style and editorial policy of Disney's 'True-Life Adventures'. Instead, though, the personality of the filmmaker was part of the story being told. In living rooms, when screens were smaller than those of today's portable sets, perspective and scale were harder to convey than in a cinema. The famous names of this pioneering age of films-for-television (Alan Whicker, David Attenborough, Armand and Michaela Denis, James Cameron, et al.) were as much part of the spectacle as whatever they were there to show us. These places and sights were remarkable partly because the knowledgeable, authoritative enthusiasts bearing witness said they were remarkable. However well-crafted the post-dubbed voice-over commentary may have been, the moments that viewers recalled (and still do, although subsequent 'great moment' compilations have redrafted public memory slightly) were those where the presenter spoke to us directly, at the scene, at the time. Attenborough's first glimpse of the Komodo Dragon, Whicker finding that J. Paul Getty has a payphone installed in his mansion: these moments are of someone who thought he'd seen it all being amazed all over again.

This is diametrically opposed to the American, or pre-war British, attitude towards the 'collection' of the world. When cinema began, the Lumière brothers decided to 'give the World to the World'. Their *opérateurs* (and that word translates as both 'agents' and 'mechanics') were recruited from a number of disciplines, mainly the physical sciences. Gabriel Veyre, a chemistry graduate from a village near Lyon, paid off the debts his family had accrued putting him through university by filming the world. His letters, collated a century later by his grandson, show a young man baffled by the plurality of the world. His films, however, do not. In each port-of-call he has pictures taken of himself in local garb, and shows the residents other films he had already made. These films, unedited (of course) and developed in the crudest of labs (his later, colour photos used dried potato for the emulsion), were simply what was in front of the lens. It was only on returning to France that the footage of two men in Mexico fighting a duel with pistols aroused any comment, and only then did it occur to him (apparently) that he had seen a man die ten feet from him and not felt anything. French imperialist angst about conditions in Indo-China (now Vietnam), or curiosity about Cuba, Canadian whaling villages or Meiji Japan, seem not to have perturbed him until his return. He talks more about the weather and how nice the

Crown Prince of Cambodia was (an eleven-year-old boy who was one of Veyre's more patient subjects for still photographs).

The marvel of seeing moving pictures was in itself enough for most of his first audiences in Havana, Phnom Penh, Montreal or Guadalajara. No one seems to have thought that their own lives were worthy of addition to the collection. Veyre is, once again, torn between the Victorian desire to con-sume the world (as witnessed by his self-portrait photos, in whatever local garb he could find, and the presentation of these films to paying audiences) and Victorian science's scruples about objectivity. He never appears in his films, for obvious reasons, but also never seems to have selected the event, only the vantage point. This 'stamp-collecting' zeal for getting specimens from as many places and subcultures as possible (apparently his only motive for visiting an opium den in Shanghai) is in keeping with the Victorian urge to get as much as possible from as many sources under one roof. One needn't go as far as Walter Benjamin to collect any number of examples (and the collecting of examples is part of it – the *Arcades* project is the culmination of the habit it anatomises [see Benjamin, 1999]); just a quick jaunt to South Kensington provides three. Most odd, and thus most typically Victorian, is the room in the V&A dedicated to plaster casts of the best bits of the best architecture from around the world, scattered willy-nilly. Similarly, in the 1924 Empire Exhibition at White City (now the site of BBC Television Centre), 'specimens' of all sorts of 'native' cultures were brought to London to 'perform' in a simulacrum of their 'habitat'. White City, more than Wem-bley or 'Albertopolis', was itself made to be a spectacle, a setting for marvels but a marvel in itself. Paris in 1900 had something similar, including the projection of Veyre's films, a travelator and a big metal tower.[4]

However much the spectators went to have fun, there was still a 'story' being told. The 1939 New York World's Fair had 'Democracity', and the Westinghouse 'Futurama', associating free-market competition with progress and liberty in a brazenly New York way. H.B. Kaltemborn narrated the former, and he was known for his right-wing views. The 1851 Great Exhibition had a strongly stated theme of industry and good taste being one and the same, but at heart the message was simple: you are a citizen of an empire almost too big to comprehend (or, for foreigners: behold, an empire that can beat yours any day). Like London Zoo, the British Museum or the Louvre's collection of the best bits of every culture Napoleon overpowered, the eclecticism was the message.

The cinema had its own way of doing this. In documentary mode, the selection, editing and above all the narrative or captions maintained authority. In the extreme version, the Disney True-Life Adventures, nature was, to a certain extent, made to perform for the audience: 'dancing' to the music (the scorpions apparently performing a Square Dance being only the most grotesque example) or doing their 'tricks' (providing a whole new metaphor in their – literal – handling of lemmings). All of this was presented to us as being 'captured' as it happened, and simply set into its wider context by the narrative. Once again, the 1939 New York World's Fair presents us with a clear precedent, Frank Buck's 'Bring 'Em Back Alive' shows. Wild animals were there to be conquered, and shown off like giant cash registers, melamine plates or television.[5] The spectacle presented, of the world in 1960 (brought to you by Westinghouse – driverless cars and all) or of 'specimen' patches of the cultures of the world (except Czechoslovakia), was nonetheless 'closed'. Like a narrated documentary, the 'subject' (viewer or visitor) is presented with something finished and non-negotiable. The subject is not engaged, simply told what's what.

So in the imperial phase, presentations of the world to the domestic audience were couched in the language of scientific objectivity, presented as a matter of consumption and 'narrated' (overtly or by implication) as placing the domestic audience 'above' the 'exotic'.

I've laboured this point a little to make it clear what *Doctor Who*, in common with most of early BBC television, refused to do. In the *Zoo Quest* (1954–64) phase of non-fiction presentation, the 'correct' response, as the presenters indicated, was to be slightly awed, slightly bemused but above all glad the world is still surprising and inexhaustibly wonderful. Humility and gameness were the watchwords. In 'authored' pieces, this was often a means of undercutting the presumed southern, middle-class demographic of early television, and former *Picture Post* journalist René Cutforth can be seen as having a definite 'mission' to bring to light under-represented portions of the British Public. *Tonight* (1957–65) may have had the apparently 'safe' anchorman Cliff Michelmore, but Fyfe Robertson had only to open his mouth to remind the viewers that Britain was being addressed. Within the public service rubric the BBC had found a way to be more regional than the supposedly more 'representative' local ITV stations. A reporter, rather than being an emissary from the Home Counties to the funnily accented realms, was our representative but speaking to them on their terms. For the five minutes of the piece, *he* was the outsider with the anomalous accent.

The Doctor, Ian, Barbara and Susan arrive somewhere and try to figure out how where they are 'works'. They often don't impose 1960s British values, and they listen to what the locals tell them. Above all, they are alert to the risks of each new setting, and thus to the wonders. To use the current term, these arenas, either alien planets or known historical events, are 'chora': to be a mere eye-witness or consumer proves first logistically impossible and then, once the Doctor has become less circumspect, a moral dereliction of duty.[6] This is, of course, a function of *Doctor Who*'s being an adventure series. 1960s British values are important and are usually the means by which the good guys win, but this is through example. Ian's dress sense 'goes native' as often as Gabriel Veyre's, but Barbara will never abandon her sensible shoes, even when impersonating the divine reincarnation of the High Priest Yetaxa ('The Aztecs' [1964]).

Mentioning 'The Aztecs' brings up the problem of 'authenticity' with regard to known (and knowable) history. Whilst anyone is free to invent a planet and say 'this is how my world works' (although internal consistency and those pesky laws of physics can be used to mark the author's homework), a 'visit' to Earth's past presents epistemological complications. The presentation of history on television has always been a tussle between re-enactments 'as-it-happened' or a presenter revisiting the real locations and showing real artefacts and attempting to tell us a story. The storytelling element reached one extreme in A.J.P. Taylor's talks to camera, which told the viewer as much about the problems of certainty as about what, if anything, 'took place'. No such doubts beset *Doctor Who*. If Marco Polo's account to Rusticello of Pisa is partially true, it's all true. And it all happened to Marco Polo. Contingency is inadmissible. The agency of the Time Travellers is only effective if that's how history was 'meant' to happen. The idea of altering it, which begins to be introduced once Dennis Spooner becomes story editor (midway through the second season in 1965), is explicitly ruled out at the end of 'The Reign of Terror' (1964). No matter what they did, the Doctor argues, history would have accommodated their actions. Now, under Spooner, the Battle of Hastings can be rewritten ('The Time Meddler' [1965]). The past, heretofore, was a 'place' and could therefore be visited like anywhere else, rather than a negotiated 'process'. And if the history books deny that Marco Polo actually got anywhere near China, or that Napoleon was as tall as the actor playing him in 'Prisoners of Conciergerie', the books are wrong, not *Doctor Who*.

The tutelary spirit of L. Du Garde Peach hovers over the first 'historical' adventures. The author of many *Children's Hour* (1924–64) scripts and Ladybird books, Peach was a clear, linear storyteller. In many ways the Ladybird version of Marco Polo's voyages (du Garde Peach, 1962) is a template for the way any other series might have dramatised *A Description of the World*. All the minor incidents John Lucarotti mentions are present in twenty-five two-paragraph pages of text (and as many illustrations). But, once again, by having Ian and the Doctor talk to him we get a person, not a Great Figure, one whose understanding of the world is challenged by the TARDIS crew in such a way as to be articulated. If he has seen Buddhist priests levitate soup bowls, how can he doubt that the TARDIS functions as it is claimed to? Moreover, the Doctor is downright abrupt with him, rather than awed at meeting someone from a history book (and the later confrontation with Mighty Kublai Khan, aside from its comedy value, again reminds us of Alan Whicker meeting Getty). In his divergence from the TARDIS crew, who are themselves heterogeneous, we have a measure of the world in which the Doctor operates as a more effective heuristic than if a narrator had merely told us all this. In a curious way, then, he is part of the spectacle as much as the remarkable sets.[7]

In using the term spectacle, a reference to Laura Mulvey's 'Visual pleasure and narrative cinema', first published in 1975, is inevitable (Mulvey, 1999). To summarise crudely, the developing child has an 'ideal' alter-ego (the reflection in the mirror), according to Jacques Lacan. If we presume that the male characters on a cinema screen include one who approximates to the male viewer's ideal, and that watching a film is a kind of daydream, it would explain why women are presented as being there for their 'worth' as items to be possessed. To be female is to be somehow 'lacking'. Audiences, of either sex, are encouraged to 'identify' with male protagonists and 'objectify' female ones. The thirty years since this was first mooted have seen revisions and attempts to confound it, not least by Mulvey herself. For our purposes, we have another aspect to draw upon which might need rethinking in this light: monsters.

The majority of *Doctor Who* monsters are lacking a piece of human personality whilst possibly gaining in physical prowess; that's why they're 'monsters' and not just 'aliens'. Returning to the idea of a move from montage to mise-en-scène, think about how often the first proper look at a monster is at a cliffhanger, and the look *of* this being is reacted to by one or more of the TARDIS crew. They are there to be looked at, and the character doing the looking is as often as not female and regularly in the story. Once again, we are looking at someone who is looking at something on our behalf. Once again, our yardstick for how to react is the reaction of a regular protagonist. And whilst the reaction might be a scream, or a look of disgust, it is the being eliciting this reaction which is now the visual object.[8]

If the 'lack' signified by the arrival of a woman in a male world is a suggested castration, as Mulvey argues, what is the monster's 'lack' telling us? Often the monster is some kind of Freudian 'component', a being lacking ego, superego or id or having these elements alarmingly out of balance by human standards. This anomaly is usually signified by the difference between the monster and a human, either visually or in voice production. Yet, for all that they may be psychically denatured, they are generally represented as being 'male'. Even Noah, in 'The Ark in Space' (1975), is provided with a growly voice despite being transformed into an egg-laying insect and absorbing the memories of others through ingesting their bodies (sort of). He's somatically female, but while a human mind remains he keeps his old voice, however distortedly. It is worth noting that in the pioneering Hartnell years only three 'alien' voices were processed electronically (the Daleks, obviously, the Mechonoids [in 'The Chase'] and WOTAN, the sinister computer in 'The

War Machines' [1966], which was merely a stage whisper put through as much tape echo as Gene Vincent had used on 'Be-Bop a-Lula').[9] Even the original Cybermen in 'The Tenth Planet' (1966) were simply Roy Skelton in a sing-song voice putting the stress on the wrong syllables. This latter example is the only significant time that an emasculated voice is applied to aliens, and the Cybermen, as the name implies, are in every other way represented as male. As surgical freaks, they were monstrous in precise relation to what they had done to their bodies, so in this one instance the castration motif is licit (note though that the subsequent appearances of these monsters in the 1970s and 1980s had them given butch voices).

The paradox is that as displays of the fear of homogeneity, the Cybermen as originally conceived are only monstrous in comparison to the diverse humans around them. Like many *Doctor Who* creatures, their uniformity is part of their display. In this regard, and several others, it might be worth thinking of the spectacle of the monster as being akin to the homogenised and reified women in Busby Berkeley musical items. The cliffhanger to part three of 'Earthshock' (1982) (Figure 4) has a procession of Cybermen, first shot from waist height as they pass in an eroticised display of masculinity, then finally approaching the camera in single file. This last shot is tripled with a digital effect, intended presumably to show three times as many actors as there were, but as the fringes of each 'column' are disrupted the effect is closer to Berkeley's 'My Forgotten Man' routine from *Gold Diggers of 1933* (1933). Many iconic moments have arisen when large numbers of identical beings approach a human space, especially a familiar one like St Paul's Cathedral ('The Invasion' [1968], an echo perhaps of the Odessa Steps scene from *Battleship Potemkin* [1925]).

All of the 'pageants' of knowledge we've seen (London Zoo, the New York World's Fair, Veyre's Home-Movies-from-Abroad and 'pedagogic' *Doctor Who*) could be said to 'degrade' being to having and having to seeing. In this view of things, David Attenborough's efforts to find the rare and endangered is – televisually – redundant, if they can fake it in Lime Grove Studio G. Yet, unlike the 'closed' stories of the World's Fair or Disney's documentaries, the

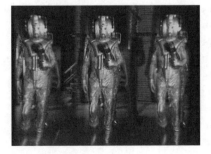

Figure 4 *Gold Fearers of 1982 –* shades of Busby Berkeley in 'Earthshock' (1982)

viewer was not supine but a willing participant. As we watch our heroes struggle to make sense of each new world they encounter, we are doing so too. For Attenborough, as for Ian and Barbara or their later replacements, the 'necessary' information is located within a lot of 'colour', partly in the interests of making a good story but also because, realistically, that is how it happens. The form of early *Doctor Who* to a certain extent mimics that of *Zoo Quest*, as we've seen. Thus each new element, be it a sight or a sound or some piece of information provided by the convenient info-dump characters (who always seem to be on hand to tell an entire planet's history or tutor one or more regular character in the cultural codes), is assimilated by us even if the TARDIS crew ignore it or are unaware of it. We don't 'own' the sights and sounds presented to us, but then neither does the Doctor. His effort to 'learn the secrets of the universe' is more a haphazard, open-ended curiosity than a quest with a definite end-point (like those of Odysseus or Captain Nemo).

Here, again, we must hastily acknowledge Freud's original conception of scopophilia as the infantile discovery of 'secrets' and the reification of others (Freud, 1977). The first of these is clearly what the Doctor and the series are about, the second is what (within the stories) bad people do but also what television does. The controlling gaze of security and surveillance technology was always associated with evil regimes: in 'The Green Death' (1973) CCTV is linked to a megalomaniac computer, BOSS, which was responsible for an eco-catastrophe as a side effect of a bid to brainwash humanity. This later phase of villainy was foreshadowed by the computer's comments on 'unauthorised footsteps' in the complex.[10] In the 1970s, when such levels of supervision and surveillance were insane science fiction paranoia, much of the Doctor's activities were conducted in 'blackouts'. In 'The Sun Makers' (1977) not only does he override the system to provide a 'ghost' image of himself to elude security, but he uses the coms and PA system to engineer a revolution by telling everyone that one has already taken place.[11] Several stories have being-put-on-display as a fate worse than death. 'Carnival of Monsters' (1973) and 'The Space Museum' (1965) are simply the most overt. These stories and others like them ('The Mind Robber' [1968], 'The War Games', 'Vengeance on Varos' [1985], 'The Greatest Show in the Galaxy' [1988–9]) all risk rupturing the fourth wall by commenting on the 'cruelty' of anyone watching the suffering of others for 'kicks'. 'Carnival of Monsters' goes further than most by having the aggression of the human 'specimens' manipulated by a control on the Scope (as a pretext for the inevitable Pertwee fight scene). Whilst he reserves the right to see anything he wants to, almost defining himself as the man who can do this, the Doctor is not to be gawped at by anyone else inside this story. Almost invariably, he tries to avoid being too widely known-about, and takes care to avoid being mentioned in official reports of the situations he has just resolved. Thus the events of the Tenth Doctor's debut story, 'The Christmas Invasion' (2005), might be seen as a transgression. The Prime Minister goes on live television to ask for the Doctor's help, and the people of the present-day Earth now definitely know about aliens. The 're-set' button, with which all present-day stories conclude by reasserting normality so it can be wrecked again next time aliens land in the Home Counties, is emphatically unpressed. Viewers 'inside' the story know about the Doctor and have seen alien spaceships on television. Yet the story withholds the final sight, members of the public watching the TARDIS arrive and the Doctor step out, even in this instance. We, watching *Doctor Who*, have that privilege but characters in *Doctor Who* stories who do it are typically baddies.

So if being seen by an invisible 'controller' is deemed intrinsically bad, what does this say about the Time Lords? Whilst the heroically engaged Doctor is happily 'botanising on the asphalt' (to borrow Benjamin's self-description), the appreciation by his own people of the universe they merely observe is consistently described as impoverished. Are they necessarily evil? There is no curiosity, sexual or otherwise (and the species is routinely described as sexless, but this essay isn't the place to get embroiled in that discussion), in their supervision of history. They are archivists first and foremost, with a disciplinary function retained as a last resort ('The War Games' introduces them as austere clergy, but the Doctor later calls them 'galactic ticket-inspectors' ['The Time Warrior', 1973–4]). Academically minded fans have had no end of fun connecting the name of the Time Lord central register, the 'Panopticon', with Gallifrey's Benthamite, Utilitarian approach to the 'lesser' mortals (explicitly stated in 'The Hand of Fear') and Foucauldian readings of this and the source of this ability, the Eye of Harmony (both introduced in 'The Deadly Assassin'). Yet within the terms of the series' discourse, the worst fate the Time Lords can bestow isn't execution, or unpicking one's existence from the cosmos so that one never existed, but amnesia or a job in the bureau of records. Knowledge, categorised and filed (and the Time Lord files contain powerful secrets, which the Master routinely exploits), is 'dead'. Indeed, the assumption has always been that they already know everything, so direct observation is redundant. For the Doctor, and the viewer at home, the difference between fact, spectacle and experience is crucial. Time Lords are oblivious to how the events they administer are experienced by the victims.

In the terms of documentary filmmaking, the 'pageant' style of Veyre and Disney is less applicable to *Doctor Who* than the traditions of Humphrey Jennings, Denis Mitchell and Norman Swallow. This was journalistic, and addressed the viewers as 'eavesdroppers' as much as attendees at a lecture. The people being interviewed and filmed weren't a spectacle, or 'specimens', but the previously disenfranchised public. Even here, music was used to accentuate the narrative, on occasion specially commissioned songs. (Again,

Jennings' emphasis on sound and flamboyant camera moves to – as we would say now – 'suture' the viewer into the story-making is influential. The title *Listen to Britain* [1943] was a bit of a give-away.) As would later happen with Attenborough, Whicker et al., the presenter's job was to connect the world being displayed and the viewer, offering personal opinions but letting the people speak for themselves. The imperial assumption of 'rightness' was shelved in favour of simply asking questions and hoping the viewers were listening to the answers. How this material is later presented is also shifted away from making an audience feel 'safe' (by bringing the drama and spectacle of 'abroad' into our homes or cinemas) to taking us 'into' the world of the subjects.

The viewer was complicit. A story was being told, with the intermediary figure being part of the story rather than the 'boundary layer' of a narrator speaking after-the-fact. The sensual engagement of the viewer was achieved through music and 'special sound'. Indeed, in the late 1960s, stories were made where the 'soundscape' was seamless, and where music ended and 'atmosphere' began was a matter of personal taste (e.g. 'The Krotons' [1968– 9], 'The Daleks' or 'The Wheel in Space' [1968]). Whilst we can't really apply film theory where a small screen in 405-line monochrome and a tiny, tinny loudspeaker are concerned, the use of sound to 'lock in' the viewer is worth an essay in itself (and Louis Niebur accepts the challenge elsewhere in this collection). I will confine myself to the observation that the more flexible approach, where story-by-story or world-by-world the decision was made as to what manner of storytelling was appropriate, extends to the sound-realm as well.

Roland Barthes wrote a piece in *Mythologies* (1993: 65–7) comparing Jules Verne's Captain Nemo to the narrator of Rimbaud's *Le Bateau ivre* (1999).[12] Nemo is a significant figure for *Doctor Who*: not only are the name 'nemo' (no one) and the title 'captain' suggestive, but the Doctor's reason for taking Ian and Barbara with him on his travels was exactly the same as that Nemo gave for abducting Ned Land et al. Nemo's secret, revealed, like the Doctor's, years later, was cause for him to withdraw from the world in disgust, and live in the submarine *Nautilus*. He observes and collects, but does not participate. For Barthes this makes him the archetypal bourgeois. Rimbaud's drunkboat is an egoless psychic traveller/participant. As an Englishman, I am inclined to use slightly different examples. If we set Tennyson's Ulysses, a traveller who is 'part of all that I have met', against G.K. Chesterton's *The Napoleon of Notting Hill* (1904), and the grocer's shop which contained the Empire, then the comparison is more stark.[13] In the Chesterton passage, the world has been processed and tinned, dry tea from 'the Empire of the Dragon' is on sale in twists of paper; moreover the whole world is subordinate to Notting Hill, as the focal point for all trade and exploration. Tennyson's poem, tainted now with associations of the botched imperialist amateurism of Robert Falcon Scott, is not about conquest, nor indeed exploration, but about self-transformation and not dishonouring the dead as much as it is concerned with travel as a cure for death.[14] Tennyson is only the most explicit of the Victorian writers who equate journeying with evading entropy. The empire, the world, existed to be seen, and seeing it, in 'Ulysses', is infinitely preferable to the living death of 'an idle king', even if the last voyage into the West is a symbolic death. Domesticity and ownership are anathema to a true explorer. Yet, for Chesterton, the whole point of seeing the world is to consume it. 1950s British television, as we have seen, squares this circle by allowing us to see (and thus 'consume') the world in our living rooms because of the Odysseys of others.

Right up until 1989, *Doctor Who* was routinely and reflexively echoing the form of television narrative that this produced. Experiments with *verité* style and hand-held cameras were inserted into the narrative as fragments. (For instance, fake news reports – 'The War Machines' [1966], 'The Daemons' [1971], 'Day of the Daleks' [1972] – were meticulously done with the same graphics as real BBC news, and on the same film stock. The 1966 story had newsreader Kenneth Kendall reading the bulletin. The comparison with 2005's 'Aliens of London' [with political correspondent Andrew Marr] and 'The Christmas Invasion' breaks down because the latter examples are rendered into the same frame-removed 'film-look' format as the rest of the series.) These were clearly flagged up as 'interruptions' to the usual style of address, just as the 1985 season's habit of people looking at the camera and commenting was, to begin with, intriguing and novel.[15]

So the Doctor and his companions are both observers and observed. They are 'permitted' to view the universe for their pleasure and instruction by virtue of the fact that they are part of what is being seen. Not only does this resist the temptations of reification, objectification (if that isn't the same thing in this case) and imperialist 'stamp-collecting' display and taxonomy, but it does so by being part of a once radical challenge to such processes which has been incorporated into BBC television's remit.[16] Furthermore, the alternative process, what we are calling 'imperialist' or 'Disney', is routinely identified with villainy.[17]

Notes

1   The process of watching television has always been part of the programme's rhetoric: from the Doctor's argument with Ian about how the TARDIS is all crammed into a police box (analogously, a TV set is a small box with infinity inside it), to the scanner having been in colour once, to the Doctor's farewell to Susan in the programme's second season. In that season's last story ('The

Time Meddler'), not only is one of the ship's key controls a 'Vertical Hold' but the Monk teases the Doctor with the idea of Shakespeare, in his new version of history, getting to write for the medium. The scanner, when the ship malfunctions in 'The Edge of Destruction', is the means by which the ship contacts the crew 'intelligently' (a system reprised in 'The Wheel in Space' and suborned in 'The Mind Robber' – and in each case appropriate music accompanies benevolent images). Yet, when the Doctor is given the option of never leaving the ship and *still* learning all the secrets of the universe, he elects to treat the Time-Space Visualiser like you would a sandwich-toaster or eight-track cartridge-player; play with it for a few days then leave it in a cupboard. It was a challenge to get it working, nothing else about it matters. Note also the similarity between this gizmo and the central conceit of American TV's first space heroes *Captain Video and his Video Rangers* (1949–55). The doughty Captain kept in touch with his 'agents' (i.e. old film clips) via an 'Opticon Scillometer'. The Captain was announced as 'Master of Time and Space'. But he never went anywhere much.

2   As so often in Nation–Spooner collaborations, New York in particular and America in general is shown as the source of all vitality and modernity. The city of Millennius in 'The Keys of Marinus' is Manhattan with archbishop Makarios in charge; in 'The Chase' not only is the Empire State Building visited but we have a 1996 'Festival of Ghana' clearly modelled on New York in 1939. The Daleks are confirmed as the most evil beings in the cosmos when they destroy Manhattan in the 22nd Century, in 'The Dalek Invasion of Earth' (1964). Note, however, that the historical events in the 'Visualiser' scene are presented exactly like the Disneyland animatronic President Lincoln and the Flora Robson version of Elizabeth I's court.

3   I am grateful to Andrew Pixley for noting that *Quatermass and the Pit* (1959) does feature a vast Martian energy form in the sky over Knightsbridge; but the effect of this, I would argue, is different to that of a physical, corporeal alien presence marching or rampaging through the city.

4   I contend, however, that the real 'heirs' of the Crystal Palace were Oberammergau and the Nuremberg Rally. In these, the spectator was at the focal point of the show; in fact the number of spectators *was* the show. Whereas in the various World's Fairs and the Festival of Britain one visited a funfair to 'see the future', these 'perlocutionary' events were geared towards removing the will, to being swamped and cowed and ultimately subsumed by the event. It wasn't the world you saw changed, it was yourself. Anyone not entirely comfortable with what was being promoted was shamed into thinking that he or she is the only one; being stared at by a crowd, or a building (as it might seem) was enough to quell any rebellious feelings. Visitors to the Great Exhibition were 'remade' as part of the empire, given their bearings in the big picture, told what 'good taste' meant.

5   It's interesting to note the difference in a generation between the subjects of Veyre's work, happy to be photographed but only able to be filmed when they didn't know the cameras were on them, with the Westinghouse visitors who were so keen to see themselves on this electrical picture radio doohickey that

many went through the whole exhibit again. The 'Hello Mum' phenomenon begins here, and the implied audience seems to be the main difference. When abstract people in another country or time are going to see you it's 'science', but when someone you know is watching it's 'entertainment'.

6   Wearing and Wearing (1996) discuss the difference between the tourist or *flâneur* and what they call a 'choraster', one who collaborates with the locals to charge the space they both temporarily share with a new (and supposedly richer) meaning. By 2005, the Doctor has made this transition completely, to the point where, in 'The Long Game', he can liken time travel to going to Paris ('You can't just read the guidebook, you've got to throw yourself in: eat the food, use the wrong verbs, get charged double and end up kissing complete strangers') as opposed to the 'look but don't touch' stereotypical Englishman abroad.

7   The odd thing is that this approach is now mainstream in non-fiction. The use of CGI reconstructions of ruined cities, actors out-of-focus to provide visual 'accompaniment' for letters or documents read out, or even people acting *as* historical figures is now depressingly familiar. Moreover, in series such as *Walking with Dinosaurs* (1999), viewers have the past and the experts mediated through the conventions of drama-documentaries about present-day events. Kenneth Branagh narrates a 'story' about the life of a prehistoric animal much as Simon King would narrate cheetahs or lions he'd filmed since birth. If the standard model for a history documentary is a historian (ideally one good on camera) walking around the site, intercut with actors in period dress grunting and getting hacked about in battle, and the alternative is members of the public trying to live 'authentically' like them, there is no room for the historical drama of the 'trad' BBC variety.

8   Historically, the screaming girl had a practical function. Cutting between Fay Wray wriggling in a giant plaster gorilla hand and a stop-motion clip of Kong with a tiny wriggly object clutched in his fist, the sound recordist dubbed the scream across the edit, to ensure that we associated the two shots as being the same from different distances.

9   One reason may have been time, or directors preferring effects they could hear in 'real time' in the studio (which became more practicable with radio mikes), but it has to be said, simple intelligibility is a factor. The Mechonoids aren't required to say anything more profound than 'Stop!' and recite numbers, but even this is garbled.

10 Anyone doubting that Freud is applicable to computers, mad or otherwise, has missed not only 'Robot' (1974–5) but also the end of 'The Green Death'. BOSS is conjoined to the mind of his creator, Professor Stevens, in a process the machine describes as a 'wedding'. That BOSS also quotes Oscar Wilde, has pet-names for Stevens and engages in some sardonic humour has led some to speculate on whether the programme's most articulate and witty megalomaniac machine is also the most overtly gay character in the entire run of the series (excluding the Master, obviously). Intriguingly, another mad computer with a dry wit, Xoanon, is the villain in a story flagrantly echoing Hollywood's Freud-on-a-Rope space opera *Forbidden Planet* (1956), namely 'The Face of Evil' (1977).

11   The similarity between this and the events of Christmas 1989 in Romania is
     intriguing. It was an erroneous report of a crushed revolt in Timişoara which led
     to the overthrow of Ceauşescu. The Doctor's methods in 'The Sun Makers'
     (simulating a revolution) may well, I imagine, have impressed Baudrillard. Had
     I more space, this essay would discuss Baudrillard's notion of the simulacrum
     (Baudrillard, 1988: 166–84), as well as Guy Debord's work on spectacle (1977),
     in far more detail in this connection. One thing does need to be recalled,
     however: for the audience, at least until well into the 1970s, the experience of
     watching the strange world(s) presented to us was unrepeatable. Spectacle was
     not a physical commodity but a communal event. Even when one story was
     repeated ('The Evil of the Daleks' [1967, rebroadcast in 1968]), this was 'sanc-
     tioned' by a scripted reason for the Doctor to be showing one of his previous
     adventures to a new friend. Similarly, flashbacks to earlier events were seen by
     the characters as well as us (the first of these was in a fantasy adventure, 'The
     Celestial Toyroom' [1966], which can charitably be described as 'an experi-
     ment'). The Doctor will put his own past on the screen as a warning (and does
     so again in his defence in 'The War Games', when put on trial by the Time
     Lords for the first time) but the programme's past is invoked rather than being
     transmitted as reruns with these exceptions. It is in the process of sharing and
     rehearsing this collective memory that fandom arose, by the same process that
     led to pre-video-era kids being word-perfect on *Python* sketches – a Zone of
     Proximal Development.

12   It might have been interesting to consider, in this light, the role of the TARDIS
     as observer and the Doctor as observed. For the first few years, until 'The War
     Games', the Doctor was as mysterious as any world visited, and was part of the
     display. He regenerated before our very eyes, and was thus turned into a special
     effect, a process confirmed six months later with the new title sequence 'bleed-
     ing' the face of Patrick Troughton into the abstract electronic patterning. His
     subsequent transformation, left incomplete at the end of 'The War Games', has
     him turned into an image and manipulated on a screen on which he had previ-
     ously displayed his memories. This merely completes a cycle of use of Troughton's
     face as a storytelling device. This was done with people being given photos, or
     graphic demonstrations used by 'hunting' machinery ('The Krotons' [1968–9]),
     or most frequently with him peering out of a TV screen built into the set and
     talking to his friends as though he could see them from 'inside' the box ('The
     Wheel in Space' has the best surviving example). If the ship is hollowed out and
     purely an 'eye' as Barthes (1993: 67) suggests, then a 'hollow' TARDIS would be
     a threat to the Doctor, objectifying him. It might be significant that the 'hallu-
     cination' story 'The Mind Robber' features photo blow-ups treated as real
     bookcases or companions, and a photo of the TARDIS traps the Doctor into
     (almost) turning himself into a fictitious character. Note that 'The Mind Robber',
     'The Krotons', 'The War Games' and 'The Deadly Assassin' are all directed by
     David Maloney.

13   The Doctor as 'gentleman amateur' is something of a minefield. The individual
     stories generally imply that he has simply wound up in a hair-raising scrape and

has to improvise a way out. Yet not only does this happen every single time, with increasing absurdity when we reach Peter Davison's 'doctorate', but we never see whatever the Doctor 'does' that he would have been doing had not this crisis intervened. In the later Tom Baker stories it is explicitly stated that he saves planets for a living, but this was deemed 'silly' by the hardcore fans. Only once, in 'The Trial of a Time Lord' (1986), does the Doctor ever suggest that he still writes academic monographs.

14 For a discussion of the 'amateur' Scott and the 'professional' (and thus 'cheating') Amundsen, see Chapter 3 of Tulloch, 1990. Tulloch seems concerned with 'professionalism' (see Tulloch and Alvarado, 1983: 61–97). I am less sure that the Doctor counts, and prefer to use the Benjamin model of the Doctor as a *flâneur*.

15 The whole thing began a year earlier, with an accident during rehearsals for 'The Caves of Androzani' (1984). The director, Graeme Harper, suggested that the actor's sotto voce aside ('the spineless cretins') be delivered with his head slightly towards the camera. John Normington delivered it looking directly at the camera, and the use of such asides, in what was in any case a space-age Revenge Tragedy, seemed appropriate, so they kept it and did it again in later scenes. Script editor Eric Saward liked the idea of 'greek chorus' figures commenting on the story, and so in a story about a surveillance-mad world where the citizens are pacified by 'reality TV' he expanded two minor figures to allow them to observe the revolution ('Vengeance on Varos' [1985]). Later, in his own 'Revelation of the Daleks' (1985), everyone was talking to the camera and some of them, notably the evil Davros, could hear what the others were saying. As we have seen, the next story, 'The Trial of a Time Lord', has the Doctor and the jurors observing the evidence by, in effect, watching three *Doctor Who* adventures and passing comment on them.

16 Which BBC we're talking about is a good question. As Robert Rowland (2000) points out, early 1960s Lime Grove personnel were often younger and more 'with-it' than is traditionally thought. His description of the Richard Dimbleby-era *Panorama* production team is suggestively close to the 'youthquake' which *Doctor Who* is commonly supposed to have embodied within the Corporation. Indeed, the 'guerrilla' filming of items with the reporter operating the camera in some instances, and a crew of five at most (as opposed to ITV's *This Week* with eight as standard), chimes with the surreptitious filming of London under Dalek rule in 'The Dalek Invasion of Earth'. Budgets were tight, but (again the comparison with Verity Lambert is interesting) this meant that a film which might have been vetoed was presented at the last minute as a *fait accompli* and management had no option but to screen it rather than have wasted resources. Unlike *Tonight*, however, the reports in *Panorama* were delivered to the nation as statements ('closed' in the terms used in the rest of my essay here), somehow 'in the public interest', and so do not entirely fit the proposition I am putting forward. (Arthur Marwick's Introduction to *Windows on the Sixties* (Marwick, 2000) includes a nine-point set of 'hallmarks' of 1960s British culture, and *Doctor Who* fits it to a T, but is only mentioned in an essay on *The Avengers*.)

17 Since completing the first draft of this paper in December 2004, my attention has been drawn to the use of similar observations in Margaret King's essay 'The Audience in the Wilderness' (King, 1996: 60–8). However, she seems unaware that it was Disney stage-hands chucking lemmings over the cliff to furnish a good ending (for the film, if not the hapless mammals), which would have made her case stronger. She also seems to think that these films exist out of context with dramas setting up an urban–rural opposition.

References

Barthes, Roland. [1957] 1993. *Mythologies*. Trans. Annette Lavers. London: Vintage, pp. 65–7, 'The *Nautilus* and the Drunken Boat'.

Baudrillard, Jean. 1988. *Jean Baudrillard: Selected Writings*. Ed. Mark Poster. Stanford: Stanford University Press, pp. 164–84, 'Simulacra and simulations'.

Benjamin, Walter. 1999. *The Arcades Project*. Trans. Howard Eiland and Kevin McLaughlin. Cambridge, MA: Harvard University Press.

Chesterton, G.K. 1904. *The Napoleon of Notting Hill*. London: Bodley Head.

Debord, Guy. 1977. *The Society of the Spectacle*. Detroit: Red and Black.

Du Garde Peach, Lawrence. 1962. *Marco Polo: An Adventure from History*. Loughborough: Wills and Hepworth Ltd.

Freud, Sigmund. [1905] 1977. *On Sexuality: Three Essays on the Theory of Sexuality and Other Works*. Ed. Angela Richards. Trans. James Strachey. Harmondsworth: Penguin.

King, Margaret J. 1996. 'The audience in the wilderness'. *Journal of Popular Film and Television*, Vol. 24, No. 2, pp. 60–8.

Marwick, Arthur. 2000. 'Introduction: locating key texts amid the distinctive landscape of the 60s'. In Anthony Aldgate, James Chapman and Arthur Marwick (eds). *Windows on the Sixties: Exploring Key Texts of Media and Culture*. London: I.B. Tauris, pp. xi–xxi.

Mulvey, Laura. [1975] 1999. 'Visual pleasure and narrative cinema'. In Leo Braudy and Marshall Cohen (eds). *Film Theory and Criticism: Introductory Readings*, 5th edn. New York: Oxford University Press, pp. 833–44.

Rimbaud, Arthur. 1999. *The Drunken Boat*. Trans. Geoff Sawyers. Reading: Two Rivers Press.

Rowland, Robert. 2000. '*Panorama* in the sixties'. In Anthony Aldgate, James Chapman and Arthur Marwick (eds). *Windows on the Sixties: Exploring Key Texts of Media and Culture*. London: I.B. Tauris, pp. 154–82.

Sobchack, Vivian. 1987. *Screening Space: The American Science Fiction Film*. New York: Ungar.

Sontag, Susan. 2004. 'The imagination of disaster.' In Sean Redmond (ed.). *Liquid Metal: The Science Fiction Film Reader*. London: Wallflower (Originally published in 1965).

Tennyson, Alfred. [1851] 1999. 'Ulysses'. *The Collected Poems of Alfred Lord Tennyson*. Ware: Wordsworth Editions Ltd, pp. 147–8.

Tulloch, John. 1990. *Television Drama: Agency, Audience and Myth*. London: Routledge.
Tulloch, John and Manuel Alvarado. 1983. *Doctor Who: The Unfolding Text*. London and Basingstoke: Macmillan.
Wearing, B. and Wearing, S. 1996. 'Refocusing the tourist experience: the *flâneur* and the choraster'. *Leisure Studies*, Vol. 15, pp. 229–43.

Chapter 6

The ideology of anachronism: television, history and the nature of time

Alec Charles

Time and the Time Lords

In 1905 a pair of British scientists – Lord Rayleigh and the magnificently named Sir James Jeans – produced one of the most unlikely ideas in the history of physics: namely that if electromagnetic waves are emitted at an infinite number of different frequencies, then any hot object must necessarily emit an infinite amount of energy. This is patently untrue: if Rayleigh and Jeans had been correct, the simple act of flicking a light-switch would have fried the universe. As Stephen Hawking (1989: 57–8) points out, their theorem reduced to absurdity the central tenets of late nineteenth-century scientific determinism: it suggests how right Max Planck had been when five years earlier he'd postulated that the nature of wavelengths is neither infinite nor arbitrary, but that energy is packaged out in specific quanta.

One recalls in this connection Zeno's paradox of Achilles and the tortoise: that ancient Greek conundrum that appears to prove that in a race between the two, the narcissistic warrior could never manage to catch up with the chelonian if the latter were given any kind of a head start – the argument being that by the time Achilles had caught up with the tortoise's starting position, the tortoise would have moved on, and by the time Achilles had reached the point to which the tortoise had moved on, the shelled athlete would have moved on some more – and so on, and so on.

The flaw in Zeno's logic may be seen as advancing evidence in favour of the Greeks' atomic view of material reality just as Rayleigh and Jeans (perhaps inadvertently) prove the quantum perspective. Zeno's paradox only works if you can divide distance into infinitely small amounts: if there's a limit on the infinitesimal – once the atom, today the latest subatomic particle – then there's a point at which the distance between Achilles and the tortoise is so small that it is not only negligible, but is in fact non-existent.

The particulate nature of matter – and of space and time – is why Achilles can beat a tortoise with a head start, and why a hot cup of tea doesn't irradiate the cosmos into oblivion. This is excellent news for philosophers, physicists, bookmakers and caterers, but it poses certain problems for post-Saussurean cultural theorists (the 'granular structure of time' is also, incidentally, a premise on which Robert Sloman based some of the pseudo-science of his 1972 *Doctor Who* story, 'The Time Monster': 'Time isn't smooth. It's made up of little bits [. . .] Temporal atoms, so to speak').

Reality, as we know, is like a rainbow: it is a spectrum, a wave or a flow. Language, as they say, is like a child's drawing of a rainbow: it takes the infinite blur of the rainbow's colours and posits them into a sequence of labelled blocks: red, orange, yellow, green, blue. These blocks (or signifieds) are as arbitrary as their labels (their signifiers): the Japanese language, for example, has a single word – and thus a single concept – for the English 'blue' and 'green-blue', and therefore distinguishes colour (at the semantic level) in a different way. Through its discrete divisions of a continuous reality, language shapes our perception and consciousness: turning Julia Kristeva's *pulsions* of the preverbally semiotic into the arbitrarily and phallogocentrically symbolic (Kristeva, 1984: 26).

Yet, as Rayleigh, Jeans and Planck demonstrate, a rainbow doesn't in fact have an infinite number of colours or wavelengths. Reality isn't a wave, but a sequence of particles. Perhaps we always knew this: rainbows after all are made of drops of rain. The material universe is a series of discrete particles: or, rather – as Heisenberg and Schrödinger propose – it is made up of waves and particles at the same time. The same, strangely, can be said of *Doctor Who*.

There are, according to traditional models of television, two main kinds of long-running TV drama programmes: serials and series. A classic example of a serial is a soap opera: its open-ended continuousness marks it out as the wave of the televisual world. A common instance of the series is the situation comedy: as David McQueen (1998: 57), amongst others, has argued, the narrative format of the sitcom requires resolution and closure at the end of each episode. This conservative model of the sitcom has attracted the attention of various critics on both sides of the Atlantic. Mick Eaton proposes that 'its basic parameters can be taken up without change, without narrative progress from week to week' (1981: 33); while David Marc adds that 'sitcoms depend on familiarity, identification, and redemption of popular beliefs' (1989: 24).

This, at least, is the traditional view of the sitcom. However, since the success of such soap-sitcoms as *Cheers* (1982–93), *Frasier* (1993–2004) and *Friends* (1994–2004), all this has changed. This was also the model for the science fiction series: from *Lost in Space* (1965–8) and *Star Trek* (1966–9), to *Blake's 7* (1978–81) and *Quantum Leap* (1989–93), every episode had to be, more or less, self-contained. It was only in the 1990s that the serial quality of the so-called 'story arc' came to dominate television science fiction: most obviously in certain episodes of *The X-Files* (1993–2002), in *Babylon 5* (1994–8) and in the later versions of *Star Trek*.

Doctor Who started life as a serial – as an extended miniseries (confusingly, a miniseries is invariably a serial) in the style of the *Quatermass* serials of the 1950s. As it progressed, however, the programme began partially to discard its serial status as it transformed into a series of miniserials. The miniserial – or 'story' – format had already come into existence well before the programme chose, in 1966, to drop its preference for individual episode titles (which, although individuating each episode, had suggested a greater sense of continuity within each season – a continuity emphasised by the cliffhangers which tended to conclude, or to refuse to conclude, each story block) in favour of titled stories comprising blocks of two to fourteen episodes. Each story is a serial; each season – consisting of a collection of generally self-contained stories – is a series. John Tulloch and Manuel Alvarado (1983: ix) explain that *Doctor Who* is 'an episodic serial [. . .] characterised by there being narrative discontinuity, but for a limited and specific number of episodes'. Tulloch and Alvarado go on: 'The long-running form of the series delays endlessly the "return to order" [. . .] The narratives of *Doctor Who* [. . .] threaten to generate their own "resistance"' (1983: 83–95).

Like the programme's sixteenth and twenty-third seasons, the 2005 series – by virtue of its all-encompassing story arc – may be viewed as a single, continuous wave; but, unlike those two earlier seasons, it posed for much of its run as particulate (as a sequence of discrete stories) until, as it approached its climax, it revealed its deeply integrated thematic and narratorial flow. This is the equivalent of what a physicist might describe as wave/particle duality.

There is an inherent awkwardness to this duality: and to the implications it has upon the ways in which we might read this text, this sequence of texts. It calls into question our senses of continuity, tradition and history. In its 'resistance' to conventional modes of reception and interpretation, this anxiety is a typically postmodern and postcolonial concern.

Continuity is an ambiguous concept. In the uncritically judgmental circles of *Doctor Who* fandom it was latterly a term which implied aesthetic value or even moral rectitude: a loyalty to tradition within a nostalgic present which constantly invites invasions from the past. This is most obvious in fandom's once overwhelmingly appreciative response to *Doctor Who* producer John Nathan-Turner's remorseless (and eventually, for some critics, unconscionable) raids upon the programme's history for his episodes' characters, settings and storylines during the 1980s. While his predecessors had often chosen to pastiche genres and specific texts of cinema, science fiction, horror fiction and mythology, John Nathan-Turner elected to pastiche – or simply to paste together – elements from the programme's own past with an incongruously unironic self-referentiality. This wasn't the experimental postmodernism of a Buñuel, a Godard or a Kubrick so much as the industrial postmodernity of a Spielberg or a Disney.

In certain schools of cultural theory, the term 'continuity' might suggest a deeper level of material reality inadequately shadowed by our linguistic distinctions. When John Fiske advocates the 'political and cultural respectability' (Fiske, 1987: 280) of the soap opera, and goes on to posit TV news programmes within the genre of serial drama, one suspects that his fondness for seriality is related to a quasi-poststructuralist perspective upon continuity which is at once comforting and radical. The serial comes to seem the preferred textual mode, both for the fan and for the theorist. The discrete, self-contained nature of the series, on the other hand, bespeaks the artistic conservatism of the seventies sitcom or of 'classic *Trek*'.

The more that *Doctor Who* caught itself up in its own internal continuity (continuity as traditionalism), the more its narrative structures came to follow this conservative model of narrative closure. Its potentials for progression and for progressivism gave way to an aimless bricolage amidst the bric-à-brac of its own – and indeed of its nation's – marvellous and misremembered past. Perhaps the most striking instances of this tendency towards historical conflation materialised during the programme's twenty-fifth anniversary celebrations, when – during 'Remembrance of the Daleks' (1988) and 'Silver Nemesis' (1988) – the Doctor did battle not only with Daleks and Cybermen, but also with British Fascists and German Nazis, against the backdrops of 1960s London and Windsor Castle. By this time, the programme's – and its protagonist's – senescent peregrinations had long since lost both their point and their edge. This invisibly sutured conceptual montage bereft of counterpoint, this theme park of flashbacks to better days, this halcyon fantasy, came to recall what you get when you take the dialectical disruption out of the work of Sergei Eistenstein: all that remains are, in Robert Stam's words, 'the commodified ideograms of advertising' (Stam, 2000: 41).

Yet in the era of relativity and relativism, it is not continuity but discontinuity which defines us. In a postmodern time – a period which paradoxically announces its status as projected beyond the present – it is a sense of ahistoricality or anachronism which makes us who we are. While Martin Heidegger (1962: 458–64) argued that being was constituted by existence in time – and therefore by the existence of time – Jacques Derrida proposes that time (and therefore being) can only come into existence through a paradoxical and anachronistic process of mutual self-affirmation: that is, a process of mutual affirmation of being by which the self which affirms must itself have been affirmed in advance by the other which it affirms, in so far as the affirming self must already have been affirmed in order that it should have the capacity to affirm the other into being. Or, as Derrida himself puts it, '*Yes*

[. . .] addresses itself to some other which it does not constitute, and it can only begin by asking the other, in response to a request that has already been made, to ask it to say yes. Time appears only as a result of this singular anachrony' (Derrida, 1992: 299).

This ontological chicken-and-egg situation recalls the temporal paradoxes that lie at the heart of Terry Gilliam's film *Twelve Monkeys* (1995) and Louis Marks's *Doctor Who* story, 'Day of the Daleks' (1972) – and indeed the entirety of the programme's 2005 season: it is the philosophical opposite of the grandfather paradox. Existence is at once self-generating and therefore self-contradictory; nothing is any longer equal to itself. Newton knew that space is relative; Einstein showed us that time is too. This dissolution of our defining absolutes takes place not only at the level of the material universe, but also in the realm of social history. This may perhaps to some extent explain why Russell T. Davies's 'Bad Wolf' mystery and paradox so gripped the public and media imagination.

The shift towards radicalising perspectives upon the relationship between history and time has been going on for a while, and indeed it seems to be an enduring legacy of those totalitarian-imperialist projects whose echoes survive in our own era's post-historicality. George Orwell, in *Nineteen Eighty-Four*, writes of the Party's wish to 'freeze history' (1954: 172), while the historians Robert Lifton and Eric Markusen refer similarly to those modes of totalitarianism – from Nazism through to nuclearism – which seek to 'stop history' (Lifton and Markusen, 1991: 88). The deconstruction – or condensation or confusion – of time and history performed by such Modernist writers as Joyce, Eliot, Woolf, Pound and Proust anticipates the anti-rationalist syncretism and fantastical anachronism attempted by Adolf Hitler, Benito Mussolini and Joseph Stalin – and, for that matter, by Margaret Thatcher and George W. Bush – and by such postmodern artists as Thomas Pynchon, Salman Rushdie, Baz Luhrmann and the creators of *Doctor Who*.

The recreation of the Roman Empire in Fascist Italy, or of Victorian values in Thatcherite Britain, or of medieval crusades in modern America – or, conversely, the introduction of atomic bazookas and police boxes into eleventh-century England, or of Britpop into the Moulin Rouge – shift the scientific deconstruction of time onto the political and cultural stage. Past and present intermingle in a style foreseen by Marshall McLuhan's vision of the informational and societal *implosion* provoked by modern media technologies: 'Mechanization depends on the breaking up of processes into homogenized but unrelated bits. Electricity unifies these fragments once more' (McLuhan, 2001: 385). We inhabit an era of historical *mélange*.

As David Harvey suggests in *The Condition of Postmodernity*, 'we have been experiencing [. . .] an intense phase of time-space compression' (Harvey, 1990: 284). Jean-François Lyotard has similarly proposed that in postmodern times 'there is no single time; a society [. . .] is not synchronous with itself [. . .] It is the observer's timepiece that judges what is present-day, just as in the universe, except that one wonders what in human history, especially in the history of the arts, functions as the speed of light' (Lyotard, 1989: 186).

What then constitutes the cultural equivalent of the speed of light: the constant that deconstructs the relational structuration – the chronological hierarchisation – of history? Appropriately enough, a prime candidate is a medium which propels its photonic messages at nearly 300,000 kilometres per second: the medium of television.

As John Ellis (1992) has said, one of the characteristic features of television is its feeling of liveness, of a constant contemporaneity. Raymond Williams (1990) points out that television has deconstructed traditional notions of distance and geography: but it's also reshaped our senses of history and time. Just as, for Jean Baudrillard, the Gulf War was no more than a simulacrum or a media event – an instance of the 'hyperrealist logic of the deterrence of the real by the virtual' (Baudrillard, 1995: 27) – so the age of television has compressed and homogenised history into a single moment: this is the essence of that crucial feature of postmodernity observed by Francis Fukuyama – its post-historicality: 'Our deepest thinkers have concluded that there is no such thing as History – that is, a meaningful order to the broad sweep of human events' (Fukuyama, 1998: 3).

Doctor Who is primarily, as Rose Tyler (Billie Piper) immediately recognises, about time and timelessness; and yet the real time machine is not the telephone box but the television itself – 'the box'. Television puts us, to quote from an episode of *Doctor Who* – Douglas Adams's 'City of Death' (1979) – in a 'special relationship to time': it posits us as history's 'perpetual outsiders'.

In the opening episode of the *Doctor Who* story 'The Space Museum' (1965), the Doctor and his companions arrive on an alien world to discover that they are 'not really' there: 'the TARDIS jumped a time-track'. They soon come face to face with their own bodies preserved timelessly (in the style of Jeremy Bentham) in the display cases of the eponymous museum. Like them, we all, as the progeny of televisual postmodernity, find ourselves caught in an eddy – an anomalous fold – between the now and the now, between 'the dimensions of time': we discover, as Hamlet put it – rather more elegantly – that our 'time is out of joint' – or that, like Pete Tyler in 'Father's Day' (2005), or like Billy Pilgrim, Kurt Vonnegut's chronological kangaroo, we have come 'unstuck in time' (Vonnegut, 1991: 53).

Television is the one true key to time – or, rather, to timelessness: a lucent cube that can reshape the course of history. Television freezes time: even more so than what Susan Sontag (1979: 15) calls the 'elegaic art' of photography, a medium which preserves, in Roland Barthes's words, 'the living image of a dead thing' (Barthes, 1993: 79), and which, as André Bazin put it, 'embalms time' – just as film preserves 'change mummified' (Bazin, 1967: 14–15).

The early Hungarian film theorist Béla Balázs described moving pictures as simply 'the flickering of [. . .] bloodless shadows' (Balázs, 1970: 280). The world of film is, according to Christian Metz (1982: 45), 'not really its object, it is its shade, its phantom, its double'. Yet the cinematic fantasy becomes more urgently real than material reality itself. Nothing is ever itself any more: there is no space, no time – no geography, nor any history. As Jean Baudrillard has proposed: 'Instead of unfolding as part of a history, things have begun to succeed each other in the void' (2005: 122).

Television takes this postmodern process even further than film. It is the cultural equivalent of the atom bomb: its confusion between the old and the new, between the archived and the live, has dissolved the distance between the past and the present – has killed history at the speed of light. This is more than anachrony: this is ahistoricality. This is more than nostalgia: this is denial. Its mode of preserving the past combines the revisionism of John Rambo with the conservatism of John Reith, and makes television a peculiarly able medium in which a late imperialist nation might hearken back to its days of glory.

Television/history

The Second World War was a historical event; the Iraq War was (and is) a televisual one – not only in its meanings but also in its motives. In our readings of the past, the break between the pre-televisual and the televisual ages seems as significant as that between events before and during our own lifetimes or memories. Television represents a cultural memory that super-sedes personal memory: a direct access to the past, a myth of timelessness, of eternal return and relentless reruns combined seamlessly with the immediate present. We therefore tend to forget its historical contexts.

The Second World War was history, but 22 and 23 November 1963 – the death of Kennedy and the birth of *Doctor Who* – were not: they were tele-vision. They were – they *are* – part of a timeless time which we (certainly the 'we' of our own immanently televisual generation) continue to recognise as the present. Let us therefore, for a moment, try to rehistoricise.

Doctor Who began eighteen years after the Second World War had ended: that's shorter than the gap that separates us now, as of writing, from Chernobyl, the Challenger disaster and 'The Trial of a Time Lord' (1986). *Doctor Who* began sixteen years after India had gained its independence: a shorter period of time than that which now divides us from the last episode of the original series of *Doctor Who* and the fall of the Berlin Wall. *Doctor Who* began seven years after the Suez crisis. That's how long John Major was

Prime Minister. That's how long Tom Baker was Doctor Who. A week may be a long time in politics, or when you're waiting (behind the sofa) for the latest instalment of your favourite TV show, but seven years – in historical terms – that's *nothing*.

Ghana and Malaysia had broken free of the British Empire six years before the first episode of *Doctor Who* was broadcast; Nigeria three years before; Sierra Leone and Tanzania just two years before. During the programme's first year, Britain lost Kenya. During its second, Zambia won its independence; over the next few years, Botswana, Zanzibar, Gambia, Aden and Swaziland, among others, would go the same way. In consigning the pre-televisual (and then the pre-colour) to the realms of history, we children of the ahistorical age of television may neglect to recall how urgent and current such events must have been.

Doctor Who was a product of those dying days of empire. During the programme's opening season (1963–4), the Doctor and his companions used their superior technology to interfere in the internal politics of a primitive tribe ('An Unearthly Child'); recognised their kinship with a clan of Aryans and taught them the arts of war ('The Daleks'); saved the paternalist empire of a white-robed mind-controller from the liberation politics of a cell of black-clad anarchists ('The Keys of Marinus'); were careful to preserve the historical conditions that would pave the way for Cortés and Napoleon ('The Aztecs' and 'The Reign of Terror'); and, when faced with a gang of rogue colonials on an alien world, improvised a disconcertingly happy ending for Joseph Conrad's *Heart of Darkness* ('The Sensorites'). Most significantly, they did battle with the Nazi-like Daleks, in the first of a relentless sequence of reconstructions of Britain's finest hours.

In the programme's second year (1964–5), its protagonists would free Vortis, Xeros and England from colonial oppression ('The Web Planet', 'The Space Museum' and 'The Dalek Invasion of Earth'). At the same time, they helped to promote, abet and inspire the ambitions of William the Conqueror, Richard the Lionheart and the Emperor Nero ('The Time Meddler', 'The Crusade' and 'The Romans'). This paradox is epitomised by a story halfway through the programme's third season – 'The Ark' (1966) – during which our heroes are content to witness the subjugation by humans of a group of cycloptic aliens, but join the resistance when this power relationship is reversed. This hypocrisy echoes the sophistic mindset of the British colonialist unable to equate his own civilising mission with the brutal opportunism of other imperial powers – from the Boers to the Nazis – the Englishman who, time and again, trains the natives to fight for what *he* believes is right – invariably in order to secure the acquisition of materials required by the imperial metropolis . . . just as the good Doctor himself, on his first visit to the planet Skaro – in 'The Daleks' (1963–4) – provokes a little war so that he might get his hands on a component necessary for his mobile home.

Late imperialist influences pervade British TV classics of this period. The *Quatermass* serials had, during the 1950s, desperately attempted to maintain a patrician sense of Britain's importance in the world – as civilisation is saved from alien invasion by the head of the British space programme! However, in the 1960s and 1970s, British televison developed a more mature sense of irony on the subject of empire. *I, Claudius* (1976) charted the corruption and stagnation of imperialism; and *Dad's Army* (1968–77), *The Avengers* (1960–9), *Monty Python* (1969–74) and *Fawlty Towers* (1975, 1979) offered a mixture of apology and apologia, anxiety and nostalgia, for England's glory days.

On the rare occasions when *Doctor Who* directly addresses the British Empire, it presents a similar portrayal of the imperialist as the kind-hearted, upper-class nitwit of bourgeois comedy. Major Daly, Professor Litefoot and Redvers Fenn-Cooper – from 'Carnival of Monsters' (1973), 'The Talons of Weng-Chiang' (1977) and 'Ghost Light' (1989) – represent soft stereotypes in the nice-but-dim style of Captains Mandrake and Mainwaring, Majors Bloodnok and Gowen, Brigadiers Farquar-Smith and Lethbridge-Stewart – the stiff-upper-lipped military clichés of *Dr Strangelove*, *Dad's Army*, *The Goon Show*, *Fawlty Towers*, *Monty Python* and *Doctor Who*.

Like the bullied child who uses humour as a defence, these ironies reflect a sense in which, even if we're no longer as strong as the new global superpowers, we're at least able to laugh at ourselves – in order, at least, to preempt the rest of the world's ridicule. Britain's former emphasis on military, political and economic power is therefore exchanged for the self-styled moral superiority of 'cultural maturity'.

When Russell T. Davies finally allows the programme's protagonists to take the reins of government (or at least control of Downing Street's Cabinet Room), they can't pass up the chance to make a few sarcastic comments about contemporary British foreign policy; but, at the same time, in the style of Nigel Kneale's *Quatermass* serials, the programme seems secretly to relish the idea that Britain still boasts a missile defense system that might prove the envy, and the downfall, of extraterrestrial life.

Empire of the Aunt

In 1904, Joseph Chamberlain spoke of 'that potent agency for peace and for civilization that we call the British Empire' (in Browne, 1974: 96). At the start of the twenty-first century, as George W. Bush declares – and sets out to prove – America's status as 'the greatest force for good in history' (August 2002), we can at least console ourselves that the world's greatest cultural influence remains the BBC. And within the traditional ideology of everyone's favourite broadcasting Auntie – as mirrored in the geographical parochialism of *Doctor Who*'s alien invasion stories – the world is England. (*Doctor Who*'s aliens rarely bother to visit other countries, and, when they do, they don't seem keen to stay and never deign to invade. Scaroth-the-last-of-the-Jagaroth – in 'City of Death' (1979) – Omega – in 'Arc of Infinity' (1983) – and the Sontarans Stike and Varl – in 'The Two Doctors' (1985) – prove as eager to leave Paris, Amsterdam and Seville as any other Englishman, or English-monster, might be.)

Doctor Who, in its much-vaunted 'quintessential Britishness', addresses the nation's postcolonial ambivalence in a series of ideological contradictions and U-turns. The protagonist is represented as a restoration of the tradi-tional colonial hero. Even his costumes – Edwardian frock-coats or cricket whites, smoking jackets or Bohemian garb – recall the period of the height of British imperial power. He's presented as the ideal of colonial liberalism: an objective, asexual saviour-explorer – a scientist whose only greed is for know-ledge – a man who's out neither for himself nor for a bit of the Other – a post-gendered gunless wonder – an upper-middle-class eccentric licensed by the establishment – a revolutionary who can't change history (a point which William Hartnell repeatedly stresses in his early adventures). Just as *Star Trek* has relentlessly justified its heroes' transgressions of their own 'Prime Directive' with questionable moral absolutes that gloss over the hypocrisies of contemporary American foreign policy, so *Doctor Who*'s protagonist's con-stant violation of his own people's policy of non-intervention – in (to quote Joseph Chamberlain again) 'the interests of humanity and civilisation' (in Hobson, 1987: 270) – reinstates the very imperialist agendas and alibis which that character's liberal humanism purports to oppose. When you vanquish the Jagrafess, you may well end up letting the Daleks in through the back door. It's not often – indeed it's almost unheard of – that the resolution is unproblematic and conclusive, and that everybody gets to live. In fact it's so rare it's enough to make Christopher Eccleston's Doctor dance for joy.

The contrast between the conservative paternalism of William Hartnell and Jon Pertwee's portrayals of the protagonist, and the revolutionary indi-vidualism exuded by Patrick Troughton, Tom Baker and Christopher Eccleston's anarchic performances, elaborates such problems and contradic-tions not only within the programme's ideological structure, but also within imperial liberalism itself. The hypocrisies of liberal colonialism (of benevolent assimilation, exploitation and oppression) are also underlined in the work of perhaps the programme's only writer who self-consciously attempts to debunk this model: the author of two of the series' stories of the early 1980s, Christopher Bailey – 'Kinda' (1982) and 'Snakedance' (1983). Both stories focus on the decadence of imperialism; both also offer non-violent (virtually non-interventionist) methods of re-establishing the liberal-humanist status quo; both also present the programme's only adult representations of sexuality prior to the coming of Jack and Rose.

After the programme's debut episode, in which it transpired that the school-girl Susan wasn't – as her suspicious teachers had hypothesised – meeting a boy in a junkyard for a nocturnal rendezvous, but was in fact returning home to her alien, time-travelling grandfather, the programme's intimations of romance became increasingly childlike and chaste. Susan Foreman herself ends up with a gaminesque chap who offers her the possibility of family and stability; Jo Grant goes off with an eccentric and intellectually passionate scientist, who, obviously enough, represents the Time Lord she can't have; Grace Holloway sees in the Doctor himself a sensitive and sexless soulmate, the perfect replacement for her discarded ex. Only Tom Baker and Lalla Ward (as their off-screen relationship started to affect their on-screen personae) gave any hints of the playful sexuality with which Billie Piper would come to treat Noel Clarke (Mickey), Christopher Eccleston and John Barrowman (Captain Jack) in the programme's 2005 season – as she flirted between their stereotypical male virtues of dogged reliability, moral strength and naked machismo.

Doctor Who may blush at the mention of sex, but the blush is an involunt-ary sign of shame rather than a symptom of innocence. The more it protests its naïvety the less naïve it seems to be. In a similar fashion, imperialism itself has, despite its official and officious claims to the contrary, always been a sexual activity – a substitute for, and a source of, erotic satisfaction (one might suggest that, for certain adolescents, science fiction has had a similar function). Empire-builders speak of penetrating virgin territories, while their opponents decry those rapes of distant lands. Romanticists have twisted these metaphors back on themselves since the days when that early American colony was named in honour of the virgin queen, when John Donne dubbed his mistress his 'new-found-land', and Andrew Marvell witnessed his love growing 'vaster than empires'.

Sigmund Freud famously described female sexuality as a 'dark continent'; and those repressed Victorian gentlemen who sought to sow their wild oats in the fertile tropics seemed to find the temptations of all that foreign flesh similarly alluring and disturbing. Edward Said (1985: 59) writes of the imperialist's simultaneous 'shivers of delight in' and 'fear of' the 'sensuality' of the colonial Other. As the historian Ronald Hyam (1999: 61) points out, the British Empire was 'deeply agitated about the dangers of mixed race unions'. John MacKenzie (1999: 277) writes that, in many popular British plays of the early nineteenth century, 'interracial couples (almost always a white male and an Asian female) featured prominently [...] Later, the increasing concern with the [...] moral superiority of Britain [...] was expressed [...] in chauvinistic language and violent events'.

The allure of the Other and the moral ambiguities of miscegenation threaten to explode imperialism's defining illusion of its own unassailable identity and integrity, and are reflected in the emasculating fantasies of female power displayed in such populist late-imperialist texts as Bram Stoker's *Dracula* and Rider Haggard's *She* – and in Sherlock Holmes's unwonted impotence in the face of Irene Adler: 'the woman'. In *Doctor Who*, the protagonist's similar discomfort in the presence of female eroticism (most notably in Tom Baker's extravagantly adolescent responses to alien dominatrices) – and his denial of his own sexuality (in William Hartnell and Peter Cushing's grandfatherliness, in Patrick Troughton and Peter Davison's false innocence) – these repressions seem to stem from a colonial tradition of sexual neurosis. There's something – indeed, quite a lot – of the 'boys' own' adventure in the Doctor's escapades . . . with all that this entails. That's underlined by the fact that two of the actors to have played the character – Peter Cushing and Tom Baker – have also taken the role of Sherlock Holmes, and that Cushing is best known for his portrayals of *Dracula*'s Professor Van Helsing, and also appeared in the 1965 film of Rider Haggard's *She*.

The puerile, sexless fantasies of these late imperial texts represent an attempt to defer development, both on a personal and on a historical level. The boy who never grows up never has to watch the sun set on his empire. This attempt to 'freeze history' is, as has already been suggested, a central and defining theme of the totalitarian-imperialist project. It is to Russell T. Davies's credit (or it is, some might say, merely testimony to his failure to comprehend and capture the nature of the franchise) that, in resurrecting *Doctor Who* within a socially and sexually aware world of council housing and flamboyant sensuality, he has attempted not only to restart the programme's history but to restart the programme, for the first time, within history – within material and psychical history. It's not just that the 2005 series breathed new life into the format – it's that it breathed life, real life, into the format for the very first time – and thus began to overcome the stagnant decadence of postcolonial nostalgia in which the series had been steeped.

The five *Doctor Who* stories that most directly explore the subject of British imperialism – Malcolm Hulke and Terrance Dicks's 'The War Games' (1969), Robert Holmes's 'Carnival of Monsters' (1973) and 'The Talons of Weng-Chiang' (1977), Christopher Bailey's 'Kinda' (1982) and Marc Platt's 'Ghost Light' (1989) – each present similarly sympathetic views of the bumbling British imperialist, but also offer increasingly ambivalent perspectives on the freezing of time and the ending of history: almost as if, as the programme grew ever more obsessed with its own past, it became blind to the problems of historical conflation. Hulke, Dicks and Holmes – workmanlike screenwriters grounded in the traditions of television drama – censure the efforts of the War Lords (who are assembling an elite army from different eras of human history), of Vorg (who has trapped his victims in a remorseless and anachronistic cycle of repetition) and of Magnus Greel (a war criminal from the future who's messing around with time machines in Victorian London). For Christopher Bailey, however, it's the heroes themselves who must halt the historical process – while the villain's desire is to restart time, and to overthrow the empire. Taking this anti-historicist stance to extremes, Marc Platt's deus ex machina, a character called Light – a taxonomically compulsive, amoral, colonial explorer who plans to put a stop to human history in order to complete his inventory – is portrayed as virtually divine, while his nemesis plots to bring down Queen Victoria. It may in fact be that Bailey and Platt, in depicting their protagonists' reactionary stances, are demonstrating that they're well aware that *Doctor Who*'s – and indeed the entire BBC's – covert project (disguised beneath a host of liberal platitudes) is to restore and sustain the greatness, or the dregs, of the British Empire.

One further *Doctor Who* story takes the British Empire for its backdrop: Terence Dudley's 'Black Orchid' (1982). It tells the tale of the murderous madness of an imperial explorer who – on his return to his native England – is hidden away in the attic like the guilty secret he is. Yet, just as Brontë's Mrs Rochester looks set to meet Conrad's Mr Kurtz, the presence of other – less controversial – elements of colonial culture intrudes. The story appears to take its title from Rex Stout's crime novel of 1942, *Black Orchids*. For this isn't the world of colonial history, but of detective fiction and its consoling postcolonial fantasies. It is specifically the unreal realm of Wilkie Collins's *The Moonstone* or of Agatha Christie's *The Mysterious Affair at Styles* – complete with its country house and its racist attitudes to the black servants. They're even drinking cocktails and playing cricket. One recalls in this context the nostalgic pathos of John Major's risible vision of England, as enunciated to the party faithful one conference time: 'What does this England mean to me? I shall tell you. It means lukewarm beer, the sound of cricket ball against willow, old dears cycling to church […]'. It was this absurd posturing which eventually ended eighteen years of Conservative rule; it was as a result of a similarly crippling nostalgia that John Nathan-Turner, the producer of *Doctor Who* through the 1980s, in isolating and emphasising this characteristic as the programme's defining feature, eventually brought stagnation and cancellation upon the show.

In the end, then, this televisual text which offers itself in the guise of anti-imperialist liberal humanism ends up as a paradigm of ideological and ontological conservatism. In this sense, *Doctor Who*, and the BBC itself, aren't unlike much of the mainstream of British politics. They may proudly proclaim the colour-blindness of their multicultural, postcolonial credentials – they may lament and decry the evils of empire, and cast members of ethnic minorities in supporting parts – but we're about as likely to see an Afro-Caribbean or an Asian in their top jobs (the Doctor or the Director-General or the

Prime Minister) as we are to see David Tennant, Mark Thompson or Tony Blair taking the title role in the life of Nelson Mandela.

In 'Doomsday' (2006), David Tennant's Doctor discovers that the Torchwood Institute, an organisation founded by Queen Victoria, is active in contemporary London, using alien technologies in a bid to restore the British Empire – and that, in doing so, the Brits have inadvertently provided a launchpad for both a Cyberman and Dalek invasion of Earth. This situation is obviously ironic and absurd: yet isn't the true absurdity not the hubris and the incompetence of the neo-imperialists, but the fact that even the possibility of this vision of the resurrection of British greatness could be taken seriously – or at least credibly – as a dramatic device on popular television at the start of the twenty-first century?

Doctor Who's echoes of imperialism represent not only an ideological anachronism but also an ideology *of* anachronism. Its ahistoricism recalls the junking of history which Terry Eagleton (1987) identifies as a defining characteristic of postmodernity and of totalitarianism. Its pseudo-pluralistic conflation or assimilation of all times, places, histories and societies is at once eminently televisual, totalistic and imperialistic – and as such is both typically and radically postmodern, and classically, tragically British.

References

Balázs, Béla. 1970. *Theory of the Film*. New York: Dover.

Barthes, Roland. 1993. *Camera Lucida*. London: Vintage.

Baudrillard, Jean. 1995. *The Gulf War Did Not Take Place*. Bloomington: University of Indiana Press.

Baudrillard, Jean. 2005. *The Intelligence of Evil or The Lucidity Pact*. New York: Berg.

Bazin, André. 1967. *What is Cinema?: Volume 1*. Berkeley: University of California Press.

Brontë, Charlotte. 2003. *Jane Eyre*. London: Penguin.

Browne, Harry. 1974. *Joseph Chamberlain, Radical and Imperialist*. London: Longman.

Christie, Agatha. 2001. *The Mysterious Affair at Styles*. London: HarperCollins.

Collins, Wilkie. 1994. *The Moonstone*. London: Penguin.

Conrad, Joseph. 1994. *Heart of Darkness*. London: Penguin.

Derrida, Jacques. 1992. *Acts of Literature*. London: Routledge.

Donne, John. 1971. *Poetical Works*. Oxford: Oxford University Press.

Doyle, Arthur Conan. 1981. *The Adventures of Sherlock Holmes*. Harmondsworth: Penguin.

Eagleton, Terry. 1987. 'Awakening from Modernity'. *Times Literary Supplement*, 20 February.

Eaton, Mick. 1981. 'Television Situation Comedy'. In Tony Bennett, Susan Boyd-Bowman, Colin Mercer and Janet Woollacott (eds). *Popular Television and British Film*. London: British Film Institute, pp. 26–52.

Ellis, John. 1992. *Visible Fictions*. London: Routledge.

Fiske, John. 1987. *Television Culture*. London: Routledge.

Fukuyama, Francis. 1998. *The End of History and the Last Man*. New York: Avon Books.

Haggard, H. Rider. 1991. *She*. Oxford: Oxford University Press.

Harvey, David. 1990. *The Condition of Postmodernity*. Oxford: Blackwell.

Hawking, Stephen. 1989. *A Brief History of Time*. New York: Bantam.

Heidegger, Martin. 1962. *Being and Time*. Oxford: Blackwell.

Hobson, J.A. 1987. *Imperialism*. London: Allen & Unwin.

Hyam, Ronald. 1999. 'The British Empire in the Edwardian Era'. In Judith M. Brown and Wm. Roger Louis (eds). *The Oxford History of the British Empire: IV*. Oxford: Oxford University Press, pp. 47–63.

Kristeva, Julia. 1984. *Revolution in Poetic Language*. Columbia: Columbia University Press.

Lifton, Robert and Eric Markusen. 1991. *The Genocidal Mentality*. London: Macmillan.

Lyotard, Jean-François. 1989. *The Lyotard Reader*. Oxford: Blackwell.

MacKenzie, John M. 1999. 'Empire and Metropolitan Cultures'. In Andrew Porter (ed.). *The Oxford History of the British Empire: III*. Oxford: Oxford University Press, pp. 270–93.

McLuhan, Marshall. 2001. *Understanding Media*. London: Routledge.

McQueen, David. 1998. *Television*. London: Arnold.

Marc, David. 1989. *Comic Visions: Television Comedy and American Culture*. Boston, MA: Unwin Hyman.

Marvell, Andrew. 1972. *The Complete Poems*. Harmondsworth: Penguin.

Metz, Christian. 1982. *The Imaginary Signifier*. Bloomington: University of Indiana Press.

Orwell, George. 1954. *Nineteen Eighty-Four*. Harmondsworth: Penguin.

Said, Edward. 1985. *Orientalism*. Harmondsworth: Penguin.

Shakespeare, William. 2001. *Hamlet*. London: Arden.

Sontag, Susan. 1979. *On Photography*. Harmondsworth: Penguin.

Stam, Robert. 2000. *Film Theory*. Oxford: Blackwell.

Stoker, Bram. 1998. *Dracula*. Oxford: Oxford University Press.

Stout, Rex. 1992. *Black Orchids*. London: Bantam.

Tulloch, John and Manuel Alvarado. 1983. *Doctor Who: The Unfolding Text*. London and Basingstoke: Macmillan.

Vonnegut, Kurt. 1991. *Slaughterhouse 5*. London: Vintage.

Williams, Raymond. 1990. *What I Came to Say*. London: Radius.

Chapter 7

Mythic identity in *Doctor Who*

David Rafer

A fascinating relationship develops between *Doctor Who* and myth, with myth emerging as a narrative sequence, in images, symbols and worldviews, as a form of thought and through the development of the central character into a mythic hero. Exploration of the mythic in *Doctor Who* brings deeper insight into the function of myth within this popular television phenomenon, enabling us to identify different types of myth that often contend for dominance. We are able to observe critical reaction to myth in *Doctor Who* balanced against the theoretical views of seminal myth theorists. It is surely time to consider this broader approach to the problem of myth in *Doctor Who*. The Doctor himself is a carrier and purveyor of his own myth but also encounters images and patterns drawn from ancient world mythology. The way that the Doctor confronts and feeds into myth reveals something of the enduring nature and appeal of mythic narratives and symbols and is a contributory factor in the mysticism of the character.

The many changing portrayals of the Doctor have provided a rich and vivid fictional form. Whilst the Doctor is an ostensibly rational being, tensions occur with the release of irrational, alien forces and through the mentalities and worldviews inherent in the various myth systems that the programme seeks to exploit. The programme sustains both modern myth influences and supplants ancient mythic materials but myth also has a form-ative effect on the series. Thus as well as considering political myth, ideology and film myth, for example (for which there is a body of extant research), there's also a need to account for the programme's use of ancient myth drawn from Greek, Egyptian, biblical, Norse, Eastern and Arthurian mythological materials. The unending adventures have given way to a new form of psychosis, a fictional character that can now be diagnosed as suffering from a mythic identity crisis!

Initially, in the programme's televisual beginnings, a strong factor in the mythic creation of *Doctor Who* was the aura of mystery surrounding the

Doctor.[1] The character was a largely unexplained figure and developed from an irascible, selfish old man in his earliest stories into the more identifiable heroic figure of 'The Dalek Invasion of Earth' (1964). The First Doctor (William Hartnell) engaged opponents in battles of wits and dispensed wisdom drawn from age and experience. These aspects reflect the 'wise old man' archetype which particularly contrasts with Peter Davison's portrayal of the Fifth Doctor as a more simplistic and chivalrous kind of hero.[2] The Doctor as wise old man dispenses wisdom to the more straightforward hero figures of Ian, Steven or Ben through adventures that recall myth theorist Joseph Campbell's 'trials and terrors of the weird adventure' (Campbell, 1993: 9). However, although the promethean archetype might describe Ian Chesterton's fire-making in 'An Unearthly Child' (1963), the archetypal significance of the Doctor remains more elusive as his different personas developed.

Like the heroes of classical antiquity the Doctor seems touched by divinity, being almost immortal and generally considered to be alien in the BBC series. Heroes of ancient myth, such as Heracles, were often the result of a union between god and mortal and the Doctor is identified as half-human in the McGann TV Movie (1996). But whereas Heracles proved himself through physical labours, the Doctor generally relies upon his intelligence to solve complex problems and often conceals his intellect beneath layers of humour, satirising situations and mocking opponents.[3] The Doctor can be wildly eccentric, particularly in his fourth incarnation (Tom Baker), making him unpredictable as he defuses tensions and societal problems through satire and comedy. This technique was developed considerably through Patrick Troughton's portrayal (typically referred to as 'Chaplinesque') of the Second Doctor in which humour masked the workings of a powerful intellect. Writers and analysts of *Doctor Who* have therefore often identified the Doctor with the Trickster archetype.[4] This suggests that the Doctor is a curiously contradictory character, a cultured figure who operates on an often instinctual, childlike level. He is both the product of a highly technological civilisation and an archetype drawn from ancient, primitive hero myths and thus has an unconscious quality.[5] The Trickster can give free expression to both rational and irrational acts and the Doctor emerges as a maverick, having stolen the TARDIS and fled his own kind. The Trickster's capriciousness can also initiate trouble and this has certainly been true of the Doctor – as, for example, when tricking his companions leads to their radiation poisoning in the first Dalek story and when his arrival into situations initiates the disruption of order.

Exploring myth in *Doctor Who* is complicated because of the *ad hoc* nature of the programme and because of the inherent contradictions in myth. Whilst myth still dominates modern thought, particularly politics, it is also viewed as having emerged from primitive mentalities. Both modern and ancient myth draw from our irrationality, yet in apparent contradiction to this there is also a kind of 'logic' inherent in myth that can be delineated through structuralist enquiry. When discussing myth we might take the view of Roland Barthes, who interprets myth as ideology: 'myth has the task of giving an historical intention a natural justification, and making contingency appear eternal. Now this process is exactly that of bourgeois ideology' (Barthes, 1972: 142). Critics have drawn on examples of *Doctor Who* stories that carry political myths such as 'The Green Death' (1973) and the Peladon adventures.[6] Clearly the institution of the BBC also, possibly unwittingly, promotes ideology not only of the political variety but also through the generic body of ideas, factors and influences permeating the lives and worlds of writers and production staff. Revolution is also a popular theme in *Doctor Who*, with the programme projecting myths of revolt against totalitarianism.[7] These kinds of tale exploit ideology or myths generated by the modern mind but the programme has also projected myths produced by ancient mentalities that are inscribed quite differently. Myth is sometimes viewed as lies but is more widely thought of as a traditional story involving supernatural beings and fantastic events and, in this sense, it is thus quite different to ideology circulating through modern cultural myths.

Generally myth can be conveyed in a narrative pattern or an image and a mythic symbol lends itself to multiple interpretations whilst an allegory generally has only one meaning. In addition, Darko Suvin (1979: 3–15) has observed that science fiction can have a quality of estrangement that echoes that of myth. Thus *Doctor Who* can project a mythlike quality through stories set on alien planets even though these episodes do not draw directly on any specific myth pattern. For Jungian psychoanalytical critics myth has a dream-like quality and involves the unconscious and archetypes, or original patterns or images, returning to consciousness (Jung, 1959: 3–53). Jung proposed that archetypes are part of the collective psyches of humanity. Myth's resonance or appeal to the unconscious recalls the way that *Doctor Who* has exploited mythic imagery to terrify impressionable young audiences. The mythic character of the Doctor can be delineated through examination of his archetypal encounters. For a seminal theoretical view of the mythic hero we can turn to Joseph Campbell, who drew upon Jung for his development of the 'monomyth' or rites of passage of the universal mythic hero. Campbell identified different stages of the mythic hero's journey including *separation*, *initiation* and *return*. The Doctor doesn't easily fit into these stages because viewers never saw his initial departure from his home planet and he has never been given the closure of a final homecoming. He does, however, have 'exceptional gifts' (Campbell, 1993: 37) and addresses the 'call to adventure' (Campbell, 1993: 58) subsection of Campbell's *separation* stage, and continually faces danger through 'a succession of trials' (Campbell, 1993: 97), associated with Campbell's *initiation* stage. He is also resurrected through Time Lord regeneration.

The survival of ancient myth patterns suggests the irreducible nature of myth and symbol but, whilst critics generally agree that *Doctor Who* has an undoubted mythic dimension, their analyses have often been highly reductive. Debra Jane Latourette (1990: 86–104) reduces the vibrant, holistic qualities of *Doctor Who* stories down to Propp's functions of the fairytale, resulting in 'moves' denoted by letters and numbers. Gwendolyn Marie Olivier draws upon Jung and Campbell to explore the programme as 'a living mythology' (Olivier, 1987: vii and 1) for fans. She looks for symbolic psychological meanings such as the TARDIS labyrinth suggesting 'an archetype of the unconscious' (Olivier, 1987: 174). Whilst *Doctor Who* may have significance for the unconscious, and has certainly been a cause of children's nightmares, it also operates through more overtly and consciously exploited mythic symbols.

Media studies research by John Tulloch, John Cook and John Fiske emphasises the importance of ideology in the shaping of *Doctor Who*. Tulloch has proposed that the neutrality of the BBC helped position *Doctor Who* within the 'national imaginary' (Tulloch, 2000: 376) for 'The Monster of Peladon' (1974) and he sees *Doctor Who* partly emerging through myths of societal forces and ideology (Tulloch, 1990: 76–83). Cook suggests that the 'Daleks films recycle simple heroic myths of the Second World War' (Cook, 1999: 125) whilst playing on national fears of nuclear holocaust. Similarly, John Fiske argues that 'The Creature from the Pit' (1979) is a story that 'acts mythically in that the logic of its chain of events overcomes the contradictions inherent in a society whose ideology reconciles apparently unproblematically the totalitarianism of science with democracy and individualism' (Fiske, 1984: 194).

Fiske sees readers'/viewers' worldviews as contributing to the construction of meaning. Yet ancient myth has also been widely used in the programme and brings with it often quite radically different mythical worldviews, codes and ideology. These stand somewhat obliquely to the discourses of viewers' own history, politics and morality, although some viewers may have greater or lesser familiarity with ancient myth. As an example we might consider the *Doctor Who* story 'The Aztecs' (1964) in which human sacrifice is at odds with viewers' cultures and rather like a cosmic Tao or path that the Aztecs follow, since writer John Lucarotti recognised that it structured their way of life. Thus whilst the Doctor's companions see what Fiske might term as an 'unbalanced situation' (Fiske, 1984: 176), to the high priest of sacrifice Tlotoxl's point-of-view things have a stability that is, in fact, destabilised with the arrival of the strangers. As Ian points out to Barbara, 'you keep on insisting that Tlotoxl's the odd man out but he isn't', and later, 'you can't fight a whole way of life, Barbara' ('The Aztecs' episode three). The majority of Aztecs follow the way of Tlotoxl whilst only Autlock is the more reasoned exception. 'The Aztecs' presents a fascinating example of a *Doctor Who* story that confronts the TARDIS travellers with an historically documented civilisation and what was once a believed mythical worldview. Feigning the role of a goddess, Barbara sets about trying to open the minds of the Aztecs to her twentieth-century, rationalistic worldview by attempting to break the Aztecs' myth but fails to realise that this is what binds their reality. Similarly, in the Tom Baker story 'The Ribos Operation' (1978), Binro-the-Heretic has been persecuted for rejecting the mythical worldview of Ice and Sun gods battling for supremacy over Ribos.

Other critics have responded variously to *Doctor Who*. Margery Hourihan maintains that the programme 'endlessly repeats the confrontation between the Doctor, the rational, humane and rather dandyish embodiment of all the best qualities of Western culture, and one or another tribe of evil opponents' (Hourihan, 1997: 141). This rather narrow view sees the Doctor as simply reinforcing Western, even imperialist, superiority in the form of the hero. In contrast, James Hodge identifies the Doctor as 'the best possible example of the shaman, the wizard-king, the wise magician' and compares the Doctor to Odin, whom Hodge recognises as 'master-by-force-of-knowledge-and-intellect' (Hodge, 1988: 40). Hodge's notion, however, of the wise magician evokes a sense of the character's mysticism rather than rationalism. Clearly the Doctor's mythic identity is more complex and multifaceted than might be supposed. The Doctor remains a generally anti-establishment hero. Even though the Third Doctor (Jon Pertwee) worked for UNIT on sufferance during a period of exile, he was often in conflict with the establishment and with the Brigadier.

The programme can function through cognitive, transcendental levels as demonstrated in the Platonist themes running through 'The Time Monster' (1972) or the Eastern influence of Buddhism in 'Planet of the Spiders' (1974) and 'Kinda' (1982). *Doctor Who* has drawn upon not only Eastern myth but many mythologies from different cultures, ancient and modern, and thus an eclecticism inevitably emerges since the programme ranges freely through all time and space, limited only by budget and imagination. These limitations may go some way to explain why, besides the great conceptual SF *Doctor Who* stories, we also find in the programme what Ursula Le Guin identifies as science fiction's own cultural sub-myths, in a Jungian 'collective' sense, such as mad scientists, supermen, all powerful computers and alien invaders which she separates from the more ancient, even mystic mythic material that has survived and given inspiration and pleasure down the centuries because it is able to connect 'idea with value' (Le Guin, 1989: 64–5).

Gallifrey, the Time Lords and the Daleks' civil wars are part of the programme's home-grown 'internal myths' (Marson, 1987: 41). Thus as Tulloch and Alvarado observe, *Doctor Who* 'can play on its own history in order to seal it off as an ever denser mythic reality' (Tulloch and Alvarado, 1983: 89).

It is this sense of the programme's mythic reality that is reinforced with Christopher Eccleston's Doctor confronting Autons and Daleks. In contrast to its own myths *Doctor Who* has imported ancient myth on many occasions. *Doctor Who* has encountered Ursula Le Guin's 'true myth' (Le Guin, 1989: 65) and what C.S. Lewis, in *Experiment in Criticism* (1961), called 'great myths' (Lewis, 1996: 42). Thus we find the mythological Devil and popular English myth being exploited in 'The Dæmons' (1971). Greek myth emerges in 'The Myth Makers' (1965), 'The Mind Robber' (1968), 'The Time Monster', 'Underworld' (1978) and 'The Horns of Nimon' (1979–80). Allusions to biblical myth occur in the two 'Ark' stories and the McGann TV Movie whilst Egyptian mythology forms the foundation for 'Pyramids of Mars' (1975). Arthurian mythology structures 'Battlefield' (1989) and Norse mythology emerges in 'Terminus' (1983), 'The Greatest Show in the Galaxy' (1988–9) and 'The Curse of Fenric' (1989). These more overtly mythical stories sit amongst Le Guin's cultural sub-myths of SF and mythic materials drawn from horror films that have given *Doctor Who* 'The Brain of Morbius' (1976) and 'State of Decay' (1980), amongst many others. These considerations lead to the question of what *Doctor Who* does with myth and to the equally intriguing problem of what myth does to *Doctor Who*.

Superficially, the 'scientific' rationalist Doctor continually seeks out the irrational and the disordered and then imposes order and brings about resolution and the return to harmony. He frames mythical and monstrous opponents within a scientifically orientated worldview, providing pseudo-scientific rationalisations for the fantastic, the irrational and preternatural. The Doctor is thus positioned as scientist-hero and generally imposes a logical worldview upon myth and the fantastic. This aspect of *Doctor Who* recalls Olivier's suggestion that audiences find it easier to believe in science than in myth,[8] rather as though science has in fact become a new myth, a notion supported by the way that scientific results are 'written up' for public presentation as well as through the involvement of myth in the formative activities involved in propounding scientific ideas (see Gerhart and Russell, 2002: 191–206). It is as though we cannot quite lose the mythical, primordial aspect of our consciousness, the poeticising faculty that persists in some degree in all human activities however ostensibly rational and analytical we consider ourselves.

The Doctor has also offered several explanations for the origins of myth. In the novelisation of 'The Dæmons' we find the Third Doctor explaining that an Egyptian god can be traced to another source:

Khnum [. . .] A Hindu Demon [. . .] Pan [. . .] The Minotaur [. . . and] the Devil with the head of a goat [. . .] Creatures like that have been seen over and over again throughout the history of man, and man has turned them into myths – into gods or devils [. . .] But they're neither. They are creatures from another world. (Letts, 1974: 82–3)

This notion echoes the historicist view that myths have a kernel of fact and that their explanation is thus to be sought in history.[9] *Doctor Who* has often exploited this kind of approach, perhaps most notoriously associated with the now discredited author Erich von Däniken, who proposed that ancient gods were really aliens. Thus *Doctor Who* has invented entire alien races around myths, identifying medieval trolls with a Sontaran, and suggesting that the truth about the Loch Ness Monster comes down to the Skarasen and the Borad whilst the Abominable Snowmen are really robot servants of the Great Intelligence (although the first Yeti story closes with the revelation of a genuine Yeti almost as if in a restorative gesture for the programme's reductive treatment of this myth). Of course we don't believe in the literal truth of these *Doctor Who* explanations for myth but what is interesting is the programme's process of supplanting 'original' myths.

Another theory of myth crops up in 'Underworld' when Tom Baker's Fourth Doctor muses that Jason's quest for the Golden Fleece culminated when he found it 'Hanging on the Tree at the End of the World. You know, Leela, perhaps those old legends aren't so much stories from the past as prophecies of the future' (Dicks, 1980a: 122–3). Whether in the past or the future, myths emerge from an archetypal event in time from which ripples can go back and forth. Whilst the notion of a kernel of fact reduces myth to history, thus giving us legend, there is also C.S. Lewis' view (Lewis, 1996: 40–9) that historicism and other approaches to myth such as allegory, psychoanalysis, ritual, etc., are all attempts to explain myth that ultimately partially fail because myth continues to evoke the feeling that there is something more, something that cannot be rationalised, that is involved in our experience of myth. It is as though myth and the mythic pulls us into mythical modes of thinking that are more intuitive and stand outside the rational.

True, the Doctor can help or become part of myth, but he is more often the enemy of myth. It is a convenient 'device' for writers to put the Doctor into situations in which the breaking of myth is dramatically exploited. Thus in 'The Power of Kroll' (1978–9) the Doctor encounters primitives whose society is ordered according to Kroll, who is their central totem. Ritual worship of Kroll forges the Swampies' mythical worldview and it is up to the Doctor to break the source of Kroll's power and the hold of his myth upon the Swampies. When Romana and the Doctor are about to be ritually sacrificed, Ranquin, the High Priest of Kroll, explains that

'When the servants of Kroll appear in his guise, they are as part of him, doing his bidding'.

'Nonsense', said Romana spiritedly. 'All you're doing is keeping alive a myth. None of you here have ever even seen Kroll. You weren't even born at the time of the third manifestation.' (Dicks, 1980c: 70)

The primitive Swampies' thinking recalls what myth theorists describe as 'mythical thought' (Cassirer, 1955).[10] Their tribe exhibit a more relational kind of thought process, believing that their rituals can influence Kroll whereas the Doctor's thought processes are more logical and are based upon inference from observed empirical evidence, induction and the scientific rationale of cause and effect. Thus he infers that the methane gas drawn up by the humans' refinery is coming from a giant organism lying dormant in the swamp. The rationalist Doctor is a far more 'conscious' persona than the intuitive Trickster identified earlier, giving the Doctor a kind of duality between his irrational, intuitive nature and the dominance of reason and rationalism. The Doctor can synthesise these opposing qualities and thus rise above their individual limitations to aspire to new forms of knowledge.

In the early 1900s a school of myth criticism developed that was associated with Cambridge scholars such as Jane Harrison who saw myth as emerging primarily from ritual (Harrison, 1980 and 1989). Whilst the patterns of myth may originate in ritual, this factor certainly plays a significant role in generating the mythic in *Doctor Who*. In 'Power of Kroll' the Swampies support their mythical worldview through rituals, particularly of blood sacrifice. It is their way both to dispose of enemies and to forge a relation with their god. Moreover, many *Doctor Who* stories have returned to ritual themes, exploiting their dramatic potential. 'The Dæmons' sees the Master conjure Azal through the Satanic rites of the Coven. The Metebelis spiders forge a link through the ritually meditating monks in order to transport themselves onto the mandala, and the Druids in 'The Stones of Blood' (1978) undertake blood sacrifice that is not simply ritual but actually feeds the alien Ogri. The Fendahl also requires the energies of a specific number of coven members and uses the pentagram as a mark of power to recreate its image. The Doctor himself is not always averse to using magic, for example when he marks out a chalk circle to protect Ace and Shou Yuing in 'Battlefield' or when countering Azal's powers with incantations that give the impression of magic. The Doctor thus has to engage with the mentality or peculiar 'logic' with which he's confronted. *Doctor Who* rituals often evoke the feeling that these ceremonials draw out alien or mythological beings and powers, making them manifest and corporeal. As Mother Tyler suggests in 'Image of the Fendahl' (1977), 'when most believe, that do make it so' (Dicks, 1979: 77). Thus these stories suggest the sense of ritual forging communal belief, turning myth into reality.

However, more generally, aesthetic problems can emerge through the inclusion of ancient myth in *Doctor Who*. A tension emerges between science fiction, which generally implies a 'logical' narrative based upon the imaginative extrapolation of science, and myth which is more about feelings, intuitions and the unexplained. In 'Pyramids of Mars' writers Robert Holmes and Lewis Greifer turned Egyptian myth into science fiction, relocating the Eye of Horus to a Martian pyramid. This is realised as a red orb that maintains Sutekh's paralysis, all of which is in the spirit of the myth of the Eye of Horus that was believed to have 'fought the enemies of light and was itself seen as fire' (Lurker, 1980: 67).[11] Despite reinterpretation within what is ostensibly a science fiction story, the Eye retains a mythic quality when refashioned for 'Pyramids of Mars' since no 'logical' explanation is provided and thus it remains the unexplained astral influence of an Egyptian god. The notion of a paralysis being transmitted to earth to imprison a godlike alien also has a mythic resonance in itself: the Egyptian *Book of the Dead* refers to the eye being lost during a battle with Seth.[12]

Refashioning Egyptian mythology confronts the audience with ancient archetypes. The archetypal pattern of 'Pyramids of Mars' emerges through the battle of two brothers, the gods Horus and Seth, whose cosmic struggle is played out in the earthly conflict between Laurence and Marcus Scarman. The Doctor's mythic role in the story is to oppose Sutekh by drawing upon his knowledge of the god's powers, science and symbols, bringing his own Time Lord myth to bear upon the appropriated Egyptian material. For the audience, the Doctor represents the power of the individual to effect macro-cosmic change. He identifies Sutekh as Set, Satan and the Typhonian Beast and Sutekh declares himself with some relish as 'the Destroyer'. This is his archetypal and primal role drawn from ancient myth. Egyptian myth commentator Donald Mackenzie observes that Sutekh was 'the prototype of the Egyptianized Set, the terminal "kh" signifying "majesty"' (Mackenzie, 1913: 307). Set, known also as Typhon, trapped and killed his brother Horus and later tore the body into fourteen pieces; thus, as the possessed Scarman affirms, Sutekh is the 'bringer of death' associated with disorder and chaos and a primal evil.[13] 'Pyramids of Mars' finds the Doctor immersed in myth and positioned as a mythic hero on the side of order and harmony when he fights chaos incarnate, manifested in the diabolic Set, who has been kept in check by Horus' imposition of stasis upon his demonic brother. Psychoanalytical critics identify the demonic brother figure as the shadow-self or 'dark side of the ego' (Coupe, 1997: 143) and it is no coincidence that, after becoming Sutekh's puppet, Marcus emerges from a space vortex shrouded in black. Whilst Marcus kills his brother, the Doctor has thwarted this kind of shadow-self figure literally in the Valeyard and more generally in his battles with evil Time Lords such as the Master.

If 'Pyramids of Mars' successfully delivers a mythic reinvention, commentator John Kenneth Muir remains critical of *Doctor Who*'s attempts to offer explanations for 'the origins of ancient mythology' (Muir, 1999: 262), pointing out that *Quatermass and the Pit* (1958–9) had already developed the concept. Consequently, Muir argues that the reworking of this idea makes the programme 'a subscriber to formula, not an inventor' (Muir, 1999: 262).

Overusing mythical materials can be aesthetically adverse, with the resulting tale ending up as a confusion of clashing elements, as happens in 'Silver Nemesis' (1988). In this story Wagnerian roles are proposed for villains with the 'living metal' Validium becoming a kind of Rhinegold for the Cybermen, ultimately bringing about their destruction. However, the tale descends into a pretentious mish-mash in which necromancy clashes with alien invaders, Nazis, the Nemesis super-being and Time Lord mythology (as well as the perpetuation of the scientifically flawed idea that Cybermen, being creatures made of metal and plastic, could somehow be allergic to gold).

Myth is refashioned with fewer jarring elements when the mythic materials are drawn from the same mythology. In 'Underworld' the Doctor initially finds Jackson's ship reminiscent of the Flying Dutchman but soon realises that the structuring myth in this adventure is Jason's quest for the Golden Fleece, the object conferring immortality being the Minyan Race Bank. Phonetically Jackson's ship, the *P7E*, echoes Persephone, the name of the daughter of Zeus and Demeter, associated with fertility by the Greeks, who was kidnapped and taken into the Greek Underworld by Pluto. Idmon, Idas and Heracles are part of the *Argo*'s crew,[14] and in 'Underworld' these names are either revised (Herrick for Heracles) or transferred exactly (Idmon and Idas, who become Trogs living in Underworld). In Apollonius of Rhodes' version, Jason takes along a Seer called Idmon whilst in 'Underworld' the Seers are bionic extensions of the ship's computer which calls itself the Oracle,[15] their second sight alluded to through the visual symbol of a third eye on their metal heads.

'Underworld', like 'The Horns of Nimon', reworks a particular pattern of events from Greek myth. Thus the clashing rocks episode from the *Argonautica* (Book II: 533–620) is transformed into interstellar debris forming around the Minyan Patrol Vessel *R1C* (Argosey). In 'The Horns of Nimon', however, scriptwriter Anthony Read sets the myth of the Minotaur on an alien planet, positioning the Doctor very much as Daedalus, helping the Anethan's equivalent of Theseus and Ariadne to escape the Nimon's labyrinthine positronic circuit. Whilst Daedalus gives the ball of string to Ariadne, the Doctor uses K9 to trace a path out of the labyrinth. The labyrinth is reinterpreted as a cosmic power complex for the alien Nimon. The 'original' myth's undercurrents of sexuality are dropped. Thus, whilst there's no mention of Pasiphaë's liaison with a bull resulting in the Minotaur, the Nimon are bull-headed half-humanoid aliens. With their energy-charged horns they symbolise technology and power under bestial control, this latter aspect translated not through sexual lust but through the Nimon's corruption of human bodies when drawing away the life forces of the sacrifices.

In contrast, in 'The Stones of Blood' it is not the pattern of a myth that is important so much as the use of mythic elements for setting and atmosphere.

The Doctor is faced with a goddess from Celtic myth, 'The Witch-Hag [. . .] Morrigu [. . .] Morridwyn' (Dicks, 1980b: 63) who is concealing herself as Vivian Fay. She is identified by the local chief Druid as having 'many names. Morriga [. . .] Hermentana [. . .] the Cailleach' (Dicks, 1980b: 35). Morrigan was a Celtic war goddess called 'the old Battle Crow' (Campbell, 2001: 303) and Chief Druid Mr de Vries tells the Doctor that the raven and the crow are the eyes of the Cailleach. Campbell observes that 'Morrigan [. . .] in later romance [. . .] was to become the fateful sister of King Arthur, Fata Morgana, Morgan la Fée' (Campbell, 2001: 302).[16] In light of Vivian Fay's ultimate fate, it's also interesting that Morgan Le Fay turns herself into stone to escape Arthur in *Le Morte Darthur* (Malory, 1485, IV: 14) and that stone monoliths were worshipped as manifestations of the Cailleach Bheur.[17] Fay's goddess-like powers serve to position the Doctor's mythic role as Merlin in this tale. In contrast, the Seventh Doctor (Sylvester McCoy) story 'Battlefield' is less subtle, seeing the Doctor directly identified as Merlin by Mordred and Morgaine, and this puts the question of the Doctor's mythic identity crisis much more overtly into contention.

Intimations of the crisis can be traced back to the confusion of identity arising when the Doctor became involved in the myth of the fall of Troy in 'The Myth Makers' (1965). Here it is Hartnell's Doctor who helps Odysseus trick the Trojans with the ploy of the wooden horse. Thus we have a journey into the myth of the Trojan horse for the Doctor, who takes on a mythic role when he is identified as Zeus. In 'The Mind Robber' Troughton's Doctor takes the TARDIS to a realm of fiction. A metafictive and intertextual adventure ensues in which the time travellers have to avoid being turned into 'fiction' when encountering, amongst other things, the Unicorn, the Minotaur and Medusa. 'The Mind Robber' also gives us the classic hero quest, with the Doctor and Zoe negotiating the labyrinth, Jamie climbing Rapunzel's hair and the travellers surviving various tests in order to reach a mysterious citadel. 'The Mind Robber' culminates in a battle of wills as the Doctor denies the reality of fiction in order to avoid losing certain life-qualities, such as free will, and becoming simply the puppet of a cosmic author. The Doctor's mythic identity, however, became a particularly dominant theme in the McCoy era when Norse mythology was brought more forcefully into the programme in the form of the Gods of Ragnarok in 'The Greatest Show in the Galaxy' (1988–9) and with Norse mythical materials in 'The Curse of Fenric' (1989). These stories again elevated the Doctor into an archetypal opponent of ancient, primordial evil made corporeal in the latter tale in the form of Fenric. The Ancient Haemovore is identified as the Great Serpent (suggestive of primal evil) and consumes his own future when destroying Fenric, who brought about that evil. This act should prevent that future and so the Ancient Haemovore, through consuming himself, echoes the

Midgard-serpent of Norse myth, a symbol of time and the doom of the gods, which swallowed its own tail.

It was also during the McCoy era that an attempt was made to inject new mystery into the Doctor. 'Remembrance of the Daleks' and 'Silver Nemesis' hinted that the Doctor was more than just a Time Lord and possibly had some involvement in 'the old time' of Gallifrey, linking him to a more mythical era of Time Lord 'Dark Age' history. The Doctor's own personal myth has not been the only one to need rejuvenation in this extremely long-running programme, since the all-powerful, godlike Time Lords encountered by viewers in 'The War Games' (1969) were later treated reductively. The Time Lords are depicted as exhibiting recognisable human weaknesses such as greed for power and physical decrepitude in 'The Deadly Assassin' (1976) and subsequent Time Lord stories. Producer Graham Williams' answer to these 'explained' Time Lords was to replace them with the more mythic, unexplained conception of the Guardians of Light and Time for his epic quest season in which the Doctor searches for the six segments of the Key to Time (1978–9). This season culminated with the Doctor's irrational, intuitive choice of placing one human life, Princess Astra's, above the rest of the cosmos when he breaks up the Key. Thus in the final scenes the Doctor reaffirms compassion, intuition and freedom of choice within the rigidly ordered cosmos structured by the godlike black and white Guardians who stand for chaos and order respectively.[18]

As we have observed, a number of stories see the Doctor directly confront ancient myth, as the programme draws upon different mythologies. Myth, however, is not a passive material and a struggle can ensue between the art of the writer and production team and the mythic materials they seek to exploit. The programme's longevity has seen the Doctor's own myth refashioned for new audiences. Whilst the programme adopts a supposedly rationalistic stance when approaching myth, science and myth present conflicting worldviews that nevertheless acquire a kind of unity when considered as products of the imagination. The Doctor often works to realign mythical elements according to the myths of popular science but he is also a carrier of his own myth of Time Lords and the TARDIS. His mythic hero role reaffirms the power of the individual to effect cosmic change, recalling Campbell's (1993: 349–54) mythic hero as world redeemer. The Doctor assumes various archetypes from scientist-hero, Trickster, wanderer, wise old man and young fool. He functions on multiple levels and is thus the multifaceted mythic hero whose transforming archetype defends civilisation whilst continually running away from it, fights for order but exists in chaos.

The programme has addressed some basic theories of myth but there remain tensions within the series between its projection of mystery and its often pseudo-scientific rationalisations, between myth and science fiction.

Ancient myth provides *Doctor Who* with symbols and worldviews from dead civilisations that were structured by mythical thought. Whilst we recognise myth as providing symbols in the televisual art of *Doctor Who*, these were not symbols for ancient civilisations but part of their believed reality. Ancient myth can provide *Doctor Who* with infusions of past cosmologies but also evokes problems of hierarchy and the limitations of a rigidly ordered universe, and the question of fate versus free will. *Doctor Who* stories playing with witches, Sabbaths and cultist ritual belief give expression to irrational forces that have to be countered by the Doctor. These forces look back to instinctual human mentalities. Promoting the mythic, however, supplies a modern need since civilisation and science continue to demythologise the world. This is where *Doctor Who* comes into its own as a mythical framing device that offers a syncretistic mythology for time and space. Long before *Stargate* (1997–) and *Babylon 5* (1994–8) popularised ancient myth within television science fiction, *Doctor Who* was a pioneer of the re-mythologising of outer space.

Notes

1   See Lambert in Haining (1983: 22).
2   See Tulloch and Alvarado (1983: 273).
3   See Olivier (1987: 184).
4   Bailey in Tulloch and Alvarado (1983: 270–9); Olivier (1987: 162–8). See also Jung (1972).
5   See also Olivier (1987: 162–8).
6   Tulloch and Alvarado (1983: 88, 107 and 182). See also Tulloch and Jenkins (1995).
7   See Fiske (1984: 170) and Tulloch and Alvarado (1983: 117).
8   Olivier (1987: 14–15). A notion Olivier arrives at through Jung (1964: 91).
9   Euhemerus, *c*. 300 BC, is attributed with 'the ultimate historicism' (Dowden, 1998: 50) referred to as Euhemerism. See Dowden (1998: 50–1).
10 See also Lévy-Bruhl (1923).
11 However, Lurker observes that when mentioned in the singular, the Eye of Horus more usually 'refer(s) to the moon' (Lurker, 1980: 67).
12 *The Book of the Dead*, Ch. 42. See Lurker (1980: 67).
13 See Chevalier and Gheerbrant, et al. (1996: 859).
14 In Apollonius of Rhodes' *Argonautica*, Idmon and Idas are crew members aboard the *Argo* and Idmon prophesies his own death (Book I) but goes on the voyage anyway and is killed by a wild boar (see Book II: 828–31).
15 There are two seers in 'Underworld' called Ankh and Lakh. Andrew Pixley observes that 'ankh is an Egyptian key-like cross symbolic of enduring life, while Lakh hails from an Anglo-Indian term meaning "a hundred thousand" (the length of time of the R1C's quest)' (Pixley, 1996: 26). The script comments on the third eye in the Seers' foreheads, 'The reason why they have metal heads is

bionic: they are linked to the computer/oracle and therefore have a kind of telepathy' (script notes cited in Pixley, 1996: 27).

16 See also Hodge (1988: 40).
17 See Littleton (2002: 245).
18 See Tulloch and Alvarado (1983: 126).

References

Barthes, Roland. 1972. *Mythologies*. Trans. Annette Lavers. London: Jonathan Cape.

Campbell, Joseph. 1993. *The Hero with a Thousand Faces*. London: Fontana Press.

Campbell, Joseph. 2001. *The Masks of God – Vol. 3: Occidental Mythology*. London: Souvenir Press.

Cassirer, Ernst. 1955. *The Philosophy of Symbolic Forms – Vol. 2: Mythical Thought*. Trans. Ralph Manheim. Newhaven and London: Yale University Press.

Chevalier, Jean and Alain Gheerbrant (eds). 1996. *The Penguin Dictionary of Symbols*. Trans. John Buchanan-Brown. London: Penguin.

Cook, John R. 1999. 'Adapting telefantasy: the *Doctor Who and the Daleks* films'. In I.Q. Hunter (ed.). *British Science Fiction Cinema*. London: Routledge, pp. 113–27.

Coupe, Laurence. 1997. *Myth*. London and New York: Routledge.

Dicks, Terrance. 1979. *Doctor Who and the Image of the Fendahl*. London: Target.

Dicks, Terrance. 1980a. *Doctor Who and the Underworld*. London: W.H. Allen.

Dicks, Terrance. 1980b. *Doctor Who and the Stones of Blood*. London: W.H. Allen.

Dicks, Terrance. 1980c. *Doctor Who and the Power of Kroll*. London: W.H. Allen.

Dowden, Ken. 1998. *The Uses of Greek Mythology*. London and New York: Routledge.

Fiske, John. 1984. 'Popularity and ideology, a structuralist reading of *Dr. Who*'. In Willard D. Rowland, Jr and Bruce Watkins (eds). *Interpreting Television: Current Research Perspectives*. Beverley Hills, CA: Sage.

Gerhart, Mary and Russell, Allan Melvin. 2002. 'Myth and public science'. In Kevin Schilbrack (ed.). *Thinking Through Myths: Philosophical Perspectives*. London: Routledge, pp. 191–206.

Haining, Peter. 1983. *Doctor Who a Celebration: Two Decades Through Time and Space*. London: W.H. Allen.

Harrison, Jane Ellen. [1962] 1980. *Prolegomena to the Study of Greek Religion*. London: Merlin Press.

Harrison, Jane Ellen. [1963] 1989. *Themis: A Study of the Social Origins of Greek Religion*. London: Merlin Press.

Hodge, James L. 1988. 'New bottles – old wine: the persistence of the heroic figure in the mythology of television science fiction and fantasy'. *Journal of Popular Culture*, Vol. 21, No. 4, Spring, pp. 37–48.

Hourihan, Margery. 1997. *Deconstructing the Hero: Literary Theory and Children's Literature*. London: Routledge.

Jung, C.G. 1959. *The Collected Works of C.G. Jung*, Vol. 9, Part 1. Sir Herbert Read, Michael Fordham and Gerhard Adler (eds). Trans. R.F.C. Hull. London: Routledge and Kegan Paul, pp. 3–53.

Jung, C.G. 1964. 'Approaching the unconscious'. In *Man and His Symbols*. New York: Dell Publishing Co., Inc.

Jung, C.G. 1972. 'On the psychology of the trickster figure'. In Paul Radin (ed.). *The Trickster: A Study in American Indian Mythology*. New York: Schocken.

Latourette, Debra Jane. 1990. 'Doctor Who meets Vladimir Propp: a comparative narrative analysis of myth/folktale and the television science fiction genre'. Unpub. Ph.D. dissertation, Northwestern University.

Le Guin, Ursula K. ed. Susan Wood. 1989. 'Myth and archetype in science fiction'. In *The Language of the Night: Essays on Fantasy and Science Fiction*. London: The Women's Press, pp. 61–9.

Letts, Barry. 1974. *Doctor Who and the Dæmons*. London: Target.

Lévy-Bruhl, Lucien. 1923. *Primitive Mentality*. Trans. Lillian A. Clare. London: George Allen & Unwin.

Lewis, C.S. 1996. *An Experiment in Criticism*. Cambridge: Cambridge University Press.

Littleton, C.S. (ed.). 2002. *Mythology: The Illustrated Anthology of World Myth and Storytelling*. London: Duncan Baird Publications.

Lurker, Manfred. 1980. *The Gods and Symbols of Ancient Egypt: An Illustrated Dictionary*. London: Thames and Hudson.

Mackenzie, Donald Alexander. 1913. *Egyptian Myth and Legend*. London: Gresham Publishing.

Marson, Richard. 1987. 'Myths and legends'. In *Doctor Who Magazine*, No. 120, pp. 39–42.

Muir, John Kenneth. 1999. *A Critical History of Doctor Who on Television*. Jefferson, NC: McFarland.

Olivier, Gwendolyn Marie. 1987. 'A critical examination of the mythological and symbolic elements of two modern science fiction series: *Star Trek* and *Doctor Who*'. Unpublished PhD dissertation, The Louisiana State University and Agricultural and Mechanical College.

Pixley, Andrew. 1996. 'Underworld – archive feature'. In *Doctor Who Magazine*, No. 243, pp. 23–30.

Suvin, Darko. 1979. *Metamorphoses of Science Fiction: On the Poetics and History of a Literary Genre*. New Haven and London: Yale University Press.

Tulloch, John. 1990. *Television Drama: Agency, Audience and Myth*. London and New York: Routledge.

Tulloch, John. 2000. 'Producing the national imaginary: *Doctor Who*, text and genre'. In Dudley Jones and Tony Watkins (eds). *A Necessary Fantasy? The Heroic Figure in Children's Popular Culture*. New York and London: Garland Publishing, Inc.

Tulloch, John and Manuel Alvarado. 1983. *Doctor Who: The Unfolding Text*. London and Basingstoke: Macmillan.

Tulloch, John and Henry Jenkins. 1995. *Science Fiction Audiences: Watching Doctor Who and Star Trek*. London: Routledge.

Chapter 8

The human factor: Daleks, the 'Evil Human' and Faustian legend in *Doctor Who*

Fiona Moore and Alan Stevens

Since their first appearance in 1963, the Daleks have entered the public consciousness to such a degree that they occasionally threaten to surpass the Doctor himself in popularity. This chapter, however, will argue that a large part of the Daleks' continued appeal to the public lies not in their presence in and of itself, but in the way in which their plans, schemes and motivations are revealed, interpreted and mediated to the viewer by the figure of a human or humanoid character who allies him or herself with the Daleks on some level: the 'Evil Human'. Consequently, the reason behind the Daleks' attraction to the audience is not so much that they are, as some have argued, an iconic figure of 'evil', as that, through the 'Evil Human', the viewer of a Dalek story is invited to explore the nature of human 'evil', and to confront the 'evil' within themselves and their culture.

Background

Although many factors have been advanced to explain the popularity of the Daleks – their iconic appearance, the ease with which their catchphrase and actions can be imitated by schoolchildren, their connection with the British mythos of the evil Nazi invader (see Bignell and O'Day, 2004: 62, 113; Pixley, 2003: 78; Robins, 1989) – we would suggest that the primary reason for their impact on viewers over the years is the way in which Dalek stories draw upon a particular archetype of European folk and fairytales, to wit, that of the human who makes a deal with the Devil. This section will consider the literature on the ways in which such mythological figures engage with audiences, and how they relate to the Dalek stories.

The literary genre which the Dalek story most resembles is that of the folk or fairytale. Like these, Dalek stories are externalised, taking place for the most part in some future time or faraway place (Bettelheim, 1978: 5); focus on the conflict between good and evil (9); feature a (normally) upbeat ending in which most problems are resolved satisfactorily (36) and, through their symbolic nature, have resonance with different age groups, adult as well as juvenile (16). In a similar way, Tulloch and Alvarado cite Verity Lambert discussing how *Doctor Who*'s role was to balance pedagogy with entertainment (1983: 42), to inculcate positive values through fantasy stories (43) and also to appeal to the older demographic, albeit in different ways than to children (55). As such, it is safe to say that Dalek stories also take on aspects of the psychological role of the folk or fairytale. Bruno Bettelheim, in his celebrated work on the psychology of fairytales *The Uses of Enchantment* (1978), argues that they teach children 'about the inner problems of human beings, and of the right solutions to their predicaments in any society' (5); specifically, they explore the dark side of human nature in allegorical/ symbolic ways, allowing children to understand that tragedy and evil are part of life, and how to deal with them, as well as reinforcing social values (7–8, 25). This is also supported by anthropological work on the use of folk or fairytales. In Audrey Richards' classic study of a girls' initiation ritual in Africa, *Chisungu* (1956), she considers how the socialisation process enacted in the rite involves the performance of stories and songs regarding pottery images, which represent exaggerated or 'monstrous' ideas of what is considered 'good' and 'bad' in society (1956: 59, 101), much as the Daleks' exaggeratedly 'monstrous' appearance allows the presentation of what society considers 'evil' (see below). The Dalek stories thus closely resemble a universal genre of storytelling which involves, at least in part, the presentation of 'good' and 'evil' behaviour, and the exploration, by storyteller and audience, of what these concepts mean.

In particular, the Dalek stories continually throw up a dramatic figure, which we shall here call the 'Evil Human'. This is a human (or humanoid) character who has made a conscious and deliberate choice to work with the Daleks for one reason or another, and whose relationship to the Daleks (and, usually, final fate at their hands) is one of the driving forces of the story. Sometimes these humans' motivations are benign, as in the case of Waterfield ('The Evil of the Daleks' [1967]); sometimes they are self-serving, as with Mavic Chen ('The Daleks' Master Plan' [1965–6]); sometimes their reasons are more ambiguous, as with the Controller of 'Day of the Daleks' (1972). All, however, are characterised by the following pattern: the human is offered something by the Daleks which they desire or need, the human agrees to serve the Daleks, the human is corrupted by association with them and is punished by death (apart from the few cases in which the human is redeemed and/or escapes retribution, which will be discussed below). Although it is true that other *Doctor Who* monsters do operate in association with humans – for instance the Cybermen – and that these relationships do occasionally involve a similar pattern of temptation and damnation, no other monster, with the arguable exception of the Black Guardian during season twenty, has relationships with humans which consistently follow this pattern. For the most part, human–monster relationships in *Doctor Who* tend to be coercive, or to involve a human pretending to work with the monster in order to deceive them. Tobias Vaughn, in 'The Invasion' (1968), does show Faustian characteristics in his relationship with the Cybermen; however, leaving aside the fact that 'The Daleks' Master Plan' was a distinct influence on the story, Vaughn differs sharply from the Evil Humans discussed below in that he neither presumes to speak for the Cybermen nor, at any point, expresses a belief that he and the Cybermen are in some way operating in sympathy. The Daleks are thus unique in the way that their relationships with their human allies follow a repeated pattern whereby a human with a character flaw is tempted into an association with them and suffers the consequences.

The most obvious antecedent for the Evil Human in European literature is the Faust legend, of which the best known is the story of Dr Faustus (Jones, 1995: 175–6). Although the legend's details vary (the significance of which will be explored below), it generally concerns a scholar who makes a contract with the Devil, offering his soul in exchange for unlimited power for a set period of time (175). As Faustus squanders his prize, using it to satiate base lusts and becoming jaded and cynical, so the audience comes to realise, first, the depths to which humans can sink when given the opportunity (176), and second, that the Devil's bargain is not, as it is presented to Faustus, a free choice: Mephistopheles deliberately plays upon Faustus' fears and desires to keep him in his power (see Goethe, 1949, 1959; Marlowe, 1965). Nation himself, in a 1992 interview, explicitly compares the Daleks to the Devil in European religious lore, and, asked to consider the Daleks' appeal, muses: 'I think it was their clear-cut blackness – they were the bad guys: no shadings, no gentle grays. They were bad' (Peel, 1992: 5). Nick Pegg makes a similar comment, referring obliquely to the pedagogic/mythological value of such demonic figures:

> The Daleks symbolise a unity. Their history and their actions are the distillation of a common fear for us as well as for the fictional characters they torment. They are a lurid representation of evil; death in pantomime garb. We need them. (Pegg, 1991: 15)

Through the Faustian archetype, then, with the Daleks as Devil and their human allies as Faust, the Dalek stories allow the author, and thus the viewer, to explore concepts of evil, reward and punishment, after the fashion of the initiates in the Chisungu.

It is perhaps worth at this point discussing briefly what we mean by 'evil' in this context. We are not using the word in the religious sense, of an absolute 'evil' opposed to an absolute 'good'. Rather, we are here considering

'evil' as 'amorality': actions and/or attitudes which go against those approved
of in the society of the time. This sense of evil is in keeping with our hypothesis regarding the Daleks as 'monsters' of the sort described by Richards
(1956), whose purpose is to define and reinforce a sense of what is considered 'wrong' in the culture which created them. Consequently, the 'evil' of
the Daleks changes as time passes and social mores also gradually change,
meaning that the Dalek/Evil Human relationship can be seen as a barometer
of changing social attitudes. Through the Daleks' relationships with their
human allies, then, changes in the concept of what is deemed 'wrong' or
'amoral' in British society are explored and, indeed, challenged.

In this chapter, we will be considering only those humans who have
more or less voluntarily agreed to work with the Daleks, and leaving aside
controlled humans, such as the Robomen or the slave-workers. We will also
confine our explorations to the original series (1963–89), and omit the
massive canon of Dalek-related spin-off material or the return of the Daleks
in the 2005 television series, for reasons of space and clarity. We will be
considering the development of the Evil Human in four stages: the 1960s, in
which the Evil Human is an overtly Faustian figure, usually an ambitious
scientist or politician, whose weaknesses the Daleks manipulate; the early
1970s, in which the concerns of the series become introspective, focusing on
the evils that society itself perpetuates (principally colonialism and environmental degradation); the later 1970s, in which this line of consideration reaches
its logical culmination in the human/Dalek figure of Davros; and finally the
1980s, in which the postmodernist movement's questioning of the concepts
of 'good' and 'evil' (see Harvey, 1989) is reflected in the fragmentation of
Dalek society in the 'Dalek Civil War' story arc. It is also worth noting that,
like Bignell and O'Day (2004), we will be considering the Daleks not as a
product of a single author/*auteur*, but as being continuously developed
through a process of collaboration and discourse between different writers,
producers and script editors over two and a half decades.

The Daleks' continued appeal to viewers, therefore, stems from their role
as 'monsters' of the sort described by Richards and Bettelheim respectively: a
pedagogical/social device educating the viewer about that which society at
the time deems 'evil'. More than this, however, the message is brought home
to the viewer not through the actions of the Daleks themselves, but through
the actions of one or more human characters, whose moral decline is held up
to the viewer as a kind of object lesson in temptation and damnation.

Evil genesis? Development of the Evil Human

The Evil Human figure first emerges in the mid-1960s, in Nation and
Spooner's 'The Daleks' Master Plan', and is built upon and elaborated by

Whitaker's two Dalek stories. Through the use of such Evil Human figures as Chen, Lesterson and Maxtible, the Dalek story is transformed from an adventure narrative into an explicit morality play, in which the ethical concerns of the 1960s are aired and explored.

The Evil Human did not emerge as a deliberate and conscious development of the Dalek formula, but developed organically out of the concept. The first two Dalek stories ('The Daleks' [1963–4] and 'The Dalek Invasion of Earth' [1964]), while not taking on the later Faustian form, do use the reactions of the human (or humanoid) characters to the Dalek menace to explore the morality of pacifism and resistance; although they are not the focus of the story, we see prototypical Evil Humans in, for instance, Susan's unwitting assistance to the Daleks in their quest to destroy the Thals, and the two women in episode five of 'The Dalek Invasion of Earth', 'The Waking Ally' (1964), who betray Barbara and Jenny in exchange for food. Although this is not the explicit focus of the plot, it appears that, with the exception of the deliberately comedic 'The Chase' (1965), the Dalek stories have never focused exclusively on combating the Daleks themselves, so much as using the Daleks as a means to explore moral concepts, including the nature of human evil.

The Evil Human first becomes the primary focus of the story in 'The Daleks' Master Plan' with the introduction of Mavic Chen. Chen is cast as a human Everyman, with a name blending Chinese and Slavonic elements and actor Kevin Stoney's performance and makeup suggesting a combination of all human races. He is an explicitly Faustian figure: a powerful and intelligent man with a fatal flaw in his overweening ambition, a flaw which anyone who aspires to better things might find themselves sympathising with. Despite being ostensibly the villain of the piece, he is not repulsive or monstrous, at least not at first; his deft manipulation of Zephon and his attempts at 'spinning' mishaps to suit his political agenda must incite at least grudging admiration, if not amusement, from the audience, and as such the audience must feel some identification with him as he sinks deeper into denial and fails to see that he has been bested by the Daleks. Finally, he is clearly the foregrounded antagonistic character; for the first time, but definitely not the last, in a Dalek story, the Daleks become shadowy, background figures, and the viewer's attention is focused on the decline of Chen, through which tale the actual plan of the Daleks is gradually revealed. The viewer is thus encouraged to see in 'The Daleks' Master Plan' a tale of temptation and damnation: above all it is the story of a man, who could be any one of us, who condemns himself through giving in to the evil in his nature.

Through Chen, we see an exploration of a social concern of the time. Chen is not only a politician, but a populist politician, gaining his support from 'ordinary people' like Lizan, Roald and Sara Kingdom. Beneath this façade, however, he is unscrupulous enough to want to betray his own people, entering into secret alliances with alien powers (and, indeed, planning to double-cross his own alien allies when their usefulness is ended). As such, he serves as a warning against the duplicity of politicians and an expression of fears of global political organisations: Chen's chararacterisation stems from Nation's fascination with the European dictatorships of the mid-twentieth century (Bentham, 1986: 120); interviewed in 1992, story editor Donald Tosh said 'A lot of his lines were based on genuine political speeches. And of course, the United Galactic Headquarters [sic] was a parody of the United Nations' (Evans, 1992: 11). In addition to reflecting anxieties about Cold War secrecy and the paranoid whispers about seemingly honourable leaders being in league with the 'Reds', and a growing distrust of authority in the run-up to 1968, the story serves as a general warning against ambition, particularly political ambition, and of letting too much power concentrate itself in a single human being. As well as being a Faustian Everyman, tempted into evil and the agent of his own destruction through a fatal character flaw, Chen is also a cautionary figure for his own time: an ambitious but unscrupulous politician who is less than careful about the company he keeps.

The first Dalek story to feature an Evil Human, then, 'The Daleks' Master Plan', sets the stage for what will be the formula of the Dalek story from then onwards. Rather than being a case of humans pitted against a monstrous antagonist, as in the Cybermen and Ice Warrior stories of the same period (with the previously noted partial exception of 'The Invasion'), the Dalek stories, uniquely, have become cautionary tales, in which a human with whom the viewer can at least partly identify is tempted, falls into evil and is punished, through the agency of the Daleks.

Development of the Evil Human: the Whitaker chronicles

It is entirely possible that the Evil Human could have been stillborn at this point, had the following Dalek stories abandoned the concept. However, David Whitaker's two Dalek stories both employed it as central to the narrative. Whitaker, though, takes the concept further, introducing multiple Evil Humans as a means of exploring the different ways in which even seemingly good individuals can condemn themselves through committing evil, even if they perceive it as a means to a 'good' end.

As with 'Master Plan', the Daleks in 'The Power of the Daleks' (1966) are not so much the antagonists of the story in their own right, as they are the catalysts for human evil. Like the Apple of Discord in the myth of the Trojan War, a Dalek is thrown into a human community to become a source of temptation and rivalry for three humans: Lesterson, Janley and Bragen. However, where, in 'Master Plan', the story focused on a single Faustian figure and his downfall through his besetting sin, here Whitaker explores the different ways in which humans can do evil, even through motives which may, at first, be praiseworthy. Lesterson, for instance, is motivated by his desire for knowledge; the Dalek plays upon this, answering Lesterson's queries with apparent obedience, building a meteorological computer, and speaking to him in ways echoing his own scientific curiosity, much as Mephistopheles distracted Faust with gifts and temptations (see, for instance, Marlowe, 1965: scene xviii). Janley's motivations are more obscure (it is never totally clear whether she is an idealist or a ruthless self-aggrandiser); however, in her idealistic statements at the start of the story, and her interest in using the Dalek to support the rebel movement, we can see the common cautionary fable of the late 1960s of the naive socialist or hippie whose politics bring them under sway of Communists or exploitative leaders (compare, for instance, the near-contemporary *Star Trek* episode 'The Way to Eden' [1969]). Bragen, finally, seems like a less ambitious reincarnation of Mavic Chen. By giving us three different Fausts with three different sets of motivations, then, Whitaker demonstrates that there are different ways of falling into evil.

More than this, however, Whitaker's first iteration of the Evil Human brings the concept of evil sharply, even uncomfortably, into the viewer's home. As noted, Bragen's ambition is not galactic in scale, but one which would be familiar to anyone who has worked in an office or joined a volunteer group; similarly, most viewers would be familiar with political idealists and, even if they did not know obsessive scientists like Lesterson personally, the 1960s was the era in which popular scientists like Magnus Pyke, David Attenborough and Patrick Moore dominated television and radio programming, courtesy of the Reithian doctrine (Tulloch and Alvarado, 1983: 36 –7). Through these desires, too, otherwise-decent humans are led to evil acts; we see Lesterson in particular first induced to manipulate the governor, extolling the potential use value of the Daleks when he himself is interested only in their scientific value, and second, becoming trapped into complicity through the incidents surrounding Resno's death. Ultimately, Lesterson, like Chen before him, is driven insane through his association with the Daleks. Through the Evil Human figure established by Nation, then, Whitaker employs the Dalek story as a way of exploring how ordinary desires and beliefs, with which the viewer might even be sympathetic, can lead to temptation and, from there, to insanity and death.

As in 'Master Plan', also, the Evil Humans of this story reflect the concerns of the 1960s. As noted, Janley's idealism places her within the trope of the hippie becoming an unwitting dupe of the Communists and/or an unscrupulous leader. The figure of Lesterson, furthermore, stems from the 1960s ambivalence towards hard science; as Banks notes, the 1960s were a time at which scientific advances were being held up as wonders of the age and their discoverers extolled as heroes, and yet there was also a fear in the general public, most prominently exemplified in the film *Dr Strangelove* (1964), of the consequences of 'science run mad' or 'mad' scientists (Banks, 1988: Section One). This is a common tension in *Doctor Who* – with the Doctor's own scientific curiosity, for the most part, being held up as a benign, praiseworthy trait, and yet such figures as Professor Zaroff and the Cybermen being denounced as villains. However, it is only here that both sides of the coin are presented, through the Faustian paradigm, with a benign if slightly weak-willed scientist being led into evil through his own curiosity. Even more than 'Master Plan', then, the emotional impact of 'The Power of the Daleks' comes less from a humans-versus-Daleks storyline than from the way in which the viewer is drawn into a cautionary tale, in which 'people like them' are led into evil by the Mephistophelian Daleks.

Whitaker's subsequent Dalek serial, 'The Evil of the Daleks' (1967), brings out the Faustian aspects of the Evil Human scenario more strongly. This time, the story focuses on the contrast between the two Evil Humans: the 'good' one, Waterfield, whose motivation is simply love for his daughter, and the 'bad' one, Maxtible, a businessman who is tempted into helping the Daleks by the promise of a formula to turn base metal into gold. The viewer is thus more inclined to condemn Maxtible and sympathise with Waterfield. However, Waterfield's behaviour is in many ways less excusable; he, like Maxtible, continues to deal with the Daleks knowing full well that they are devious and destructive, and he is induced to deceive and kidnap the Doctor and Jamie; although he also saves the Doctor's life in attempting to allow Victoria to escape Skaro, he is killed in the process, in an indication that evil is still evil, even when done for the best of motivations (a theme which Nation would later pick up on himself for 'Genesis of the Daleks' [1975]). Whitaker's portrayal of Waterfield thus owes more to Goethe's Faust, a decent man who does evil but redeems himself through his love for Gretchen, than to Marlowe's more pessimistic portrayal, with Victoria perhaps acting as a kind of Gretchen-figure (cf. Goethe, 1959), indicating that the Evil Human paradigm is subject to as much variation as the Faustian one. Through this, Whitaker makes explicit the idea that temptation can cause even basically good people to behave amorally, even if they believe it is for a noble cause.

Maxtible's final fate is also worthy of note within this paradigm. Throughout the story, Maxtible wilfully blinds himself to the truth, attempting to find justifications for the Daleks' behaviour which fit with his own materialistic worldview. The Daleks, in turn, reward him by imbuing him with the Dalek Factor, turning him, effectively, into a human Dalek. Whitaker had used a similar concept earlier, when the insane Lesterson parrots Dalek-like phrases, but here the connection between doing and becoming evil is more explicit. Rather than being tempted, yielding, doing evil and dying as a result, Maxtible is transformed into the very being used as a signifier of evil. The message is plain: through collaborating with evil, and excusing evil, a human being incorporates evil into their very being, with, apparently, no hope of redemption.

The later 1960s Dalek stories thus follow a similar pattern, in which the Daleks serve, not as villains in and of themselves, but as catalysts for cautionary tales in which human beings are induced to do evil through temptation. Whitaker, however, does not simply reiterate the Faustian paradigm, but uses it, like Goethe, to explore the idea that even good people can become evil through adopting amoral attitudes and behaviour. In the process, Whitaker highlights 1960s concerns about authority, the anti-war movement and the dangers of scientific discovery, in such a way that the viewer can relate a fictitious morality tale to their own experiences.

Through a glass darkly: the early 1970s

With the early 1970s, however, we see a subtle shift in the role of the Evil Human. Rather than reveal the Daleks' hidden plans gradually to the viewer as they become drawn into the plot, the Controller in 'Day of the Daleks' and Galloway in 'Death to the Daleks' (the two key Evil Humans) instead interpret the Daleks' motivations to the viewer, voicing their own beliefs about why the Daleks are acting as they are, and why collaboration is a good strategy. The Evil Human paradigm is taken a step further, such that the Dalek stories are no longer about the Daleks, nor even about the temptation of a Faustian human by Mephistophelian Daleks, but represent the Daleks as a signifier for moral conflicts being played out in the mind of a particular human individual.

The Controller in 'Day of the Daleks', for instance, is a man explicitly working closely with the Daleks for reasons which he attempts to justify, but which ultimately involve the betrayal of his fellow humans. His role, however, is not to act as a kind of object lesson in temptation and damnation; the temptations involved in his becoming Controller are not foregrounded. Instead, his role is to articulate the ethical nuances of collaboration versus resistance. His position bears a strong resemblance to that of colonial leaders who collaborated with European invaders, or to the controversial Jewish ghetto leader Mordecai Chaim Rumkowski, who collaborated with the Nazis in order to save as many of the people under his care as possible (Gilbert, 1986: 141). The rehearsal script describes him as 'a hard, pitiless man. As we get to know him, we shall see in him the inner guilt of the quisling, for that is what he is' (Pixley, 2001: 29). He argues, in defence of people making such a choice, that if he did not take on the mantle of leadership, someone else, possibly with less desire to do good by his people, would take it (which, of course, is precisely what happens at the end of the story): 'We have helped make things better for the others, we have gained concessions. I have saved lives!' he says, at the same time criticising the rebels' decision to actively resist instead. The Controller does not, as earlier Evil Humans did, enter into a compact with the Daleks for open self-aggrandisement (although it is acknowledged that he lives a more comfortable life than most of his fellow humans). His evil lies in the fact that he recognises the Daleks as oppressors, but chooses to do nothing to prevent this, and instead acts to promote the system.

In this, the Controller reflects the changing moral agenda within the Dalek stories. In 1970s *Doctor Who* in general, the production team began an explicit shift towards using the programme for social comment, focusing particularly on concerns about colonialism ('The Mutants' [1972], 'Colony in Space' [1971]) and environmentalism ('Invasion of the Dinosaurs' [1974], 'The Green Death' [1973]) (Marson and Mulkern, 1985: 37; Pixley, 1995: 26, 2002: 28; Tulloch and Alvarado, 1983: 53, 181–3). As such, the narratives are moving away from a concept of evil as an external force (as in the Cold War fears of Communist infiltration), and towards an idea of evil coming from within the characters themselves. It is not insignificant that this is the point at which the Daleks begin, as it were, to lose their voice: whereas in earlier stories, there was always a master plan to reveal and a secret to expose, in 'Day of the Daleks' the Daleks are simply a conquering force, and the viewer's interest is focused entirely on the Controller's moral struggle as he decides whether to continue supporting the Daleks or to give aid to the resistance. It is also significant that, like Waterfield, the Controller achieves a kind of salvation, sacrificing his own life to save the Doctor's and give him a chance at thwarting the Dalek invasion; if evil comes from within us, the message reads, then we ourselves can conquer it and become good in the end. As the Daleks' role in the stories becomes simpler, so the figure of the Evil Human becomes more complex, in line with the 1970s shift away from fears of invasion and conquest, and towards fears that our own shortcomings are destroying the world we live in.

It is worth pausing here to mention 'Planet of the Daleks' (1973), the sole story since 1965 *not* to feature an Evil Human character. Probably because Nation was primarily drawing on his first two Dalek stories when writing it, we do not encounter anything closer to the Evil Human than a slightly impetuous Thal. This may well be one of the things which has made this particular serial such a failure with critics and audiences (e.g. Robins, 1987). Without an Evil Human to articulate the moral lessons of the story to the viewer through their actions, the Daleks become what they are often erroneously accused of being: boring pantomime Nazis, enacting a loosely sketched plan for invading the galaxy/solar system. The Thals, the Doctor and Jo do not interact with the Daleks in any way bar treating them as cardboard villains, which ironically means that not only are the Daleks not very interesting, but the protagonists are also singularly dull and lightly sketched. 'Planet of the

Daleks' is thus the exception that proves the rule: it is not the Daleks as villains in and of themselves which gives them their interest to the viewer, but their role as a signifier of evil at work among the human characters, who are the story's true focus.

What is more interesting is that Nation seems to realise this, and, in his subsequent serial, 'Death to the Daleks' (1974), gives us a story with many of the elements of 'Planet' (plagues, alien slave-workers, friendly natives and resistance movements; the story was also planned to take place on a jungle world, until Terrance Dicks, fearing that the two stories were too similar, urged Nation to change this [Pixley, 1999: 38]) but with an Evil Human added in the form of Galloway. Galloway, like the Controller, articulates a 1970s concern with the ethics of colonialism: he is an unapologetic racist, treating the Exxilons as an inferior species even after seeing evidence that they have had a highly developed civilisation. He is also, as the dying Commander Stewart notes, 'a glory seeker'. He allies himself with the Daleks not out of temptation, but out of a combination of necessity and self-aggrandisement, with his racism leading him to fatally underestimate his allies. As with the Controller, also, the focus of the story is not on the temptation of a human by an outside force, but on the amorality already within Galloway being given full rein by the presence of the Daleks. Nation, however, takes a more pessimistic view of human nature than Louis Marks. Galloway's act of self-sacrifice at the end of the story, interpreted by many (including Terrance Dicks [1978]) as a redemptive act, is perfectly in keeping with his self-serving character: it ensures that he is remembered as the man who died saving the crew and ten million colonists from the Daleks rather than as the man who did a deal with the Daleks and enslaved the Exxilons. As in 'Day of the Daleks', then, 'Death to the Daleks' presents us with a Faustian character not as an object lesson or morality tale, but as someone through whose behaviour the complexities of colonialism and the politics of hero-making are explored for the viewer.

Nation, however, goes further, making Galloway the catalyst for evil behaviour in others. Galloway's justifications for his own actions lead Hamilton and Tarrant, seemingly decent people, to acquiesce in the enslavement of the Exxilons and the attempted killing of the Doctor and Sarah. He manipulates the other humans into doing his bidding, playing on Hamilton's feelings about his dead father and undermining the authority of the expedition's commanders. In line with the 1970s concern about evil coming from within rather than outside, Galloway is thus absorbing the Daleks' traditional role as the catalyst for human evil; although the Daleks are the catalyst for his own evil behaviour, in the traditional Dalek/Evil Human mode, they act in the story more as a signifier for evil, while Galloway himself is the main figure practising, and perpetuating, amoral behaviour.

In the 1970s, then, the Faustian aspects of the Dalek/Evil Human relation-ship become less significant to the story, and the focus instead is placed on the moral conflicts within the Evil Human himself, with the Daleks as simply the catalyst and/or a signifier for his evil behaviour. This development stems from changes in the concept of amorality in the wider British culture – from fear of outside alliances, to a fear of what we ourselves are capable of doing – thus articulating to the viewer not cautionary tales about temptation, so much as ones warning us to beware of our own motivations. It is thus not surprising that the next development in the Evil Human story would be the physical melding of humans and Daleks into a single being.

Davros: the logical culmination

Davros is, in many ways, the ultimate embodiment of the Evil Human. He makes his appearance at a point at which the entire Dalek mythos becomes, effectively, reset, and their relationship to humans, evil and otherwise, becomes transformed. Nation's two Davros stories establish a new paradigm both for the Daleks and for the role of the Evil Human, one at once more complex and simpler than what has gone before, and which sets the stage for the fragmented scenarios of the 1980s.

Davros makes his first appearance in 1975's 'Genesis of the Daleks', at a time when the Evil Human was a firmly established figure. He incorporates elements from earlier Evil Human figures of the 1960s: he is both a scientist and a politician and later, in 'Revelation of the Daleks' (1985), he will demon-strate that he is also an astute businessman. He is driven by his relationship with the Daleks to ruthlessly sacrifice his people and allies to support them. At the end of the story, he is destroyed by the Daleks due to overestimating the degree of control he has over them. However, in keeping with the 1970s, he himself embodies the evil of the Daleks; his Daleklike wheelchair, single eye and voice synthesiser make him symbolically half-Dalek, as such incorporating signifiers of evil within himself as well as entering into compacts with them. Nation himself, in a 1992 interview, described him as embodying 'the *essence* of the Daleks' (Peel, 1992: 4). His appearance and speech patterns echo the ways in which Lesterson and Maxtible came to actually imitate Daleks at the end of their lives. Davros is thus the logical culmination of the Evil Human portrayals that we have seen thus far: he is tempted to work with the Daleks for personal gain, does evil and is (apparently) killed, and also, through his physical appearance, articulates the idea of evil coming from within.

Davros' hybrid appearance, significantly, places him firmly in the category of pedagogic 'monster' as described by Richards (1956: 59). The 'monsters' used in such contexts as initiation and folk tale are frequently liminal, that is to say, neither one thing nor the other, a mix of different, normally separate categories (van Gennep, 1960: 20). According to Douglas, liminal creatures have the power to disturb through their hybrid appearance, to cause people to think about the separate categories represented, and the boundaries between them (1966: 54–5). Davros, as Bignell and O'Day note, is such a boundary-straddling creature, incorporating two different and opposed categories within himself (2004: 148; see also Peel and Nation, 1988: 77); Laight implies that his hybrid appearance makes him 'more interesting than his creations' (2003: 15). Furthermore, Davros is a visible, constant reminder to the viewer of the connection between humans and Daleks: whereas before, the fact that the Daleks were once human in appearance could be largely ignored in favour of presenting them as mechanical aliens, the presence of Davros continually reinforces the idea that the Daleks came from humans, and humans can, in turn, become Daleks, if only symbolically. As Pixley notes, 'Davros could be treated as a humanoid villain and used normal dialogue to exhibit ambition and even wit' (1992: 24); yet he is inescapably Daleklike at the same time. Much as the earlier Evil Humans encouraged the viewer to reflect on human evil through their own progress, so Davros, in a different way, causes the viewer to think about what it is to be human, as opposed to being a Dalek, by virtue of his membership in both categories.

Davros' relationship with the Daleks is, however, at once more complex and simpler than that of his predecessors. The character flaw from which Davros acts is also different to what we have seen before: he is not aiding the Daleks for money, or political power in the conventional sense (as he is willing to destroy his own people rather than allow the Kaled politicians to close down the project), but he is acting from a kind of twisted parental urge, the desire to be the man who brought forth a being capable of destroying all life in the universe. Nor does his downfall come from an arrogant assumption that he is superior to the Daleks; it never seems to occur to him until the end that the Daleks might view him as different to themselves, even though he has encouraged in them their trademark xenophobia. The catalyst for Davros' evil actions is, interestingly, not entering into an agreement with the Daleks, but Davros' own emotions and feelings towards them: he is, in effect, the author of his own Faustian bargain. Davros speaks for, and interprets the actions of, the Daleks, it is true, but at this stage the Daleks are incapable of speaking for themselves, being merely prototypical 'travel machines' for Kaled mutants, and Davros, as their creator, is the closest person to their mindset in the universe. Davros thus has a closer, more parental, relationship to the Daleks than that of the earlier Evil Humans.

At the same time, however, Davros' appearance marks a simplification of the Dalek/Evil Human relationship. It has often been remarked that 'Genesis' is the point at which Dalek history and culture change (Cornell et al., 1995:

173–5): because of the Doctor's intervention, Davros sends the Daleks out unfinished, and with a simple computer program controlling their actions; when they return, they destroy Davros and his scientists before they can finish the work. In subsequent stories, the Daleks appear diminished, no longer the Machiavellian, Mephistophelian figures they once were, formulating alien, clever plans. It is thus significant that at this point they acquire a permanent spokesperson in the form of Davros. When he returns, in 'Destiny of the Daleks' (1979), his relationship to them becomes very like that of the Mekon to the Treens in the comic *Dan Dare*, a shrunken, megalomaniacal villain with an army of evil cyborgs (as noted by John Friedlander in Clark and Handley, 1994: 11; see also Tulloch and Alvarado, 1983: 126). In the explicitly 'monstrous' figure of Davros, then, the viewer is confronted with the ultimate articulation of the idea that evil comes from within us, and yet the subtlety, the potential for viewer identification and for seeing the evil that the Evil Humans do as part of the viewer's own experiences, is also lost.

Davros is thus the culmination of the path which the Evil Human figure took in the 1970s, in which the focus of the narratives shifted from tales of temptation and damnation to a more introspective look at the evil within humans. Through Davros, the Evil Human merges with the Daleks and becomes their spokesperson; the human, not the Daleks, has become the 'monster'. From here on in, the human/Dalek relationship differs from what has gone before: while the Daleks now have a permanent, as it were, human spokesperson, the exploration of the concept of evil now becomes more fragmented and complicated.

Breakdown: the Dalek civil war

In the 1980s, Eric Saward's Dalek stories introduced the ongoing plotline of the 'Dalek Civil War', focusing around a split between Daleks loyal to Davros and those opposing him. Significantly, although this can scarcely be conscious on Saward's part, this is the era which sees the development of the 'multi-faction' Evil Human story, in which the various factions of Daleks each have their own human or humanoid collaborators, mediating the complexities of the war to the audience. In keeping with the postmodernist spirit of the 1980s, then, the Dalek/Evil Human relationship articulates multiple positions on what it is to be, and do, evil, and what its consequences are. The 1980s, as David Harvey (1989) notes, was the point at which postmodernism as a philosophy became most strongly articulated through the mainstream. This involves, in part, the questioning of linear Grand Narratives along the lines of the Dalek stories we have seen before: evil external force tempts human, human is tempted, falls and is either killed or becomes Daleklike himself, or alternatively human is placed in morally dubious position by external circumstances, and must choose between redemption and damnation. 1984's 'Resurrection of the Daleks' sets up the questioning of such narratives straight away, first introducing what seems to be a conventional Dalek/Evil Human relationship in the Mavic Chen or Maxtible mould – that between the Supreme Dalek and the mercenary Lytton – and then subverting it by introducing Davros into the mix, creating two factions, one led by a conventional Dalek/Evil Human dyad, the other by a Dalek/Evil Human physical hybrid. 'Resurrection' thus indicates a clear shift away from what has gone before: rather than, as Whitaker did, using multiple Evil Humans linked to each other and the same group of Daleks to explore ideas about what induces people to do evil, Saward instead sets up different factions of Daleks with accompanying humans, as if to indicate that there are different ways of defining evil (and as such, of defining an Evil Human), without particularly singling one out for attention.

This questioning of linear modernism can also be seen in the portrayal of Lytton. While the possibility has been raised by some commentators (e.g. Peacock, 2000) that Lytton is not human, but a manufactured duplicate, he can be treated as 'human' for our purposes by virtue of the fact that he demonstrates himself to be capable of independent thought and action. He is a type of Evil Human that is particular to the 1980s: he does not ally himself with the Daleks through the temptation to achieve power or to become rich, or through an innate colonialist bigotry, but, as we are repeatedly informed in the sequel story 'Attack of the Cybermen' (1985), simply to make a living. In this, he is very much in keeping with the 1980s celebration of the money-making anti-hero, such as the protagonists of *Working Girl* (1988) and *American Psycho* (Ellis, 1991). Lytton is amoral, then, in that he will sell his services to anyone, regardless of the morality of that action; however, he is not punished for his amorality, but in the end – unlike every other human ally the Daleks have had up until this point – he escapes to fight another day. The character, who emerged out of Saward's fascination with the mentality of people who kill for a living (Marson, 1984: 24), is thus the focus not of a cautionary tale, but of a questioning of these: the message is less 'if you are tempted, and succumb to it, you will be punished' or 'evil is within us, and we must combat it or suffer the consequences', than 'evil is a part of everyday business, and it can go unpunished'. Through having multiple human or quasi-human spokespeople for the Daleks and through having one of them go unpunished for his actions, the idea is brought across that evil is not so much absolute as relative.

This idea of multiple Evil Humans, all articulating different positions, is further developed in Saward's corporate satire 'Revelation of the Daleks'. As well as Davros, the serial gives us three pairs of humans allied with different factions of Daleks in different ways: Tasambeker and Jobel, Takis and Lilt, and Kara and Vogel. Not only is the presence of these multiple factions of Evil Humans, each with their own shifting alliances, a means of mediating the complex struggles between the various factions of the Daleks to the viewer, but the audience is once again presented with a variety of different ways of defining evil, from the openly Faustian relationship the Daleks have with Kara, to Tasambeker, falling into evil through her frustrated love for Jobel, to Takis and Lilt, who turn out to have been duplicitous double-agents all along (and who, like Lytton before them, go unpunished at the end of the story, a fact which contemporary reviewer Jackie Marshall is quoted as saying is 'unfair to younger viewers' [Anonymous, 1999: 26]). Interestingly, also, where the earlier Dalek stories held up becoming a Dalek, or at least Daleklike, as the ultimate in ignominious fates for Evil Humans, here Davros offers the chance to become a Dalek to Tasambeker as a reward, highlighting that evil can be a thing to be desired as well as shunned. Again in the 1980s, the Evil Humans are less the subject of morality tales than explorations of different ways of being amoral.

The other interesting aspect of 'Revelation' is the role of Davros. In this story, Davros simultaneously plays the role of the Evil Human, acting as spokesperson for the Daleks and receiving his comeuppance at the end, and that usually played by the Daleks; it is he who instigates the corruption of Tasambeker, and it is he, rather than the Daleks, whom Kara and Vogel are trying to outwit. The Daleks have become background figures to the conflict played out between the Evil Humans, being more symbols of evil than players in and of themselves, with even their corruptor role having devolved onto one of the Evil Humans.

The postmodernist exploration of evil can also be seen in 'Remembrance of the Daleks' (1988), in which we again get multiple factions of Daleks allied with multiple Evil Humans, in diverse relationships. Unlike the Saward serials, however, writer Ben Aaronovitch had an agenda of reinterpreting the series, including its concepts of evil (Parkin, 2003: 21). In the tradition of the 1980s comics and films which reinterpret the popular culture of the past, such as *The Dark Knight Returns* (Miller, 1986), Tim Burton's *Batman* films (1989, 1992), *The Watchmen* by Alan Moore (1987) and *The Prisoner* sequel *Shattered Visage* (Motter and Askwith, 1990), Aaronovitch pastiches elements from earlier Dalek stories by Saward and Nation, but reinterprets them in terms of late-1980s racial politics and fear of neo-Nazism. He attacks the contemporary tendency to portray the 1960s nostalgically, as in, for instance, the films *Stand by Me* (1986) and *Dirty Dancing* (1987), and subverts the series' conventions (Parkin, 2003: 21). It is thus not surprising that the first Evil Human, and the one most in the traditional mould, is Ratcliffe, a neo-Fascist who allies himself with the Daleks out of a belief that his ideology is compatible with theirs. The twist in the character comes in the fact that Aaronovitch appears to believe that this is in fact true, as he reinforces the belief that the Dalek civil war is simply about racial superiority through Ace's explanation to Rachel and Alison which the Doctor does not refute. As has been noted elsewhere, this interpretation is strongly at odds with the civil war storyline set up by Saward, in which the conflict is overtly cast in terms of internal politics and the actions of Davros against the Supreme Dalek (in fact, in 'Revelation', the Daleks are perfectly willing to accept Davros's converted human Daleks into their ranks, showing that racism seems to have little to do with it). Ironically, however, Aaronovitch unwittingly gives the lie to his interpretation through his use of Ratcliffe as a mouthpiece for the Daleks, in that he forgets that it is the role of the Evil Human to deceive himself – to falsely interpret Dalek behaviour in terms of his own belief system, and usually to perish as a result of his misinterpretation. In Ratcliffe, then, we see a villain for the 1980s, not only in that he is a neo-Fascist, but in that the careful viewer will spot the inconsistencies within his interpretation and be thereby called upon to question the messages of the serial.

This subversion of the Evil Human concept is supported in the person of the second Evil Human figure, the little girl. Normally, the role of the Evil Human is to mediate the Daleks to the viewer, allowing the audience to use the Human's emotions as a kind of cultural reference point. The little girl, however, remains an enigma throughout the story: we get no sense of her motivations, or even whether or not she was coerced into her alliance with the Daleks. The little girl is thus a kind of anti-Evil Human, rejecting rather than inviting viewer identification. Instead of presenting a Faustian morality tale, then, or causing the viewer to consider the evil within, the figure of the little girl encourages the viewer to speculate on her reasons for allying herself with the Daleks, and, ultimately, to assign their own motivations to her, in the ultimate expression of postmodernist philosophy in Doctor Who.

Davros, finally, makes his appearance briefly at the end of the story, and again, is cast as a mouthpiece, a spokesperson, for the Daleks, seated in a chair which is an explicit visual link to the Emperor Dalek of the TV Century 21 comics. The significant point about his appearance is, however, to highlight the role of the Doctor. At the time, script editor Andrew Cartmel (a self-confessed admirer of Alan Moore [Bishop, 1995: 46]) had been attempting to introduce to the series the concept of the 'dark Doctor', in which the series' central character would be reinterpreted as a slightly sinister anti-hero whose motivations were not always pure, an idea which would reach its culmination in the Virgin New Adventures novels (Parkin, 2003: 21). Correspondingly, throughout 'Remembrance', Aaronovitch portrays the Doctor, for the first time, as no better than Davros. Rather than, as in earlier stories, simply landing in a place and becoming caught up in the flow of events, the Doctor deliberately precipitates the conflict. There is an interesting parallel between the Seventh Doctor's actions here and the Fourth Doctor's refusal to blow up the Dalek incubator room in 'Genesis' ('if I kill [. . .] then I become like them. I'd be no better than the Daleks'); if the inversion reads logically then the Seventh Doctor has indeed become 'no better than the Daleks'. The final change rung on the *Doctor Who* mythos sees the Doctor himself recast as an evil figure, going out of his way to commit acts of genocide (see Brown, 2002). Much as the comics and films of the late 1980s made a specialty of recasting beloved childhood heroes, such as Batman, into sinister, villainous figures, so 'Remembrance' reinterprets the Evil Human role to render the beloved childhood figure of the Doctor little better than Davros.

The Dalek civil war storyline thus sees new changes rung on the Evil Humans, in light of the more postmodern, less linear concepts of evil of the 1980s, culminating in Aaronovitch's reworking of the *Doctor Who* formula to suggest that even the eponymous hero himself could be drawn into evil (a notion explored further in Christopher Eccleston's interpretation of the Doctor in the new series' Dalek episodes). Although the Evil Human formula changes over the decades, then, the driving force of the Dalek stories continues, in the 1980s, to be the interpretation and challenging of concepts of amorality through the figures of the Daleks' human allies.

Analysis and conclusions

It thus seems that the Evil Human character, central to almost all Dalek stories from 1965 onwards, lends the Dalek stories their power and viewer appeal, not through simply portraying the concept of 'good versus evil', but through inducing the viewer to reflect on the concept of evil as it applies to the concerns of the day. The flexibility of the concept, and its links to archetypal folk tales and other forms of traditional narrative pedagogy, have allowed it to develop with the times, keeping the Daleks fresh and contemporary at points when other monsters have gone out of fashion.

While the Daleks are undoubtedly signifiers for evil within the Dalek story, the strength of the Daleks as villains does not stem so much from this characteristic: the same, after all, could be said to apply to the Cybermen, the Zygons and numerous other *Doctor Who* monsters. Rather, the key attraction for the viewer is the way in which they draw on the European folkloric archetype of the Faustian bargain – or even, arguably, the biblical tale of Adam and Eve – to explore the concept of human evil, by foregrounding the Daleks' human allies as the most interesting villain within the piece. Furthermore, the flexibility of the concept allows it to change with the times: much as Faust legends run the gamut from Marlowe through to the animated cartoon *The Devil and Daniel Mouse* (1978), so the Dalek stories serve as a barometer for the changing moral concepts of British society throughout the series' run.

The Dalek/Evil Human relationship fulfils different functions with differ-ent audience members. While its purpose, like Richards' Chisungu monsters, is partly to educate children in the values of their culture, highlighting the social concerns of the day and either presenting a cautionary tale regarding them, or exploring the morality of action when presented with an ethically difficult situation, its appeal also lies in the fact that these images have similar resonance with older viewers. In particular, the more complex and/or chal-lenging Evil Human figures, such as the Controller and Lytton, encourage older viewers into considerations of what the concept of 'evil' is, and whether the fact that they are general throughout the culture makes them 'right' or 'good'. Through the Evil Human, the viewer is encouraged to reflect on evil within their own lives and even within themselves; this allows children to learn about standards of behaviour within their society, and allows adults to consider and question their own cultural values.

In sum, then, the Evil Human figure has been an integral part of the Dalek story since the mid-1960s, providing both a figure through which the viewer can explore concepts of evil and redemption, and a tragic subplot in which the Daleks act as the catalyst for human weakness to lead individuals and, in some cases, whole groups, into committing evil acts. However, the Evil Human does not remain a static figure; it changes both in line with develop-ments in the onscreen history of the Daleks, and to reflect the social mores and preoccupations of the time in which the story was made. As we move into the twenty-first century, a time in which concepts of evil are being rapidly reinterpreted in light of the new political arena, it will be interesting to see how the role of Evil Humans and their relationship with the Daleks develops.

References

Anonymous. 1999. 'Audiences and references'. *In-Vision*, No. 84, pp. 26–7.

Banks, David. 1988. *Cybermen*. Bournemouth: Who Dares Publishing.

Bentham, J. Jeremy. 1986. *Doctor Who: The Early Years*. London: W.H. Allen.

Bettelheim, Bruno. 1978. *The Uses of Enchantment: The Meaning and Importance of Fairy Tales*. London: Penguin.

Bignell, Jonathan and Andrew O'Day. 2004. *Terry Nation*. Manchester: Manchester University Press.

Bishop, David. 1995. 'Dark Times'. *Doctor Who Magazine*, No. 225, pp. 44–7.

Brown, Anthony. 2002. 'A game in two halves'. *In-Vision*, No. 100, pp. 21–2.

Clark, Anthony and Derek Handley. 1994. 'The man behind the masks: interview with John Friedlander'. *Dreamwatch*, No. 1, pp. 10–12.

Cornell, Paul, Martin Day and Keith Topping. 1995. *Doctor Who: The Discontinuity Guide*. London: Virgin.

Dicks, Terrance. 1978. *Death to the Daleks*. London: W.H. Allen.

Douglas, Mary. 1966. *Purity and Danger*. London: Ark.

Ellis, Brett Easton. 1991. *American Psycho*. London: Vintage.

Evans, Andrew. 1992. 'Script editing *Who*: Donald Tosh'. *Doctor Who Magazine*, No. 191, pp. 10–13.

Van Gennep, Arnold. 1960. *The Rites of Passage*. Trans. Monica B. Vizedom and Gabrielle L. Caffee. Chicago: University of Chicago Press.

Gilbert, Martin. 1986. *The Holocaust: A Jewish Tragedy*. London: Fontana Press.

Goethe, Johann Wolfgang. 1949. *Faust Part One*. Trans. Philip Wayne. Harmondsworth: Penguin.

Goethe, Johann Wolfgang. 1959. *Faust Part Two*. Trans. Philip Wayne. Harmondsworth: Penguin.

Harvey, David. 1989. *The Condition of Postmodernity: An Enquiry into the Origins of Cultural Change*. Oxford: Blackwell.

Jones, Alison (ed.). 1995. *Larousse Dictionary of World Folklore*. Edinburgh: Larousse.

Laight, Rupert. 2003. 'Genesis of the Daleks'. *Doctor Who Magazine Anniversary Special: We Love Doctor Who*, p. 15.

Marlowe, Christopher. 1965. *The Tragical History of Doctor Faustus*, ed. Paul H. Kocher. Arlington Heights, IL: Harlan Davidson Ltd.

Marson, Richard. 1984. 'Eric Saward interview'. *Doctor Who Magazine*, No. 94, pp. 20–5.

Marson, Richard and Patrick Mulkern. 1985. 'The Pertwee Years'. *Doctor Who Magazine Winter Special*, pp. 4–13; 37–46.

Miller, Frank. 1986. *The Dark Knight Returns*. London: Titan.

Moore, Alan. 1987. *The Watchmen*. New York: DC Comics.

Motter, Dean and Mark Askwith. 1990. *Shattered Visage*. London: Titan.

Parkin, Lance. 2003. 'Remembrance of the Daleks'. *Doctor Who Magazine Anniversary Special: We Love Doctor Who*, p. 21.

Peacock, Matthew. 2000. 'Jacob's Ladder'. *Tides of Time*, No. 25, pp. 6–7; 27–8.

Peel, John. 1992. 'Nation states: interview with Terry Nation'. *In-Vision*, No. 39, pp. 4–5.

Peel, John and Terry Nation. 1988. *The Official Doctor Who and the Daleks Book*. New York: St Martin's Press.

Pegg, Nick. 1991. 'Review: The Sontaran Experiment/Genesis of the Daleks'. *DWB*, No. 93, p. 15.

Pixley, Andrew. 1992. 'Archive feature: Revelation of the Daleks'. *Doctor Who Magazine*, No. 188, pp. 23–30.

Pixley, Andrew. 1995. 'Doctor Who archive: The Mutants'. *Doctor Who Magazine*, No. 230, pp. 23–30.

Pixley, Andrew. 1999. 'DWM archive: Death to the Daleks'. *Doctor Who Magazine*, No. 278, pp. 36–43.

Pixley, Andrew. 2001. 'DWM archive: Day of the Daleks'. *Doctor Who Magazine*, No. 301, pp. 26–33.

Pixley, Andrew. 2002. 'DWM archive: The Green Death'. *Doctor Who Magazine*, No. 320, pp. 26–34.

Pixley, Andrew. 2003. 'Greatest contribution to Doctor Who: #2–20'. *Doctor Who Magazine Anniversary Special: We Love Doctor Who*, pp. 78–81.

Richards, Audrey. 1956. *Chisungu: A Girls' Initiation Ceremony among the Bemba of Northern Rhodesia*. London: Faber and Faber.

Robins, Tim. 1987. 'Story Review'. *Planet of the Daleks – Doctor Who: An Adventure in Time and Space*, No. 68, pp. 5–6.

Robins, Tim. 1989. 'The Dark Knight Doctor'. *The Frame*, 12 November, pp. 11–13.

Tulloch, John and Manuel Alvarado. 1983. *Doctor Who: The Unfolding Text*. London and Basingstoke: Macmillan.

Part III

The seeds of television production:
making *Doctor Who*

Chapter 9

The Filipino army's advance on Reykjavik: world-building in Studio D and its legacy[1]

Ian Potter

Doctor Who is, like the TARDIS, a vehicle that can go anywhere to tell its stories, a genre-hopping serial with a device at its centre that allows it free movement through space and time, and even permits travel into other dimensions in which the usual rules of televisual naturalism cease to apply. In practice, of course, fulfilling this infinite potential has been absolutely impossible. Its stories have been limited from the start by what audiences would accept or expect from the programme, the preferences of the production team and BBC management, and, perhaps most obviously, the practical circumstances in which the show was made. In *Doctor Who*'s original 1963–89 run, this show with infinite scope very rarely ventured beyond the M25 circular around London, and, more tellingly, hardly ever left the confines of the BBC's electronic TV studios. Even as casual viewers we're quick to spot the occasional uncomfortable performance or unconvincing special effect this resulted in, but we're sometimes blinded to some of the subtler repercussions of the programme's production methods.[2] In this short chapter I hope to briefly touch on some of the technical aspects of the programme's early years, and explore a few of their possible consequences. For while students of the programme are used to looking at its direction as being defined by a combination of factors – the BBC's Reithian ideals, the commercial sense of BBC Head of Drama Sydney Newman's production team decisions and audience responses – we sometimes neglect the hard practicalities behind the show's production which helped shape it from the very beginning.[3] As a June 1963 memo to the BBC's Head of Serials Donald Wilson from Sydney Newman about the proposed first episode pointedly requests: 'I implore you please keep the entire conception within the realms of practical live television' (Newman in Hearn, 1994: 37).

    Doctor Who, while never strictly broadcast live, was until the late 1960s generally constructed in the television studio 'as live', because despite being recorded onto videotape, it could not be edited on that format for practical reasons. Videotape had been invented by Ampex in 1956 and adopted by the BBC in 1959, but for most of the 1960s the only way it could only be edited was by physically cutting and resplicing the tape, using a microscope to ensure the fields were correctly aligned. This was a costly and time-consuming process to get right. A half-hour reel of videotape cost around a hundred pounds in the early 1960s, a not inconsiderable sum, which meant tape was routinely reused. Any editing would require that the tape be purchased by the programme using it, because the process effectively prevented its reuse by creating a weak point on the tape and momentary image loss at the edit point. Given that *Doctor Who*'s initial programme budget was only £2,500 per show, editing was strongly discouraged, and it's notable that where edits did occur they often seem to be on tapes reaching the end of their usable lives which could be purchased cheaper![4]

In lieu of a capacity to edit, programmes were recorded with a number of built-in recording breaks, typically two or three, at which the screen would fade to black and it was possible to rewind the tape and remount a section of a programme from one of these points if its recording had not gone satisfactorily.[5] However, because the total recording time available to record twenty-five minutes of *Doctor Who* was likely to be an hour and a quarter, including time for any required costume, set or camera changes, the potential number of retakes was extremely limited.

As the 1960s progress we do start to see some limited video editing on *Doctor Who*. Known examples from the early years include the remounts of the end credits for 'The Bride of Sacrifice' ('The Aztecs' episode three [1964]) and a short sequence from 'A Desperate Venture' ('The Sensorites' episode six [1964]); Verity Lambert's trim to the climax of 'The Centre' (episode six of 'The Web Planet' [1965]) to remove a shot she felt was incomprehensible; the out of sequence recording of the fight in 'The Death of Doctor Who' ('The Chase' episode five [1965]), and the late addition of the cliffhanger into 'Mission to the Unknown' (1965) at the end of 'Galaxy Four' episode four ('The Exploding Planet' [1965]). The first large-scale out of sequence video recording occurs with 'The Ark' episode four: 'The Bomb' in 1966. These examples are, however, exceptions rather than the norm, and, as electronic editing wasn't possible at the BBC until around 1968, were all presumably physical edits to the tape or carefully timed assemble edits.[6]

For the main part, though, early *Doctor Who* was almost entirely shot in the order it would appear on screen with only minimal recording breaks, often in the BBC's tiny Lime Grove studios, with the shots that ultimately appeared on screen being selected live in the production gallery. All incidental music and sound effects were played in live, and any complex sequences (for example fight scenes, scenes set in expansive landscapes, and some visual effects) that could not be achieved in the live studio environment would be

Figure 5 The Doctor and
companions gaze on the Dalek city,
courtesy of Inlay in 'The Daleks'
(1963–4)

played in from pre-recorded film. Almost all this 'film effort' as the BBC
termed it would be shot at the studios in Ealing, with location material
almost absent from the early years of the programme, in large part due to the
difficulties of freeing the cast from rehearsals to film on location.[7]

In terms of special effects the series typically had recourse to Inlay, by which
the output of two cameras could be combined electronically to produce simple
matte shots (as ever, live), a small number of film inserts and ingenuity. In
the first series, for example, Inlay was used to show the regular cast looking
down on the Dalek city (Figure 5) and to produce the illusion of working
elevators within it in 'The Daleks' (1963–4), and to depict teleportation in
'The Keys of Marinus' (1964).

TARDIS materialisations and dematerialisations were generally achieved by
cross fading caption slides (stills depicting the set with TARDIS prop present
and absent as appropriate), or as film inserts.[8] The resultant programme was,
not surprisingly, essentially dialogue-based punctuated with, by necessity,
very brief spectacle, and indeed *Doctor Who*'s signatures arguably become
suspense, rich dialogue and storytelling which tells rather than shows as a
result. Incidental music, being unable to react to live studio action, was
generally used to enhance mood, rather than underscore specific action as in
later years.

Another more concrete effect of studio production, particularly during the
early 'as live' years, was a natural tendency for action to be presented outwards,
through an 'invisible fourth wall' as on a proscenium arch stage. This arises
from TV studio sets generally being constructed around the edges of the
studio with space for multiple cameras to move from one to another in the
centre. As a result, exploration of location in the series tends to be linear (see
the petrified forest in 'The Daleks', the Earth spaceship in 'The Sensorites',
the trap-filled caves of 'The Rescue' [1965], for example). Furthermore,
because the reverse reaction shot we're used to in film drama can't be
easily achieved without the presence of other cameras or the absence of a far
wall to the set being revealed, dialogue is often directed artificially forwards towards the viewer with characters' reactions covered either in angled

close-ups, three-quarter profile two shots, or variations on the classic *Corona-tion Street* three shot, with two characters framed tightly in discussion (typically in three-quarter profile) with a third overhearing, seen full-face directly between them. Indeed, William Hartnell's oft-noted performance tics as the Doctor (darting eyes, hands high on the lapels or in motion around the face) seem to be deliberate attempts to work within a medium in which the extreme close-up and head to chest medium close-up dominate.[9]

A perhaps more unexpected consequence of this is that the 'invisible fourth wall' becomes at times the location of the unknown in the series. This is exploited expertly in the cliffhangers to 'An Unearthly Child' and 'The Daleks' episode one 'The Dead Planet', where the threat to our heroes is a presence between the viewer and the foreground that we can only guess at; the figure casting the misshapen shadow in front of the TARDIS, or the being through whose point-of-view (POV) we are menacing Barbara Wright (Figure 6).

In the 1970s and 1980s this monster's point-of-view shot saw regular service as a suspense-building device in the series, arguably not just because it's an effective tease, allowing the audience to speculate on the nature of the unseen horror, but also because it's easily achievable in the studio, whereas cutaways revealing details of the monster, the other classic filmic technique to achieve similar ends, are not. More significantly for the drama's shape, 'as live' produc-tion meant that *Doctor Who*, a programme ostensibly about free movement in time and space, tended to tell stories almost entirely in straightforward chronological order in restricted settings. Almost all the 1960s episodes were based in a single small set of locations, with action largely moving forward in real time, barring time lapses signified by fades to black. While this restriction often makes for focused drama, and helped accentuate the sense of jeopardy and battling against the clock the series traded on, it's also by far the easiest way to construct a narrative you'll be recording live in limited space. Even the early 'quest' stories ('Marco Polo' [1964], 'The Keys of Marinus' and 'The Chase'), which flit from location to location as their narratives unfold, observe an almost Aristotelian limitation on time and place, whereby each

Figure 6 The monster's point-of-view in 'The Daleks' (1963–4)

episode's action, excluding film inserts, occurs in a small number of sets often specific to that episode alone.[10]

The flashbacks in the first episode, 'An Unearthly Child', highlight the difficulties of mounting these sequences in the 'as live' studio setting and may help explain why *Doctor Who* used the device of non-linear time so rarely. They're mounted as POV shots from Ian and Barbara's view with Susan playing straight to the camera. This is because the teachers' recollections of Susan's bizarre classroom behaviour cannot feature the actors playing them in shot without either pre-recorded film inserts or time-consuming studio breaks as the actors are now in the car outside the junkyard set. Consequently Carole Ann Ford (Susan) plays the scenes without them, reacting to pre-recorded audio. While this is a valid stylistic choice for handling flashback it's once again the easiest one to achieve in the 'as live' setting and it's possible the technical difficulties they initially present help ensure that flashbacks (bar recaps of the previous episodes' cliffhangers) never really enter the series repertoire, occurring only another three times during the 1960s and indeed only seventeen times in the whole of the original twenty-six-year run.[11]

Doctor Who's avoidance of flashback may of course have been for any number of reasons other than just production practicalities. It may perhaps have been felt that it was confusing for a series literally travelling in time to have featured mental time slips too, but there appears to be no major stylistic objection to flashback in popular TV drama in the 1960s. Indeed, each episode of *Dixon of Dock Green* (1955–76), one of the BBC's most successful shows of the period, was constructed as a flashback topped and tailed by monologues directly addressed to the audience by the central character.[12]

A broader look at the shape of 'An Unearthly Child' shows just how this 'as live' production with limited recording breaks and film inserts could work to the show's advantage. The story's mystery is built almost entirely through dialogue in what appears to be real time within just two initial locations: Coal Hill School and the nearby Totters Lane. Its first spectacle, the entrance to the TARDIS interior is achieved in the episode's single recording break, managing to maintain an illusion of continuous action while moving into a clearly impossible space. Following this unsettling moment, the episode continues world-building through dialogue until the climactic TARDIS take-off sequence. This uses the episode's entire film allocation in a two-minute-long dialogue-free sequence combining the police box's disappearance (a caption slide mix), abstract howlround patterns, live studio action and the police box's arrival in a barren landscape (filmed at Ealing) larger than any location seen in the rest of the episode. This sequence is an impressive one even in isolation but seems all the bolder and more spectacular when juxtaposed with the preceding twenty-three minutes of conventional studio dialogue. It's an artful and intelligent marshalling of resources to heighten impact and, whether we realise it consciously or not, part of the sense of wonder we experience on entering the TARDIS and when it takes off surely comes from the way the style established in the rest of the episode suddenly falls away without warning at both these points, the first time subtly and the second dramatically.

This bravura use of suspense and spectacle is perhaps best seen again in the construction of 'The Space Museum' ('The Space Museum' episode one [1965]), which holds its fire to similar effect as the dialogue-based mystery built up in the episode is capped by a surreal visual sequence at the cliff-hanger. Other particularly effective early examples of the use of extended film inserts to expand the impact of the series include the way the exploration of Aridius is supplemented by location shots in episode one of 'The Chase' ('The Executioners'), the impressive model work and battle sequences in episode six of the same story ('Planet of Decision') and the transference to Mira sequence in 'Counterplot', 'The Daleks' Masterplan' episode five.

In later years, the introduction of new electronic effects, routine out of sequence recording and electronic editing lessened the need for film to carry the weight of spectacle in the series, but the importance of balancing the resources remained, and from 1972 it became common for at least one story a season to be entirely made in studio in order to allow increased location filming on others. One particularly interesting example of continued artful use of the series' film allocation is the lengthy location-filmed mental duel in the otherwise studio-based story 'The Deadly Assassin' (1976), which exploits the difference in the media within the narrative stylishly, flipping us between the dialogue-heavy world of the Time Lords in the studio and the imagistic dream world of the Matrix on location film.

Doctor Who was of course far from unique in BBC drama in constructing stories to fit the technical resources available. For further examples, one only has to look at the way both *The Wednesday Play* and *Play for Today* saved up film allocation for specific plays and Alan Bleasdale's series *Boys from the Blackstuff* (1982) to see this was a situation that affected 'high culture' as much as popular drama. The latter series was constructed so that three of its five episodes could be made on OB video, with a fourth shot almost entirely in the studio. This marshalling of resources then allowed the key episode, 'Yosser's Story', to be made entirely on film, rather than as a potentially disconcerting mixture of film and video.

Where *Doctor Who* was unique was in being a BBC drama in continuous production for twenty-six years with a large number of production personnel staying with the programme for extended periods through that run, and while it may be legitimately argued that many of the considerations that influenced early 1960s *Doctor Who* should not have informed its production in the 1970s and 1980s, it's also worth remembering how practices can remain ingrained within both an ongoing production like *Doctor Who* and a large corporation like the BBC.

In 1968, for example, the programme was still routinely being made essentially 'as live', despite electronic editing being available, with several episodes edited from film telerecordings. In fact the first story to be made substantially out of sequence on video was 'Inferno', two years later in 1970 (and one suspects the practicalities of most of the regular cast playing dual roles that required costume changes was the initial spur to this change in production). Indeed, while the most obvious of the changes introduced to *Doctor Who* production at the beginning of the 1970s was the programme's move to colour recording, it's arguable that in production terms the biggest changes were the reduction to twenty-six episodes a year, making more extensive location filming with the regular cast feasible, and the adoption of out of sequence recording, both of which broke up the series' earlier ingrained patterns. The series was now able to spend more time away from the studios and studio resources could now be more effectively deployed, maximising resources by grouping similar activities together.

One major consequence of this change was the regular adoption of a system in which a studio day per story was devoted to electronic effects sequences, most crucially Colour Separation Overlay (the BBC name for Chromakey), the TV matte system, which with the advent of colour recording superseded Inlay as the series' key electronic effect. The effects added on these studio days remained essentially live, however, with unearthly glowing effects achieved either in camera via front axial projection or at the mixing desk with a colour synthesiser, and composite shots being mixed straight to tape, rather than being created in post-production, as we might now expect. Post-production at this stage in the show's history amounted to the compilation of the scenes in the edit suite and the subsequent addition of sound effects and music to the soundtrack, which as a result could now be timed to fit specific on-screen action. A revealing example of the extent of resources available is 'The Sontaran Experiment' (1975). As the first *Doctor Who* story shot all on video on location, it had no studio effects time. It consequently featured no electronic visual effects beyond a simple mixed shot of a red painted board and the location action to depict a laser beam, a brief accelerated video sequence created on location using the videodisc machine normally used by Outside Broadcast Video units for slow-motion replays of sporting action and a number of jump cuts introduced in the edit. The production was, however, able to use special sound and music to help 'sell' the practical visual effects achieved on location.

These changes in production method had an obvious effect on the style of the programme, allowing it a greater sense of spectacle, scale and speed. It's often mentioned that the show's shift to a contemporary Earth setting and the Doctor's attachment to the military intelligence organisation UNIT in the early 1970s allowed budgets to stretch further but it's not always stressed just how these fictional changes mirrored changes in production that allowed the programme to change format from what had been essentially a suspense-based drama into an action series. The Doctor's new establishment position allowed him to be speedily briefed at the start of stories rather than having to stumble across events as an outsider, and the larger regular cast UNIT supplied also gave more scope for multi-stranded storylines told with greater pace. The fact that the new regular characters were for the most part soldiers also aided the series reformatting.

Even with the slow relaxation of the 'contemporary-Earth-only' rule over the 1970s, and the return to smaller regular casts, this relatively film-heavy, action-based format continued for some time, with only two stories ('The Curse of Peladon' [1972] and 'The Monster of Peladon' [1974]) being entirely studio realised during producer Barry Letts' five years on the show. After Letts' departure in 1974, the series slowly drifted from its action format, with new producer Philip Hinchcliffe concentrating once again on suspense and character interaction, reasoning that strong performances could sell a story more effectively than any spectacle the budget could stretch to. The studio-bound story began to reappear more regularly again, almost exclusively for stories set in outer space or on alien worlds (the exceptions being the two period chamber pieces 'Horror of Fang Rock' [1977] and 'Ghost Light' [1989]), ultimately making up between a third and half of all stories from the late 1970s onwards.[13]

The final major refinement to the series' production model came in 1977, with the cinema release of *Star Wars* changing expectations of what televisual science fiction would deliver. Although producers always denied they were trying to compete with *Star Wars*' spectacular effects, *Doctor Who* undeniably shifted in reaction to it, with the programme finally being granted a gallery-only post-production session in which more complex electronic effects could be added, giving the series a production method radically different from any of the BBC's other regular studio-based drama series for the first time in its history in the process (A.J. 'Mitch' Mitchell in Howe et al., 1994: 117). The resultant production model saw out the final twelve years of the series' original run.

For all the massive changes in television technology the passage of time brought, some things remained more or less unchanged throughout *Doctor Who*'s initial twenty-six-year run: stories by and large followed the templates established in the series' first four years, shots continued to be selected live during multi-camera studio recording, and a typical four-episode story continued to be essentially recorded over four evenings. While putting together this chapter I thought it could be useful to apply Lez Cooke's methodology

(Cooke, 2003: 15) of establishing average shot lengths in television dramas to episodes of *Doctor Who* at different points in its history – to help provide a snapshot indication of changes to the show's visual grammar over the years. I arbitrarily picked the first episodes of serials from the start of season one, the middle of season six, the start of season thirteen, the middle of season nineteen and the start of season twenty-six, expecting to be able to trace a slow shift in shot length as production methods became more sophisticated. I was surprised to discover the average shot length barely changed. 'An Unearthly Child' (1963) featured 132 shots in 25 minutes, 'The Krotons' episode one (1969) 131, 'Terror of the Zygons' episode one (1976) 152, 'The Visitation' episode one (1982) 155, and finally 'Battlefield' episode one (1989) 255, giving an average shot length of eleven and a half to ten seconds for most of the series' run. The lack of any marked acceleration over the first nineteen years perhaps reflects a continuation of the programme's essentially discursive studio-bound nature, or possibly indicates that while technologies changed, audiences, industry practitioners and the BBC did less so. Whatever the reason, the continuity is surprising.[14]

The most recent television reinventions of *Doctor Who* in 1996 and 2005 both come from an era in which the studio-based TV drama format from which the programme sprang is regarded as an anachronism, one that now survives only in the form of soap opera. Both the 1996 and 2005 models have budgets the original series never approached and draw their visual cues and production methods, albeit in different ways, from the cinema (and perhaps ironically, the OB based production techniques *Doctor Who* was beginning to develop at the end of the 1980s for financial reasons, which have since become TV industry norms). However, the stories they've continued to tell, in which ideas, characters and suspense take precedence over action, draw directly on the programme's origins as a weekly serial trying to deliver the Universe from an electronic studio for around £600 a week.

Notes

1   The Filipino army's advance on Reykjavik is a presumably epic battle in the 51st century, referred to in the *Doctor Who* story 'The Talons of Weng-Chiang' (1977). I use it in my title as it sums up for me *Doctor Who*'s treatment of the epic through most of its original run. For obvious budgetary reasons, this kind of grand spectacle is kept off screen, and generally features only in dialogue as the trigger or consequence of the more compact, television-shaped, stories that unfold on screen. My spelling of Filipino comes from the published script of the story (Holmes, 1989: 138), and is backed by the subtitles on its DVD release, though both Justin Richards' book *Doctor Who – The Legend* (2003) and Terrance Dicks' novelisation of 'The Talons of Weng-Chiang' (1977) offer the variant spelling Philippino.

2   This is a difficulty exacerbated in recent years by DVD releases of the series
    'correcting' production 'errors' of the 1960s, 1970s and 1980s with modern
    post-production techniques, which can give a misleading impression of what
    was achievable at the time with the resources available. This has involved at
    various times: the cleaning and regrading of film inserts (on occasion changing
    the composition of shots on screen), the smoothing of video edits and sound
    effect tape loop joins, reduction of studio noise, insertion of background sound
    effects, the painting out of boom mikes or unwanted background action and
    attempts to make the fringing around Colour Separation Overlay shots less
    obvious. These are all interventions that make a television production seem
    more professional by current broadcast criteria, but which do not reflect the
    programme as made entirely truthfully. Indeed, VIDfire, a process designed to
    restore some of the look of 1960s video to film telerecording copies of the
    programme, has actually been used on episodes originally transmitted from film
    telerecordings ('The Mind Robber' episode 5 [1969] and 'The Seeds of Death'
    [1969]), 'restoring' a quality to the episodes that was not actually present on
    transmission.

    Doctor Who is not alone in suffering this re-presentation of television archive
    material. For example, the commercial release of arguably the most famous epis-
    ode of *Hancock*, 'The Blood Donor' (1961), has, since the 1980s, been re-edited
    at the wish of the writers to trim a lengthy film insert at the end, which tightens
    the pace of the episode but distorts our conception of British TV comedy
    at the time. The insert (featuring an ambulance rushing through the streets) was
    deliberately long to permit Tony Hancock to change costume and move to
    another set for the pay-off to the episode, and while truncating the sequence
    may marginally enhance a modern viewer's enjoyment of the comedy, it also
    disguises the conditions in which the programme was made. It's regrettable,
    given the care and dedication of those involved, that the criteria for television
    'restoration' are still so widely at variance with those for archive film where
    practitioners seek to avoid making editorial changes to the material to suit
    contemporary tastes in the restoration process. Sadly, I suspect this disparity is
    likely to continue until the cultural importance of television is more widely
    respected, and a general audience's ability to read the grammar of old television
    as a product of its time is allowed to mature as a result.

3   I'm hugely indebted to legions of researchers into the series' production history
    for much of the specific background information relied on in this piece, but
    I feel special praise has to be meted out to Andrew Pixley for his exceptional and
    exhaustive archive features for *Doctor Who Magazine*; Stephen James Walker for
    his pieces on early *Doctor Who* in *The Frame* fanzine, *Doctor Who Magazine* and
    his work on the *Handbook* series alongside David J. Howe and Mark Stammers
    (2005); Richard Bignell, for his impressively researched *Doctor Who: On Location*,
    and J. Jeremy Bentham for his book *Doctor Who: The Early Years* which, while
    occasionally slightly inaccurate looked at twenty years on, set an impressive
    standard for later authors. The blame for any confusion I may bring to the picture,
    through my interpretation of their work, lies squarely with me not them.

4   Video costs thanks to John Trenouth, Head of Television, National Museum of Photography, Film and Television, whose BBC contacts came up with a figure of £120 a reel in 1960. The production costs come from the First Doctor 'Production Diary' in Howe et al., 2005: 46–179. An alternative price for a reel of tape is provided in Denis Norden, Sybil Harper and Norma Gilbert's book *Coming to You Live!* (1985), which, while anecdotal and aimed at a general reader, contains much valuable first-hand testimony from a wide range of people working in British TV during the 1950s and 1960s. Here Bob Wright, BBC Head of Lighting recalls videotape as costing around £90 a reel at the time of Philip Saville's BBC production *Hamlet at Elsinore* in 1963. He also states that a physical tape edit would take an experienced editor about ten minutes. This figure tallies closely with the estimates for physical edits on *Rowan and Martin's Laugh In* (1968), by far and away the most edited tape show of the period which reputedly required 60 hours' edit time to make the 350 to 400 edits each instalment demanded. *Doctor Who*, which had a run-in time from recording to transmission of between two to three weeks for much of the 1960s, did not have the luxury of that kind of edit time. The cost of videotape and its routine reuse goes some way to explaining why most surviving British TV output of the 1950s and 1960s exists now only in the form of telerecordings, filmed copies of the programmes played on a TV monitor screen. The other reason telerecordings proliferate from this period is that making a 16mm film copy of a programme tended to be the best way of making it viewable on foreign TV systems and thus saleable overseas in the days before easy video standards conversion.

5   It is likely that most of the early fade to black edits seen in *Doctor Who* are physical cuts to the tape rather than 'in machine' assemble edits, but with the original tapes long wiped it's not always clear. The original unscreened version of 'An Unearthly Child', for example, was clearly made with the assumption that one of the remounted versions of the programme's final sequences could be spliced to the opening later, though whether the plan was to achieve this by cutting the videotape or the surviving telerecorded film copy remains uncertain.

    The ability to roll back and re-record video arrived in the mid-1960s when second-generation quad machines which could switch from playback straight into record and perform a 'clean' assemble edit became available (for example the Ampex VR1100 marketed in 1962), but exactly when *Doctor Who* first has this facility is unclear. Thanks again are due to John Trenouth for this information.

6   Thanks once again to John Trenouth and his BBC sources for information regarding electronic editing. This information, like much anecdotal testimony from the period, is disputed, and there is some evidence to suggest electronic editing may have actually begun in 1967. It's also notable that many more physical edits begin to occur from 1967 on following the arrival of new producer Innes Lloyd. In addition to the video edited stories, a handful of 1960s episodes of *Doctor Who* were edited on film, from telerecordings made of the studio output. There is some debate as to whether this was primarily done for artistic reasons (i.e. ease of editing) or simply because of availability of equipment. The episodes in question are, 'The Ambush' ('The Daleks' episode four), 'Crisis'

('Planet of Giants' episode three), 'The Waking Ally' ('The Dalek Invasion of Earth' episode five), 'The Power of the Daleks' episode six (1966), 'The Wheel in Space' episodes five and six (1968), 'The Dominators' episode three (1968), 'The Mind Robber' episode five (1968), 'The Krotons' episode one (1968), 'The Seeds of Death' episode five (1969) and 'The Space Pirates' episode two (1969). It seems likely that 'The Ambush' was edited from a telerecording of the studio output due to its heavy visual effects content, notably a complex Inlay shot combining studio recording with a film insert of bubbling metal and a negative effect during the Dalek–Thal fight sequence. On the other hand, the transmission of 'The Waking Ally' from telerecording apparently stems from the BBC's videotape machines being committed to coverage of the 1965 General Election. Certainly the one major edit that occurred on *Doctor Who* in the early 1960s, the conflation of the original third and fourth episodes of 'Planet of Giants' to produce a more satisfactory single episode ('Crisis'), would appear to have been achieved on 35mm film telerecordings because of the much greater complexity of video editing.

7   It's worth remembering that the series remained primarily studio based until the production schedule was reduced to twenty-six episodes a year in 1970. The episodes of William Hartnell *Doctor Who* that seem most similar to the 1970s and 1980s run of the series in the level of their location work ('The Dalek Invasion of Earth', 'The War Machines' and 'The Smugglers') are atypical stories made at the beginnings and ends of the series' recording runs, which could consequently have additional time spent on their filming, and although the level of location shooting during Troughton's time on the series increased this was often at the cost of breaks for the regular cast and was sometimes only achieved through the use of doubles.

8   Perhaps unsurprisingly, given the limited resources, some of the most striking visual effects in the series' early years come as a result of abuse of the electronic studios in which the programme originated. The famous 'howlround' title sequence was created using feedback from a camera viewing its own monitor, the negative Dalek extermination effect was a creative application of 'peeling', the tendency of the CPS Emitron cameras' tubes to show bright objects in negative, and the grainy, high-contrast transition from Hartnell to Troughton in 'The Tenth Planet' episode four was the result of using a serendipitously faulty mixing desk at the Riverside studios. All these effects, by virtue of their basis in the electronic studio, help to give the series a texture quite unlike any filmed science fiction series of the time.

9   Hartnell's professionalism as an actor with regard to knowing his position on camera and how he was being framed is regularly remarked on and series regular Peter Purves (Steven) has often talked of his use of small close-to-the-face gestures for the camera (see, for example, Howe et al., 2005: 28). There is a definite logic to Hartnell's idea, with his performance being well suited to consumption on small 405-line domestic television receivers and capture by the CPS Emitron cameras at Lime Grove, which being turret cameras without zooms, were likely to hold still shots of a performer longer than we might currently expect. An alternative approach to building suspense within the series' limited

studio resources arose in the late 1960s (most prominently in 1967–8), with a run of stories under producers Innes Lloyd and Peter Bryant built around large single sets (christened 'base under siege' stories by *Doctor Who* fandom) in which cameras and actors have increased scope for movement and we are allowed to closely observe characters' reactions to an alien threat. Stories adopting this approach include 'The Moonbase' (1967), 'The Tomb of the Cybermen' (1967), 'The Ice Warriors' (1967), 'Fury from the Deep' (1968) and 'The Wheel in Space' (1968).

10 'Marco Polo' is unusual in its treatment of time, in that in charting a six-month journey it covers a longer period in its seven episodes than any other *Doctor Who* story (excepting 'The Ark', with its convenient seven hundred year break between episodes two and three). Despite this, the majority of the action still takes place over just nineteen days, with the rest of the epic journey covered by narration in the form of entries from Polo's diary.

11 The flashbacks I've identified occur in the first episode, 'An Unearthly Child' (1963), 'The Dalek Invasion of Earth' episode two (1965), 'The Celestial Toymaker' episode one (1966), 'The Wheel in Space' episode six (1968), 'Planet of the Spiders' episodes one, five and six (1974), 'The Ark in Space' episode three (1975), 'The Keeper of Traken' episode one (1981), 'Logopolis' episode four (1981), 'Earthshock' episode two (1982), 'Mawdryn Undead' episode two (1983), 'The Five Doctors' (1983), 'Resurrection of the Daleks' episode two (1984 [as originally transmitted]), 'The Trial of a Timelord' parts one–eight and fourteen (1986) and 'Ghost Light' episode three (1989). I exclude from this list the stills sequences in 'The Mind of Evil' (1971), 'The Day of the Daleks' (1972) and 'The Brain of Morbius' (1976), and the 2005 series' flashbacks in 'Father's Day' and 'Bad Wolf'. Interestingly, only the first two examples are 'pure' flashback in which a character's spoken recollections lead directly into a visual representation of their memories. The later sequences are, with just six exceptions, projected images of the past achieved, within the story's fiction, by technological means, and for the most part involve relating the current story to earlier shows rather than resolving points in the present narrative. It's hard to unpick to what extent this avoidance of flashback might be a symptom of a general move away from the device in British TV drama, a hangover from the production methods of the first seven years of the series, or a result of the series consciously developing a predominantly naturalistic house-style in which to tell its fantastical stories, but it's undeniable that the programme avoided flashback almost entirely until the 1980s, when the technique was predominantly used to celebrate the series' heritage.

12 It's perhaps also worth mentioning as a footnote the apparent absence of resistance at this time to direct address in UK TV drama we're used to constructing as naturalistic. Leaving aside the arch introductions to camera of *The Saint* (1962–9) and the regular fourth-wall breaking of George Dixon, episode six of *Coronation Street* in 1960 features a direct address to the audience which makes the Doctor's Christmas wishes to the audience from 'The Feast of Steven' ('The Daleks' Masterplan' episode seven [1965]), so loathed by many *Doctor Who* fans, seem positively ambiguous in comparison. It almost seems the fan resistance to

this moment in *Doctor Who* and the three occasions Tom Baker unequivocally attempts something similar ('The Face of Evil' [1977], 'The Invasion of Time' and 'The Pirate Planet' [both 1978]) come from a reading of breaking the fourth wall as a Light Entertainment technique that destroys a drama's reality. Certainly, there seems to be no similar resistance to the Doctor's out of vision narrations at the openings of 'The Deadly Assassin' (1976) and the 1996 TV Movie, or indeed to incidental music or any number of other non-naturalistic devices in the show. To pick just a handful of these, they include characters' thoughts being heard in voice over in both 'The Underwater Menace' and 'The Moonbase' in 1967, Morgus's pieces to camera and the expressionistic representation of the regeneration in 'The Caves of Androzani' (1984), and the lighting effects accompanying Ace's auditory flashback in 'Ghost Light'.

13 The rise in studio-only stories coincides with a relative shrinkage in *Doctor Who*'s budget with respect to inflation through the late 1970s, and it could be argued that the drift from action series back to a suspense model during that period is as much an economic decision as an artistic one. The series' increased reliance on location work in the late 1980s was similarly economically driven, when the availability of lightweight Outside Broadcast cameras meant it became more cost effective to shoot a number of stories entirely on OB video rather than mount them as a combination of studio and location work.

14 Unlike Lez Cooke's average shot lengths in *British Television Drama* (2003), which are calculated from camera scripts and programme running times, mine were generated by watching the episodes and recording shot changes with a pencil stroke on paper, which leaves some potential for inaccuracy, particularly during some of the faster sequences in 'Battlefield', and one montage of close-ups on the Zygon creatures in 'Terror of the Zygons' in which it was hard to determine precisely how many shots were seen. All my figures exclude opening and closing titles.

The acceleration in pace to an average shot length just under six seconds in 1989 is only partly a reflection of the unusually high degree of OB video content in 'Battlefield', which could be more frenetically edited than multi-camera studio work. Surprised by the shot length, I checked the first episode of the all-studio recorded 'Ghost Light' from the same year. 'Ghost Light' features 201 shots with an approximate seven and a half second shot length, suggesting a deliberate policy to change the visual grammar of the programme in its final years. My instinct is that this change occurred at the start of season twenty-four in 1987, but as yet I've not been able to confirm this. I hope in future it may be possible to examine this apparent shift in more detail with a less arbitrary selection of episodes. A similar acceleration does not appear to have taken place in, say, *Coronation Street* at the time. My suspicion is that the increasing editing speed reflects the rise in home video during this period, and an increased expectation of filmic pace of work in the science fiction and fantasy genres that may be linked to that. It may also have been part of an attempt to combat claims that the programme was looking both old fashioned and cheap. The change certainly predates the generally noted acceleration in pacing within terrestrial TV drama which many observers have linked to the launch of Sky Television in February 1989 and the resultant loss of major films to terrestrial networks.

References

Bentham, J. Jeremy. 1986. *Doctor Who: The Early Years*. London: W.H. Allen.

Bignell, Richard. 2001. *Doctor Who: On Location*. Richmond: Reynolds and Hearn.

Cooke, Lez. 2003. *British Television Drama: A History*. London: BFI.

Hearn, Marcus. 1994. 'The Giants'. *Doctor Who Magazine*, No. 209, pp. 34–6.

Holmes, Robert. 1989. *Doctor Who: The Scripts – The Talons of Weng-Chiang*. London: Titan.

Howe, David J., Mark Stammers and Stephen James Walker. 1994. *Doctor Who: The Seventies*. London: Virgin.

Howe, David J., Mark Stammers and Stephen James Walker. 2005. *The Handbook: The Unofficial and Unauthorised Guide to the Production of Doctor Who*. Tolworth, Surrey: Telos.

Norden, Denis, Sybil Harper and Norma Gilbert. 1985. *Coming to You Live!* London: Methuen.

Pixley, Andrew. 1987–2003. 'Archive feature'. *Doctor Who Magazine*.

Chapter 10

'Who done it': discourses of authorship during the John Nathan-Turner era

Dave Rolinson

This chapter explores authorship in television drama by contrasting the authorial influence of producer John Nathan-Turner over 1980s *Doctor Who* with the claims to agency made by his writers, directors and script editors. The problematic authorial reading in the title, which describes the period between 1980 and 1989 as 'the John Nathan-Turner era', is one with which *Doctor Who* fans are familiar. They anticipated academics' descriptions of drama series as a 'producer's medium' by periodising the programme by producer ('the Hinchcliffe era') just as readily as they periodised by leading actor ('the Hartnell era'). The Nathan-Turner 'era' provides a useful test case for series authorship, given the extent to which fans attributed the programme's perceived success and failure to his personal input.

Authorship was attributed to writers in the title sequence of every episode (for instance, 'The Leisure Hive ... by David Fisher'), but this practice obscured the extent to which writers' space for individual expression was contested. For instance, Jonathan Bignell and Andrew O'Day (2004: 28–9) observe that, because *Doctor Who* was an ongoing, episodic series, 'an individual writer's storyline or script must contribute to the overall whole of a programme' and, because it was part of the science fiction genre, writers were expected to employ 'specified generic characteristics'. In short, the 'personal signatures' of writers were subsumed within 'generically coded formats'. John Tulloch and Manuel Alvarado (1983: 173–4) contrast the 'Great Tradition' of television 'artists' like Dennis Potter, who were seen to assert their individual voices within 'serious' play strands like *The Wednesday Play* (1964–70), with 'the "craft" tradition' of 'craftsmen' who were 'enmeshed within the cramping restrictions of a ratings-oriented industry'. Tension between these traditions was manifested in Christopher Bailey's troubled attempt to 'appropriate a space for authorship' and 'serious creativity' in 'Kinda' (1982); by contrast, Stephen Gallagher's autobiographical references in 'Warriors' Gate' (1981) were hidden 'to the producer's satisfaction' within the format (Tulloch and Alvarado, 1983: 175–6, 247–306).

Accepting the 'craft' tradition, fan critics have celebrated features which would be seen as obstacles to authorship within the 'artist' tradition. Writing about Robert Holmes, Matthew Jones (1995: 37) has argued that *Doctor Who* is 'formula television. Almost every single story is made up of the same basic ingredients [. . .] the skill in writing *Doctor Who* comes from exactly how the ingredients in the formula are mixed'. Jones operates within what Tulloch and Alvarado (1983: 176) describe as the 'space for authorship [. . .] appreciated by fans' which 'works within and expands the mythology of the institution'. Therefore, fans responded to writers who adhered to the formula like Terry Nation or Terrance Dicks, who contrasted his *New Adventures* novels with those of his more experimental contemporaries to argue that 'I'm still selling you steak and chips' (Binns, 1996: 9). Writers who combined a distinctive voice with an adherence to the formula were highly valued, like Holmes, Brian Hayles or Malcolm Hulke. This reading of authorship is shaped by the acceptance that viewers of series, like spectators of genre cinema, derive pleasure from 'novelty-within-convention' (Tulloch and Alvarado, 1983: 64). If success is defined by the extent to which writers serve existing generic features, in a sense writers both write *Doctor Who* and are written by *Doctor Who*.

However, there are problems with the opposition between 'craftsmen' restricted by genre and 'artists' who assert their agency. Writing on Potter, Rosalind Coward disputes the use of the 'author' construct, imported from other disciplines arguably to legitimise the study of television, because the idea of 'transparent communication' between authors and audiences denied the collaboration inherent in television production and restricted understanding of mass production (Coward, 1987: 82, 87). As this chapter will demonstrate, collaboration was ingrained in the process of 'authoring' *Doctor Who*.

These restrictions have not displaced the assessment of authors in *Doctor Who*. Tulloch and Alvarado (1983: 176) note that, within the '*continuity* of professional concerns' there remained a 'variety of signatures'. Fanzines have isolated individual figures for study, aware of the differences between stories written by Terrance Dicks and Douglas Adams or directed by Graeme Harper and Fiona Cumming. One of the consequences of fandom's displacement of the 'canon' inadvertently established by Jeremy Bentham during the growth of organised fandom in the 1970s has been the re-evaluation of individual contributors. As occurred with the typology of French critics during Film Studies' construction of a 'canon', fan writers sought out contributors whose work was distinctive, within a production format which appeared to stifle individual creativity. To take one of many examples from fanzines, Theo Robertson (1995: 31) elevates Malcolm Hulke above others who treated *Doctor Who* as a children's programme. Robertson argues that, given the moral complexity of his work, Hulke could be set against writers like Terry Nation and described as an 'exception'.

For over twenty-five years, *Doctor Who Magazine* (produced by Marvel and, more recently, Panini) has interviewed and devoted features to individual contributors, including Hulke (Macdonald, 1992a) and Robert Holmes, who was the subject of a special issue (see Macdonald, 1994). The fact that Holmes is also covered in this book demonstrates continuity between treatments of authorship by fans and academics, which is reinforced by Bignell and O'Day's book on Terry Nation. Just as developments in film theory have displaced orthodox 'auteurist' approaches, so Bignell and O'Day qualify their focus on Nation with theory and by questioning where 'authority' lies in collaborative media. However, Nation's agency is not entirely displaced. Responding to Rosalind Coward, John R. Cook (1998: 4) has written that the 'complexity of production' which Coward thought invalidated 'notions of authorial expression' could 'be seen to resolve itself into a clear hierarchical system of creative power relations whereby traditionally in British television, the writer was privileged'. This is true of certain writers of single plays, but does the more regimented 'hierarchical system of creative power relations' in series drama resolve itself in this manner?

'The Leisure Hive' (1980), the first story produced by John Nathan-Turner, would suggest not. It introduces season eighteen's defining tone and themes. It is set on the planet Argolis, whose people and landscape were rendered sterile by nuclear war. In a conceptual pun typical of the season, one citizen uses the leisure facility known as the recreation generator to attempt the re-creation of society by constructing a new generation. The serial's foreshadowing of later themes includes its sense of recursion, as the aggressive use of technology is used to escape the consequences of the aggressive use of technology, and its depiction of an embattled society in thrall to its own history, like the underground society of 'Meglos' (1980), the querying of descent which reveals evolutionary recursion in 'Full Circle' (1980), the apparent retreat into medievalism and vampire legend of 'State of Decay' (1980) or the Gateway as temporal focal point in 'Warriors' Gate'. Philip Macdonald (1992b: 42–3) observes that season eighteen stories portray 'objects, societies and planets [. . .] being dragged backwards by their very efforts to move forwards', reinforcing the season's dominant themes of entropy and 'reclaiming humanity from the ravages of corrosion'.

However, it would be problematic to attribute this story's introduction of the season's themes to David Fisher, despite his credit as writer, because of the programme's 'creative power relations'. Arguing that 'Nathan-Turner made his mark on the series from the word go', David J. Howe and Stephen James Walker (1998: 381–2) employ the common reading of 'The Leisure Hive' as a site for 'changes' implemented by Nathan-Turner. These changes largely related to production values, as he used his experience of BBC budgets as production unit manager to 'put the money on the screen'. There were also stylistic changes, including a new title sequence and theme tune, his decision to replace incidental music composed by Dudley Simpson with less conventional electronic scores by the Radiophonic Workshop, and an insistence on a 'more sombre' performance by Tom Baker which was reflected in his new costume and the tone of scripts.

Nathan-Turner and script editor Christopher H. Bidmead asserted their agency by contrasting their 'serious', hard science fiction with the 'undergraduate humour', 'childish silliness' and poor production values of *Doctor Who* under the previous regime of Graham Williams and Douglas Adams (see Tulloch and Alvarado, 1983: 193–246). Bidmead sought the 'scientification' of *Doctor Who* and a greater thematic unity which resulted, according to Philip Macdonald (1992b: 42–3), in 'probably the most consistent and carefully constructed progress' of any *Doctor Who* season, a more sophisticated and *authored* incorporation of running themes than the season-long 'Key to Time' arc of season sixteen (1978–9) or 'The Trial of a Time Lord' story which ran throughout season twenty-three (1986). Privileging Bidmead's authority throughout the season, Macdonald credits the Bidmead-scripted season finale 'Logopolis' (1981) with 'bringing to a climax the mood and the themes of the preceding six adventures'.

Script editors are junior to producers within television's creative hierarchy, but *Doctor Who*'s specific production circumstances, and the format's lack of prescribed features, gave its script editors such influence over style that they become markers of 'sub-eras' which are more accurate than periodisation by producer alone; therefore, Nathan-Turner's criticism applies more to 'Williams/Adams' than to 'Williams/Holmes'. Their relative autonomy was reinforced by the fact that 'script editor' was, according to Bidmead, 'an utterly undefined job title' (Griffiths, 1997a: 9). David J. Howe and Stephen James Walker quote a BBC Editors' Guide which argued that 'The primary function of the editor is to find, encourage and commission new writers', but also contained responsibilities which sometimes conflicted, for instance in 'encouraging writers to practise their art with as much freedom as possible' while guiding them on 'necessary disciplines'. Reflecting this, Bidmead estimated that he wrote 70 per cent of season eighteen, in two distinct ways: the 'legitimate' authoring which took place in 'brainstorming sessions with each of the writers' to which script editors would 'contribute at least half the ideas', and the 'less rewarding' work of substantially rewriting material which did not 'achieve what was required' (Howe and Walker, 1995: 176–7). Paradoxically, therefore, although season eighteen's 'intellectual' scope connotes authorial freedom, the application of Bidmead's dominant themes restricts the agency of its contributors.

Bidmead sympathised with writers who interpreted the process as 'that bugger Chris Bidmead took my stuff and did it his own way' (Griffiths,

1997a: 10). In similar terms, Stephen Gallagher complained that 'Warriors' Gate' was 'heavily edited between leaving my hands and appearing on air'. However, Gallagher's discovery that he had not been personally 'singled out' reveals the typicality of this practice: 'I found out that every writer who worked on the show in those couple of seasons had the same complaint' (Travers, 1988: 9). Eric Saward similarly argued that, during his time as script editor, 'I could have gone up as co-author on almost every story' (Howe and Walker, 1995: 195). Bidmead hit upon a more amenable job description when recalling his rewriting of 'Full Circle' after discussions with writer Andrew Smith: 'I just incubated the script we had originally hacked out between us' (Griffiths, 1997a: 11).

This 'brainstorming' is closer to Andrew Cartmel's definition of his work as script editor. His defining strategies, which included restoring mystery to the Doctor's character and bringing depth to the companion's character-isation, impacted upon the narrative structure suggested to writers, who employed the 'plot device' of the Doctor as 'a distant mountain range seen through a mist [. . .] manipulating everything' (Bishop, 1995b: 44) and configured plots around Ace. However, despite proposing a controversial re-visioning of the Doctor's past, known as the 'Cartmel Masterplan', this was never imposed as an authorial framework like Bidmead's recurring themes or structures such as the 'E-Space trilogy'. Indeed, Cartmel stressed his writers' autonomy. Noting Rona Munro's use of 'feminist/occult sym-bology' in 'Survival' (1989), including the 'cat symbol' and 'reflections of the moon in water' as images associated with 'wise-women through the years', he argued that Munro was an example of 'someone writing from her own obsessions and inspirations on a path that was parallel to *Doctor Who*; that was what I wanted' (Bishop, 1995c: 42–3). However, Munro also experienced the generically coded format. She recalled Cartmel discussing the '*Who* Concept [. . .] where the writer comes up with the story and the produc-tion team make it fit into the world of *Who*' (Rudden, 1992: 10–11). This included the incorporation of the Master. Munro noted her intentions to show the Cheetah People as 'very very sensual' and Ace having a 'relation-ship with a Cheetah woman as a kind of lesbian subtext', but argued that 'nowhere did that appear on screen' (Tulloch, 1999: 22). This omission is striking because Munro's intentions reflected Cartmel's desire to explore Ace's character, and because Ace was shown to be attracted to the male Sorin in 'The Curse of Fenric' (1989), although the fact that the latter story portrayed emerging sexuality through the more acceptable generic coding of vampirism implies a restriction by format as much as by sexuality.

Unlike Cartmel, Bidmead was a script editor who also wrote stories, and 'Castrovalva' (1982) heightens an authorial reading of the work which he edited. Although overseen by a different script editor and written as the beginning of both season nineteen and the Davison era, it can be read as the culmination of season eighteen. It closes a themed trilogy, as Shardovan sacrifices himself to thwart the Master just as the new Keeper and the Doctor do in 'The Keeper of Traken' (1981) and 'Logopolis' respectively. 'Castrovalva', like the Cartmel-edited 'Survival', shows the Master lure the TARDIS crew into a trap – a world over which he appears to have creative agency until it turns on him. These ideas of agency and escaping history could be read as a comment on the programme's need to emerge from Tom Baker's long era, symbolised by the new Doctor's unravelling of the Fourth Doctor's iconic scarf while mapping the labyrinthine TARDIS. The Doctor is trapped on Castrovalva, whose history and the memories of its people are false because they were invented by the Master. Echoing the self-perpetuating tasks of 'Full Circle' and the TARDIS-within-a-TARDIS of 'Logopolis', the Doctor is trapped within a recursive landscape. Escape from Castrovalva requires a dynamic individualism which closes the Bidmead 'arc' of season eighteen, in which individuals battled the universal scale of entropy. Although season eighteen was too multifarious and philosophical to be reductively described as a study of scientific determinism, 'Castrovalva' could be read as a redemptive exorcism of individuals' inability to escape the universal scale of entropy in that season, as personified by the Watcher, a harbinger of doom from which the Doctor could not escape. Here, individuals discover their free will. Escape from Castrovalva is foreshadowed in the TARDIS's escape from Event One, a site of history and creation (the 'big bang'). Observing that 'people escape from gravity all the time', Nyssa and Tegan learn that 'if' must be turned 'into a fact', because freedom as an aesthetic concept must be understood imaginatively before it can be enacted. This idea is grasped by Shardovan, who negotiates Castrovalva's bafflingly recursive spatial topography 'in my philosophy' and ultimately revolts against his creator, the Master, in a sacrifice which asserts individual agency and, unlike the sacrifices which closed the previous two stories, leads not to the perpetuation of the status quo but to the realisation that 'we are free!'

Like Shardovan, writers attempt to assert their agency from within Bidmead's creation, as his themes unify the stories from 'The Leisure Hive' to 'Castrovalva'. Therefore, the credit 'Stephen Gallagher' refers less to the noted horror novelist Stephen Gallagher than to a nominal 'Stephen Gallagher' who becomes an organising structure (in the language of the auteur-structuralism with which film theorists challenged auteurism by contrasting, for instance, John Ford the director of Westerns with 'John Ford' the agent constructed by critics). Is there, then, a distinction between Gallagher, Fisher and David Agnew, that most elusive of *Doctor Who* writers? Any critic seeking Agnew's authorial signatures would struggle given that, before writing 'The Invasion of Time' (1978) and 'City of Death' (1979), Agnew wrote such 'serious' plays as 'Hell's Angel' (1971) for *Play for Today* and *Diane* (1975). Of course, this auteurist reading is indefensible because, like Norman Ashby, Robin Bland and Stephen Harris, 'David Agnew' did not exist; the name was used as a pseudonym for disputed credits. The idea of constructing an 'Agnew' signature seems laughable; Mark Shivas, the producer of *Diane* (from which Jonathan Hales removed his credit after extensive revisions by director Alan Clarke) was amused by 'the idea of someone doing a PhD thesis on "Agnew's" work some years down the line' (Kelly, 1998: 77). However, is it substantially different from constructing a 'Gallagher' or 'Fisher' signature in work which has been institutionally reworked? Do we need a different form of credit which does not, in Coward's terms, 'hide knowledge of the media' (Coward, 1987: 87)?

The assertion of Nathan-Turner/Bidmead's agency in *The Unfolding Text* has been widely questioned. Gareth Wigmore (1996: 22) summarised the standard view with facetious acuteness: 'And lo, the great Hinchcliffe had his power cruelly ripped away [...] [under Williams] Anarchy was loose: robotic dogs, gigantic prawns, dancing bulls, glowing green phallus-monsters, yay, even unto Catherine Schell', until Nathan-Turner 'dragged things back from the brink of disaster'. One of the ways in which Wigmore discredits this view is by citing complications of authorship: for instance, 'The Leisure Hive' and 'Meglos' were 'written for the Williams house style' and were arguably weakened by their 'serious' treatment. In a review of 'The Leisure Hive', Philip Macdonald (2004b: 56) included a plot synopsis which was revealed to be that of 'The Horns of Nimon' (1979–80), in order to stress their similarities: 'a complex cautionary tale of scientific hubris' full of 'iconic images' including 'lurking alien infiltrators' in a landscape devastated by war and 'the neurotic remnant of a once-proud race of conquerors [...] retreating to the insular protection of their many-spired city'. These innate similarities, according to Macdonald, proved that 'The Horns of Nimon' had a poor reputation because of its 'camp' atmosphere and poor production values as markers of the Williams style, whereas 'The Leisure Hive' was prioritised because of the signifiers of the 'serious' Nathan-Turner era. Disputing this, Macdonald (2004a: 4) argued that season eighteen is less authorially discrete, and the Williams era more sophisticated, than is often thought (presumably also by Macdonald himself – see 1992b).

For instance, 'State of Decay' was written for season fifteen but withheld because of the BBC's sensitivity towards their contemporaneous *Count Dracula* (1977). The transmitted version features an abundance of signatures: a script by Terrance Dicks (Pertwee-era script editor and writer for several eras), with vampire iconography redolent of Hinchcliffe's 'Gothic horror' era, simultaneously inflected by Bidmead's dominant themes (including decay, hence the retitling from 'The Witch Lords') and witty interplay between Tom Baker and Lalla Ward largely unseen since season seventeen (preserved by director Peter Moffatt despite an attempted late rewrite by Bidmead). These stories demonstrate the impact of new production teams, alongside other *Doctor Who* stories written by figures from previous eras, including the UNIT romp 'Robot' (1974) which provided an uncharacteristic beginning to the Hinchcliffe era, and Pip and Jane Baker's 'Time and the Rani' (1987), which was an equally uncharacteristic opening to the Cartmel era. With these qualifications in mind, David Fisher can be removed from debates over how different production teams reshaped his work, to regain a level of autonomy. Macdonald (2004a: 8) notes that 'The Leisure Hive' revisits themes from earlier Fisher stories, including time-bubble experiments from 'City of Death', 'inter-species communication' from 'The Creature from the Pit' (1979) and 'space-age courtroom drama' from 'The Stones of Blood' (1978).

In this reading, Nathan-Turner's 'signature' is less creative than administrative, in keeping with the definition by Bignell and O'Day (2004: 35) of television as 'a producer's medium' in which the producer 'controls the process of making a programme and fulfils a responsibility to the television institution [. . .] by overseeing the format, budgets, personnel, the production schedule and the delivery of the finished product'. Fans welcomed this signature, as Nathan-Turner's budgetary expertise resulted in improved production values despite the series' low budget, but his reputation declined when Nathan-Turner blurred the roles between producer and script editor. Fans' interpretations of a producer's duties were explored publicly following the 'cancellation crisis' of 1985 and Cartmel's fraught first season. Nathan-Turner was criticised by disgruntled fans on television and by his former script editor Eric Saward in the fan press. In contrast to the agency enjoyed by Bidmead, Saward felt that he and his writers were constricted by the producer's influence over scripting, particularly through increased references to the series' past. Saward disliked the 'very heavy brief' given to Peter Grimwade for 'Planet of Fire' (1984), as he 'had to write out Turlough, introduce Peri [. . .] use the Master and [. . .] the Lanzarote location' (Howe and Walker, 1995: 155), while Robert Holmes's brief for 'The Two Doctors' included an overseas location, a multi-Doctor reunion and the Sontarans. Regardless of one's subjective opinion about Nathan-Turner's decisions, it is noteworthy that he was criticised for exercising his legitimate powers as producer. For instance, interviewed alongside Saward in *DWB*, fan Ian Levine attacked Nathan-Turner's casting and his choice of writers and directors, and was disappointed that Nathan-Turner decided on the Sixth Doctor's tasteless jacket 'against the advice of the costume designer *herself*!' Levine alleged that Nathan-Turner excluded writers and directors from the series' past so that his control (or agency) was 'untempered by anyone else' (Leigh, 1992: 19–20).

Nathan-Turner was being attacked for his support for new talent, which had been seen as one of the reasons for the success of season eighteen. One of the most celebrated examples is Lovett Bickford, whose contribution to 'The Leisure Hive' raises the final member of the creative team: the director. Helping to assert Nathan-Turner's signature of modernity, Bickford opens the story with a long pan across a deserted out-of-season Brighton beach, which eventually finds the Doctor asleep in a deck chair. Bidmead has argued that 'It was full of great meaning for Lovett [. . .] but I think at the expense of the rest of the episode' (Griffiths, 1997a: 9). This response seems surprising, given that it creates an atmosphere of regret and desolation in leisure, and – perhaps inadvertently – establishes the recurring theme of 'doing nothing', which becomes the Doctor's defence against entropy. Bickford brought what he described as his 'particularly idiosyncratic visual style' (Hearn, 1992: 40) to give a semantic weight to visuals which was almost unique for pre-1996 *Doctor Who*. This sequence ends with a highly unusual transition between Earth and Argolis, a zoom out from Earth, across space to Argolis, using a light as a metonym for a sun, before the camera seems (due to an inventive edit) to move through a wall.

Directors are also subject to the restrictions of genre which I have touched upon with regard to writers. For instance, there is a shot in the first part of 'Horror of Fang Rock' (1977) in which the Doctor and Leela talk at a table, during which the camera zooms in to a medium close-up in which the Doctor is foregrounded while Leela is adrift in the background asking questions (Figure 7).

This shot structure is determined by the patriarchal restrictions of the format, which is particularly striking given that this story was shot by one of the series' few women directors, Paddy Russell. As with writers, some directors could be labelled 'craftsmen' serving the format, others combine serving the format with personal touches (for Holmes and Hulke, read Douglas Camfield and David Maloney), while others exercise true individuality, including

Figure 7 Patriarchal shot composition in 'Horror of Fang Rock' (1977)

Waris Hussein, Michael Imison and Ken Grieve, whose direction of 'Destiny of the Daleks' (1979) featured inventive compositions and a pioneering use of Steadicam. In Nathan-Turner's first season, Paul Joyce can be considered alongside Bickford, employing a disjointed montage of tracking shots at the start of 'Warriors' Gate' which heralds one of the programme's most consistently inventive pieces of direction.

Doctor Who directors remain critically neglected, but this is true of television directors in general. When John R. Cook (1998: 4) argued that the creative 'hierarchy' resolved itself in favour of the writer, he added that writers were prioritised over directors, who were 'relegated to the secondary role of interpreter' of writers' ideas. A rare academic investigation into the impact of a television director upon a script occurred in another article entitled 'Who done it?', in which Joost Hunningher (1993) explores director Jon Amiel's influence over Dennis Potter's *The Singing Detective* (1986). This was a radical angle to take in television analysis, unlike in film analysis, in which it is the norm to discuss writers 'serving' directors. I have proposed readings of television direction in my book on Alan Clarke (Rolinson, 2005). Although Clarke benefited from being able to direct some plays entirely on film as a result of institutional support denied to *Doctor Who*, he also worked within the same restrictive structures which affected *Doctor Who*, and asserted a level of creative authority over and above that of *Doctor Who* directors. They too faced the stressful time restrictions of multi-camera studios (throughout the programme's history), 'piebald' productions which combined studio interiors with a small amount of location material shot on film (*Doctor Who*'s dominant form between its first filming in 1964 and its last in 1985), and video location material shot on Outside Broadcast. Location video featured experimentally in season twelve's 'Robot' and 'The Sontaran Experiment' – alongside its increasing use across television drama – but only became the norm from 1986 onwards for budgetary reasons.

Multi-camera studio has been criticised by many practitioners for its fraught atmosphere, which *Doctor Who* fans can now sample in behind-the-scenes DVD extras. Time restrictions compromised directors' ability to assert a personal signature in terms of composition and editing, as they had to mix between cameras recording simultaneously rather than composing and lighting each shot separately and editing them together. Just as Clarke was able to make distinctive work within this system, so Lovett Bickford recalled 'pushing the boundaries of a studio-based system that wasn't ready for it', using a time-consuming single-camera approach which the producer initially welcomed as an assertion of his own signature: 'John Nathan-Turner and I were striving to do something new and different' (Hearn, 1992: 39). Graeme Harper also brought a distinctive approach to 'The Caves of Androzani' (1984) and 'Revelation of the Daleks' (1985), with striking visual ideas, unusual compositions and editing strategies and a use of hand-held camera in the studio which reinforced the scripts' themes of paranoia and changing identities. Whether it is a coincidence that similar strategies are employed in 'Warriors' Gate', to which Harper contributed without a screen credit after Paul Joyce fell ill, is a subject fit for further research. Bickford, Joyce and Harper complicated the director's place within the 'creative power relations' of the programme, particularly since Bickford and Joyce claimed to have rewritten their respective scripts.

However, this hierarchy of relations is again resolved in favour of the producer because producers shape the 'house style' of series drama. Indeed, criticisms of the programme's direction in the mid-1980s were related to Nathan-Turner: while Bickford and Joyce's dynamism reflected his search for modernity in season eighteen, criticisms of Peter Moffatt's direction of 'The Two Doctors' (1985) were used to reinforce criticisms of the producer. Moffatt initially withholds the identity of an alien aggressor through an archetypal *Doctor Who* shot taken from the alien's point-of-view (Figure 8), but there is little dramatic impact in the moment at which the viewer finally discovers that the aggressors are Sontarans, because the first Sontaran is framed in a placid very long shot (Figure 9).

Criticisms of this shot constitute it metonymically as the producer's privileging of style over dramatic content, as its display of landscape maintains the languid, travelogue pace of the scenes shot on location in Spain. Eric Saward has argued that Nathan-Turner's use of overseas locations was not motivated by dramatic purpose; for instance, he asserted that video footage of a recce of Singapore locations for a proposed Auton story was shot at the last minute after Nathan-Turner had enjoyed 'a good time [. . .] at the BBC's expense' (Leigh, 1992: 19). Whether or not Saward's view is justified, the producer's accountability for failures of direction is noteworthy. Equally, the relatively gruesome stabbing of Oscar, which jars unpleasantly with the story's frivolous tone, reinforced criticisms of violence which Michael Grade, then Controller of BBC 1, used to defend his attempt to cancel the series.

Figure 8 How to introduce your monster in 'The Two Doctors' (1985)

Figure 9 How *not* to reveal your monster in 'The Two Doctors' (1985)

Nathan-Turner contested the idea that he imposed a 'house style' on directors. He argued that 'I am very keen that directors bring their own interpretation to it', noting that, unlike on *Rockliffe's Babies* (1987–8) and other series, on which directors 'are told the house style is this, and that is how you should shoot it', there were 'no house rules in *Doctor Who* that I have ever imposed, apart from "favour the Doctor", "shoot a cliffhanger in a certain way", and "start a first episode in a certain way"' (Nasse and Penswick, 1988: 6). However, some of his former collaborators have noted his influence on the series' pace and style. Bidmead told Peter Griffiths (1997b: 29) that 'He was still stuck with the language of the Sixties. If you cut from you and I sitting here [...] to the same situation two hours later, John would say that in order to understand that time had passed you had to put in a cut-away [...] if nothing happens, why are we messing about with it?' There is a jarring example of this during 'Dragonfire' (1987), when the viewer is removed from a dramatic situation to see a very brief scene of Mel and Ace playing 'I Spy'. However, the script editor of this story, Andrew Cartmel, had a different impression of Nathan-Turner's editing capabilities: 'probably half the battle in television is getting the script and shooting it [...] Editing is a whole separate creative process. John was fantastic at it. He'd say, "Cut all that, reverse the next two scenes, put that there", and it would work' (Bishop, 1995a: 7). This editing practice has a distinct impact upon the pace and style of *Doctor Who* in the late 1980s, as is proved by a comparison of the original version of 'The Curse of Fenric' (1989) with the special edition version released on DVD in 2003. The original features scenes which were halved and moved around, which enables it to pack in lots of information from an overlong script and results in a frenetic pace, with, arguably, a dissipation of moments of atmosphere and characterisation by these devices and 'topping and tailing' the beginning and ending of scenes for timing reasons.

However, other perceived failings of the Nathan-Turner era's visuals were rooted in technological restrictions. Andrew Cartmel attributed fans' accusations that Nathan-Turner's later stories were 'pantomime' in style to 'the bright, artificial lighting' of the studio, which 'gives a brashness and a lack of depth' to images (Bishop, 1995a: 7). The lack of location filming also harmed Cartmel's era. This meant that the show was shot entirely on videotape, which, with the exception of Alan Wareing's work, restricted atmosphere – Cartmel argued that 'Shooting on video really doesn't help' – and hampered the reputations of directors working on the programme at this time. Just as film critics neglected television directors until the convergence of film and television around *Film on Four*, so the 1996 TV Movie's status as a 35mm all-filmed production inspired detailed analyses of director Geoffrey Sax's substantial personal contribution (see Blum, 1996). It seems ironic that the trend in film and television now is towards digital video; the 'Russell T. Davies era' has been substantially shot in a studio, albeit on single camera and with increased time and money.

Davies's appointment has both resolved and further problematised this chapter's investigation into agency. As writer and executive producer, Davies has an unprecedented degree of control within the 'hierarchy' of 'creative power relations'. He has written most of the episodes and overseen the rest. Steve O'Brien and Nick Setchfield (2005: 38) described Davies as 'the most powerful' producer in the programme's history, to the extent that the 2005 series was 'almost auteur television'. As this implies, Davies's highly distinguished pre-*Who* career creates new fissures in the attribution of agency, because *Doctor Who* is simultaneously a continuing series with a 'generically coded format' and an artefact from a writer in the 'artist' tradition. The authorial discourses which circulated around John Nathan-Turner may make Davies wary of being identified in these terms, but one thing is beyond doubt: when it comes to the new *Doctor Who*, Russell T. Davies 'done it'.

References

Bignell, Jonathan and Andrew O'Day. 2004. *Terry Nation*. Manchester: Manchester University Press.

Binns, John. 1996. 'Still selling steak and chips'. *Matrix*, No. 52, pp. 6–10.

Bishop, David. 1995a. 'Dark thoughts'. *Doctor Who Magazine*, No. 224, pp. 4–8.

Bishop, David. 1995b. 'Dark times'. *Doctor Who Magazine*, No. 225, pp. 44–7.

Bishop, David. 1995c. 'Dark deeds'. *Doctor Who Magazine*, No. 226, pp. 40–3.

Blum, Jonathan. 1996. 'From script to screen'. *Matrix*, No. 53, pp. 11–13.

Cook, John R. 1998. *Dennis Potter: A Life on Screen*. Manchester: Manchester University Press.

Coward, Rosalind. 1987. 'Dennis Potter and the question of the television author'. *Critical Quarterly*, Vol. 29, No. 4, pp. 79–87.

Griffiths, Peter. 1997a. 'Coming of age'. *Doctor Who Magazine*, No. 257, pp. 6–12.

Griffiths, Peter. 1997b. 'Fifth man in'. *Doctor Who Magazine*, No. 258, pp. 26–31.

Hearn, Marcus. 1992. 'Directing *Who*'. *Doctor Who Magazine*, No. 191, pp. 39–42.

Howe, David J. and Stephen James Walker. 1995. *The Fifth Doctor Handbook*. London: Doctor Who Books.

Howe, David J. and Stephen James Walker. 1998. *Doctor Who: The Television Companion*. London: BBC.

Hunningher, Joost. 1993. '*The Singing Detective* (Dennis Potter): Who done it?'. In George W. Brandt (ed.). *British Television Drama in the 1980s*. Cambridge: Cambridge University Press, pp. 234–57.

Jones, Matthew. 1995. 'The Mastercraftsman'. *Doctor Who Magazine*, No. 233, p. 37.

Kelly, Richard (ed.). 1998. *Alan Clarke*. London: Faber and Faber.

Leigh, Gary. 1992. 'From the inside: Behind the scenes on *Doctor Who* 1980–85'. *DWB*, No. 106, pp. 18–21.

Macdonald, Philip. 1992a. 'Crossing the line'. *Doctor Who Magazine*, No. 192, pp. 42–5.

Macdonald, Philip. 1992b. 'Change and decay'. *Doctor Who Magazine*, No. 185, pp. 42–5.

Macdonald, Philip. 1994. 'However improbable'. *Doctor Who Magazine*, Winter Special, pp. 4–8.

Macdonald, Philip. 2004a. 'Games without frontiers'. *Doctor Who Magazine Special Edition: The Complete Fourth Doctor Volume Two*, pp. 4–9.

Macdonald, Philip. 2004b. 'The Leisure Hive'. *Doctor Who Magazine Special Edition: The Complete Fourth Doctor Volume Two*, p. 56.

Nasse, Saul and Neil Penswick. 1988. 'From Argolis to Windsor'. *Doctor Who Magazine*, No. 140, pp. 6–10.

O'Brien, Steve and Nick Setchfield. 2005. 'Russell spouts'. *SFX Collection: Doctor Who*, pp. 36–40.

Robertson, Theo. 1995. 'Malnutrition'. *Faze*, No. 2, pp. 31–2.

Rolinson, Dave. 2005. *Alan Clarke*. Manchester: Manchester University Press.

Rudden, Liam-Michael. 1992. 'Writing *Who*'. *Doctor Who Magazine*, No. 189, pp. 10–11.

Travers, Paul. 1988. 'Valley of Who'. *Doctor Who Magazine*, No. 139, pp. 9–12.

Tulloch, John. 1999. '"Whose stories you tell": Writing "Ken Loach"'. In Jonathan Bignell (ed.). *Writing and Cinema*. Harlow: Pearson, pp. 11–28.

Tulloch, John and Manuel Alvarado. 1983. *Doctor Who: The Unfolding Text*. London and Basingstoke: Macmillan.

Wigmore, Gareth. 1996. 'Mathematical excrement'. *Matrix*, No. 53, pp. 22–5.

Chapter 11

Between prosaic functionalism and sublime experimentation: *Doctor Who* and musical sound design

Kevin J. Donnelly

In 1973, the BBC reclassified the sound of the TARDIS landing as 'music', crediting Brian Hodgson with its composition (Howe et al., 1994: 54). Although this was not noted at the time, it was remarkable as a rare acknowledgement of how music and sound effects can be conceived in similar terms. One rarely noted aspect of *Doctor Who* is the startling incidental music and sound design for the serial, which had some of its roots in more experimental practices. Although the BBC thought of it as a Saturday teatime filler programme, *Doctor Who* was a symbolic herald of the corporation's modernity and the repository of the television medium's imagination more generally. Yet the sound and music had to carry out a lot of the 'imagining' for a programme beset with cheap sets, basic lighting and unconvincing special effects. As such, it had a more prominent role than music in many other areas of television, inspired by having to span the galaxy and all of time and space.

A number of *Doctor Who* episodes from the 1960s are 'missing', destroyed by the BBC. The fact that some avid fans recorded the sound on tape during their broadcast has meant that the BBC has been able to release 'soundtrack' versions of these missing episodes with some bridging narration to retain coherence. If one listens to these soundtracks, they often demonstrate not only how well music works for the series, but also how well the soundtracks work as objects within themselves, without the missing visuals. The enigmatic 'Watcher' in *Doctor Who Magazine* noted:

> *Doctor Who* was inextricably linked with the medium of sound even when it was a television programme. Television, as media scholars have long pointed out, evolved from the manifestly non-visual tradition of broadcast radio. Using the same production techniques and often the same production people, television effectively came into being as radio with added pictures. Although the boundaries are less clear today, in many ways television still has more in common with radio than with cinema. (The Watcher, 2000: 50)

This is borne out by the success of the soundtracks of 1960s *Doctor Who* episodes divorced from their accompanying images. One important reason is that the sound effects and incidental music are so evocative, and also that there is a distinct ambiguity about what constitutes 'music' and what might be heard as sound effects. *Doctor Who* regularly functioned as a showcase for sound/music technology, while science fiction more generally offers a unique scope for screen music. As the genre is all about possibilities, the music is all about musical potential. The music in *Doctor Who* has a massive range. It has to span the galaxy, to go way beyond music for the rest of television, as well as masking the deficiencies of the programme's production values. Although the music was written and recorded very quickly, tending towards the functional in relation to on-screen activity – it had a determined edge, derived from experimental music culture.

Relative histories (1963–89)

A musical history can cut across the 'consensual' history of *Doctor Who*, which in popular literature on the subject usually follows the succession of different Doctors (William Hartnell, Patrick Troughton, Jon Pertwee, Tom Baker, Peter Davison, Colin Baker, Sylvester McCoy, etc.), or even histories that follow the succession of producers or production and transmission seasons. With respect to the programme's sound effects, its 'special sound' was produced by the BBC Radiophonic Workshop, and more precisely by Brian Hodgson from 1963 to 1972, and then by Dick Mills, from 1972 to 1989. Cutting across all these divisions, we might divide *Doctor Who* (over its initial twenty-six-year run 1963–89) into four musical periods:

1. 1963–9, seasons one–five
2. 1969–80, half way though season six–season seventeen
3. 1980–4, seasons eighteen–twenty-two
4. 1986–9, seasons twenty-three–twenty-six

In its early years, *Doctor Who* used much in the way of avant garde *musique concrète*, startling sounds produced through the manipulation of recordings on magnetic tapes. It also showcased strange sounds produced by basic electronic devices (oscillators, ring modulators, filters), which were most apparent in Delia Derbyshire's arrangement of the *Doctor Who* title music. During the 1960s, the programme used music by a number of freelance composers, some of whom were respected in art music circles or had reputations for producing avant garde music. For example, Tristram Cary produced music for 'The Daleks' (1963–4) and 'Marco Polo' (1964), amongst others, while Humphrey Searle, who was a British pioneer in using Schoenberg's twelve-tone compositional method, scored 'The Myth Makers' (1965), although with a rather traditional score. Some of Cary's musical cues were reused in later stories (his avant garde sounds from 'The Daleks', for example, would resurface in 'The Rescue' [1965] and 'The Ark' [1966]), a standard practice in television music unlike its more opulent cousin in the cinema (Donnelly, 2002: 333–5). Similarly, during the 1960s *Doctor Who* used a great deal of stock or library music, which was cheap and had been recorded for use in general contexts rather than for a specific dramatic moment or specific programmes. However, while *Doctor Who* used library music by composers such as the French composer Roger Roger and Martin Slavin, whose *Space Adventures* was used as a theme for the Cybermen in 'The Tenth Planet' (1966), 'The Moonbase' (1967) and 'Tomb of the Cybermen' (1967), 'art music' was also utilised. Some music by respected British (but Spanish-born) avant garde composer Roberto Gerhard was used a number of times in different stories, as were sounds by the Baschet brothers (also known as *les structures sonores* or *les sculptures sonores*), derived from their sound sculptures.

This opening musical period runs from 1963 to 1969 (seasons one–five), and is marked by a tendency to use avant garde music in the popular context of television. This insertion of minority culture into mass culture makes the programme's sound profile most distinct from contiguous programmes. The fact that the music of avant garde art music composers was utilised makes *Doctor Who* remarkable in itself, providing a highly singular sound world through the use of extremely dissonant and unpopular music of the sort that rarely got heard at the time outside highbrow university music departments or occasional minority-interest concerts.

The longest stable period of *Doctor Who* music ran from 1969–80, from half-way through season six to season seventeen. During this time, *Doctor Who*'s music was written overwhelmingly by Dudley Simpson, who was responsible for scoring 310 episodes. The scores usually comprised a relatively small amount of music performed by a small ensemble of traditional musicians which was usually electronically 'enhanced' by the BBC Radiophonic Workshop to make it sound less conventional and more otherworldly. From 1963 to 1970, music had been composed blind rather than to the moving images. This changed in 1970, with the onset of the adoption of timecoding on video playback, which had been brought in from Germany (Jones and Leigh, 1994: 110). This development allowed precise composition and 'through-composed' music that matched the momentary dynamics of on-screen action. Yet over the years, due to the exigencies of rapid production, plenty of the music for *Doctor Who* was written without recourse to images. Among the most impressive of Dudley Simpson's scores were 'Pyramids of Mars' (1975) and 'Horror of Fang Rock' (1977), both of which had the sort of quality usually associated with expensive film scores, yet retained a strong sense of the alien and the unsettling through the Radiophonic Workshop's treatments and Simpson's fragmented music, which was based on short and thematically unconnected musical cells. His music was written to fit action and indeed was probably one of the best examples of precise underscore in television, despite on occasions including some fairly crass 'mickey mousing', where action was mimicked by the music. For example, towards the end of episode two of 'The Talons of Weng Chiang' (1977), the music simply doubles the screen activity as props are thrown down on the Doctor from the back of the stage. This tendency in Simpson's scores is more overt during his final years on the programme when *Doctor Who* was shifting from a suspense-based ethos toward a broader and more comedic tone. Simpson's scoring during seasons sixteen and seventeen reflects that – in effect, he was responding to the scripts' and productions' new emphasis.

Seasons eight and nine in 1971 and 1972 experimented by having Simpson's scores produced electronically, and at times other composers scored occasional stories, such as Malcolm Clarke, Geoffrey Burgon and Carey Blyton, but these served only as isolated hiatuses in Simpson's impressive tenure as the musician for *Doctor Who* throughout the decade. However, by season eleven he was being denied the customary aid from the Radiophonic Workshop and accompanied his small-ensemble pieces with a synthesiser he had bought himself (Cook and Herron, 2003: 29).

Producer John Nathan-Turner's wholesale redesign of *Doctor Who* in 1980 included a notable reorientation of the programme's music: Simpson was no longer required as composer, and instead the music was produced in tandem with the sound effects for the programme by members of the BBC Radiophonic Workshop. This approach began with season eighteen and carried on until season twenty-two in 1984. One significant effect was to integrate music and sound effects in the programme, almost all of which were produced electronically, giving *Doctor Who* an absolutely unique sound signature among television programmes. The integration of music and sound effects created a sense of holistic 'sound design', where the soundtrack was conceived as a unity rather than elements that can be mixed in a complementary and conventionally hierarchised manner. Employees of the Radiophonic Workshop who produced a regular run of scores included Peter Howell, Paddy Kingsland and Roger Limb. Of these scores, one of the most interesting was Roger Limb's music for the last outing of Peter Davison as the Doctor, 'The Caves of Androzani' (1984). This demonstrated an interest in the specificity of sounds, inaugurating with some high-pitched synthetic wails that sound electronic rather than attempting to sound like traditional instruments, while the story uses copious amounts of understated music for percussion alone. Limb's music is premised upon building atmosphere and follows a through-composed pattern, matching the development of momentary dynamics of the drama. Perhaps a more characteristic score was Peter Howell's for 'The Leisure Hive'

(1980), which marked itself as the clarion call of a new era not only through its achievement of striking sounds through the use of novel synthesisers such as the Yamaha CS80, but also through the use of a revamped title theme that replaced Delia Derbyshire's *musique concrète* sounds of the original with the seemingly more 'modern' sounds of integrated keyboard synthesisers.

After having music produced 'in house', *Doctor Who* then reverted to its earlier division of labour, where the Radiophonic Workshop created sound effects and a small roster of freelance composers made the music. This final period ran from 1986 to 1989, seasons twenty-three to twenty-six, and included music by Keff McCulloch, Dominic Glynn and Mark Ayres. All of the music was produced on electronic keyboards. McCulloch's music was largely pop-inspired, although it had more of the character of muzak (McCulloch had been a pop musician in Pickettywitch and the Climax Blues Band). It tended not to follow the dynamics of screen action and in stories such as 'Paradise Towers' (1987) habitually was controlled rather crudely by the sound editor turning its volume up and down. Dominic Glynn produced music that owed something to the developments in pop synthesiser music at the time, and has since gone on to produce synthesiser dance music. Mark Ayres, on the other hand, produced music that was more in keeping with the dominant traditions of music on *Doctor Who*, most notably Dudley Simpson's scores during the 1970s. At times, Ayres's music is vaguely reminiscent of a 'silent cinema piano' accompaniment, providing continuous development and following the dynamics of the on-screen action intricately, moment by moment (the most impressive music along these lines probably being Ayres's rich and varied score for 'The Greatest Show in the Galaxy' [1988–9]).

Such a division of *Doctor Who*'s run into four segments largely follows organisational lines. Yet there are other ways, other formations that might be used to divide up the programme's history over its initial twenty-six-year run on television. Types of sound, techniques and sonic hardware provide a very convincing set of divisions across this period. Despite the fact that traditional small musical ensembles were used from 1963 through to 1980, developments in musical technology feature strongly, arguably in a defining manner, in different periods of the series. The 1960s marks a primitive but innovative wielding of cutting-edge musical technology. The BBC Radiophonic Workshop was only able to produce effects using basic magnetic tape technology and rudimentary electronic devices, such as the ring modulator, which multiplied one signal by another. This was wielded effectively to create the distorted sound of the Dalek voices (and was later used to modify 'organic' scores such as Carey Blyton's for 'Death to the Daleks' [1974] and Geoffrey Burgon's for 'Terror of the Zygons' [1975]).

The early 1970s were characterised by the appearance of keyboard-operated modular synthesisers, most notably the BBC's massive prototype

EMS Synthi 100, which was nicknamed 'the Delaware' due to its housing in Delaware Road, Maida Vale, in London. This was showcased on season eight in 1971, where wholly synthesiser scores were first used in a systematic manner (electronic scores had appeared in season four using the Radiophonic Workshop's 'Multicolortone Organ'). The late 1970s saw the increasing proliferation of preset keyboard synthesisers. By the time that *Doctor Who*'s music was being produced solely by the BBC Radiophonic Workshop, a number of 'off-the-peg' keyboard synthesisers were being used, such as the Oberheim OBX, the Roland SY2 and the Yamaha CS80 (Ayres, 2002). These were much easier and quicker to programme. In the early to mid-1980s, 'samplers' became prominent. These were new digital synthesisers that recorded ('sampled') and then treated sounds rather then building them up through subtractive synthesis (the use of oscillators and filters, as in older generations of synthesiser). Also in the early 1980s, there were frequency modulation synthesisers, where one sine wave is modulated by another (as in the Yamaha DX7) and by the mid-1980s, wavetable synthesisers which could mix waveforms. Sampling synthesisers proliferated in the wake of the appearance of the Fairlight CMI in 1981. The music for *Doctor Who* in the later 1980s often used integrated preset digital keyboard synthesisers, such as Keff McCulloch's Emulator and Prophet 5, the former of which regularly made use of sampled orchestral stabs, sprinkled liberally throughout McCulloch's scores. It is not too difficult therefore to follow technological developments through the sort of sounds evident in *Doctor Who*. Technological determinism may be unfashionable, but it proves an attractive explanation for the programme's sonic development over time. It is certainly not controversial to suggest that hardware tends to set limitations and encourage certain procedures of construction.

Doctor Who provided a showcase for cutting-edge sound technology and musicians who were given scope to try things out that went far beyond the bounds of possibility for the vast majority of television. In this sense, the programme provided a more immediate window for musical technology than pop music or art music. The aim of its music was to express 'the otherworldly' and the principal way of achieving this was, and still is, through the use of the most recent sonic technology. These fresh, new sounds signify 'the future', or at least as near to the future as we can possibly get.

BBC Radiophonic Workshop

The BBC Radiophonic Workshop was founded in 1958 and disbanded in 1998, under John Birt's leadership of the corporation, after a few years of being run down. It produced all the sound effects (including voice effects) for the whole run of *Doctor Who* (1963–89) and produced music as well from

1980 until 1986, among its other duties. In addition to this, as I've already noted, the Workshop 'treated' Dudley Simpson's music, through adding and developing the sounds produced by an ensemble of conventional instruments. According to one of their number, Malcolm Clarke, 'We provide the basic scenery, the emotional climate, the temperature, the environment in which things are happening' (mb21, 2004).

There are two useful sources of information about the BBC Radiophonic Workshop. The first is the book by its one-time Head, Desmond Briscoe, and the second is the BBC 4 documentary *Alchemists of Sound*. The former supplies copious information about equipment and facts about the organisation, while the latter is more concerned with assessing the importance of the Radiophonic Workshop. While the documentary's brief is to be welcomed, care should be taken in such reappraisals not to overemphasise certain aspects. The documentary tends to focus on the Workshop as an avant garde entity connected to art music practice, and perhaps this historical revisionism reflects the BBC's desire to 'trade up' some of its more successful elements in an era of almost continuous questioning of the BBC's public-funded status. Nevertheless, and despite its mass media context, the BBC Radiophonic Workshop should be seen as the British manifestation of an international drive of experimentalism that embraced IRCAM in Paris (which included Pierre Boulez), Darmstadt in West Germany (including Karl-Heinz Stockhausen) and the Columbia-Princeton Electronic Music Center in the USA (including Vladimir Ussachevsky and Milton Babbitt). It is beyond doubt that the BBC Radiophonic Workshop took inspiration on the one hand from tape-based *musique concrète* inspired by French pioneer Pierre Schaeffer, and on the other from technological developments often tied to these experimental centres. Yet the BBC Radiophonic Workshop was very much an experiment within the mainstream. This makes it extraordinary not only by the standards of musical experimentation, but also in that it was a nearly unique insertion of the avant garde into a highly popular context. Indeed, *Doctor Who* includes striking examples of extreme and challenging music consumed as a mass medium.

In the sense of mainstream music, some of *Doctor Who*'s music was produced by distinct outsiders. A fine example is Workshop member Delia Derbyshire, officially one of the Workshop's 'studio managers', who had reached her position through a technical channel rather than specifically as a musician. Similarly, maverick experimentalist Tristram Cary, who was never a part of the Workshop, came to provide music for *Doctor Who* on the back of his experiments in radio and electronics probably more than his background in scoring a handful of films, including Ealing's *The Ladykillers* (1955). He went on to found the pioneering electronic music studio at the Royal College of Music in London, despite having a career that lacked the sort of institutional support enjoyed by most respected composers and music academics.

The sound effects of *Doctor Who* were always striking. These were credited as 'Special Sound' on screen and the series used sound in an iconic way far more than other television programmes. One could argue that sound 'starred' rather than simply being there to convince audiences of the veracity of screen representations. In addition to this, certain sounds were reused constantly and thus had more status than simply 'sound effects'. The relaunched 2005 series of *Doctor Who* has demonstrated great awareness and respect for these 'sonic stars', with returning effects including the TARDIS materialisation/dematerialisation, the Autons' handgun and the throbbing ambience created for the Dalek control room. So distinctive and foregrounded were *Doctor Who*'s sound effects that several recordings were available commercially as well as the programme's music. An LP called *Doctor Who Sound Effects* was released in 1978, and included sounds such as 'Dalek hatching Tanks on Skaro', 'Sutekh Time Tunnel' and 'Styre's Scouting Machine (Approach, Stop, Search, Depart)', among others. More recently, the BBC has released two CD recordings of many of these sound effects (re-released by Mute in 2005). Yet these were more than simply sounds, often functioning thematically or even emotionally – like music. For example, each episode of 'Fury from the Deep' (1968) began with a heartbeat-like sound created by Brian Hodgson, which had been developed from a multi-track recording of a heel squeaking on linoleum (and was also used to represent the Nestene consciousness in 'Spearhead from Space' [1970]) (Pixley, 1999: 18).

From season eighteen (1980–1), all the music in *Doctor Who* was produced electronically by the BBC Radiophonic Workshop. However, season eight (1971) was an experiment where all the musical scores were realised electronically by the Workshop after having been written by Dudley Simpson. This phase included the synthesised supernatural wind sound that dominates the first episode of 'The Daemons' (1971). Tristram Cary noted that he '[. . .] did quite a lot of the sound effects too' (Cary, 1994: 18), while Dudley Simpson commented on Cary's electronic music: 'you couldn't tell the difference between the sound he made and the sound they made for effects' (Jones and Leigh, 1994: 109).

The television work of the Radiophonic Workshop evolved from its origins in the manifestly non-visual tradition of radio rather than the dominant visual tradition of film. Yet, *Doctor Who*'s sound and music situation should be noted as 'sound design'; indeed, this innovation was the forerunner of the current 'sound design' wave in feature films, particularly the creative sound design of the 1990s. Rather than being premised upon noise-reduced multi-speaker set-ups, the Radiophonic Workshop's *Doctor Who* soundtrack in the early 1980s reflected an integrated and holistic approach. We might conceive of an

aural version of the dominant regime of television drama, that of 'naturalism',
where a minimal visual language attempts to erase any sense of style and
instead presents what an audience reads as a seamless window on the world
(Cooke, 2003: 64). Such audio naturalism would probably be characterised
by a strict divide of incidental music and diegetic sound effects, or at least a
strong demarcation between the two, but this was not the case on *Doctor Who*.

The space between functionalism and experimentation

While the BBC has been more than happy to emphasise its experimental
music credentials in relation to the Radiophonic Workshop (see the aforementioned BBC's 'Alchemists of Sound' documentary), it should never be
forgotten that that the musicians produced relatively cheap functional music.
This was underlined by the fact that cutting the programme's music budget
was an easy and common production economy. In season six, for example,
there were two stories that contained absolutely no music. From *Doctor Who*'s
inception, the Radiophonic Workshop took up some of the slack, as they were
not included as part of the programme's music expenditure. Consequently,
there was always something of a mix of sound effects and music. An example
of this is Brian Hodgson's piece called *Thal Wind*, which appeared in 'The
Daleks' (1963–4) as a supplement to Tristram Cary's music. Nominally at least,
this was a piece of ambient sound effect, although when heard contiguously
with Cary's austere avant garde music, it sounds more conventionally musical.
Later in the 1960s (as Louis Niebur discusses in detail in the following
chapter), Brian Hodgson's 'sound effects' increasingly included an aspect of
incidental music, in some cases (such as 'The Krotons' [1968–69]) with no
credit, while in others, Hodgson and the Radiophonic Workshop were given
a full credit ('The Wheel in Space' [1968]).

   Economy was, and still is, paramount in the vast majority of television
production. In the 1970s, *Doctor Who*, although having an original score for
each episode, had them performed mostly by small ensembles (usually of less
than ten musicians) and augmented by electronics from the BBC Radiophonic
Workshop (Jones and Leigh, 1994: 112). Dudley Simpson asserted that 'You
can't ask the costume department to use tissue paper. And you can't ask the
graphics department to use thin lines instead of thick ones [...] but you
can ask the composer to write for two players instead of four' (Cook and
Herron, 2003: 28). Simpson had to make as much variation in sound as
possible with a very limited palette, and regularly included an organ to give
more body to the sound, a brass instrument or two to boost the middle
register and percussion to add more colour (Cook and Herron, 2003: 28).
Yet music could still prove important, adding vitality and atmosphere where
it was sometimes sorely required. *Doctor Who* has often had a somewhat

undeserved reputation for a budget that fell short of the programme's imagination. Here the music became an essential area of support, compensating for cheap sets, effects, monsters and saturation lighting. As an essential part of this process, music was thus able to attempt more in the way of overt experimentation than might have been expected. It had to do what the other elements in the programme could not, to make locations convincing and imagine the unimaginable for *Doctor Who*.

In musical terms, *Doctor Who* produced some moments that should go down in television history as significant. Perhaps the first of note was during 'The Web Planet' (1965), where recordings of sound-music derived from the Baschet brothers' sound sculptures was used. These French artists (with collaborator Jacques Lasry) produced esoteric sounds that were at home in art galleries but had never been heard on primetime British television before. The same recordings were also used later on 'Galaxy Four' (1965). In fact, the Baschets had been approached in 1963 to provide *Doctor Who*'s theme music but had proved too expensive (Pixley, 2004: 14).

The close relation between individual composer/performer and the music can allow a certain scope. A most unique score for a television programme was composed and performed by Malcolm Clarke of the BBC Radiophonic Workshop for the *Doctor Who* story 'The Sea Devils' (1972). Clarke's music is startling in its range of obtrusive electronic timbres and relative melodic paucity. In fact, this programme manifests an interesting point in time when mainstream television (momentarily) embraced avant garde music. This electronic music was a featured aspect of the programme rather than simply being an unheard musical backdrop. The shocking new sounds, conjured from the BBC's brand new prototype EMS synthesiser, mixed music and sound effects, and presented uncomfortable sounds to a substantial early evening audience on Saturdays in a way not duplicated in Britain before or since. The score was a last-minute replacement, as another Radiophonic Workshop member, John Baker, was unable to write the score commissioned (Howe et al., 1994: 51). *The Television Companion*, an authoritative source on the serial, notes that:

> Clarke [...] came up with a score that can best be described as experimental. It is in effect a collection of atonal sounds that punctuate action, in some parts melodic but in others simply background noise (for example a low bubbling for the sequences set in the submarine). Opinions differ as to the merits of this approach, but one thing that is certain is that no-one who watched 'The Sea Devils' can possibly fail to miss what is arguably its most striking aspect. (Howe and Walker, 2003: 306)

The score had been commissioned from the BBC Radiophonic Workshop to save money, rather than hire Simpson and his musicians (Pixley, 1992: 29).

The malignant 'sea devils' of the story's title are accompanied by a theme derived from the *Dies Irae*, the medieval mass of the dead. This is potentially one of the few recognisable melodic aspects of Clarke's score that makes external reference. The complexity of this sort of television underscore allows for musical references and the opportunity for the music to signify on different levels: one for the viewer who is only a casual listener to the score and one for the more attentively listening viewer. What is immediately striking is how timbre – the qualities of the sounds themselves – is more important than melody, harmony or rhythm. What is also apparent is that there is difficulty in differentiating what might be non-diegetic music from what appears to be diegetic sound effect. Music and sound form is derived largely from technological capabilities. Malcolm Clarke was literally 'let loose' on the brand-new prototype synthesiser, 'the Delaware', which Radiophonic Workshop Head Desmond Briscoe noted was 'probably the most advanced synthesiser in the world' (Briscoe and Curtis-Bramwell, 1983: 129).

There are isolated precedents to *Doctor Who*'s sound on film, most notably Louis and Bebe Barron's 'electronic tonalities' for *Forbidden Planet* (1956), and also Jerry Goldsmith's electronic music for the Africa section of *The Illustrated Man* (1969). But *Doctor Who*'s boldness in terms of incidental music's sound was unique to television during the 1960s and early 1970s. Science fiction shows such as *The Twilight Zone* (1959–65), *The Outer Limits* (1963–5), *Star Trek* (1966–9) and *Raumpatrouille* (1966) all used much more traditional music.

The most common process for creating television underscores is through the use of smaller ensembles, solo instruments and composers recording their own music on electronic keyboards – good examples being *Doctor Who* and *The X-Files* (1993–2002). There is thus a tendency towards sparer textures than in film music. This is owing first to the cost restrictions on television production in relation to mainstream film production, and secondly, to television's more intimate character.

One year after 'The Sea Devils', Pink Floyd released their best-selling album *Dark Side of the Moon* (1973). This not only seemed to evince a form of 'sound design', mixing songs and sound effects, but also showcased another EMS synthesiser, the VCS3. It is interesting to note that both the BBC and Pink Floyd endorsed the use of synthesisers from a British company, Peter Zinovieff's EMS, rather than use the more internationally prominent Moog synthesiser. EMS's instruments potentially had more capabilities through facilities for careful calibration, although this required quite leisurely programming time and EMS synthesisers failed in the long run to match the popularity of more immediate Moogs. A sense of modernity is often tied to technology, and this is truer for music than for many other areas of culture.

Technology offers the promise of the 'future', with its developments always incomplete and tied to a discourse of progress, no matter how covertly, but perhaps most obviously through the cycle of (hardware) redundancy. As I pointed out earlier, new, unfamiliar sounds appear to be forward looking, modern through being 'futuristic', and *Doctor Who* made much of its singular sound profile. This mixture of music and sound effects amounted to a musically inspired sound design. In the 1980s, it was even the beneficiary of early broadcasts in NICAM stereo, allowing for a spatialisation of sound. Interestingly, in the late 1970s the Musicians' Union in the UK waged a campaign against the use of synthesisers, which it characterised as doing musicians out of a job. On the one hand, this appealed to the possibility of synthesisers to replicate the sounds of other instruments, but on the other it played to the suggestion that such things were 'devices' manipulated by 'operators' rather than instruments used to make music as such. The Radiophonic Workshop, although employing a number of musicians, had its origin in studio technology and management rather than the musical areas of the BBC.

Conclusion

On rare occasions, you can see what *Doctor Who* would have been like with more conventional music. An isolated example is in the episodes scored by Carey Blyton, most notably in 'Death to the Daleks' (1974), where the Dalek appearances are converted into a comic turn by jocular saxophone music. In fact, a whole dimension of the programme is lost through its lack of musical 'alienness', despite some attempts to treat Blyton's music with minimal electronics. *Doctor Who* more characteristically represented the future or the otherworldly through the use of cutting-edge sound technology and techniques that by their rarity would sound unfamiliar to the vast majority of the audience.

The music for *Doctor Who* retains a certain cultural prominence. While it may not be the subject of detailed analyses in university music departments, it has a place in popular history through an increased commercial availability in recent years. Many of the BBC's DVD releases (for the 1980s programmes) have isolated scores, allowing the music to be listened to along with the images but without the hindrance of dialogue or sound effects. This experience underlines how far sound effects and music interacted. In its pioneering years, *Doctor Who* married art music experimentation and the exigencies of cheap television drama. Even when the music had a less than experimental character, it used the sort of synthetic sounds that were only appearing furtively in the margins in television at the time. Significantly, *Doctor Who* blurred the distinction between music and sound effects, reconceiving screen sound as a unity that included both 'musical' sound effects and music that made some sound effects. In this way, it prefigured the current process of sound design in feature films. This was partially the result of *Doctor Who* providing a space that allowed the extremes of experimental music, previously only open to highbrow musical elites, into the homes of Britain's wider populace. To popular ears, this was not necessarily recognisable as music but was distinctly recognisable (even to the Queen, as her response when introduced to Radiophonic Workshop staff at the Centenary Conversazione of the Institution of Electrical Engineers at the Royal Festival Hall indicated [Tulloch and Alvarado, 1983: 13]) as *Doctor Who*.

References

Ayres, Mark. 2002. Sleeve notes to *Doctor Who at the BBC Radiophonic Workshop Volume 4: Meglos and Full Circle*. Music by Peter Howell and Paddy Kingsland. BBC WMSF6053-2.

Briscoe, Desmond and Roy Curtis-Bramwell. 1983. *The BBC Radiophonic Workshop – The First 25 Years*. London: BBC.

Cary, Tristram. [March 1988] 1994. 'The musicians: Tristram Cary'. In Gary Leigh (ed.) *The DWB Interview File: The Best of the First 100 Issues, no. 2*. Brighton: DreamWatch.

Cook, Benjamin and Tom Herron. 2003. 'Bohemian Rhapsodies' [interview with Dudley Simpson]. *Doctor Who Magazine*, No. 330, pp. 26–30.

Cooke, Lez. 2003. *British Television Drama: A History*. London: BFI.

Donnelly, K.J. 2002. 'Tracking British television: pop music as stock soundtrack to the small Screen'. *Popular Music*, Vol. 21, No. 3, pp. 331–43.

Jones, Dallas and Gary Leigh. 1994. 'The musicians: Dudley Simpson' [interview]. In Gary Leigh (ed.) *The DWB Interview File: The Best of the First 100 Issues, no. 2*. Brighton: DreamWatch.

Howe, David J., Mark Stammers and Stephen James Walker. 1994. *Doctor Who: The Seventies*. London: Virgin.

Howe, David J. and Stephen James Walker. 2003. *The Television Companion: The Unofficial and Unauthorised Guide to Doctor Who*. Tolworth, Surrey: Telos.

mb21. 'BBC Radiophonic Workshop'. www.mb21.co.uk/ether.net/radiophonics/quotes.shtml (accessed May 2004).

Pixley, Andrew. 1992. 'Archive feature: Series LLL, The Sea Devils'. *Doctor Who Magazine*, No. 192, pp. 23–30.

Pixley, Andrew. 1999. 'The DWM Archive: Fury From the Deep'. *Doctor Who Magazine*, No. 277, pp. 14–22.

Pixley, Andrew. 2004. 'Do you want to know a secret?' *Doctor Who Magazine Special Edition: The Complete First Doctor*, pp. 11–21.

Tulloch, John and Manuel Alvarado. 1983. *Doctor Who: The Unfolding Text*. London and Basingstoke: Macmillan.

Watcher, The. 2000. 'It's the end, but . . .'. *Doctor Who Magazine*, No. 292, p. 50.

Discography (CD unless noted)

Doctor Who at the BBC Radiophonic Workshop, Volume 1: The Early Years, 1963–69. BBC WMSF6023-2, 2000.

Doctor Who at the BBC Radiophonic Workshop, Volume 2: New Beginnings, 1970–1980. BBCWMSF6024-2, 2000.

Doctor Who at the BBC Radiophonic Workshop, Volume 3: The Leisure Hive (music by Peter Howell). BBC WMSF6052-2, 2002.

Doctor Who at the BBC Radiophonic Workshop, Volume 4: Meglos and Full Circle (music by Peter Howell and Paddy Kingsland). BBC WMSF6053-2, 2002.

Doctor Who – The Curse of Fenric (music by Mark Ayres). Silva Screen FILMCD087, 1991.

Doctor Who – Devils' Planets: The Music of Tristram Cary. BBC WMSF6072-2, 2003.

Doctor Who – Earthshock: Classic Music from the BBC Radiophonic Workshop, Volume 1. Silva Screen 1FILMCD710, 1992 (re-release of *Doctor Who – The Music* (1983) LP).

Doctor Who – The Five Doctors: Classic Music from the BBC Radiophonic Workshop, Volume 2. Silva Screen FILMCD709, 1992 (re-release of LP from 1985).

Doctor Who – Ghost Light (music by Mark Ayres). Silva Screen FILMCD133, 1993.

Doctor Who – The Greatest Show in the Galaxy (music by Mark Ayres). Silva Screen FILMCD114, 1992.

Doctor Who – Music from the Tenth Planet. Ochre OCH050, 2000.

Doctor Who – Pyramids of Mars: Classic Music from the Tom Baker Era (music by Dudley Simpson, realised by Heathcliff Blair). Silva Screen FILMCD134, 1993.

Doctor Who: Terror of the Zygons/The Seeds of Doom (music by Geoffrey Burgon). BBC WMSF6020-2, 2000.

Doctor Who Sound Effects, no. 19, BBC Radiophonic Workshop. BBC Records REC 316, 1979.

Evolution: Music from Doctor Who (music by Keff McCulloch). Prestige, 1997 (re-release of LP *The Doctor Who 25th Anniversary Album* [1988]).

Music from The Tomb of the Cybermen. Via Satellite V-SAT ASTRA 3967, 1997.

Out of this World: Atmospheric Sounds and Effects from the BBC Radiophonic Workshop. BBC, REC225, 1976 (LP).

Sherlock Holmes meets Doctor Who – Music for Brass and Saxophone by Carey Blyton. Upbeat Classics URCD148, 1999.

Space Adventures: Music from Doctor Who 1963–1971. Julian Knott JPD2CD, 1998 (re-release of cassette, Doctor Who Appreciation Society; 1987).

The Worlds of Doctor Who. Silva Screen FILMCD715, 1994.

Chapter 12

The music of machines: 'special sound' as music in *Doctor Who*

Louis Niebur

'Doctor, what is it?'
'It sounds like electronic machinery.
It sounds like a computer.
But the pitch is all wrong!'
     ('The Ice Warriors', episode one, 1968)

What do alien machines sound like? Perhaps a more interesting question could be, what do alien *planets* sound like? In the latter half of the 1960s, the *Doctor Who* crew explored these questions in a fashion unlike any other science fiction production before or since. Due to exigencies almost entirely outside the production team's control, including declining ratings and smaller budgets, each individual serial's director was responsible for finding a way of making a new, 'more serious' *Doctor Who* on less money than his predecessor. Often, one of the most cost-cutting contingencies for individual episodes was the sacrifice of an original musical score. Directors for these episodes instead assembled music tracks from the BBC's stock music library, a collection of recordings composed generically to fit into a variety of situations.

To their credit, directors often fashioned soundtracks rivalling many of the best original scores, maintaining a continuity with the programme's 'house' sound; a blend of original and electronic instruments, or traditional instruments treated electronically to create an 'otherworldly' effect. Often these stock compilations (such as those for 'The Web of Fear' [1968] and 'The Tomb of the Cybermen' [1967]) benefited from much larger musical forces than those available to the weekly original composer. But there can be no denying the feeling that something is missing from these 'scores'.

The constant contribution of serious contemporary musicians of the calibre of Stanley Myers, Tristram Cary, Norman Kay and Humphrey Searle imbued *Doctor Who* with an aura of musical contemporaneity that no amount of anonymous stock music ever could. And, prestige aside, the composition of a specially written score offered the possibility of providing the audience with a much more precise 'commentary' on the action, with the composer's music acting as a continuous observer and respondent. This aspect of the programme was not lost, however, during these years, as another sonic element always featured prominently; that of 'Special Sound', provided by Radiophonic Workshop composer Brian Hodgson. In a science fiction series like *Doctor Who*, this indispensable aspect of each episode provided each alien weapon, monster and machine with a distinctive sound unique to that world. But during these years in particular, Hodgson was also called upon to provide a less clearly defined service, that of creating a more 'musical' backdrop for each episode. For episodes that utilised stock scores, and even those that had no score at all, Hodgson's 'special sound' continuously functioned *as music*, and as a result generated suspenseful, truly alienating soundworlds, of a kind previously unheard on television. These scores create a greater feeling of unease and suspense than more traditional scores could ever hope to achieve; Hodgson's music lacks the traditional markers of tonality, instead wrapping listeners in a cocoon of alien sounds and atmospheres.

This chapter examines two stories from 1968, and explores the way Hodgson's contribution complicates the boundaries between 'sound effect' and 'music'. Hodgson joined the BBC as a studio manager in the Drama Department, where he worked on numerous plays. After two years in Drama, he was inspired by a visit to the Radiophonic Workshop, and requested a three-month attachment. He ended up staying, excluding a brief time away, nearly twenty-five years, becoming Senior Studio Manager in 1970. Hodgson was not trained as a musician, but had an extensive practical knowledge of electronic music and electronic sound creation, working in the theatre with avant garde composers such as Marc Wilkinson. Rather than creating extended musical works based in tonality, Hodgson's *forté* was finding and assembling the right noises: component sonic elements that combined to create unique sound collections for a work.

The institutional separation in the BBC between 'special sound' and 'music' is too broad a topic to enter into here, but existed as a very real schism which served, on the one hand, to distance the work of the Radiophonic Workshop from other contemporary electronic and traditional musicians, but also shielded Workshop composers from prejudices from within the often myopic musical establishment of Britain. This division, however, obscures the very real arbitrariness and flexibility of the definitions of 'sound effect' and 'music'. It is true that Hodgson's work on *Doctor Who* fulfils the original mandate laid down in 1958 for the role of the Radiophonic Workshop to provide 'an additional "dimension" for radio and television productions [by] provid[ing] an aid to productions which neither music nor conventional sound effects can give' (BBC WAC R53/483/1, 22 May 1958). It would be shortsighted, however, to think that this 'additional dimension', in functioning between the borders of music and sound effect, does not exist in reality as a *blending* of the two. Hodgson's scores are so effective precisely because our minds are unable to distinguish the role of the sounds we hear. They often function as traditional non-diegetic film music; creating a feeling of unease, suspense and shock, and reflecting the emotions of the characters on screen. This function precisely articulates the goals of the Workshop in official documentation, 'to produce sounds which convey to the listeners' imagination the *mood* or *emotional idea* behind the author's theme of his radio or television drama' (Brooker, 1963: 5). But they also fulfil the role of diegetic sound effects, realising the sounds of the future through the technology of the future.

Although, according to composer Delia Derbyshire at the Workshop, 'The BBC made it quite clear that they didn't employ composers and we weren't supposed to be doing music' (Hutton, 2000: 3), the change towards contributing more 'musical' soundtracks to commissions was noted in an internal document from 1963, probably written by Desmond Briscoe, the first Studio Manager of the Workshop. Briscoe explains (most likely in an attempt to encourage more commissions) how much more comfortable the Workshop composers are with purely musical projects:

> It would seem that the work which the unit is called upon to create has steadily become more sophisticated, more precisely designed and shaped and above all more musical in nature, whether the source of this musical sound be electronic (in this respect we have increased our equipment, having twenty-two tone generators with two associated keying units, as compared with two generators when most of our work was special effects) or the sound of musical instruments played either by members of the unit or by professional musicians on contract for the particular programme. (BBC WAC R97/9/1, May 1963)

Several earlier *Doctor Who* composers employed this evocation of the 'ineffable', in particular the electronic scores of Tristram Cary. In his music for 'The Daleks' (1963–4), Cary tended towards abstract, tune-free soundscapes as a way of representing the threat of the robot alien monsters. Here, the composer wasn't going for a musical mickey mousing of the visual events, but a more generalised evocation of menace. One advantage of this technique was its flexibility, as Cary noted: 'It is much easier to time music that isn't melody based. If you have music that just conveys the alienness of the situation, you can shorten or extend the music quite easily, where as in melodic 8-bar structure that isn't nearly as easy. I tend to use tape loops that can be adjusted in length' (Cary, 1998). The difference between Cary's practice and the regular employment of stock music of a similar character was that Cary's sonic creations emerged out of the context of the story and situation, indelibly linking themselves to their time and location. For example, in much the same way as Dudley Simpson's later melodic 'Master' leitmotiv became indelibly linked to his character, Cary's more ethereal sonic representations of the Dalek city and the Dalek headquarters in 'The Daleks' emerged for future Dalek stories as *the* sound of the Daleks – in effect, their theme.

The mid-1960s were an important period for the BBC's Radiophonic Workshop. They had seen a change in production from abstract sound effects intended for radio drama to more literally 'musical', more 'tuneful' productions. In addition, the standard methods for producing the music itself were changing as synthesiser technology became more readily available. In particular, the development of the EMS VCS3 synthesiser (a smaller version of the more famous enormous Delaware Synthesiser that featured so prominently in *Doctor Who*'s music throughout the 1970s) meant that musical noises or sound effects that had once been created by assembling bits of recorded natural (or 'concrete') sounds could be manufactured more easily by purely electronic means. The shift towards pitched, electronically generated sounds in the generation of both incidental music and 'special sound' makes the interpretation of the scores created under their influence easier to understand using the basic rules of film music theory as it has evolved in the last twenty years.

If one of the basic goals of film music seeks to represent the internal thoughts and feelings of the characters and their struggles in the onscreen drama, then another use could certainly be a more symbolic representation, one step removed from the direct expression of emotion – not the more common use of musical semantics as shorthand for dramatic parallelism, but rather the taking advantage of the effectiveness of this shorthand to instantly convey *genre* conventions. For example, it is difficult to know whether or not an audience responds to tremolo strings with a feeling of suspense because tremolo strings naturally evoke this feeling, or because audiences have learned to expect, through generations of experience with melodramatic conventions, that such an effect *tells* them to feel suspense. Film music holds, by its manipulation of generic signs, the ability to generate the emotion itself, evincing from its listeners the feelings required to place the film, radio play or television show into a specific intended category. The signs, as complex as they are, present film music scholars with a problem, as Caryl Flinn notes, in 'how to talk concretely and specifically about the effects generated by a signifying system that is so abstract' (Flinn, 1992: 7).

This kind of detachment includes by extrapolation any musical representation of genre, mood or tone, as a stereotype, such as 'sentimental' (strings), 'heroic' (diatonic brass) and, of course, 'frightening' (dissonance or electronics). The establishment of these characteristics' symbolic meanings often dates far back into musical history. But some of these meanings date only to the creation of the sound-producing machines themselves, and these 'meanings' are sometimes more subtle than are given credit. Creating commentary through symbolic sound bites is one of film music's most basic and powerful tricks. Understanding a musical commentary forged by the sound design of imaginary technology is not quite as straightforward, but by expanding sound theorist Michel Chion's concept of the *acousmêtre* to these sounds a more nuanced reading appears.

When a character in a film or television programme picks up a violin and begins to play on screen, we the audience members understand both what the sound is and where it is coming from. We see the source of the sound and recognise the sound itself as belonging to that object. There is synchronisation between the image and the soundtrack. Michel Chion has labelled this an example of synchresis, a 'sound with both a visual and auditory component' (Chion, 1994: 63). Synchresis does not rely on an absolutely literal representation of a sound; rather, the combination of synthesis and synchronisation make the listener believe an image and sound belong together. Again, the sound and image don't necessarily have to be exact analogues: Chion uses the example of an axe chopping a log at the precise moment the visuals show a baseball player hitting the ball as an example of 'the forging of an immediate and necessary relationship between something one sees and something one hears at the same time' (Chion, 1994: 224). What happens if the violinist walks off camera, out of the frame, with the violin before beginning to play? How does the audience know the sound is meant to be diegetic – sound that both the characters in a film and the audience can hear – or non-diegetic – sound only the audience is meant to hear, like a film score? Why should an audience believe in a sound emerging from a source technically invisible to them? This type of sound, one heard without an accompanying visual analogue, Chion has labelled *acousmatic*, and the absent object an *acousmêtre*. The *acousmêtre* exists as a spectral phenomenon, evoking an inherently mysterious unknowableness. The *acousmêtre* functions as a staple of the horror genre, as, for example, the all-knowing, all-seeing killer's voice on the telephone; or as a voice echoing out in a dark seemingly empty theatre, calling to his frightened victim who frantically looks around in search of the invisible voice; or the humanoid robot, with the voice emerging from a motionless metal face.

Science fiction film and television such as *Doctor Who* presents a different kind of problem, but one for which Chion's concept of acousmatic sound serves as a launching point. When, in science fiction, the audience sees a piece of noisy 'advanced technology', it assumes that the artificial noise emerges from the piece of fictional machinery. While certainly a kind of synchresis, this noise is also a more specific kind of acousmatic sound, since the audience has no idea *what* kind of sound that particular piece of equipment should make, and has no prior characteristic sound associated with it.

This problem is different again from the *acousmêtre* of the robot in science fiction, who embodies mystery, wonder and fear through the presence of a recognisable human voice without the image of a human face. In the case of a ray gun or space ship, the sounds are largely part of the imaginary – combining as they do expectation of traditional sounds associated with the generic 'type' of equipment, and an ignorance of the specific object – and therefore impossible to truly understand in the sonic literalness of their representation. Chion's terms as they stand do not account for this eventuality and a more useful way of discussing fabricated sounds, sounds that exist as representations of fictional technology, should acknowledge their dual nature, both synchretic and acousmatic, here 'synchretic acousmatic'. While Chion clearly intended for synchretic sound to refer exclusively to an instantaneous coincidence of sound and image (as in his example of the chopping axe) rather than a continuously occurring sound, Hodgson's continuous 'atmospheric' tape loop compositions, embodying alien locations and technology, obviously function as diegetic real-time sounds, a kind of long-term simultaneity that I believe still validates the use of Chion's terminology.

'The Dominators'

'The Dominators' (1968) presents a clear example of this dual function. The director, Morris Barry, decided not to commission a traditional score for this adventure, instead relying exclusively on Brian Hodgson's 'special sound'. From the beginning of the first episode, Hodgson cleverly sets up a (quite musical) distinction between the simple 'unknowable' alienness of the Dulcians and the 'dangerous' alienness of the Dominators. Over the initial image of the invading ships of the Dominators, Hodgson inserts a standard electronic sound effect evoking 'flying saucers', a high, non-pitched whirring. On top of this he also includes a pitched 'note', a high D-flat, produced electronically. For a second or two, this is all that is heard; the D-flat ambiguously floating above the whirring against the image of a dozen or so ships flying in formation. The pitched note could be interpreted as either a diegetic aspect of the ship's engines, or a more abstract non-diegetic *musical* drone – an ambiguity that is resolved when, only a few seconds later, a new pitched note, a B-flat, harmonises with the D-flat, producing the interval of a minor third. Although, as mentioned above, music's apparent similarity to language encourages a tendency to 'read' its intervals and harmonies in a dangerously literal way, it cannot be denied that the traditional semantics of tonality and harmony provide opportunities for emotional expression with which simple sound effects can't compete. The minor third interval has, since at least the fifteenth century, been associated with sadness, fear and the uncanny. Musical semantician Deryck Cooke describes how the minor third 'has a "depressed" sound, and the fact that it does not form part of the basic harmonic series makes it an "unnatural depression" of the "naturally happy" state of things' (Cooke, 1959: 57). Immediately the audience is musically informed that the ships must be regarded with suspicion, an impression further encouraged by the inclusion of a final pitched note, an F, completing the minor triad.

The non-pitched diegetic sound of the ship's landing sweeps away the pitched music, and with the arrival of the Dominators on the planet Dulkis (which resembles a chalk quarry) comes a new sound: the 'music' of Dulkis itself. The planet seemingly hums. Over the sounds of Dulkis, another pitched noise, an E-flat, signals the door-opening mechanism of the Dominator's ship. This (diegetic) E-flat is 'resolved' by the following (non-diegetic) abrasive D sting that accompanies the entrance of the first Dominator from the ship. This process is repeated as the second Dominator emerges. The ship provides the E-flat, and the 'music' provides its cadential resolution with the appearance of the Dominator on a harsh D (Hodgson providing both).

At this point in the story, the planet Dulkis and its 'music', the continuous hum, contain a feeling of menace, associated as they are with the Dominators and the earlier minor mode signifier attached to them. But more than this, the noise of Dulkis provokes certain questions, encouraging a feeling of unease. Where is the hum coming from? It must emerge from the planet somehow, but where and why? Through this perfect synchretic acousmatic sound, the planet both requires a particular practical reading (the residents of Dulkis must be aware of it) and musically inclines the audience towards a feeling of suspense. A possible 'why' could be that the story centres on a part of the planet known as 'The Island of Death' due to its supposed contamination by radiation. The sound/music perhaps represents, in the manner of a Geiger counter, the presence of radiation and the threat it poses. This reading suffers logistically with the realisation that the contamination has been removed by the Dominators, cancelling both the reason for the sound and its suspenseful quality. The nature of the sound – warm, vaguely inviting and comforting, in fact not unlike the sound of the TARDIS interior – contains no abrasive or harsh elements, such as the pitched stings used at the Dominator's entrance. And, moments later, the Doctor and his companions arrive while Dulkis's music plays on, resolving in the minds of listeners that the music primarily serves to 'alienate' the surroundings, to differentiate the quarry of Dulkis from Earthbound quarries, or indeed, other *Doctor Who* quarries. If *Doctor Who*'s always diegetic electronic sound effects are symbolic representations of how something imaginary is supposed to sound (both futuristic and 'the unknown', synchretic acousmatic or acousmatic) then non-diegetic electronic music can be a symbolic internalisation and aural expression of both emotion and the 'aura of the programme'. In a perfect example of a synchretic *acousmêtre*, the radiophonic background captures the extreme enigma of the situation, i.e. there is no discernible *reason* for the sound. Although we see the planet Dulkis, its music emerges from nowhere, and seems to represent no material object or technology. There is a material analogue to the sound in the physical presence of the planet's surface, and although always diegetic, the effect of hearing these sounds on the listener corresponds to the effect of hearing a piece of contemporary music for the first time: the sounds are purely 'sound', without associative quality, and the listener struggles for comprehension, lost in a sea of unfamiliar sonic signs, listening for melodies, rhythms, anything that helps impose a formal design. The disorienting sensation, mirroring the character's initial disorientation on the screen, offers both a suspense similar to and a timbre different from a more traditional score. Perhaps more importantly, it also serves as a reminder to the audience of the genre they are watching; electronic sounds encourage a 'science fiction' reading of the programme, fulfilling and rewarding the viewer's expectation and generic knowledge.

With the entrance of the Dominator's machine servants, the Quarks, Hodgson's diegetic sound effects provide the additional menace needed to forge the Dominators as the villains against whom the peaceful Dulcians struggle. Clearly the Dominators need a 'sound' of their own after the pacifist nature of Dulkis and its citizens deprives the planet's music of menace, and Hodgson provides it at the beginning of episode two. For the first time, we see and hear the inside of their invasion ship, and it produces a much richer sound than the mellow alien ambience of Dulkis. Here, the audible traces of technology are heard. High-pitched rhythmic electronic pulses (recognisable as 'the sound of technology'), rapidly repeating, provide the background against which more abstract atmospheric tape music swirls. Again, the mechanical, computerised nature of the Dominators, foregrounded by the almost familiar sound of machinelike pitched electronic music, is distanced, made dangerous, by the synchretic acousmatic vagueness of the thicker background texture. And the contrast between the now benign ambience of Dulkis's Island of Death and the actively mechanical, functioning *acousmêtre* of the spaceship's interior creates the audible threat the Dominators pose to the peaceful people of Dulkis.

Hodgson had explored the use of ambient musical diegetic sound textures eighteen months earlier in his contribution to the second series of *Out of the Unknown*, 'The Machine Stops' (1967). E.M. Forster's sole science fiction story concerns the attempt by a young man and his mother to escape dependence on the machines that rule life in the enclosed cities of the future. The sound of the machines infiltrates everything in this underground world, a relentless, mechanical pulsation that is seductive and trance-inducing as well as oppressive and claustrophobic. The surface of the Earth has supposedly been rendered unliveable due to radiation poisoning, but when our protagonist finally makes it to the surface, he not only finds this to be untrue, but that the Earth is a beautiful, flourishing place. Musically, however, the surface screams with noise – ambient textures obviously agonising to the protagonist, as his ears bleed. This synchretic acousmatic sound effect reflects the degree of unfamiliarity our hero has with 'natural' sound: noises which to us would pass by unrecognised, the ordinary sounds of the world. Rather than hearing a literal interpretation of the sonic background, the audience is presented with an internal perspective; the perspective of one whose only aural perception of reality has been carefully filtered to eliminate unnecessary sound.

'The Wheel in Space'

'The Wheel in Space' (1968), concluding only three months prior to 'The Dominators', also contains 'special sound' that ventures into the domain of music, although with 'The Wheel in Space' Hodgson composes much more obviously musical material. He appears to deliberately differentiate noises meant to be understood as music from those intended to be heard as sound effect. This makes the moments of boundary-blurring all the more shocking.

The dialogue-free opening of the surviving episode three, for example, combines complex sound effects with simple traditional diatonic harmony to create a mysterious, sinister atmosphere. The episode begins with a traditional dominant–tonic progression from a G-sharp down a fifth to C-sharp. Hodgson makes it 'radiophonic', however, by producing the sound electronically and giving it an otherworldly echo. This echo reflects the 'outer space' nature of the shot it accompanies, recreating like a sound effect the conventional emptiness of space, and yet musically functioning to reinforce the same effect. The open fifth, C-sharp to G-sharp in this case, without an internal third, has traditionally signified 'lack' or 'emptiness'. This is a purely musical use of sound – and possibly a reference to the famous rising fifth and octave in the opening of Richard Strauss's *Also sprach Zarathustra*, which was making waves in theatres during the broadcast of 'The Wheel in Space'. It also arguably signifies the isolation of space and mankind in a vast universe. The reverberant, cavernous nature of the sound fades against the next shot, a timer clock of sorts which replaces this electronic sound effect with a new pitch, somewhere between an F-sharp and G. This between-the-keys note, impossible to achieve on a traditionally tuned keyboard, evokes both the artificial nature of the sound and its new, non-musical context. It is now placed firmly in the diegesis as a synchretic acousmatic sound, in line with the accompanying bleep synchronised with a flashing light on the timer. Another pitch enters, a simple sine tone hovering above the G-ish note, a C-sharp. The lower pitch begins to pulsate as the shot changes again, this time to a series of orbs containing the embryonic Cybermen. Visually reflected in the disintegration of the Cybermen's 'shells', the pulsation increases, grinding in pitch against the C-sharp. The interval between them, incredibly out of tune as only electronically generated sounds can be, known as the augmented fourth, occupies a unique position in traditional harmony as the most dissonant, ugly, threatening interval in music. In fact, in medieval and renaissance times, this interval was referred to as 'the devil in music'. While on the one hand, the higher-pitched C-sharp accompanies shots in synchronisation with a flashing electronic light, it also functions according to the semiotics of traditional tonal musical language. This interval continues pulsing away as yet another element enters: the sound of the shells falling apart at the molecular level, created by the addition of unpitched white noise and random sounds in pulses. Hodgson effectively makes the transition between the vastness of space and the threat of the Cybermen in purely musical terms, all the while accurately depicting and supporting the onscreen action.

Like Dulkis in 'The Dominators', Hodgson creates an ambient sound for the Wheel, one that reflects the relative safety of that location in opposition to the Cybermen. The Wheel's sound, a high-pitched G supported by a quieter D, creates a stable, comforting fifth. This same interval Hodgson produced for the TARDIS interior, where it often has the same effect. Recall 'The Daleks', when Susan returns to the TARDIS to retrieve the crew's anti-radiation drugs, and how the sound of the TARDIS seems to embrace her like a blanket as she enters. This same feeling of security, trust, and reliability is evoked in the Wheel; in this way the familial feeling of closeness between the Wheel's inhabitants is reinforced.

Place this against Hodgson's background texture for the Cybermen's base, and a clear difference emerges. For the villains, instability lurks everywhere. Against an abrasive cyclical whirring, a quieter electronic melody plays over and over. This low-pitched melody rocks back and forth between B, D and D-sharp, an alternation of minor and major, unstable and unsteady. Here again, the dual nature of the synchretic acousmatic 'special sound' blurs its place in the diegesis. Understandable both as 'music' and 'sound effect', the Cybermen's environment betrays them as evil without their uttering a word or relying on traditional music to tell the story for them.

This use of sound alone – what a decade later would be called 'sound design' in Hollywood – as a means of creating a 'mutual implication' between the image and the audial remains revolutionary (Gorbman, 1987: 15). That such innovation occurred as a result of purely economic reasons makes it all the more remarkable. Still, Hodgson's contribution to *Doctor Who* remains one of the least understood aspects of the programme's well-documented history, perhaps because, like most music, his musical evocations generated through the medium of 'special sound' operate largely at a subconscious level. With the introduction of Dudley Simpson as the programme's regular composer in 1970, Hodgson was no longer called upon to fulfil the dual function of composer and sound effects producer. For better or worse, the domain of 'special sound' moved largely to the foreground, to the realisation of more standardised sound effects; primarily ray guns, monsters and computers, leaving alien worlds to fall silent, their music a thing of the past.

References

BBC WAC R53/483/1, 'Technical General Electronic Effects and Music 1956–8'.
BBC WAC R97/9/1, 'Radiophonic Workshop Radiophonic Effects Committee and Electronic Composition Workshop 1956–68'.
Brooker, F.C. 1963. *BBC Engineering Division Monograph: Radiophonics in the BBC*. London: BBC.
Cary, Tristram. Letter to author, 9 February 1998.
Chion, Michel. 1994. *Audio-Vision: Sound on Screen*. Trans. Claudia Gorbman. New York: Columbia University Press.
Cooke, Deryck. 1959. *The Language of Music*. Oxford: Oxford University Press.
Flinn, Caryl Flinn. 1992. *Strains of Utopia: Gender, Nostalgia, and Hollywood Film Music*. Princeton, NJ: Princeton University Press.
Gorbman, Claudia. 1987. *Unheard Melodies: Narrative Film Music*. Bloomington, IN: Indiana University Press.
Hutton, Jo. 'Radiophonic Ladies'. www.sonicartsnetwork.org/ARTICLES/ARTICLE 2000JoHutton.html (accessed 13 January 2003).

Part IV

The parting of the critics:
value judgements and canon formations

Chapter 13

The talons of Robert Holmes

Andy Murray

The original UK edition of Trivial Pursuit contained a glaring factual error fit to get any self-respecting *Doctor Who* fan foaming at the mouth. Players requesting a pink question ('Entertainment') risked being asked, 'Who created *Doctor Who*?' According to the reverse of the card, the answer was 'Terry Nation'.

Terry Nation? He didn't even want to write for the series at first. He only caved in when Tony Hancock sacked him, and he needed the work. Fair enough, he wrote the second story, as a freelancer, and thereby spawned the Daleks, but even their impact was as much to do with their iconic design, courtesy of BBC staffer Raymond Cusick, as Nation's often uninspiring scripts. Certainly, nothing he wrote for the series subsequently was remotely as significant.

I mean, come on. Terry Nation?

Everyone knows that *Doctor Who* was created by Robert Holmes.

Robert Holmes died, at the age of 57, on 24 May 1986. In a career spanning four decades, he'd written for many of the top British TV shows of the day, including *Dixon of Dock Green* (1955–76), *Emergency Ward 10* (1957–67), *Doctor Finlay's Casebook* (1962–7), *Juliet Bravo* (1980–5), *Bergerac* (1981–91) and *Blake's 7* (1978–81). He'd never established himself as a writer of his own original work, however, and was regarded an industry stalwart rather than a household name. Arguably his greatest claim to fame was as writer of a total of fourteen *Doctor Who* stories, and a three-year stint as the series' script editor. Indeed, he contributed more *Doctor Who* scripts than any other writer. In itself, of course, that's just a statistic. 'Most' doesn't necessarily mean 'best'. But Holmes was a uniquely talented writer, with a particular knack for *Who*. He was, as this chapter will argue, the finest writer the series had.

Holmes' *Who* tales often drew on a simple technique: taking a scenario familiar from contemporary popular culture and transposing it to a space adventure setting. (Often this was so blatant it was even signalled in the title. A tale of pirates in space? Hello 'The Space Pirates' (1969). An adventure aboard an ark in space? That'll be 'The Ark in Space' (1975). Even 'The Ribos Operation' (1978), about a galactic con-man, was originally commissioned under the title 'The Galactic Con-man'.) Holmes delighted in the 'ripping yarn' and, in the main, his stories could be characterised as SF adventures with strong elements of humour and edgy thrills. At times he would increase the wry, satirical humour and go comparatively easy on the action: most obviously, in 'The Sun Makers' (1977), but also with 'Carnival of Monsters' (1973) and 'The Ribos Operation'. On other occasions – particularly while he was installed as the series' script editor and guiding its overall texture – he kept the humour sparse and black and emphasised the menace with lurking megalomaniacs. Such 'Gothic horror' tales include 'Pyramids of Mars' (1975) and 'The Talons of Weng-Chiang' (1977). Some of Holmes' very best work, such as 'The Deadly Assassin' (1976) and 'The Caves of Androzani' (1984), blends these various approaches together.

For inspiration, Holmes plundered everything from Sherlock Holmes, Mark Twain and Hammer's horror films to Fritz Lang's *Metropolis* (1927) and Nigel Kneale's BBC *Quatermass* serials (1953–9). By the time of 'The Mysterious Planet' (1986), he was even plagiarising his own early story 'The Krotons' (1968–9). The provenance of the story wasn't really important. Of course, when working on a series like *Doctor Who*, made at speed and with a tight budget, which demanded a constant influx of new ideas, looking elsewhere for those ideas was virtually inevitable. Indeed, it could be a boon. As Holmes told *Doctor Who Magazine* in 1985, 'If an audience can say, "Ah yes, that's a cowboys and indians story", as opposed to a Zaags versus Zoombers story, they can relate to it much easier' (Russell, 1985: 15).

Holmes' *Who* career wasn't plain sailing from the start, however. His first story, 'The Krotons', for the series' sixth season, is solid but unspectacular. The titular Brummie-accented monsters aren't remotely menacing, and the adventure is largely standard-issue fare, albeit with a nice line in humorous dialogue. His next effort, 'The Space Pirates' (1969), is painfully overlong and uninspired. Despite the dubious comic potential of space miner Milo Clancey, the story, replete with 'real-time' spacecraft effects, is slow and uneventful. In amongst the talk of Beta Dart ships and Argonite theft, there's precious little for the audience – or indeed, the writer – to engage with. Perhaps, though, it represents Holmes on a learning curve. Having got writing *Doctor Who* a little bit wrong, he learns how to do it right next time. It's perhaps surprising that Holmes got another chance at all after such a shaky start, but he had proved himself to be a reliable, imaginative professional, at a time when the production team were suffering major difficulties getting workable scripts in place. Crucially, he'd won the respect and friendship of the show's script editor, Terrance Dicks. As Dicks explains, 'I always had faith in Bob as a good and original writer, and when we wanted an opening show [in 1970], I chose him for it. You'll tend to go back to people you like working with and that you feel you can rely on' (Dicks, 2005).

That 'opening show' was 'Spearhead from Space' (1970), which rewired the *Doctor Who* format, as the previous season had ended with revelations about the Doctor's Time Lord origins – the first major dispelling of the air of mystery since the show began. It's not a particularly substantial tale: the invasion by the plastic Autons doesn't really get going until the final episode, and even then it's seen off pretty easily. The bulk of the running time is spent introducing the new elements of the series' format – the regenerated Third Doctor, Liz Shaw, the ongoing UNIT set-up (this last seeded in previous adventures by other writers) – and setting the tone for what's to follow. Indeed, what plot exists is hugely derivative, not least of the 1965 film *Invasion*, for which Holmes had provided the story. There's also the matter of the gleeful plagiarising of Nigel Kneale's BBC serial *Quatermass II* (1955) . . .

Despite this, 'Spearhead from Space' is Holmes' first exceptional *Doctor Who* story. It allows the writer to fully flourish his impressive facility with character and dialogue. Freed from writing about space pirates and robotic overlords, Holmes can create characters he appreciates: hapless soldiers, disgruntled employees, secretive poachers. There's a sparkle to the dialogue, and the interchanges between the Doctor, Liz and the Brigadier – often off to one side from the main plot – are a delight. The Autons themselves are a fantastic, topical invention. At a time when plastic objects were desirably ultra-modern and fashionable, Holmes turned the commonplace substance into an alien killer. The scenes of shoppers and commuters being petrified, if not gunned down, by living mannequins are powerful and surreal. Holmes communicates the terror to the audience by having it occur to highly average figures: poachers, bobbies and the proverbial man-on-the-street.

Throughout the Pertwee era, Holmes became a linchpin of the series' writing pool. He was called upon almost every year to write the first story of each season. Terrance Dicks insists this wasn't intentional: 'You wouldn't choose a writer who was good at doing new companions: that's not how you think about it. That's kind of Hollywood!' (Dicks, 2005). But whether by accident or design, it became a significant accolade. In practice, it meant that Holmes was entrusted to introduce any new regular characters each year, from the new Doctor on. Indeed, he minted each new companion from Liz to Jo Grant and Sarah Jane Smith. As script editor, he later helped devise and oversee the introduction of the Fourth Doctor, Harry, Leela and K9, and once he'd left the post, he wrote the debut of Romana, too. That's besides the subsidiary recurring characters he was responsible for debuting: the Master (in both his Pertwee and Tom Baker incarnations), the Black and

White Guardians, and his own creation, the Sontarans. His involvement in the genesis of most of these characters didn't stretch to creating them: for instance, Jo, Sarah and the Master were jointly devised by Barry Letts and Terrance Dicks. But Holmes' crucial task was to make these new additions play: for the actors, for the audience and for other writers.

Holmes' flair for writing vivid characters and effective dialogue was the secret of his success. He was certainly no slouch with structure and storytelling, but by and large he kept such matters simple and tight and let his characters do all the work. Not unconnectedly, he's recognised as a terrific writer of double-acts. Essentially a double-act is the basic ingredient of drama, or indeed of comedy. Two characters can spar, or discuss the plot and convey exposition, or move events on. Two characters is, of course, the bare minimum for this, but it's an economical unit. Three can be a crowd (that's not to mention the fact that employing two actors is possible on a BBC budget, whereas employing five starts getting expensive). Holmes was acutely aware of the value of double-acts and, accordingly, his stories are full of them. They are used dramatically, as with Scarman and Sutekh in 'Pyramids of Mars', or Li H'Sen and Greel in 'The Talons of Weng-Chiang'. They're used for comic effect, as with Gatherer Hade and Marn in 'The Sun Makers', Vorg and Shirna in 'Carnival of Monsters' or Jago and Litefoot in 'The Talons of Weng-Chiang'. At almost every turn, Holmes populates his tales with pairs of characters, often with a similar purpose, but with sufficiently different attitudes to generate drama, comedy and dialogue. Skilful use of these pairings could create an entire story. Almost exclusively, 'The Ribos Operation' revolves around the interactions between Garron and Unstoffe, Graff Vynda-K and Sholakh, and the Doctor and Romana.

This last pairing is of particular interest. Over the years Holmes succeeded in structuring the Doctor's relationship with his companion as a double-act – albeit unintentionally. Before 1970, the Doctor had never travelled with just one on-screen companion for any significant duration. Thereafter, it became the model. Throughout that period, it fell to Holmes to introduce the new companions, and establish their rapport with the Doctor, repeatedly as one based on humour and mutual affection, but which could erupt into mild dramatic tension. The wider UNIT set-up lurked in the background throughout; then, with Holmes fully installed as script editor, the Fourth Doctor was initially given Harry Sullivan as a one-man UNIT substitute. However, Harry was quickly dispensed with, and the classic double-act TARDIS crew – the Fourth Doctor and Sarah-Jane – was born. The Doctor and his 'girl companion' became the model thereafter (and, indeed, has now been adopted for the show's 2005 incarnation).

As Holmes was leaving his post, the crew immediately gained an extra member – K9 – which Holmes considered an encumbrance and a 'one season gimmick' (Kahane, 1981). In years to follow, with Holmes estranged from the show, the TARDIS found itself home to several companions at once, reaching a peak at four. Poetically, when Holmes returned to the show, the companion count had fallen back to one for the first time since he'd left.

At heart, writing good *Doctor Who* is about sleight of hand. The viewers have to believe they're witnessing the thrilling adventures of a charismatic alien travelling through time and space. In fact, they're watching a huddle of actors in a small BBC studio, wholly reliant on production staff short on time and funds. The trick is to beguile the audience, firing their imagination so that the fantastic events in question appear sufficiently three-dimensional and convincing. Holmes makes regular use of several devices to pull this illusion off. Driven by economic necessity, they add immeasurably to the effectiveness of the finished result. One, basic but very effective, is to have the characters casually but vividly refer to whole worlds and situations that are never shown on screen. In 'The Sun Makers', we're told that mankind has fled the dying Earth, tried to survive on Mars, and finally settled in five megropolises on Pluto. On screen, we see a handful of characters scurrying about within one megropolis (similarly, 'The Ark in Space' is an intimate, low-key piece about the fate of humanity). In 'The Time Warrior', Linx talks vividly of amassed Sontaran military academy hatchings, but he's only ever seen alone. In 'The Brain of Morbius', we learn that Morbius, scourge of the galaxy, previously arrived on Karn with hordes of devoted followers before being executed. Helpfully, we only see the aftermath: six speaking parts living on an otherwise deserted planet. Thus a whole series of events are implied with dialogue alone. Yet Holmes does not reserve this generosity with 'world building' dialogue just for the great and intergalactic: he is equally adept at fleshing out the worlds and lives of his 'ordinary' characters on Earth (e.g. the brief history of failed thespian, Oscar Botcherby, in 'The Two Doctors' [1985]: 'we Botcherbys have never shirked public service. My dear departed father was an air-raid warden in Shepton Mallet throughout the War. Slept in a steel helmet for five years').

   Similarly, Holmes' villains are made to appear wildly monstrous without doing much at all. Greel in 'The Talons of Weng-Chiang' is described as the vile 'Butcher of Brisbane', a slaughtering fugitive from the fifty-first century, but mostly just skulks in a cellar barking orders. In 'Pyramids of Mars', Sutekh barely moves throughout, only managing a brief spot of standing up towards the end of episode four. But through his whispered heart-stopping dialogue, and the Doctor's recollections of the Osirans and Sutekh's evil, his threat becomes credible. It's a hugely effective verbal con-trick.

   Another favourite Holmes technique involved making the most out of what actually was on screen by putting as much distance as possible between what the sets are representing. It's a useful means of adding scale and scope to an economical TV narrative. Hence, 'The Space Pirates' takes place in a whole succession of space-going settings; 'Pyramids of Mars' occurs in England, Egypt and Mars; and 'The Two Doctors' is spread over a futuristic space station and contemporary Seville. Obviously all these sets were, in reality, the self-same BBC studios. This technique is by no means unique to Holmes: on a show like *Doctor Who* it was, of necessity, common currency, but Holmes had a particular skill with it. He often used it in 'above/below' combinations: in 'The Sun Makers', some sets represent the upper levels of Megropolis One, and others the underground catacombs. Much the same goes for Ribos in 'The Ribos Operation', Gallifrey in 'The Deadly Assassin' and the Palace Theatre in 'The Talons of Weng-Chiang'.

More cunning yet, Holmes would lend depth to his tales by featuring 'worlds within worlds', often by means of location filming. 'Carnival of Monsters' takes place on the planet of Inter-Minor, but also within the assorted worlds contained inside the Minascope; whereas the action of 'The Deadly Assassin' is spread across the hallowed halls of Gallifrey, the planet's murky catacombs, and within the boundless dreamworld of the Matrix. Suddenly, the BBC's cash-strapped adventures appear to take place on a cosmic scale. Such nimble scripting techniques were, therefore, of paramount importance to the show's success.

While steering the show as script editor, Holmes, in conjunction with producer Philip Hinchcliffe, made specific plans for the direction of each new season, devising the basic trappings and tone of each individual story. Not surprisingly, given Holmes' own tastes, many classic horror tales were reworked as *Doctor Who* adventures. The results included outer-space versions of *Frankenstein* ('The Brain of Morbius'), *The Mummy* ('Pyramids of Mars') and *The Hands of Orlac* (1935) ('The Hand of Fear'). Holmes' script editing of 'The Ark in Space' and 'Pyramids of Mars' amounted to complete rewrites and he would contribute less visibly to every story during his tenure, devising the basis for each one. The enormous popular success of the series at the time can be attributed to the magnetism of new lead Tom Baker and the skilful guidance of Hinchcliffe. But Holmes begins to look like the true creator of the distinctive and hugely popular mid-70s *Who*. In February 1977, at the height of his reign in the post, Holmes was interviewed by Jean Rook of the *Daily Express*. Under the headline 'Who do you think you are, scaring my innocent child?', a rather combative Rook seems eager to depict her subject as an irresponsible villain cheerfully wishing nightmares on the nation's children (Holmes, it seems, is a great admirer of Edgar Allen Poe, Michael Arlen and Ray Bradbury). However, it contains a Holmes quote that has since passed into *Who* legend. The writer admits he personally wouldn't allow any child under the age of ten to watch the series any longer, and suggests instead that it is now 'geared to the intelligent fourteen-year old' (Rook, 1977).

Today, the Hinchcliffe–Holmes axis is highly regarded for making *Doctor Who* in a fashion that refused to talk down to their audience. The acclaimed scriptwriter and primary writer on the new series of *Doctor Who*, Russell T. Davies, nominated the partnership's debut adventure, 'The Ark in Space' – alongside the luminary likes of *Pennies from Heaven* (1978), *Twin Peaks* (1990–1) and *The Sopranos* (1999–present) – as an all-time television highlight in a recent *Guardian* article, saying 'Nothing creates terror and claustrophobia like the good old-fashioned walls of a BBC studio. I must have watched this a hundred times. It's not enough' (Davies, 2005).

With no disrespect intended, it's clear that Holmes wrote the sort of stories that he'd like to see himself, and that his tastes struck a chord with the programme's youthful audience. He shares an adolescent's fascination with ne'er-do-wells and rapscallions. He populates his fiction with space pirates, intergalactic con-men and lurking, disfigured villains. His writing demonstrates a penchant for the *grand guignol*: the more grisly and blackly funny the tale the better. His most bloodthirsty villains – Sutekh, Greel, Irongron from 'The Time Warrior' (1973–4), Mandrel from 'The Sun Makers' – hurl vivid threats in the same manner as playground bullies. From Hammer horror to Conan Doyle, Holmes had, in the nicest possible way, delightfully adolescent tastes.

Despite his memorable arch-villains, though, Holmes seems most fascinated by petty, shady wrongdoers. It's a more human, identifiable scale of villainy. The likes of Garron, Vorg and Glitz are rough around the edges, but essentially they're on the side of Good. It's this habit of depicting characters in shades of grey that lifts Holmes' work above that of his contemporaries. It adds sophistication and human vulnerability to his stories. Even the character of Tom Baker's Fourth Doctor, partly shaped by Holmes, seems to have darker edges than his forebears, despite being ostensibly the hero (it's tempting to surmise that in his previous occupation as a policeman, Holmes developed some insight into the potential villain within us all).

This suggestion of duality chimes perfectly with Holmes' predilection for double-acts. The tension between, say, the moral murkiness of Vorg and the good-heartedness of Shirna from 'Carnival of Monsters' seems compacted down into the aloof, alien hero of the Fourth Doctor or the tortured genius of Dastari ('The Two Doctors'). Nothing is entirely clear-cut in Holmes' space fantasies – as in real life. This makes them both reassuringly familiar and impressively sophisticated.

Holmes himself had disparaging words to say on the matter of over-intellectualising, warning that, 'If anyone decides that *Doctor Who* is an art form, its death knell will be sounded' (quoted in Hearn, 1994: 36). Despite the fruits of his active imagination, he seems by all informed accounts to have been a down-to-earth man in person, content to carve out a living as a scriptwriting 'hack'. His agent, Jon Thurley, has described Holmes as 'quiet, self-effacing, very likeable', while his friend and colleague Roger Marshall remarked, 'in his laid-back, pipe-smoking way, he was never terribly ambitious [. . .] He was a gent' (both Brockhurst, 2003). He may have been horrified at the suggestion that his collected works conspired to mean something, insisting instead that it was just work, nothing more. Nevertheless, his *Doctor Who* stories seem to share an outlook, a landscape. Often, his tales draw heavily on contemporary Western society, extrapolating an alien world or future. It's expressionistic and dreamlike – or nightmarish. Commonplace contemporary details – shop-window dummies, taxation demands, con-artists, dissatisfied workers – are blended in with alien invaders and far-off planets to deeply surreal effect. There's a good deal of humour in Holmes' approach, too. Thus, his writing seems closer to the satires of Jonathan Swift than the Boys' Own fantasies of *The Tomorrow People* (1973–9) – or, indeed, the escapist work of fellow *Who* writers such as Terry Nation.

In the Robert Holmes universe, the world 'above' is often populated by would-be free thinkers, revolutionaries, performers, even criminals, repressed by the Powers That Be via petty bureaucracy, commerce and institutionalised exploitation. Often the source of this repression lurks hidden away underground, lonely and embittered, even physically disfigured. Many of his stories feature servile, often mute, unthinking drones doing the donkey work for remote masters, from the Autons and Sharaz Jek's androids to Sutekh's mummies. Similarly, the obedient work-units of 'The Sun Makers' equate pretty directly to those of 'The Mysterious Planet': unquestioningly, they go about their business, following orders. Both the Autons and the Sontarans, Holmes' great contributions to the *Doctor Who* 'monsters' gallery, are essentially clones, acting out orders and duties. Again, it's tempting to read into this motif of selfish, irrational impulses and desires coming from 'below' that hamper the fulfilment of individuals 'above'. Given the way it had been previously established within the series, the Time Lord society of 'The Deadly Assassin' should be a thing of wonder and majesty, with the mastery of time and technology at their disposal. Instead, their world is rife with corruption, petty-mindedness and greed. At the heart of the rot, hidden below their city, the Master lurks, manipulating events, his body itself rotting and ugly. Holmes demotes the Time Lords from mythical demi-gods to vulnerable schemers, and there's no other way he could have written them. He repeatedly drew out the flawed, vulnerable 'human' side of individuals within societies. He does precisely the same to the Time Lords, making them function as people with drives, passions and weaknesses, squaring off their image of purity and

Figure 10   Masked menace in
'The Caves of Androzani' (1984)

high-mindedness against how real personalities – especially personalities in possession of power – operate.

This fascination with human vulnerability is never more obvious than when Holmes deals with fragile physicality. Many of his villainous creations – the emaciated Master, Sharaz Jek (Figure 10), Magnus Greel – are deformed, with an emphasis on facial disfigurement. The Autons are, by their nature, featureless, and the Sontarans are clones who wear helmets. Greel's pet, Mr Sin, is an expressionless dummy, and Sutekh's mummies have no faces at all. Sutekh himself exists in eternal paralysis beneath a mask. Even the humanoid work-units of 'The Sun Makers' and 'The Mysterious Planet' are homogenised and stripped of identity. It could be argued that even the enigmatic Doctor hides behind interchangeable faces and in several of Holmes' stories he has characters comment on what lies beneath the Doctor's 'mask' ('you have the mouth of a prattling jackanapes but your eyes . . . they tell a different story', observes Sharaz Jek). Of course, a masked character helps engender intrigue and mystery in viewers and guarantees Holmes at least one bankable dramatic set piece in these stories when the villain is unmasked, often to grotesque effect. Intriguingly, Holmes himself contributed a piece to *The Doctor Who File* (1986) that played down his own gifts as a writer and emphasised instead his disfiguring false front teeth, and their habit of scaring women and children.

Holmes seems fixated on contrasting interiors and exteriors (or the surface and what lies beneath.) There's a marked difference between the embittered likes of Jek and Sutekh and cheerful extroverts from Vorg and Garron to Oscar Botcherby. Both Jek and Vorg may have selfish tendencies, but Vorg is socialised and harmless. Rather than serve up straight SF heroes and villains, Holmes presents flawed personalities, but reserves caution for those who spend a lonely life skulking away, presenting these individuals as infinitely more dangerous. Perhaps it's all a matter of perception. Certainly, it's a preoccupation of Holmes': numerous tales feature characters who view the outside world through surveillance cameras and monitor screens. Some can only see at all through eye-holes in masks. Ideas such as the Matrix and the Minascope mark Holmes out as a writer fascinated with a voyeuristic worldview. This motif is underlined through the dangerous power sources of the 'Eyes' of Harmony and Horus.

If every writer puts himself into his work, where is Holmes – an unassuming 'hack' writer, Hertfordshire-born father of two, intelligent, literate, cynical, worryingly tall, pipe-smoking ex-policeman, Army officer and journalist (*Behind the Sofa*, 2003) – within the world of *Who*? Typically, it's not clear-cut. There's an element of wish-fulfilment in the series, however. Did Holmes subconsciously see himself as the Doctor – the heroic, revolutionary extrovert, intent on rooting out injustice, despotism and taxation? Or perhaps there's something of the writer in creations like Vorg. By no means a hero, Vorg's just an entertainer, trying to drum up an audience for his ricketty 'carnival of monsters' that's 'very popular with the children'. There's another intriguing possibility, though. His colleague Phillip Hinchcliffe has remarked that Holmes optimistically fancied himself as a dead ringer for the actor Bernard Horsfall, who portrays Goth in 'The Deadly Assassin' (*Behind the Sofa*, 2003). Consider, then, in Part Three of that adventure, the Doctor finds himself at the mercy of Goth within the dreamworld of the Matrix. Incognito, seen only beneath masks or as a pair of spectral eyes, Goth warns the Doctor that he is 'the creator here [. . .] these are my rules'. Seeing Goth, as Holmes' substitute, hunting down the Doctor with his imagination and resourcefulness at full tilt, becomes a psychologist's dream.

Here it seems is a man who recognises the failings of our fleshly existence, but who repeatedly highlights the notion of vision or perception. It's how we choose to see things, rather than how we are physically manifested, that counts most. The most evil characters excuse their actions as a matter of opinion. Sutekh cheerfully declares to the Doctor that 'Your evil is my good', while the rotting Master of 'The Deadly Assassin' curses his nemesis for being 'so despicably good, so insufferably compassionate'.

Much of the writer's work appears to revel in the power of words and the imagination – like a comment on the act of writing itself. Cordo of 'The Sun Makers' is a hopeless drone until the Doctor spurs him on to believe that the Company can be beaten. In addition to 'The Sun Makers' the Doctor instigates a similar rebellion in 'The Krotons'. He's an agent of the imagination, inspiring others to see things as they truly are and to dream of change. He defeats egotists like Greel by seeing them as ridiculous and pitiful, and refusing to perceive them as they do themselves – as formidable and all-powerful. The Doctor (virtually) never uses violence. Even faced with a fiend like Sutekh, he fights words with words and argues the case for his beliefs.

Possibly, Holmes' *Who* work is a subconscious tribute to the series itself. He was clearly very fond of the show and once confessed, 'I owe [it] a lot:

I ought to call my house "TARDIS"' (Kahane, 1981). But that's disingenuous; it was a job which obviously fired his considerable imagination more than *Juliet Bravo* (or indeed *Blake's 7*). It allowed him virtual creative free-rein while connecting to millions of viewers. If his stories seem to worship the power of the imagination, while decrying life as a faceless drone or a lurking physical wreck, it just might be how the writer felt about his favourite job.

Holmes' understanding of what made *Doctor Who* effective meant that he had equally strong ideas about what couldn't be done. By reputation, he could be arrogant and confrontational in the professional sphere. In Terrance Dicks' estimation, 'Bob was a very strong sort of character with ideas of his own, and he didn't suffer fools gladly!' (Dicks, 2005). Eric Saward is blunter: 'He was difficult, arrogant, highly critical and rude' (quoted in Brockhurst, 2003). Established monsters such as the Daleks and Cybermen weren't to his tastes at all: he found their restrictive personalities and monotonous plotting for power not remotely interesting (Rook, 1977). He was disparaging about the semi-educational 'historical' adventures from the show's early years (Hearn, 1994: 37) – although conversely, as in 'Talons of Weng-Chiang', Holmes relished using historical settings himself by drawing on an era's pulp fiction, rather than factual research, perhaps a further tribute to the power of the imagination. He was also unhappy writing *Who* scripts within exacting parameters or to specific requirements. Asked to lengthen 'The Space Pirates' from four episodes to six, the result was lumbered with uninspiring padding (as script editor, Holmes favoured four-part stories, which became the standard model thereafter). In writing for the 'Key to Time' season, he disliked the story arc and considered the Guardians dull and unnecessary. In particular, he loathed having to create 'the biggest monster ever seen in the show' for 'The Power of Kroll' (one of his weakest scripts). Following this story, Holmes was absent from the series for over five years, and seemed not to miss it. When asked in a 1981 fanzine interview if he would return, Holmes shrugged: 'One never knows. But I think it is unlikely' (Kahane, 1981).

And yet, during his period as script editor, Holmes repeatedly produced inspired work at the very last moment, replacing scripts by other writers that failed to make the grade. Holmes seems to have been happiest when left to his own devices, hammering out a tale that entertained and amused him. If time was tight and necessity became the mother of invention, all the better. He did not, however, appreciate his imagination and skills being hemmed in by other factors. His scripting work on other, less free-wheeling series – *Bergerac, Juliet Bravo*, in particular his four episodes for *Blake's 7* – are spirited, witty and adept, but never spring to multi-coloured life in the manner of his most imaginative *Who* work (although by the time of his final *Blake's 7* entry, the taut thriller 'Orbit' (1981), he was perhaps getting there). Even his celebrated TV adaptation *The Nightmare Man* (1981) suffers from the restrictions of a contemporary setting and the ultimately ordinary military-scientific goings-on at its source. Writing (relatively) normal fare just didn't bring out his best qualities as a writer.

Holmes never became an acclaimed writer of original work. His best *Doctor Who* work is not merely proficient by *Who* standards; it's fine writing in its own right, solid, accomplished, yet often with moments of vivid invention. But Holmes had a slightly uncomfortable attitude to 'high-brow' scripting, and is said to have lacked ambition. Reportedly, he had a standing invitation to submit to the prestigious *Play for Today* strand (1970–84), but never got round to it. Confusingly, many of Holmes' filmographies include 'The Brilliant New Testament', supposedly a 1970s *Wednesday Play* (Cornell et al., 1993; Brockhurst, 2003; Imdb, 2005) but no such play seems to have existed. Indeed, neither Holmes' close colleague Terrance Dicks nor his long-time agent Jon Thurley has any recollection of the piece, or even recognises the title (Dicks, 2005; Thurley, 2004). Holmes was a family man and perhaps needed the security of the likes of *Juliet Bravo* and *Bergerac* rather than risking original work away from his chosen field of the established series with a proven framework. He was given to describing himself as 'the [Citroen] 2CV of script-writers' (Holmes, 1986:) and insisting 'I think I'm not a serious writer' (Russell, 1985: 14). According to Dicks, 'Bob was always a very modest self-deprecating kind of writer in a way. He would say, "Look, I'm just a hired hack. You give me a job on a workaday programme – *Doctor Who*, police series, hospital drama – whatever it is, I'm a scriptwriter for hire", and he would have thought trying for *The Wednesday Play* pretentious' (Dicks, 2005).

Phillip Hinchcliffe has said, of the dissolution of his partnership with Holmes after leaving *Who*, 'perhaps Bob and I should have gone to Hollywood' (Rigelsford, 1995: 103). There had, in fact, been attempts to launch new projects. Together, Hinchcliffe and Holmes devised a potential new science fiction series, *Lituvin 40*, and there was talk of a spin-off series featuring the Jago and Litefoot partnership from 'The Talons of Weng-Chiang', but the BBC passed on both. In later years Holmes harboured pet ideas for black comedies concerning the inhabitants of a nuclear bunker or the adventures of two escaped convicts. They never went ahead. Instead, after leaving the *Doctor Who* staff, eager for a change, Holmes continued writing scripts for the show (taking in a five-year layoff). He also contributed to several other popular TV series, with stints as script editor of *Armchair Thriller* (1978–80) and *Bergerac* (having turned down the same post on *Blake's 7*).

Holmes did not devise *Doctor Who* – far from it – but his writing shaped it immeasurably. It was never the same series after his contributions to it. His style, and his additions to the show's mythos, had a massive impact on all that came after. Producer Graham Williams, Hinchcliffe's successor, seems to have been fascinated by the Time Lord mythology Holmes developed. 'The Invasion of Time' (1978), written by Williams and script editor Anthony Read, is, in effect, a sequel to 'The Deadly Assassin'. Indeed, under Williams, the whole series resembles a family adventure show for which 'The Deadly Assassin' was the harder-edged pilot. Writers like David Fisher, Chris Boucher, Philip Martin and Stephen Wyatt seem to owe more to Holmes' version of *Who* – eccentric, wryly humorous, imaginative yet often derivative, built from gripping stories and memorable characters – than any other.

After contributing a story or two, most of the programme's scriptwriters became – in producer John Nathan-Turner's neat phrase – '*Who*'d out'. Yet although leaving the show in 1978, Holmes would return. Eighties *Who* script editor, Eric Saward, watched tapes of Holmes' stories and became determined to bring the writer back. A first attempt, for the twentieth anniversary project that became 'The Five Doctors' (1983), ran aground (typically, Holmes was dismayed by the provisos of the project – namely five leading men, a whole flotilla of assistants and assorted returning villains). Holmes bonded with Saward, though, and would eventually write the following season's much-lauded 'Caves of Androzani'. He became irritated, again, by the limitations placed on his next script, for 'The Two Doctors' (1985): asked to include the Sontarans, the Second Doctor and Jamie, he was also requested to set the piece in New Orleans – and then, subsequently, told to relocate it to Seville – leaving him, not surprisingly, unimpressed (according to Cook, 2004: 16). A further script intended to feature the Autons (plus the Master, and the Rani) in Singapore stalled when the series was put on hiatus in 1985.

Such was the trust that Saward had in Holmes that meetings were held with potential new writers Holmes recommended, such as Jack Trevor Storey and David Halliwell. When the programme returned from hiatus for the epic fourteen-part 'Trial of a Time Lord' (comprised of four separate stories with the linking narrative of the Doctor's trial by his own people) Holmes was commissioned to write its first and last segments. Already valued as a 'writer's writer', Holmes was also appreciated by his leading actor. When asked in 1986 by *Doctor Who Magazine* to nominate his favourite stories from the programme's history, Colin Baker replied, 'Basically anything by Robert Holmes' (Holme, 1986: 22).

Holmes would never complete the 'Trial of a Time Lord' commission and died while working on the (aggravatingly complex) finale to the season. Shortly after, Saward quit out of sheer frustration, never meeting his successor, Andrew Cartmel. Once settled in his new post, Cartmel sifted through tapes of old stories for inspiration. His conclusion was that the show's highlights, from 'Pyramids of Mars' to 'The Talons of Weng-Chiang', had all been written by Holmes (Bishop, 1995: 44).

Once the television series itself ceased production at the end of 1989, a host of young new writers, including Paul Cornell and Mark Gatiss, were enlisted to pen a range of novels for Virgin Books continuing the *Doctor Who* narrative in print. The so-called *New Adventures* were often gleefully replete with continuity references, and drew heavily on the Doctor's identity as a Time Lord. References to Gallifrey and Rassilon abounded. The deepening of the character's mythos, largely spearheaded by Holmes, was being embraced by a whole new generation. Virgin's *New Adventures* were brought to a close when the BBC piloted a new American co-production of *Doctor Who* in 1996. The pilot itself resembles a welding of 'Spearhead from Space' – the regenerated, befuddled Doctor in the hands of human medics – to an Earthbound retelling of 'The Deadly Assassin', with an incarnation of the Master, hell-bent on renewing himself, planning to draw apocalyptic power from the Eye of Harmony. Freely namedropping Gallifrey, Rassilon, dimensional transcendentalism and the constellation of Kasterborous, it plays like a tribute to Holmes' contribution to *Doctor Who* mythology (embryonic versions of the American project went even further, spinning out Holmes' neat Gallifreyan legends into a cack-handed would-be epic).

Doctor Who has become a pop culture legend, referenced in everything from *Queer as Folk* (1999–2000) to *Dead Ringers* (2002–present) and *The Simpsons* (1990–present). And yet, the popular image of *Who* owes a great debt to Holmes. The series now adored across the globe is not the same one sketchily devised by Sydney Newman. Nor is it quite the one fleshed out by David Whitaker, Verity Lambert and Terry Nation at its inception. If anything, it most closely resembles the vision of the show forged by Holmes, and not only in terms of tone and format. So many of the details of the *Doctor Who* mythos – Gallifrey, the isomorphic TARDIS, the co-ordinates 'one-zero-zero-one-one-zero-zero by zero-two from Galactic zero centre' – were dreamt up by the writer. Admittedly, the *Who* legend is a patchwork assemblage of other influences – literature, legend, current affairs, cinema – conjuring up a strangely familiar 'other world', but the same can be said of every major modern mythology, from *Lord of the Rings* to *Star Wars* and *Harry Potter*.

Indeed, Holmes' concepts have had a healthy life beyond the series. 'The Deadly Assassin' introduces the Matrix – a computer housing a vast array of information which, when interfaced with via a headset, takes the form of a surreal virtual reality world. The *Matrix* film trilogy (1999–2003) borrows this concept wholesale, even the name, but in amongst the discussions of the source of the films' ideas – philosophy, Lewis Carroll, graphic novels, martial arts cinema – Robert Holmes is rarely given credit (see, for example, Clover, 2004).

With *Doctor Who* back in production, the signs are strong that Holmes' influence will continue. In his inaugural adventure, the Ninth Doctor combats Holmes' Autons. During his first public interview about the role, actor Christopher Eccleston dredged up his hazy childhood memories of the show, and came up with the 'Sontarins' (sic) (Eccleston, 2004). *Who* fan and Holmes admirer Russell T. Davies is now installed as head writer and executive producer. As the series launched, Davies uncannily echoed Holmes' own 'Zaags versus Zoombers' comments, declaring, 'Every single story will involve the human race. I'm not interested in planet Zog. I don't care! [...] If you have planet Zog, you have to be with that human colony who are fighting things like in the Wild West and they're pioneers and there's an emotion there' (O'Brien and Setchfield, 2005: 47). Meanwhile, contributing writer Steven Moffat recently eulogised Holmes' writing in a *Doctor Who Magazine* special as 'crisp [...] economical [...] blindingly good' (Moffat, 2004: 18). The Time Lords may be gone now, but the likes of 'The Ark in Space' or 'Pyramids of Mars' have been mentioned on numerous occasions as preliminary blueprints for the new episodes. Officially, Holmes never created his own original TV series; but then, given his remarkable impact on *Doctor Who*, he as good as did.

References

Brockhurst, Colin. 'Robert Holmes – The Eighties'. *Circus*. www.circus.edendev.co.uk/doctorwho (accessed September 2003).

Bishop, David. 1995. 'Interview with Andrew Cartmel – part two'. *Doctor Who Magazine*, No. 225, pp. 44–7.

Clover, Joshua. 2004. *BFI Modern Classics: The Matrix*. London: BFI.

Cook, Russell and Benjamin Cook. 2004. 'Interview with Eric Saward – part three: stormy waters'. *Doctor Who Magazine*, No. 348, pp. 14–19.

Cornell, Paul, Martin Day and Keith Topping. 1993. *The Guinness Book of Classic TV*. Guinness World Records Ltd: London.

Davies, Russell T. 2005. 'Have a Russell T. Davies TV festival'. *Guardian*, 1 January.

Dicks, Terrance. 2005. Interview with the author. 23 June.

Eccleston, Christopher. 2004. Interview with Christopher Eccleston. *BBC Breakfast Time*. BBC 1, 2 April.

Hearn, Marcus (ed.). 1994. 'Holmes on Holmes'. *Doctor Who Magazine Winter Special: Robert Holmes – The Grand Master of Doctor Who*, pp. 36–41.

Holme, Penny. 1986. 'Interview with Colin Baker'. *Doctor Who Magazine*, No. 118, pp. 18–23.

Holmes, Robert. 1986. 'A life of Hammer and tongs'. In Peter Haining (ed.). *The Doctor Who File*. London: W.H. Allen, pp. 205–10.

Imdb (Internet Movie Database). 'Robert Holmes – mini-biography.' www.imdb.com/name/nm0392025/bio (accessed January 2005).

Kahane, John M. 1981. 'Interview with Robert Holmes'. *The Time Meddler*, No. 3, October. www.circus.edendev.co.uk/doctorwho (accessed September 2003).

Moffat, Steven. 2004. 'Killer Queen: The Ark in Space'. *Doctor Who Magazine Special: The Complete Fourth Doctor – Volume One*, pp. 17–18.

O'Brien, Steve and Nick Setchfield. 2005. 'Carry on Doctor – interview with Russell T. Davies'. *SFX Magazine*, No. 128, March, pp. 42–8.

Rigelsford, Adrian. 1995. *Classic Who: The Hinchcliffe Years*. Boxtree: London.

Rook, Jean. 1977. 'Who do you think you are, scaring my innocent child? Interview with Robert Holmes'. *Daily Express*, 11 February.

Russell, Gary. 1985. 'Interview with Robert Holmes'. *Doctor Who Magazine*, No. 100, pp. 12–16.

Thurley, Jon. 2004. Interview with the author. 23 July.

Chapter 14

Why is 'City of Death' the best *Doctor Who* story?[1]

Alan McKee

> Romana: You mean an alien's trying to steal the Mona Lisa?
> The Doctor: It *is* a very pretty painting.

The fans of *Doctor Who* like to argue. They like to argue about the best actor in the lead role. They like to argue about the best era. They like to argue about obscure pieces of trivia – such as the best spaceship in the programme (Jenkins, 1997: 25). But most of all, fans love to argue about which is the best *Doctor Who* story (McKee, 2001).

The answer, for many of us, is 'City of Death' (Howe and Walker, 1998: 368; MacDonald, 2000: 46), a story broadcast in 1979 in which the Doctor (Tom Baker) and Romana (Lalla Ward) take a holiday in Paris and find themselves enmeshed in a plot to steal the Mona Lisa in order to finance dangerous time-travel experiments.[2]

Opening shots

'City of Death' has a head start in discussions of what makes good *Doctor Who*; it comes from that era of the programme that has 'by far the best' title sequence and title music that it ever boasted (Harries, undated). While many programmes simply edit together some clips of characters running around, *Doctor Who*'s title sequence has always been a piece of abstract art, a non-representational distillation of the essence of the programme to follow. To the eerie sound of discordant electronic music, we hurtle through a strangely shaped tunnel of twisted blue light, rushing towards an empty darkness that keeps receding from us.

The music is layered with alien noises (created by Delia Derbyshire): they do not replicate any instruments available on Earth, neither do they aim for a clean sound of the purely electronic. The bass notes are rough; they rub you up the wrong way. The noise that carries the melody is piercing and discordant, while in the background we can hear strange alien winds. Iconic shapes, lodged in the subconscious of a generation of children in Britain and its colonies, rush towards us: the Doctor's time machine, shaped like the antiquated British 'police box'; the face of Tom Baker, an actor who became famous across the world for playing this benevolent but disturbing alien and could never then be taken seriously in any other role; and finally, the words themselves: 'Doctor Who', so familiar that we forget that they pose an un-answered question (a radical way to name a family programme broadcast at Saturday teatime) – the character is not called 'Doctor Who'; he is called 'the Doctor'. We don't ever really know 'who' he is, who is asking the question, or why this is the title of the programme.

This title sequence, designed by Bernard Lodge, represents the pinnacle of the visual pleasure offered by *Doctor Who*. It's all downhill after this in terms of looks. This isn't one of the criteria on which fans judge the programme, simply because it isn't very good at it:

> The fact that *Doctor Who* was cruder visually than flashy American series or big-budget cinema films is fantastically irrelevant. The programme's success has not been built on special effects, but on solid storytelling. (Gray, 1997: 114)

Doctor Who should not be judged by the fact that its sets are obviously sets, that its models are obviously models, that its forms of representation are so resolutely non-naturalistic. The programme doesn't claim to be visually stunning. And so *Doctor Who* fans, developing criteria for judging which are the best stories, avoid the question of visuals to focus on those areas in which it does excel. 'Solid storytelling' is one of these.

Plotted so hard you can sing it

'Strong storytelling' is a phrase that fans often use to explain 'that indefinable magic of *Doctor Who*' (Darlington and McGown, 2000: 8; see also Tulloch and Jenkins, 1995: 145). And 'City of Death' – written by the creator of *The Hitch Hiker's Guide to the Galaxy* (*HHGTTG*), Douglas Adams (in conjunc-tion with series producer Graham Williams, under the joint pseudonym of 'David Agnew'), is 'plotted so hard that you can sing it' (Cornell, Day and Topping, 1995: 239).

The story is complex, but presented in a straightforward and entertaining manner that impeccably follows the first rule of drama; show, don't tell. An alien spacecraft attempts to take off from prehistoric Earth. It malfunctions and explodes, throwing the pilot – Scaroth – through time. He emerges as twelve splintered fragments at different points in Earth's history, living indi-vidual but linked lives. He sets about manipulating the evolution of human-kind to the point where it will sustain the time-travel technology that will carry him back to the moment of take off, so he can prevent himself from pushing the button and destroying his ship. In order to finance his time experiments in the present day (1979), he uses his unique transtemporal perspective to gather up (what will become) cultural treasures from throughout history, which can then be sold. As the story starts, Scaroth – disguised as wealthy aristocrat Count Scarlioni (Julian Glover) – is about to steal the Mona Lisa from the Louvre, so he can sell it and six other genuine copies of the painting (which he had Leonardo da Vinci paint in the sixteenth century) to seven separate collectors. The obscene sums of money he makes from this transaction will finance his final experiment. Of course, there is a problem: the same explosion which destroyed his spacecraft also provided the spark of energy that created life on Earth. If he succeeds in his plan, Earth will be forever a dead planet. The Doctor and Romana must intervene to protect humanity.

This is a pleasure in *Doctor Who* which is not a camp one: it is not 'so bad it's good'. Writers like Robert Holmes, Christopher H. Bidmead, Terry Nation and Terrance Dicks all craft a good story. Even Douglas Adams (famously bad at plots) here puts together a beautiful narrative. It's not easy to write a good story. Many of the academics who write about culture don't appreciate this, as narrative is not high on the list of criteria by which to judge the value of a work of art. Indeed, from reading the critical theory that condemns narrative as a reactionary form, you might think that producing a well-crafted story was something that was so easy you have to work hard *not* to do it. This isn't true – as anyone who has ever attempted to write a compelling narrative knows (I speak here as the author of seven unpublished *Doctor Who* novels that didn't quite manage it). It is easy to produce texts that don't have strong, coherent narratives – as many children's television drama series attest (see *Into the Labyrinth* [1981–2] and *The Tomorrow People* [1973–9]). Narratives are valuable for sensemaking, are much enjoyed in many human cultures and are very difficult to get right.

There are guidelines for producing a well-crafted narrative; but as human beings are not computers (as *Doctor Who* never tires of telling us: the programme's philosophical thinking is not one of its most sophisticated points) there aren't exactly *rules*. We never know for certain whether a narrative works or not until it is set free into the mediasphere and audiences are allowed to go to work on it.

In a classical narrative, there should be an opening equilibrium (even if it is not shown in the story itself); a disruption to that narrative, which involves the protagonists; a crisis which threatens them; a resolution which restores the equilibrium and moves the central characters forward in some way. During this process, a number of sub-questions must be set which are not only of interest to the viewer, but which are resolved in a satisfactory manner within the narrative – in ways that are original enough to be surprising, but obvious enough to seem convincing.

Ideally, each scene should progress the story in a way that contributes to the overall movement of the narrative but is not repetitious. It should allow characters to be delineated. The characters themselves should be interesting enough to drive the narrative, and believable as they do so. It will be obvious that most of the criteria I am listing here are very much subjective ones – it depends on who is asked to 'believe' in a character, for example. The decision about whether or not a plot succeeds on these criteria is taken by community discussion, and there will always be dissenters. In the *Doctor Who* community, some viewers insist that the 'City of Death' has a 'crap' plot (Velazquez, 2002: unpaginated). Gary Russell, one of the driving creative forces behind Big Finish's audio *Doctor Who* dramas has argued that the production has 'an air of embarassment' and is 'so terribly average', albeit acknowledging its moments of 'grandeur' and 'superb' story (Russell, 2004: 36–7).

These guidelines for storytelling have been developed over centuries of R & D, from traditional myths onwards, and provide a craftsperson's framework for producing a text that is likely to retain the attention and engage the emotions of an audience. 'City of Death' follows these rules remarkably well: over the course of the four episodes the story moves forward in a coherent and linear fashion, continually setting and resolving narrative puzzles and revealing an ongoing and complex plot. This is the base line of *Doctor Who* storytelling. But 'City of Death' does more than this.

The two cardinal sins of *Doctor Who* plotting are the 'infodump' and padding. The infodump is 'blatant exposition' (MacDonald, 1999: 8), the infelicitous presentation of plot information in ways that don't serve character or bother about the use of language. One obvious example is the tendency of characters in television drama to tell each other things that they both already know, as in the 1964 *Doctor Who* story 'The Sensorites', where one creature asks another: 'Are the hearts of the human creatures on the left or the right side of their bodies, or in the centre as in ours?' (quoted in MacDonald, 1999: 9).

'City of Death' avoids this trap, presenting its plot information in ways that are visual (we find out that Count Scarlioni is the alien Scaroth when he rips off his human mask to reveal the monstrous face beneath) or funny (we are introduced to the Count's plans to finance time experiments by selling artworks when he calls his henchman into the room: 'The Gainsborough didn't fetch enough. I think we'll have to sell one of the Bibles ... the Gutenberg [...] sell it discreetly [...]' 'Sell a Gutenberg Bible discreetly?' 'Well, as discreetly as possible').

Padding is the term used to describe those story events whose internal logic is fine, but which serve no purpose of progressing the larger plot. *Doctor Who*'s most common padding trope is the 'recapture': the heroes have been captured by the villain; they are locked up; they escape; they run up and down some corridors; they are recaptured; they escape again. 'City of Death' is free of padding: even when the heroes are 'recaptured' and locked in the alien's cellar on multiple occasions (following the logic of a cheap television programme that has to make the best possible use of a limited number of sets), the situation is slightly different each time, as is its resolution. The stock scenarios, necessary for an adventure narrative, are rewritten to suit the context of the story and to become entertaining in their own right – as when the first 'capture' becomes a matter of carefully negotiated etiquette. When the Count has found our heroes, he tells his henchman to lock them up in the cellar of his fabulous Parisian mansion. The hardboiled detective Duggan (whom our heroes have accidentally picked up in the Louvre) picks up a chair to throw at him. The Doctor turns on him:

> Duggan! What are you doing, for heaven's sake? That's a Louis Quinze! Just behave like a civilised guest! I beg your pardon, Count. If you'd just be kind enough to show us to our cellar, we'd be terribly grateful.

As they stand in an aristocratic drawing room, decorated with the most expensive of French works of art and heirlooms, such a mode of address almost makes sense; and in the next scene it is justified diegetically as the Doctor explains: 'What's the point of coming all the way here, just to escape immediately? We stay here, let them think they've got them safe – then we escape'. The narrative function is served perfectly; character is explored; and all this is done with a third layer of pleasure – that of finding a novel and entertaining way, inspired by the situation, to address the first two. Douglas Adams is the perfect writer to augment the narrative this way (as long as a co-writer takes care of the mechanics of the storytelling for him): he is, after all, the man who explained to us in *HHGTTG* that the reason for the number of unlikely coincidences in the storyline of his space opera was the fact the heroes' ship was powered by the 'Infinite Improbability Drive'. In 'City of Death', the conventions of adventure narrative dictate that, sitting in a French café, our heroes are held up by villains with guns and kidnapped (twice, in the same café). The Doctor goes in the next day to speak to the patron: 'Do you remember those two people I was in with yesterday? We kept being held up and attacked, smashing things?' The programme confronts the generic implausibility (if such a thing happened in a café, there would be police, questions, post-traumatic stress) straight on, as though there were no implausibility at all: the patron merely looks bored.

Don't be so portentous

We could multiply the aspects of the storytelling at which 'City of Death' excels. The story's cliffhangers, an absolute necessity in the adventure serial

format, and which provide 'much of *Doctor Who*'s edge-of-the-seat appeal'
(Barnes and Ware, 1997: 7) are, in 'City of Death', 'mucho brilliant' (Daniel
O'Mahony, quoted in Howe and Walker, 1998: 368), relying on clever
hermeneutic twists as much as the threat of immediate physical danger to
pull viewers back for the next week's episode. The story's structuring logic is
charmingly poetic rather than realistic. The Doctor and Romana discover the
time experiments in Paris when a pavement artist sketches Romana: as he
paints, the world flickers and when they see his drawing of her he has put, in
place of her head, a clock face with a fracture running across it: 'Almost like
a crack in time', as the Doctor says. Scientifically this is nonsense – why
should a time experiment cause an artist to draw such a picture? – but meta-
phorically it makes perfect sense. This logic runs consistently through the
story. This is also the 'wittiest' *Doctor Who* story (Cornell, Day and Topping,
1995: 237): the most famous scene in this respect occurs when the Doctor
meets Scaroth/Count Scarlioni for the first time. He is thrown into the room
by the villain's henchman. 'I say, what a wonderful butler, he's so violent,
hello, I'm called the Doctor, that's Romana, that's Duggan, you must be
the Countess, this is clearly a delightful Louis Quinze chair may I sit in it, oh
I say, haven't they worn well?'

Rather than discuss all these qualities in detail, let us instead take the last
of them as a perfect example of 'City of Death's' ability to fulfil another
criterion for judging the worth of a *Doctor Who* story: it contains 'the humour
that should always be present in *Doctor Who*' (Daniel O'Mahony, quoted in
Howe and Walker, 1998: 368). It doesn't take itself too seriously.

The best *Doctor Who* should, many fans agree, exhibit a form of camp
(although it's worth acknowledging that there are a great many fans who
would react with horror to this suggestion, emphasising instead the show's
predilection for, say, Gothic mystery; perhaps the balanced view is to acknowledge, as David Herman does, a tendency for the programme to be both
'part country house Gothic, part Carnaby Street camp' [Herman, 2005:
unpaginated]). To paraphrase the Doctor's own account of his actions, he
should always be completely serious about what he does, but not necessarily
about the way that he does it. The programme is not realist, in the sense that
it tries to convince you to suspend disbelief and believe you are watching an
actual event. It insists on its own status as an entertainment.

Given the fact that *Doctor Who* was made so quickly and so cheaply, to
validate such qualities was perhaps a necessary step in developing aesthetic
criteria for evaluating the programme. In the opening scene of 'City of Death',
we see a model spaceship in a wasted landscape. It is obviously a model. We
cut to the alien Scaroth inside the spaceship: the actor is wearing gloves of
green, wrinkled skin over his hands, but they have come loose and his own

skin can clearly be seen underneath them. The programme cannot match films like *Star Wars* (1977) for the quality of its effects, sets and costumes. Rather, it matches other elements of the production to its own amateur effects, never taking itself too seriously. When the Doctor and Romana experience a time slippage, the Doctor becomes thoughtful:

The Doctor: You and I exist in a special relationship to time, you know – perpetual outsiders.
Romana: Don't be so portentous.

The programme includes the same kind of verbal playfulness that we now see in *Buffy the Vampire Slayer* (prefigured by twenty years), where lines not only make narrative and character sense, but also delight in their own poetic play with language:

The Countess: My dear, I don't think he's as stupid as he seems.
The Count: My dear, nobody could be as stupid as he seems.

In this way, the amateurism of the production becomes something to be celebrated rather than apologised for. Indeed, it fits the character of the programme, and the character of the Doctor, very well. He also is fallible and has a tendency to make things up as he goes along. He has no master plan, no particular end point in mind. He simply has fun and overthrows unjust regimes:

The Doctor: Make mistakes. Confuse the enemy.
Romana: Is that why you always win? [...] Because you always make mistakes? ('Destiny of the Daleks' [1979]).

Famously, 'City of Death' was written over a weekend when another script fell through: Graham Williams and Douglas Adams locked themselves into a room with coffee, and emerged two days later with the scripts. Improvisation, amateurism and not taking it all too seriously become criteria of worth. And 'City of Death' shows that this can be done so very well:

It's generally the case that heroes in TV shows improvise and celebrate individuality against big systems [...] Obviously *Star Trek* would be hypocritical to do this, being a global brand made by a giant company, but *Doctor Who* has always shown signs of being made by people who have to improvise (hence the *Blue Peter* modelwork in many cases) and who find the miraculous in the everyday. The titles for the late 1970s stories – the time tunnel that people so fondly remember – were made from meticulously zooming in, frame by frame, on polarised-light photos of polythene shopping bags. They created the noise of a time machine from a door key and a piano string. How can you NOT love a programme that does this? (Wood, 2002: 17)

Absolutely exquisite

Beyond the storytelling, it is the performances in *Doctor Who* which are usually identified as its most outstanding contribution to television art (Cornell, 1998: 15; MacDonald, 2000: 47). Most notable is the performance of Tom Baker as the alien Doctor. Of the ten people who have played the lead role on television, Baker is not the best actor in the sense of performing a convincing character. But his Doctor – with his long scarf, curly hair, bulging eyes and manic grin – is by far the best remembered by general viewers, even twenty years after he left the part (when the Doctor makes an appearance on *The Simpsons*, it is Tom Baker's version who guests). Baker's performance is by far the most charismatic and the most convincingly *odd* of the Doctors. If we had to pick a single element and say, *this* is what makes *Doctor Who* different from anything else on television, Baker's performance would be it.

Tom Baker's Doctor has proved to be larger than the actor playing him. He has not been able to replicate the success of this character in his later career, nor has any other actor made the role so popular. Perhaps this is because, as the programme makes much of the fact that its hero isn't human, the role offers a unique possibility to be an alien: to refuse conventions of how people behave realistically or naturalistically and instead simply to be *charismatic*. Baker's performance makes the most of this possibility: he produces a character that isn't human in his reactions. He shows little concern for human life, although he will occasionally stop narratives to produce great paeans to the sanctity of it. He does not make small talk. He is delighted and interested in the world around him, but it is entirely on his own terms – before he has finished introducing himself to somebody, he will have forgotten that he was talking to them as he spots something of interest behind them and strides off to have a look. His performance is unpredictable, suggesting a number of powerful forces driving this character – curiosity, outrage at injustice, delight at the interesting things the universe has produced – which overlap and are held together in a single body, even if they do not quite coalesce to produce a realistic 'character' in any familiar sense. What stability the character has comes from Tom Baker himself, his absolute confidence in the part, his obvious conviction that he *is* the Doctor. When the character – and indeed, when Tom Baker – does latch on to the here and now it is with an intensity that makes you realise that, were he so engaged all the time, the sheer energy of it would damage the fabric of the universe. And he is very funny, endlessly producing little bits of business to enliven even the most prosaic line: passing time in a French café in 'City of Death', the Doctor opens a philosophical paperback, flicks through the pages and puts it back down – 'Not bad. A bit boring in the middle' – before his attention is caught by something else.

Alongside the phenomenon of Baker's Doctor in this story, we have his companion Romana. For most of the programme's run, the narrative function of the Doctor's 'companion' was to provide a younger human perspective on this alien being, offering the possibility of identification for viewers. Romana, by contrast, is an alien like the Doctor: rather cleverer than he is, and similarly unpredictable. As played by Lalla Ward, Romana is a Time Lady to match the Doctor's Time Lord (literally – the actress is a minor member of the British aristocracy, as her accent and attitudes make clear). She is pretty, but her charm comes more from a performance that is similar to Tom Baker's: she is rather alien, disconnected in a Bohemian way, enjoying herself but with little sense of engagement with the everyday lives or concerns of petty humans. 'You know what I don't understand?', asks Duggan. 'I expect so', she replies, ignoring him. Ward is also well known in the fan community for the visual pleasure she offers by way of her frocks (not all companions did this – some had quite rigid uniforms that rarely changed). In this story, she is dressed like a schoolgirl – and more St Trinians than *Home and Away*. When the Doctor and Romana are together, these two beautiful performances catalyse to produce something else: Baker's 'on-screen rapport with Lalla Ward is justly the stuff of legend' (MacDonald, 2000: 47). It is a matter of record for *Doctor Who* fans that it was in Paris during the filming of this story that Tom Baker and Lalla Ward fell in love (they later married). This does not translate into any sexual frisson between the characters – that is not what *Doctor Who* does – but it does result in a sense of closeness. The characters finish each other's lines, perform as though they know what the other is thinking, and – most importantly – seem greatly to enjoy being together. The glances they exchange while wandering through Paris, or talking to lesser mortals, make clear that they share a world, a view, an intimacy. They smile together.

Into this world of Baker and Ward, the two charismatic aliens, come other performers and guest stars. Again, this is part of *Doctor Who*'s playful self-reflexiveness. Just as Stephen Hawking might appear in *The Simpsons* in order to fly away in his specially adapted superchair, so here Julian Glover (Figure 11) – a respected British Shakespearean actor – appears with a green, spaghetti-headed mask covering his face, as the alien Scaroth who wishes to destroy humanity. While he is in the *Doctor Who* universe he plays the game, taking quite seriously this role which is so different from King Lear: 'Just go back and watch the first encounter between Tom and Julian Glover. The great actor gives the great TV star room to get every prop and angle in the set on his side, while he stands back and times his lines to perfection' (Cornell, 1998: 15). This trend in *Doctor Who* guest stars we might call part of its 'edutainment' remit. *Doctor Who* was originally intended to have BBC-style educational purpose, with the hero visiting Earth's historical past and possible scientific futures (Glover himself appeared as King Richard I in 'The

Figure 11 Shakespeare meets
Doctor Who – Julian Glover in
'City of Death' (1979)

Crusade' [1965]). As well as these (quickly forgotten) aims, we see lurking throughout its history a desire to teach its audience about high culture: the Doctor is forever boasting about his meetings with Shakespeare and Leonardo da Vinci, quoting the former and celebrating the art of the latter. The Count's collection of 'priceless' artefacts includes Shakespeare's first draft of *Hamlet*, from which the Doctor reads:

> 'To be or not to be, that is the question. Whether it is nobler in the mind to suffer the slings and arrows of outrageous fortune, or to take arms against a sea of troubles' . . . Take arms against a sea of troubles? That's a mixed [he breaks off then continues breathlessly], I told him that was a mixed metaphor, but he would insist.

In the same way, Shakespearean actors regularly guest star, à la *Sesame Street*, adding their cultural authority to the enterprise.

Another trend in guest stars is motivated by the programme's odd positioning in the British television landscape. Generically, *Doctor Who* melds adventure serials with light entertainment, and British light entertainment stars commonly appear on the programme, playing their roles more or less straight (along with its emphasis on amateurism, this is one of the ways in which the programme's 'Britishness' is expressed): *Carry On* stalwart Peter Butterworth played recurring villain The Meddling Monk; funnyman Ken Dodd was the Tollmaster in 'Delta and the Bannermen' (1987); game show host Nicholas Parsons was the doomed vicar in 'Curse of Fenric' (1989); and so on. In this unashamed 'stunt casting', the programme draws on the explicitly British star personae of these actors. As Lance Parkin has written of the Peter Davison story 'Earthshock' (1982), only *Doctor Who* would remake *Alien* (1979), casting Beryl Reid in the Sigourney Weaver role (Parkin, 2002: 16).

'City of Death' sees two of the most spectacular examples of this stunt casting, for effects of Britishness and playfulness, as its narrative includes a short comedy sketch playing on the story's artworld setting. The Doctor has parked the TARDIS in an art gallery, where two patrons mistake it for an exhibit. They are played by British comedy stars Eleanor Bron (star of satirical revues) and John Cleese (of *Monty Python's Flying Circus*, and the new Q in the Bond movies). In this the programme is firmly implanted in the genealogy of British comedy: Douglas Adams writing for John Cleese as Tom Baker runs past, scarf flailing:

> Cleese: For me one of the most curious things about this piece is its wonderful . . . afunctionalism.
>
> Bron: Yes. I see what you mean. Divorced from its function, and seen purely as a piece of art, its structure of line and colour is curiously counterpointed by the redundant vestiges of its function.
>
> Cleese: And since it has no call to be here, the art lies in the fact that it *is* here. [The Doctor and companions run past, into the TARDIS, slam the door and dematerialise – it vanishes]
>
> Bron: Exquisite. Absolutely exquisite.

Everybody's BBC

In this single scene, and in 'City of Death' as whole, we can see what makes the best *Doctor Who* so very good: its status as 'family entertainment' (Cornell, 1998: 14), or 'cross-demographic communication' (Hartley, 1999: 31). For the youngest viewers, the art gallery visitors add tension with a thirty-second pause in the rush to save the history of humanity. For adults, they are a wonderfully ironic acknowledgement that this is a programme that knows it is daft, but doesn't care (see Parkin, 2002). The diegesis is absorbing for those who choose to suspend disbelief; the performances are there for other viewers; the sense of cultural capital and edutainment for still others.

> 'City of Death' represents the height of *Doctor Who* as popular light entertainment intended to be enjoyed by all the family. For the serious-minded adolescents there's a solid plot: the alien Scaroth, in a prefiguring of *Highlander*, exists throughout history and intends to unite all his selves, using a criminal scam to finance his brutal time experiments [. . .] For the adults, there's the fun of laughing at how the guy with one eye in the middle of his forehead sees out of that mask, and the glee of Julian Glover's purring James Bond villain. The children of the family, meanwhile, are entertained by the presence of a scary monster. (Cornell, 1998: 14)

Doctor Who managed successfully to reach these mixed audiences, perhaps better than any programme in British television history. The programme survives in public memory, and when viewers remember it, 'City of Death' is what comes to mind: Tom Baker's Doctor, *that* title sequence and music, a green-headed alien, a clever and funny plot, guest stars and dodgy special effects. These are the criteria on which we judge *Doctor Who*: this is why 'City of Death' is the best *Doctor Who* story.

Notes

1 The academic purpose of this paper is simple. Some academics have worried that postmodern challenges to traditional hierarchies of cultural authority mean that 'anything goes' and consumers no longer make judgements about what is good and bad culture (see for example Brunsdon, 1997: 128; Nelson, 1997: 218; Caughie, 2000: 232). This paper seeks to demonstrate that this is not the case. The fact that academic systems of aesthetic judgement no longer command the respect they have previously done does not mean that aesthetic judgements are no longer being made. Indeed, I would argue that we can now recognise more aesthetic thinking, not less, in the consumption of culture – as we begin to notice that many groups other than academics develop elaborate aesthetic systems for judging good and bad. *Doctor Who* fans are one such group. The approach taken to illustrate this point is one of methodological joyriding – taking standard academic methodologies without their owners' consent, taking them into places their owners would not sanction and there doing scandalous things with them. In this chapter I have taken the methodology of 'aesthetic appreciation' – common in disciplines such as Film Studies and Art History – and applied it to a popular television programme.

2 The full plot of 'City of Death' is available at www.drwhoguide.com/who_5h.htm.

References

Barnes, Alan and Peter Ware. 1997. 'And cut it . . . now!' *Doctor Who Magazine*, No. 249, pp. 6–13.

Brunsdon, Charlotte. 1997. *Screen Tastes: Soap Opera to Satellite Dishes*. London: Routledge.

Caughie, John. 2000. *Television Drama: Realism, Modernism and British Culture*. Oxford: Oxford University Press.

Cornell, Paul. 1998. 'City of Death'. *Doctor Who Magazine*, No. 265, pp. 14–15.

Cornell, Paul, Martin Day and Keith Topping. 1995. *Doctor Who: The Discontinuity Guide*. London: Virgin Publishing.

Darlington, David and Alistair McGown. 2000. 'The adventure game – part one: it's a jungle out there'. *Doctor Who Magazine*, No. 296, pp. 8–13.

Gray, Phillip J. 1997. 'Why the Nimon should be our friends: storytelling and stylistic change in *Doctor Who*'. In Paul Cornell (ed.). *License Denied: Rumblings from the Doctor Who Underground*. London: Virgin Publishing, pp. 108–15.

Harries, Simon. Undated. 'Cult: *Doctor Who*'. *TV Ark: The Television Museum*. www.tv-ark.org.uk (accessed 4 February 2003).

Hartley, John. 1999. *Uses of Television*. London and New York: Routledge.

Herman, David. 2005. 'Smallscreen'. *Prospect*, No. 110, May. Available online at www.prospect-magazine.co.uk/pdffiles/6886.pdf (accessed 12 November 2005).

Howe, David J. and Stephen James Walker. 1998. Doctor Who: *The Television Companion*. London: BBC Books.

Jenkins, Jackie. 1997. 'The life and times of Jackie Jenkins'. *Doctor Who Magazine*, No. 258, p. 25.

MacDonald, Philip. 1999. 'And those main points again . . .' *Doctor Who Magazine*, No. 281, pp. 8–12.

MacDonald, Philip. 2000. 'I'm going slightly mad'. *Doctor Who Magazine*, No. 290, pp. 46–7.

McKee, Alan. 2001. 'Which is the best *Doctor Who* story?: a case study in value judgements outside the academy'. *Intensities: The Journal of Cult Media*, No. 1, www.cult-media.com/issue1/Amckee.htm (accessed 17 September 2005).

Nelson, Robin. 1997. *TV Drama in Transition: Forms, Values and Cultural Change*. London: Macmillan Press.

Parkin, Lance. 2002. 'Nudge nudge, wink wink'. *Doctor Who Magazine*, No. 232, pp. 10–16.

Russell, Gary. 2004. 'Voulez-vous: City of Death'. *Doctor Who Magazine Special Edition: The Complete Fourth Doctor – Volume Two*, pp. 36–7.

Tulloch, John and Henry Jenkins. 1995. *Science Fiction Audiences: Watching Doctor Who and Star Trek*. London and New York: Routledge.

Velazquez, John. 2002. 'The horrible truth'. In Robert Smith? [sic] (ed.). *The Doctor Who Ratings Guide*, www.pagefillers.com/dwrg/frames.htm (accessed 5 Feburary 2002).

Wood, Tat. 2002. 'How to make fans (and influence people)'. *Doctor Who Magazine*, No. 320, pp. 12–17.

Chapter 15

Canonicity matters: defining the *Doctor Who* canon

Lance Parkin

One of the concepts most frequently employed in discussions between *Doctor Who* fans in recent years has been 'canon', but relatively little has been done to define or explore the term, to acknowledge that it has evolved a special meaning in a *Doctor Who* context, or to work through the assumptions and implications.

There are two broad uses of the word 'canon' when discussing literature. The first, and probably the most familiar to students of English Literature, is the Leavisian notion of a Great Tradition (Leavis, 1948). It would be very easy to construct a Leavisian list of *Doctor Who* stories that showcased good writing, demonstrated the development and history of the series and championed qualities felt to be admirable. Discussion of *Doctor Who* is rife with notions of 'classic' and 'seminal' stories and *Doctor Who* fans frequently conduct polls and surveys that, whatever the precise format of the question or the sample size, come to almost entirely predictable conclusions. If television stories like 'The Talons of Weng-Chiang' (1977), 'The Caves of Androzani' (1984) and 'Genesis of the Daleks' (1975), or novels such as *Human Nature* (1995), *Alien Bodies* (1997) and *The Also People* (1995) didn't appear high up in the final results, then a fan's first instinct might be to question the methodology of the survey. There is an assumption of a 'fan consensus', one that covers what the best stories are, the criteria for reaching that opinion and the basic facts of the continuity of the series. Clearly, much of the appeal of being a *Doctor Who* fan – as with followers of a sports team or rock band – is a sense of history shared with likeminded people, where high and low points are discussed in great levels of detail.

For many years now, the 'consensus' has been more honoured in the breach, and most reference books have emphasised that they aren't simply a recounting of dry facts. As *The Discontinuity Guide* put it more than ten years ago, 'if you're interested in *Doctor Who* then you will know such things already' (Cornell, Day and Topping, 1995: 2). Surveys of the series often offer critiques of individual stories that draw attention to the reviewers' iconoclastic views:

> For a certain age group this story is the most memorable example of 70s *Doctor Who*. However, 'The Daemons' isn't really very good. (Cornell, Day and Topping, 1995: 129)

or, indeed, squirm at their inability to dissent, as with *About Time 4*'s critique of 'The Talons of Weng Chiang':

> Regarded by lazy people as one of the greatest *Doctor Who* stories ever made, who are nonetheless right on this occasion. (Miles and Wood, 2004: 154)

As with Leavis' Great Tradition, nowadays the notion of a consensus held by 'certain people' only seems to be invoked to be challenged, a useful idea to underpin discussion but not something many people take literally. It's easier to find 'dissenters' than anyone holding the opinions they are 'dissenting' from.

When *Doctor Who* fans talk about 'canon', what's being discussed is more like the biblical canon. In its simplest form, it asks which texts 'count' as part of the fictional world of *Doctor Who*. Usually, the question is framed something like this:

> I thoroughly enjoyed 'Dalek' but it did state for certain that the war that destroyed Gallifrey was between the Time Lords and the Daleks. Up until now, it seemed like the series might be going with the storyline in 'The Ancestor Cell' where the Doctor destroys Gallifrey during a war with Faction Paradox. So, has the canonicity of the novels now been tossed out or has Russell Davies stated any-where that he considers the books as background for the series? (Ironheart, 2005)

It's an argument that's difficult to comprehend from the outside, but 'canon' is invoked time and again in fan debates, and such debates can get heated.

Doctor Who represents a large body of work – more than seven hundred television episodes would be plenty, but almost every episode was novelised, and there are hundreds more stories: original novels, comics, novellas, films, stage plays, short stories and audio plays. There is also a thriving spin-off industry of stories that aren't always licensed by the BBC: professional novels, comic strips and audio plays featuring secondary characters from the TV series and books, not to mention parodies, pastiche and fan fiction. Are there stories that a *Doctor Who* fan needs to see to understand the series? If some-thing is established in a book, should it be understood as a 'fact' that future stories need to take into account? Should the new TV series be beholden to the stories told in the audio plays produced since the last time *Doctor Who* was on television? Just how much background reading does a writer of a new *Doctor Who* story have to have done? The different responses to such questions are more useful as insights into the psychology and attitudes of individual fans than for coming to any definitive conclusions.

From the very early days there have been a lot of *Doctor Who* stories that haven't been on television. June 1964 saw the publication of *The Dalek Book*, a hardback collection of text stories, comic strips and articles. It took the opportunity to present Daleks, their technology and related monsters without the limitations of a BBC budget – and in colour. Within a couple of years, it was followed by a number of sequels, and (from 1965) a series of *Doctor Who* annuals, one of which, *The Invasion from Space* (1966), was a single novella-length story. From November 1964, there was a *Doctor Who* comic strip in *TV Comic*, and from January the next year, there was another strip featuring the Daleks in *TV Century 21*. Three television stories were adapted into children's novels and the first two Dalek television stories were adapted into movie versions, with Peter Cushing starring as Doctor Who. Clearly, a big market for these stories were fans. At this early stage, these were individual children who liked *Doctor Who*, not the organised, international network of adults that *Doctor Who* fandom comprises now, but for most modern fans, the annuals, novelisations and comic strips were as memorable as and perhaps even more tangible than the TV series as they were growing up.

There are two important points to be made about this. The first is that many of these spin-offs used writers from the series. The Dalek comic strip was written by David Whitaker, the first story editor of the television series. He and Terry Nation collaborated on *The Dalek Book* and its sequels. Whitaker also wrote two of the first three novelisations. Bill Strutton adapted his own television scripts for 'The Web Planet' (1965) into the novelised version, *Doctor Who and the Zarbi* (1966). In the 1970s and 1980s, when the novelisations were revived, almost everyone writing them worked or had worked on the television series.[1] The stalwart of the range was Terrance Dicks, the script editor from 1968 to 1974. By the 1980s, there was a policy (and a clause in their contract) that the writer of the TV story had first refusal on adapting their own work. Right from the start, then, the branches of *Doctor Who* shared many of the same creators.

The second point is that the adaptations of television stories often contradicted or elaborated upon the source material. A good example is the first Dalek story. There were three significant versions: the original TV episodes, a seven-part serial called 'The Mutants' (1963–4 [aka 'The Daleks']) by Terry Nation (the second story broadcast); the novelisation by David Whitaker, *Doctor Who in an Exciting Adventure with the Daleks* (1964) and the movie, *Dr Who and the Daleks* (1965). The three versions share the same basic story and lead characters with the same names. With no plans to novelise the first televised story, David Whitaker's book comes up with a new introduction to the regular characters. Here, the Doctor, Ian, Barbara and Susan are brought together following a car accident on Barnes Common, and Ian is not a science teacher, he's a research scientist. The story is told from Ian's point of view,

which means a number of scenes are reworked. Whitaker also took the opportunity to put back some of the elements that couldn't be achieved on TV,
notably a glass Dalek that gives a good view of the horrible creature inside.
The movie version is different again. The running time is a lot shorter, so the
story is considerably simplified. The lead characters have the same names,
but little else in common with their TV versions: Susan is a child, rather than
an older teen; Barbara is that older teen, rather than a frumpy history teacher;
Ian is a bumbling suitor for Barbara. The Doctor is Dr Who, an eccentric,
forgetful human inventor.

Which of these, if any, should be considered the most accurate account of
the adventure? Was the 'real' Ian Chesterton a science teacher, a scientist or
a bumbling idiot? The instinct is to say the television version, because it's
'the original' or because it fits into a large, apparently easily defined, body of
work in the same medium.[2] But both the book and the movie had the opportunity to restore scenes or to make spectacular additions that were beyond
the scope of the television adventure. In a time before video recorders (before
a lot of television was even archived by the companies making it), a hardback
book was a far more enduring and accessible record than an ephemeral
television broadcast.[3] One thing that doesn't seem to factor in is a question of
quality. A good case could be made that certain novelisations are better than
the TV stories on which they are based (I would nominate *Day of the Daleks*
and *Battlefield*). Few of those who don't consider the original novels 'canonical'
would go as far as to say that absolutely every TV serial is better than absolutely
every novel.

Even if we were to agree on a list of 'canonical stories', would that make
additions that didn't contradict them 'false'? *Doctor Who* fans in the 1970s
used the novelisations as a source of facts about old *Doctor Who* stories.
It was here that younger fans learned about the previous Doctors and the
monsters they fought. Many of the incidents and facts presented in the
novelisations are made up for the books, and didn't appear in the television
version. Indeed, many of the early stories altered the titles of the stories and
made a conscious effort to neaten up and explain parts of *Doctor Who* lore.
Some of the 'novelisations', such as *The Cave Monsters* (1975) or *Warrior's
Gate* (1982), bear little resemblance to the original TV story. I'm sure I'm not
the only fan who vividly 'remembers watching' a scene on TV that actually
only appears in the novelisation. Some things fans take as indisputable facts
of *Doctor Who* first appear in the novels – for example, the rising column in
the centre of the TARDIS console being called 'the time rotor', the description
of each actor playing the Doctor as an 'incarnation', the Sontarans being a
race of clones[4] or the device that (in theory at least) disguises the TARDIS
being 'the chameleon circuit'.[5] As the years went by, the television series even
adopted some of the ideas from other sources, either by misremembering (in

'Genesis of the Daleks', when recalling the Dalek invasion of Earth, the Doctor describes the end of the second Peter Cushing film, not the television story) or by consciously adopting something from the books (the glass Dalek missing from the first story on television eventually showed up in 'Revelation of the Daleks' in 1985). From the beginning, then, there wasn't a simple one-way process of the books feeding off the television series, there was an interchange of writers and ideas, and the books, stories in annuals and (particularly) the comic strips were willing and able to create new companions and monsters for the Doctor, and to develop things seen on television.

While the TV series was being broadcast the primacy of the 'television stories' was largely unchallenged. There were two main reasons for this: the relative size of the audiences for the television series (millions) and the books and comic strips (tens of thousands), and the impact on the fictional '*Doctor Who* universe'. However popular and long-running the series of novelisations, the annuals or the *Doctor Who Magazine* comic strip were – or, conversely, however low the television ratings dipped – the non-televised stories reached a tiny fraction of the audience the televised ones did. While there were innovations from the stories in other media that affected the television series, most such traffic was one way.

With the television show out of the way, though, there was something of a Copernican revolution – now, not everything revolved around the TV series. The main focus for fan activity in the early 1990s was the *New Adventures* range (the 'NAs'). These were original novels, published by Virgin. Quickly doubling the release schedule from bimonthly to monthly, the NAs became a large body of work in their own right. The range had two stated aims: to act as the officially licensed 'continuation' of *Doctor Who*, but also – as the back covers put it – to tell 'stories too broad and too deep for the small screen'. The two statements demonstrated the main tension in the relationship between the TV series and the original novels: there was a balance to be struck between being 'like *Doctor Who*' and innovating. The novels could not be exactly like the television series, for a number of reasons. Most obviously, they are different media. Novels are typically more introspective and less spectacular (the novels' concentration on the thoughts and feelings of the regular characters was often misinterpreted by critics – and to be fair, some of the authors – as an excuse for endless angst). The novels were also, inevitably, going to be for a different audience than the TV series – a far smaller, but much more committed readership of fans (and a subset of fans, with the time, money and inclination to read so many novels, at that). There was also the problem that the TV series had manifestly failed in recent years – audiences that had been as high as nine million in 1985 were barely above three million in 1989, and some of the most vociferous criticism of the recent series had come from fans themselves. If the TV series no longer appealed to either a mainstream or a fan audience, it would be pointless to reproduce it perfectly in book form, even if such a thing were possible. It's notable that the most 'controversial' early novels, the ones that moved furthest from the feel of the television series, were those written by Marc Platt, Ben Aaronovitch and Andrew Cartmel – key writers of the television series.

Even so, the television series still had a presence. Each extant episode was being released on VHS, but these video sales were comparable to the sales of the novels or *Doctor Who Magazine*, rather than the millions who had watched on TV. That said, now that it was possible to encompass the whole of the television series in a reference work, without the worry that it would be out of date by the time it was published, numerous books appeared, both new and reissued. The show was rediscovered – literally, in the case of episodes returned to the archives – but many fans hadn't actually had a chance to see older episodes until they were released on VHS. They learned that many of the things they had been told about the series weren't accurate, and this led to the widespread reassessment of many stories that saw the old 'consensus' vanishing. Many of the Hartnell stories with a 'classic' reputation, like 'The Web Planet' and 'The Dalek Invasion of Earth' (1964), were felt to have dated badly. Conversely, the historical stories, long regarded as pointless filler, were championed. But the ability to dip in and out of the whole television series had the effect of further codifying it, making it much more familiar and also somehow more monolithic and planned. So many things fans take for granted, like the Time Lords and UNIT, had been made up on the spur of the moment. It was tempting to imagine that *Doctor Who* had appeared in 1963, with the Doctor, his two hearts and ability to regenerate, the Daleks and Cybermen springing fully formed into existence. It seemed almost impudent to want to add things to the mix.

This is not a problem unique to *Doctor Who*. Other long-running series, such as *Star Wars* and *Star Trek*, have become 'franchises' in the same way, with many spin-offs in just about every medium that has vocal fans as its main consumers. One crucial distinction between *Doctor Who* and its two more recent rivals is that it lacks a clearly identifiable creator.[6] *Star Trek* was, as each episode was contractually obliged to state, 'created by Gene Roddenberry'. *Star Trek* was still the work of many hands:

> Over the years a lot of the very best Star Trek has been the work of people other than Roddenberry, and while they've always acknowledged their debt to him, people like Dorothy DC Fontana, David Gerrold, Gene Coon, Leonard Nimoy, William Shatner, Nicholas Meyer, Patrick Stewart and Rick Berman have often used their weight to push the series away from his vision in favour of a more light-hearted, action-packed and self-referential version. (Jones and Parkin, 2003: 7)

But it only had one *creator*, and Roddenberry used this position to make rulings about whether a story 'really happened' in the *Star Trek* universe.[7] *Star Wars* was created by George Lucas, who has, from the beginning, exercised his authority by only authorising strictly approved spin-off stories, and by declaring certain subjects off limits.[8] Lucas has also revised the original *Star Wars* movies, most notably the first, which has been altered for each re-release for cinema, television and home video (and has even, retrospectively, gained a new title, *Star Wars Episode IV: A New Hope*), each new version becoming the 'official' version upon release.[9]

Roddenberry and Lucas, then, are authorities and can act like the popes of their magisteria and make definitive, official rulings on matters of canon. This doesn't mean that fans meekly agree with these decisions, but it certainly does affect licensed spin-offs. *Star Trek* novels and TV shows are banned from featuring, or even mentioning, characters from the animated series (some writers have taken this as a challenge and snuck references in), and George Lucas has refused to allow the 'original' version of *Star Wars* a DVD release.

Doctor Who has no such single authority or anything much like it.[10] When the TV series was in production from 1963 to 1989, the producer usually had the power to approve merchandise and insist on changes, but there were twelve producers over the course of that run, and there were dozens of script editors and writers, each with different ideas about *Doctor Who* and attitudes to the audience and fans of the series. The makers of *Doctor Who* were not of one mind, but almost all those asked have insisted that telling a good story should take priority over a slavish devotion to what had gone before.

> How much more wondrous it must have been to be David Whitaker and open a script submission that began 'it is 6000 AD. The Earth is underwater [. . .]' and not worry if it conflicted with established continuity. Throw it all up in the air, I say. Nothing is sacred. Nothing is written. Start from scratch to keep the show vivid and alive. (Mark Gatiss quoted in Gillatt, 1999: 11)

When the series went off the air in 1989, official responsibilities for it became even more diffused as the producer's role passed to 'the BBC', the corporation that made (and cancelled) the television series and licensed the spin-offs. They had 'approval' of the spin-offs, but beyond basic 'brand management' – ensuring that the logo was correctly displayed and that no characters said 'fuck' in the licensed product, keeping an eye to make sure fanzines and fan fiction weren't violating any trademarks or copyrights – the BBC had little to say on a day-to-day basis. They were quite happy for the *New Adventures* to call themselves 'the official continuation' of *Doctor Who*. It's hard to imagine anyone at the BBC at that point comprehending, let alone engaging, with the 'canon debate'.

Whether the makers intended to or not, as more and more *Doctor Who* stories were broadcast, a large body of work built up and this appeared internally consistent. Characters and monsters would return, and the audience gradually learned a great deal about the mysterious Doctor. While the series was, to most intents and purposes, an anthology with different writers and directors every few weeks, the audience was encouraged to link stories together from the show's earliest days, and the regular characters would often remind each other of their previous adventures. The natural instinct for the audience of any serial drama or other long-running series is to think that the fictional world is consistent.

The big turning point, though, was 'The Dalek Invasion of Earth', the story that reintroduced *Doctor Who*'s most enduring villains. Here, for the first time, there was an attempt to explain a link between one fictional story and another. Ian is confronted by a Dalek, an alien race wiped out at the end of their first story. The Doctor explains they are 'a million years ahead of us in the future. What we are seeing now is about the middle history of the Daleks'. A *continuity* had been created. Normally, 'continuity' on television is a simple matter of making sure that the characters are wearing the same clothes on the location and studio work, and checking the script to make sure what's said reflects what the audience has already seen earlier in the episode. This didn't mean there weren't occasional contradictions or 'continuity errors', but during the 1960s, the 'fictional facts' of the series were clearly easier to keep straight – there was less to contradict, and much territory that the series had yet to touch upon.

By its tenth anniversary, *Doctor Who* had evolved. The original child viewers of the series were now in their teens. The production team, headed by producer Barry Letts and script editor Terrance Dicks, were all too aware of this – they received many letters from precocious viewers. Unusually, the programme would often incorporate viewers' notes and queries into the show. So, in 'The Sea Devils' (1972), the Doctor remarked that the Silurians weren't really from the Silurian period, and in 'The Day of the Daleks' (1972), he answered one of the viewers' most frequently asked questions about time travel, explaining why characters couldn't just keep going back in time until they got the result they wanted. Later Barry Letts would have a good-natured moan about the pedantry of the show's fans: 'To be corrected by a 15 year old about the third monster on the left in a show made before he was born can be an earthshaking experience' (Lofficier, 1981: Foreword). But this was a phenomenon he actively encouraged as producer. There had been informal fan clubs before for both the regular actors and the series, but now there was a recognised Doctor Who Fan Club. The TV production office didn't just help to organise actor interviews for the Fan Club newsletter, they arranged to duplicate it on BBC copiers.

The show's fans were starting to coalesce into a 'fandom' – strong local groups which were beginning to talk to each other. The readers of the newsletter expressed a great deal of interest in the show's past.[11] *Doctor Who* had always changed like few other series, and this encouraged comparison of different eras of the programme – fans would naturally have strong preferences between the Doctors, their companions, the monsters and the stories. Uniquely, *Doctor Who* fans were just as fascinated by what was happening behind the scenes. While some *Star Trek* analysis now differentiates between the work of different writers – and there was always a contingent of Trekkers who hero-worshipped Gene Roddenberry – many fans of that show demonstrate little or no knowledge of exactly what a director or executive producer is responsible for. It's a stark contrast with *Doctor Who* fans, most of whom would talk of the Hinchcliffe or Letts eras rather than the Baker or Pertwee ones, who are fully aware of the differing philosophies guiding individual script editors, and who are *au fait* with the names of everyone behind the camera, as this fan critique reveals:

> One of the criticisms I have about 'Mawdryn Undead' is Peter Moffatt's rather lacklustre direction. Flat and overly bright lighting even manage to make Stephen Scott's exquisite sets look dull. (Sangster, 1996: 14)

This shows a level of knowledge and attention to minute detail that puts many film critics, and indeed academics, to shame.

Unusually, this pulling back of the curtain has always been actively encouraged by the makers of *Doctor Who*, who have consistently been intent on showing even the youngest members of the audience that it's all make-believe. In the 1960s, this consisted of monsters being paraded on *Blue Peter*. 'The Making of Doctor Who' (1972) provided the first substantial analysis behind the scenes, as well as a guide to previous episodes. The *Radio Times* would publish a tenth anniversary special that did much the same, and added a wealth of photographs. Not least of all, the show brought back popular old monsters and, at the start of the tenth season, united all three actors to have played the Doctor in 'The Three Doctors' (1972), a story that added a great deal to the fictional history of the Doctor's home planet, by explaining how the Time Lords had discovered time travel. There was a large regular cast, 'the UNIT family' the Doctor found himself with during his exile to Earth, and when a story was set in the future, the Doctor was often heard to explain how it fitted with other stories.

So, *Doctor Who* fans assimilated a staggering amount of information about the series – not just the fictional minutiae, but details about the circumstances of production. They began to see their role as one of being guardians. Some fans would carefully make and compare notes, others were trading tape recordings of the soundtracks. This role was spiritual as well as material. If you love and understand something a great deal, and it changes, then there is obviously no guarantee that you will love or understand the changed version. As Jon Pertwee and Barry Letts left, replaced by Tom Baker and Philip

Hinchcliffe, many of the early fans were unhappy with the changes being made. The most famous example is the Doctor Who Appreciation Society review of 'The Deadly Assassin' (1976), that wailed (in capitals) 'WHAT HAS HAPPENED TO THE MAGIC OF DOCTOR WHO' (Vincent-Rudzki, 1977), but its harking back to a former golden age is hardly unique.[12]

There's an interesting power relationship here, one characterised by this exchange in *The Simpsons*:

Comic Book Guy:	Last night's Itchy and Scratchy was without doubt, the worst episode ever. Rest assured, I was on the Internet within minutes, registering my disgust throughout the world.
Bart:	Hey, I know it wasn't great, but what right do you have to complain?
Comic Book Guy:	As a loyal viewer, I feel they owe me.
Bart:	What? They've given you thousands of hours of entertainment for free! What could they possibly owe you? If anything, you owe them!
Comic Book Guy:	Worst episode ever.

(*The Simpsons*, 'The Itchy and Scratchy and Poochie Show', 9 February 1997)

It wasn't hard for fans to see themselves as somehow more emotionally invested in the show than the BBC that made it. The perfect symbol of this was that one fan, Ian Levine, learned that the BBC were throwing away the old episodes, and made a beeline for the skips, where he recovered (most of) the discarded film cans. By the mid-1980s, it was clear that the BBC no longer wanted to make the show . . . just as it was beginning to build a fanbase in the huge North American market. More books, toys and other items of merchandise were sold during the 'hiatus' in 1985 and 1986, when *Doctor Who* was off the air, than in the 1960s, when it was regularly in the top twenty programmes.

It's no exaggeration to say that some senior people at the BBC had contempt for the show. It's probably more balanced, though, to agree with Colin Baker, who suggested (on a 1992 Manopticon convention panel) that the real problem was that no one at the BBC was championing the show; producers wanted to make a name for themselves with their own ideas, not become just the latest in a line on an established show. *Doctor Who* fans quickly came to fill this vacuum, their long-standing sense of guardianship and love for the programme becoming a strong sense of *ownership*. While trying to downplay the importance of continuity, the following line from a survey of the series is telling:

Doctor Who's attitude to its own past can be summed up by one fact: that 'Warriors of the Deep' is a sequel to 'Doctor Who and the Silurians' written by someone who had never seen it. (Clapham, Robson and Smith, 2005: 3)

Fans had not only seen it, they had the book and the video. They argued over whether the 'Doctor Who and the' part of the title was meant to be part of the title. They knew exactly what the Silurians' third eyes could or couldn't do, they knew that the term Silurian was a complete misnomer, and they knew that 'a complete misnomer' was itself a quote from the story's sequel, 'The Sea Devils' (1972). They even had a slang term for a sexual practice based on the shape of a Silurian's mouth. The writers of the series might not know much, but *Doctor Who* fans were fluent, as it were, in Silurian.

It's a sensible question to ask: just how much should a *Doctor Who* writer know? They clearly couldn't – let alone shouldn't – watch every episode or read every book and comic strip. By placing such a value on knowledge of the past, the fans were effectively saying that only fans could write for the series. A couple of fans had written for the television series, and the production team had used fans – including Levine – as uncredited advisers, but up until now there had been a clear demarcation between Amateurs and Professionals, to the point that some prominent fans who'd sent in story ideas suspected they'd been rejected purely because they were prominent fans. This distinction even seemed to apply to *Doctor Who Magazine* (*DWM*), the annuals and the novelisations. The writers and artists on the *DWM* strips, for example, may well all have had affection for the series, but only John Peel – who wrote a handful of back-up strips – had been active in fandom. The fact that there *were* 'prominent fans' was itself an indication of how fandom had developed. By the end of the 1980s, fandom was a complex mix of different generations, with different loyalties and temperaments. Fanzines ranged from the vitriolic *Doctor Who Bulletin* to *In-Vision*, each issue featuring a forensic 'making of' of an individual story. In between, *Skaro* and *Matrix* offered personal recollection and opinion, along with close reading and imaginative fiction. Within that, most fans rejected traditional models of hierarchy, were suspicious of 'elite fans' or 'superfans', and saw 'authority' as resting with the individuals with a mastery of lore and trivia. In their 1995 survey *Science Fiction Audiences*, Tulloch and Jenkins concluded that the fans represented a 'powerless elite', one with great knowledge but no influence. That was painfully true in the 1980s, but was already an outdated model for *Doctor Who* fandom, thanks to the *New Adventures*. While the NAs started off with stalwarts of the novelisations (John Peel, Nigel Robinson), television writers (Andrew Cartmel, Ben Aaronovitch) or both (Marc Platt, Terrance Dicks), the book that set the agenda for the NAs was by a fan writer, Paul Cornell. A range for fans was soon being written by names familiar to those – and only to those – who read *Doctor Who* fanzines, like Andrew Hunt, Mark Gatiss, Gareth Roberts, Neil Penswick, Andy Lane and Jim Mortimore.[13] As the NAs started to hit their stride, though, the charge that the books were 'fan fiction' was used as ammunition by those fans who didn't like them, and who clung to the old distinction between Amateurs and Professionals. Nearly fifteen years on from the launch of the NAs, drawing a neat distinction like that seems a little quaint. The writers on the new television series all wrote for Virgin, Big Finish or both and even the Tenth Doctor, David Tennant, acted in a number of Big Finish audio plays and is a long-time subscriber to *Doctor Who Magazine.*

The problem for the twenty-first-century *Doctor Who* fan is not so much philosophical as logistic. *Doctor Who* in the last five years has become what might be described as super-fragmented. Television stories are available on VHS and DVD, and episodes where only the soundtrack survives have been released as part of the Radio Collection. Virgin published NAs and MAs (*Missing Adventures* featuring earlier Doctors). BBC Books publish Eighth Doctor, Ninth Doctor and Past Doctor ranges of novels. Big Finish released both Eighth Doctor and Past Doctor audio adventures, and also audios based on Sarah Jane, Gallifrey, UNIT, the Cybermen and the Daleks, as well as short story collections. There are webcasts and revised NAs and MAs on BBCi (who have also put up a few of the out-of-print *New Adventures*). There is the *DWM* comic strip. Telos released a series of *Doctor Who* novellas, and when they lost the licence, a new series, *Time Hunter* was launched featuring a character from one of these. The trend for spinning off a character from the spin-offs was launched by Virgin in 1997 with the Bernice Summerfield *New Adventures*,[14] and now involves stories, or whole ranges, such as *Faction Paradox, Miranda, Iris Wildthyme, Time Hunter, Guy de Carnac, Doctor Omega* and *Kaldor City*. Even a rich fan with a great deal of time on his hands would have trouble keeping up with every release, let alone assimilating and enjoying them all. Some of these are only available by mail order, or in specialist shops. *Doctor Who Magazine*'s 'Shelf Life' review section, which ten years ago had a regular single reviewer occasionally complaining about his or her workload, now employs four or five people. They, at least, get free copies. With the exception of the webcasts, and now the TV series, 'buying in' to the other ranges involves just that – spending money. A fan, then, has to pick which stories to watch, read or listen to.

It's hardly surprising, especially in a series as perennially self-aware as *Doctor Who*, that some novels have taken canonicity as a theme. One of the earliest BBC novels, *War of the Daleks* (1997), 'retconned' the ending of the television story 'Remembrance of the Daleks' (1988), revealing that the Doctor hadn't destroyed the home planet of his arch enemies after all. *Interference* (1999) rewrote the end of the Jon Pertwee era of the television series; *Unnatural History* (1999) imagined what it would be like to live in such a world, where even one's own past could be rewritten on a whim. Over the years, no part of the *Doctor Who* universe had been portrayed in so many various and mutually incompatible ways as Gallifrey, the Doctor's home planet. My own *The Infinity Doctors* (1998) tried to incorporate everything we had been told about Gallifrey and the Doctor's relationship to it, wherever we had been told it, from the TV series to the most obscure fan fiction. The (intentional) irony is that such an ultra-inclusive approach makes it utterly impossible to place *The Infinity Doctors* in relation to the rest of *Doctor Who*. The ultimate expression of this was Jim Mortimore's *Campaign* (2000), which deserves a mention if for no other reason than it was the only novel ever rejected for publication after completion, and was privately published instead, making it officially 'non-canonical'. It is a book set in the early years of the series that collides various versions of the Doctor and the first TARDIS crew in a reality-bending story that – amongst many other challenges to the 'canon' – featured the Ian of the TV series as well as the Ian who had a car accident on Barnes Common.

What's notable is that – with the exception of *War of the Daleks* – these novels all celebrate the plurality and artistic freedom that a lack of a defined 'canon' allows, but also recognise the threat to narrative.

> What's the point of controlling a universe without meaning, where nothing of consequence ever happens? Why shed tears when someone dies if they can be brought back, why cheer on your favourite team when if they lose they can also win? [. . .] That's what we've created – a universe where everything is nothing. A universe where nothing matters. (Parkin, 1998: 272)

With so much new *Doctor Who* to choose from, it must almost be at the stage where no two fans have experienced exactly the same set of stories, even among the ones released in the recent past. With no distinction any longer between 'fans' and 'professionals', with a greater exchange between media, the canon debate is now either completely irrelevant or of supreme importance.

'Canon' is a concern of fans rather than the makers of the series. As Russell T. Davies said during the broadcast of the new series, canon 'is a word which has never been used in the production office, not once, not ever' (Davies, 2005: 66). However, fans have long been a powerful influence on and even part of the production of the series, even leaving aside their domination of its critical reception and analysis. The fact that Davies knows it's a concern to (his fellow) *Doctor Who* fans is telling in itself. 'Canon' is a useful term when used as an organising principle that allows people to sort between the bewildering array of *Doctor Who* and related stories and to construct a 'shared' fictional universe. A notion of a 'canon' allows fans to 'manage' *Doctor Who* in three important ways.

The first is a simple question of an individual fan understanding what is going on in the narratives. If they want to follow the adventures of the Doctor, but don't have the time or money to follow them all, there needs to be a way of determining which are the 'best' stories to read. If the books are 'canon', then any self-respecting *Doctor Who* fan would read them, or at the very least keep abreast of the latest developments. Even those of us who have read them all often have trouble keeping track of so much information (there are something like a million new words a year to absorb). Being able to fence off areas as 'canon' makes it easier to quantify and control.

The second is perhaps related, but more negative – if 'the books aren't canon', then a dedicated *Doctor Who* fan can still be a dedicated *Doctor Who* fan if he or she doesn't read them. Declaring that a range of books 'aren't canon' becomes a way of justifying not following them. At the same time, those who do follow the books can lord it over those who don't. For both, 'canon' is used to justify a preference, or even a prejudice.

The third reason is that in a 'shared culture', something actually has to be shared. In an increasingly diverse fandom, common reference points are important. In recent years, three fans, each following the 'ongoing' adventures of the Eighth Doctor, could meet and have no common points of reference. There are three distinct series of 'ongoing adventures' for the Eighth Doctor, in the *Doctor Who Magazine* comic strip, the Big Finish audios and the Eighth Doctor Adventures novels, each with their own elaborate running storylines and specially created companions and threats.

However, in the complete absence of a 'pope' who can state officially what and what isn't 'canon', any definitions of which stories 'count' as canon are idiosyncratic to the point where fans routinely refer to their own 'personal canon' – the polar opposite of the normal use of the term, where canon is imposed by a central authority.

Fans' greatest ire is reserved for books such as *War of the Daleks* and *Interference* that seem to reverse developments in previous stories, or 'retcon' them (*retroactively change continuity*). The key to understanding the importance of 'canon' to a *Doctor Who* fan is that it represents *investment*. Fans spend a great deal of time and money on *Doctor Who*. The average Briton buys three books a year. At their height, there were that many *Doctor Who* books being published every month. *Doctor Who* fans are not lost in a fantasy world – they have as great an understanding of the circumstances of television production as any other group of viewers. Via the Internet and conventions, they have far more direct contact with the authors of the novels than any other group of readers. For this level of commitment to work, they have to know the stories matter. Fans want the writers to demonstrate at least some of the care and attention to detail that they possess. For the emotional, time and financial investment of being a *Doctor Who* fan to pay off, they have to contribute to and inform, in some way, the wider *Doctor Who* universe. They – the stories and the fans – have to *matter*.

Notes

1   This includes Ian Marter, who was an actor, not a writer on the television series. 'Warriors' Gate' and 'Terminus' were adapted by their screenwriter, Stephen Gallagher, using the pseudonym John Lydecker. By the time the range had run its course, only two writers – Nigel Robinson and John Peel – hadn't worked on the TV show.

2   Saying that only television stories 'count' sounds like a straightforward enough place to draw the line, but there are a number of problems. The story 'Shada' (1979) was made for television, but owing to a strike was never completed. Eventually, the scenes that had been recorded were made available on video along with a script and linking material. Is it 'a television story'? What about the K-9 spin-off episode, 'K9 and Company' (1981)? Most fans dismiss 'Dimensions in Time' (1993) and 'The Curse of Fatal Death' (1999) because they were broadcast during charity telethons – but, then, so was 'The Five Doctors' (1983). The pilot version of the first episode was broadcast as part of the thirtieth anniversary celebrations – so does the fact that it was broadcast legitimise it? A number of stories have been released on video with additional scenes – which of the four versions of 'The Curse of Fenric' (1989) 'counts'?

3   The first Dalek story was released on DVD in January 2006 but is not available on VHS. The movie is out on DVD and the novelisation has just been released as a talking book on CD. The VHS back catalogue has been deleted, and the stories are being released on DVD, but at the rate of roughly one every two months. At that rate, it will be well over ten years before some stories are part of the current catalogue. As the BBC has released soundtracks of stories that don't survive on video, one of the ironies is that all the 'lost' *Doctor Who* stories are actually easier to purchase now than many of the ones that aren't 'lost'.

4   The novelisation *The Sontaran Experiment*, published in January 1978, is the first place to establish that the Sontarans are clones. This was first mentioned on screen in 'The Invasion of Time', broadcast in March 1978. The closeness of those dates suggests that both were in production at the same time. The natural conclusion is that one influenced the other, but as the TV production office approved all the novelisations, it's impossible to say which way the influence ran. Another possibility is that Robert Holmes, creator of the Sontarans, made notes that both drew on. However, the novelisation of the first Sontaran story *The Time Warrior* (also published in 1978) called the Sontarans 'cyborgs' (p. 8) rather than clones (and it's generally accepted that the prologue in which the word appears was the one bit of the novelisation written by Robert Holmes, not the credited author, Terrance Dicks). Whatever the circumstances, the books established that the Sontarans were clones before the TV series.

5   The term was first used in *The Doomsday Weapon*, the novelisation of 'The Colony in Space' (1974), and not on television until 'Logopolis' (1981).

6   A third meaning of the word 'canon' is used by fans of the Sherlock Holmes stories. There 'the canon' refers to the stories written by Arthur Conan Doyle himself. Traditionally, this includes fifty-six short stories and four of novel length. However, it excludes around a dozen items written by Conan Doyle, including

articles, a plot outline, stage plays and self-parodies. *The Final Adventures of Sherlock Holmes* (1993) provides a good summary of this additional material.

7   Gene Roddenberry even considered some of his own work non-canonical – particularly the animated version of *Star Trek* and aspects of *Star Trek V: The Final Frontier* (1989).

8   Marvel Comics in the late 1970s were not allowed to show Luke Skywalker and Darth Vader meeting or duelling, as that was reserved for the movie sequel. This encounter, though, was one of the most requested in the letters pages – leading to a number of dream sequences and *doppelgänger* storylines. The list of current restrictions for novelists and comic strip writers mostly concerns territory that Lucas will cover in the new prequel movies, but there are some long-standing bans on, for example, depicting the home planet of Yoda.

9   Every time the original *Star Wars* movie has been re-released in the cinema or on video or DVD, it has been re-edited, so there's no one 'original' version. For a good survey of the changes, see Smith (2002: 68–72).

10   The original UK edition of Trivial Pursuit asked, 'Who created the television series *Doctor Who*?', causing a lengthy discussion in at least one household. The answer is a complicated one, but it most certainly wasn't 'Terry Nation', the answer given on the card. Terry Nation created the Daleks, and it's interesting to note that he (and later his manager, Roger Hancock) was careful to exercise a great deal of control over the use of his creations, in *Doctor Who* and elsewhere.

11   A good account of the early history of *Doctor Who* fandom appears in *The Seventies* (Howe et al., 1994: 173–4). It reports that Jon Pertwee was so annoyed by the newsletter's interest in the past that he tried to organise a rival devoted solely to him!

12   Nowadays, of course, one of the cornerstones of the 'fan consensus' is that the Hinchcliffe era is one of the show's great golden ages, and some contemporary fans have bemoaned the destruction of Gallifrey in the books and new TV series in much the same terms as their antecedents bemoaned its introduction.

13   One reason for employing fans to write the books, series editor Peter Darvill-Evans would state later, perhaps not even half-jokingly, was economic: we first-time authors were cheap and didn't generally have agents.

14   The current Big Finish Benny books go beyond mere spin-offs – they are a spin-off from their audio series, a spin-off from the Benny novels published by Virgin, a spin-off from the NAs, a spin-off from *Doctor Who*.

References

Clapham, Mark, Eddie Robson and Jim Smith. 2005. *Who's Next: An Unofficial and Unauthorised Guide to Doctor Who*. London: Virgin Books.

Conan Doyle, Sir Arthur. 1993. *The Final Adventures of Sherlock Holmes*. Collected and introduced by Peter Haining with a foreword by Jeremy Brett. London: Warner.

Cornell, Paul, Martin Day and Keith Topping. 1995. *The Discontinuity Guide*. London: Virgin Publishing.

Davies, Russell T. 2005. 'Production notes: the evasion of time'. *Doctor Who Magazine*, No. 356, pp. 66–7.

Gillatt, Gary. 1999. 'We're gonna be bigger than Star Wars!' *Doctor Who Magazine*. No. 279, June, pp. 8–12.

Howe, David J., Mark Stammers and Stephen James Walker. 1994. *Doctor Who: The Seventies*. London: Virgin Publishing.

Ironheart. 2005. 'Have the BBC/Virgin novels just been made obsolete?' Posted on 3 May to http://groups.google.co.uk/group/rec.arts.drwho (accessed 19 September 2005).

Jones, Mark and Lance Parkin. 2003. *Beyond the Final Frontier*. London: Contender.

Leavis, F.R. 1948. *The Great Tradition: George Eliot, Henry James, Joseph Conrad*. London: Chatto & Windus.

Lofficier, Jean-Marc. 1981. *Doctor Who – The Programme Guide*. London: W.H. Allen.

Miles, Lawrence and Tat Wood. 2004. *About Time 4*. New Orleans: Mad Norwegian Press.

Parkin, Lance. 1998. *The Infinity Doctors*. London: BBC Books.

Sangster, Jim. 1996. 'Thinker, zombie, soldier, spy.' *In-Vision*, No. 65, pp. 13–14.

Smith, Jim. 2002. *George Lucas*. London: Virgin Publishing.

Tulloch, John and Henry Jenkins. 1995. *Science Fiction Audiences: Watching Doctor Who and Star Trek*. London: Routledge.

Vincent-Rudzki, Jan. 1977. 'Review of "The Deadly Assassin"'. *TARDIS*, Vol. 2, No. 1.

Chapter 16

Broader and deeper: the lineage and impact of the Timewyrm series

Dale Smith

Ever since *The Dalek Book* (1964) was published, *Doctor Who* (1963–89) has been providing inspiration for new stories independent and outside of the television series. Comic strip adventures for the Doctor have been produced since Polystyle Publications Limited's *TV Comic* (1951–84) first introduced them in 1964, and these continue in Panini's *Doctor Who Magazine* (1979–present).

The impact and importance of the comic strips cannot be underestimated and is worthy of a discussion all of its own: they were not only the first original *Doctor Who* stories produced separate from the television series, they were also the first to present a world different to that in the TV series – such as the First Doctor travelling with his grandchildren John and Gillian, characters who never existed on screen. For their first twenty-five years, however, the comic adventures were published concurrently with the TV series, giving any fans who were unsatisfied with this universe 'real' *Doctor Who* to return to. The comic stories weren't a continuation of the *Doctor Who* series, but a side step from it. It wasn't until 1991 and the publication of *Timewyrm: Genesys* that the *Doctor Who* story continued anywhere except the television screen.

The first request to produce original *Doctor Who* novels reportedly came from Nigel Robinson, editor of the Target imprint then owned by publishers W.H. Allen.[1] Ever since David Whitaker's *Doctor Who in an Exciting Adventure with The Daleks* (1964)[2] was given a 1974 reprinting by Target, the imprint had been publishing 40,000 word 'novelisations' of television stories, primarily aimed at a young readership. These novelisations were extremely popular – in 1991 Virgin Publishing released a 'bestseller' list that indicated that Whitaker's book and *Genesis of the Daleks* (1976) had sold in excess of 100,000 copies each (see *Doctor Who Magazine*, No. 180, 1991) – and yet were dependent entirely on the *Doctor Who* TV series. When the number of episodes in a season was cut from twenty-six to fourteen in the mid-1980s, it became apparent that at some point in the future all available *Doctor Who* stories would be novelised.[3] At that point, Target would have no product to sell.

In this light, Nigel Robinson made his request for permission to create original novels featuring the Doctor in the mid-1980s, but this was turned down with the explanation that the BBC would rather all the TV stories were novelised before it considered original novels. A compromise was offered: although original fiction could not be produced featuring the Doctor, a range of fiction featuring his companions was approved.

Across 1986–7, Target published three books under the banner 'The Companions of Doctor Who'. The last of these was Terence Dudley's 1987 novelisation of *K9 and Company* (1981), a failed pilot for a *Doctor Who* spin-off series, but the other two were new, original fiction.[4] The experiment was a failure and the range was cancelled after these three books due to poor sales. According to Peter Darvill-Evans, 'the poor sales were because those tie-ins didn't have the Doctor in. You can't have *Doctor Who* without the Doctor' (Darvill-Evans in Howe, 2001: 6).[5]

This failure didn't put a stop to the idea, and Robinson's successor, Jo Thurm, made a further request as she was leaving the post in 1989. The request was followed up in March the same year by Peter Darvill-Evans, Thurm's replacement. By a fortunate coincidence, it was a few months after Darvill-Evans' request that the BBC made the decision that a twenty-seventh season of *Doctor Who* wouldn't go into immediate production. With the future of the TV series in doubt, the BBC – and in particular series producer John Nathan-Turner – were more open to the idea of original fiction being published. In October 1989, Peter Darvill-Evans was given permission to publish an original range of books.

Darvill-Evans had been confident that his new range of books wouldn't go the same way as the 'Companions of Doctor Who' because of another short-lived selection of Target novelisations: the 'Missing Episodes' stories. These were novelisations[6] of scripts that had been commissioned for the twenty-third television season but then cancelled when the show was put on hiatus. Darvill-Evans noticed that these books 'seemed to sell as well as the standard novelisations which just strengthened my view that if the Doctor was present, then the books would do fine' (Darvill-Evans in Howe, 2001: 6).

Darvill-Evans' reasons for trying to ensure that the books 'would do fine' were simple:

> My priority is *not* to produce the best possible *Doctor Who* novels. As a consultant publisher, hired by Virgin Publishing, my brief is to make profits for the company. Luckily, one way of doing this is to produce original *Doctor Who* fiction; and, not surprisingly, I work on the assumption that the level of sales is affected by the quality of the books. (Darvill-Evans, 1992)

It is often imagined in fan circles that the reason for the quality of the *New Adventures* and their frequent use of new authors was because the novels were at the centre of Virgin Books' output, and were an attempt to create a stable of writers who could go on to provide other original fiction for the company. In fact, it was the other way round: before Virgin took an interest in the company, W.H. Allen produced a wide number of books of which the Target novelisations were only a small part. The majority of this output, however, wasn't financially viable, as the company was still trying to turn itself into a major publishing house. Virgin didn't want to make the necessary investment to continue this, and instead decided to break up the company and sell off its assets.

It was in looking into this that Virgin discovered the two W.H. Allen imprints that were – unlike every other imprint – still turning a profit: the Nexus range of erotic fiction, and the Target imprint. Virgin's interests were in making an unglamorous profit, and these ranges were doing so. They were kept on, as part of a much smaller company, renamed Virgin Publishing. The quality of the *New Adventures* wasn't because they were the centre of Virgin's business plan; the *New Adventures* became the centre of Virgin's business plan because of their quality. The main reason why the Virgin *New Adventures* went beyond what might be considered necessary in terms of quality and characterisation is attributable to their first editor: Peter Darvill-Evans. Although Darvill-Evans was at heart a businessman ('I came from a background outside book publishing, and had run highly commercial operations such as the trade sales side of Games Workshop, and been a director of a magazine distribution company [...] I was interested in the bottom line' [Darvill-Evans, 2004]), he had ideas for the range right from the beginning that would involve them being more than just the average TV tie-in:

> I wanted from the start to create a series of novels that would continue from where the TV series finished – because in my opinion the later McCoy stories were becoming dense, complex, multi-layered dramas that renewed my faith in *Doctor Who* and in TV drama in general. In part, I wanted to cock a snook at the BBC for cancelling the programme just when it was getting really good. (Darvill-Evans, 2004)

The reason for Darvill-Evans' interest in 'dense, complex, multi-layered dramas' was equally straightforward:

> I wanted to tie people in for the long term. I wanted readers not to be able to just buy one book, and to get into the habit of buying all of them [...] what I was trying to create was a series of books that could exist without *Doctor Who* [...] we might need to reach a new audience and branch out. So all along I wanted to do something that would stand alone. (Darvill-Evans in Howe, 2001: 8)

Darvill-Evans knew that the best way to do this was to create individual novels of a standard high enough to entice a readership in. Rather than create novels that merely pastiched the TV series, he aimed for a range that took the ideas of *Doctor Who* and explored them, unafraid to take them past the boundaries previously established in the TV series.[7] He was aided in this by the BBC's reluctance to make a firm decision on the future of the TV series – giving him an open-ended range of books that, for five years, were free to go in any direction they wanted to, save regenerating the main character or killing off his companion, Ace. He was also helped by the fact that the *New Adventures* wouldn't be the first range of prose *Doctor Who* adventures that Virgin had produced.

For the readers, and many of the authors of the new novels, the Target novelisations were the benchmark for the *New Adventures*. Indeed, of the authors of the Timewyrm series, John Peel[8] and Terrance Dicks,[9] had both written for the Target novelisations – as had Nigel Robinson,[10] who was also an ex-editor of the range. First time author Paul Cornell was 'an avid reader' (Cornell, 2004) of the books.

Before Virgin had become involved, the Target novelisations were usually written by an author working from either the script or a video of the original TV episode. Target attempted to get the original writers of the TV stories to author the novelisations, but as they were often producing novelisations years (and even decades) after the original broadcast, in many cases it proved impossible. Sometimes the sheer number of years between TV story and novelisation meant that even when the original writer could be used, the final shooting script and/or video were as vital as they would have been with an entirely new author. There were some notable exceptions – such as David Whitaker's *Doctor Who in an Exciting Adventure with the Daleks*, which as the first novelisation produced was given a new opening sequence to introduce the characters, as well as other changes[11] which remained for the Virgin reprinting – but on the whole, the novelisations stuck very closely to the original story as broadcast. This approach, coupled with the fact that the range was intended for a young readership, often produced simple, uncomplicated representations of the TV stories involved.

However, as the novelisations caught up with the programmes in production, it became increasingly possible to get the original writers of the TV stories to provide the novelisations. This in turn gave the authors a greater feeling of control over the stories and also meant that the original inspirations were fresher in the mind. Alterations were made, correcting things that the writers hadn't thought worked well on television, or introducing scenes or concepts that had been abandoned during the production process. As early as Donald Cotton's *The Mythmakers* (1985) and *The Romans* (1987) – in which Cotton added sections and narration intended to utilise the advantages of writing prose instead of dialogue[12] – the involvement of the original writer could lead to alterations that made the books more than transcriptions of the TV stories. From Kevin Clarke's *Silver Nemesis* (1989) relocating Ace's battle with the Cybermen from a warehouse to a building site (originally deemed too dangerous for filming), to Graeme Curry doing away with the 'Bertie Bassett' design imposed by the production team for his villain the Kandy Man, and reverting to his original intention of a glucose-based reanimated corpse for his novelisation of *The Happiness Patrol* (1990), the authors were less content to simply present in prose what was seen on screen.

It was in this sort of atmosphere that Ben Aaronovitch wrote *Remembrance of the Daleks* (1990), the novelisation of his 1988 TV story of the same name and 'simply the best Target book of the last ten years, if not the best of all' (Russell, 1990a: 37–8). It is this book that is credited with being the trial run for the *New Adventures*, mostly because of the fact that it introduced the character of 'the other'[13] – who was to play such an important part in the novels over their six-year run – but also because of the sheer quality of the prose and characterisation. According to Cornell (2004) '*Remembrance* set the tone for what I was doing' and, in turn, Cornell would set the tone for the whole of the *New Adventures*.

Remembrance of the Daleks succeeds so well because Aaronovitch took full advantage of the change from TV script to prose novelisation. The introduction of fictional quotes and times instead of chapter titles gives a sense of scale to the novelisation: the characters have lives after the story ends, and the reader has a constant impression of the timeline of the action. Aaronovitch also uses the opportunity to present internal monologue, giving characters depth whilst also enriching the theme of combating hatred: from the vicar blinded at Verdun and finding God, to the Special Weapons Dalek that knows it is feared by other Daleks and exists only to destroy. Characters that had only seconds of life on the TV screen are given whole lives in the novelisation, lives that help to serve the overall message of the book: there are things so evil that they must be fought, no matter what the cost – but identifying those things isn't always easy.

Equally influential was Ian Briggs' *The Curse of Fenric* (1990), the novelisation of his 1989 television story and a book that, for Russell (1990c: 20–1), reviewing its initial release, was 'better [than] Ben Aaronovitch's approach'. Unlike Aaronovitch's novelisation, *The Curse of Fenric* isn't often mentioned as a prototype *New Adventure*, despite being very well received at the time – possibly because although it did make contributions to the overarching story of the *New Adventures*,[14] it didn't add anything as inherently recognisable as 'the other'. It may also be because Ben Aaronovitch went on to write some of the most challenging and enduring *New Adventures*, whereas Ian Briggs never wrote for the range – despite being originally intended to write the first in the Timewyrm series.

Nonetheless, the novelisation follows a similar approach to Aaronovitch's: taking full advantage of the change in medium. Depth and scale are given to the story, on an even grander scale than *Remembrance of the Daleks* as here we are afforded 'historical documents' which illuminate the back-story, from Fenric's original encounter with the Doctor to a letter 'written' by Bram Stoker showing how Fenric's Haemovores inspired the Dracula story. More important, however, is the attention paid to prose and character. Briggs' writing is, like Aaronovitch's before it, superior to its contemporaries in the range, and characters are expanded from the original TV story. It is the Doctor's companion, Ace, who gets the majority of the development: by the end of the novelisation the groundwork has been laid for much of the character development in the next few years of *New Adventures*.[15]

Both novelisations share a willingness to modify and expand on the original material to take into account the change of medium. Structure and technique are considered, and are used to serve the story. Prose is lifted above mere functional descriptions of what was seen on the TV screen, and instead gives a feeling of mood and character. Characters are explored, their histories and worldviews being used to illuminate both their actions and the themes of the stories. More than this, both novelisations share a similar theme: the nature of evil, and the nature of those who oppose it. This theme could encapsulate the entire run of the Virgin *New Adventures*.

It should be no surprise, then, that it was the quality of these books, as well as other recent Target novelisations, that convinced Peter Darvill-Evans the *New Adventures* should go ahead. More than that, with the new aspects that both books introduced to the *Doctor Who* story ('the other' and a new perspective on the Doctor's actions and history from *Remembrance of the Daleks*; a deeper understanding of the character, history and future of Ace from *The Curse of Fenric*; and common to both, a willingness to investigate the strengths and possibilities of *Doctor Who* stories in a prose medium) it is plain to see that although the Virgin *New Adventures* pretended they were a continuation of the TV series, they were actually a continuation of the series of long-running Target novelisations.

Even so, the books weren't marketed under the Target imprint but as Virgin books – for simple reasons:

> Target Books are considered as a childrens' [sic] list in the book shops and these are not childrens' [sic] books [. . .] It's the casual browser in W.H. Smith's that we're aiming for, who'll buy it out of interest, not habit, from the adult science fiction section. (Darvill-Evans in Russell, 1990b: 48–50)

It is debatable how successful this objective was, but Virgin still managed to attract a large and loyal readership. As Darvill-Evans acknowledges (2004), the *New Adventures* 'never came anywhere [near] the sales of the Target novelisations at their height. We would print 25,000 copies – but we sold virtually every one, which is why the series was successful. No returns, no wastage, predictable sales figures'.[16] In 1997, the Virgin *New Adventures* were financially viable enough for the BBC to decide that original *Doctor Who* novels should be produced in house, and Virgin's exclusive licence was allowed to expire, despite considerable effort on Virgin's part to convince the BBC otherwise.[17]

They managed to achieve this kind of following, as Peter Darvill-Evans had predicted, because 'the level of sales is affected by the quality of the books' (Darvill-Evans, 1992), and Virgin were producing some high-quality books. The Virgin *New Adventures* went far beyond what a range of TV tie-in novels needed to in terms of storytelling, prose quality, characterisation and emotional resonance. Perhaps the best example is the death of the Doctor's companion Roz in Ben Aaronovitch and Kate Orman's *So Vile a Sin* (1997), where it is clear from 'the body on page one' that the death is coming – and yet there is still a hefty impact as the Doctor suffers a near breakdown at her funeral.[18] The *New Adventures* made a lasting impact on *Doctor Who*, so much so that the executive producer and chief writer of the new series, Russell T. Davies, has not only had a *New Adventure*[19] of his own published but also requested from Paul Cornell that his script for the series ('Father's Day' [2005]) use the *New Adventures*' voice:

> I think the NA voice he was after was about emotion, about evoking strong emotional response from what happens to real characters. That wasn't on the to-do list of the old show. The NAs put human drama high on the list. (Cornell, 2004)[20]

If this approach to emotional resonance ('strong emotional response') and character ('real characters') can be traced back to the later Target novelisations (in *Doctor Who* terms, at least), it was Cornell who truly took hold of it and made it his trademark. Cornell wrote the fourth *New Adventure* and the last in the Timewyrm series, *Timewyrm: Revelation* (1991). For Darvill-Evans (in Howe, 2001: 11), Cornell's book was 'a darn good story' that 'impressed with [its] writing style'. Today, the book is generally credited as setting the tone for the *New Adventures* (see for example Michael [2000]; Walker [2002]): although fan opinion is difficult to clearly determine, few *New Adventures* supporters or detractors disagree that *Timewyrm: Revelation* was the first example of what the series became typical for.

There was a lot riding on the Timewyrm series, and the fact that the range it started continued for six years with the Doctor's presence (and two without) shows that it was a success. Shortly after their publication, Peter Darvill-Evans observed that 'one of the tasks of the TIMEWYRM [sic] novels was to introduce the idea of original fiction gently [...] This is why each TIMEWYRM novel was progressively more complex and experimental than the last' (Darvill-Evans, 1992). Darvill-Evans was possibly imposing a retrospective pattern, but it is an interesting way of looking at the Timewyrm sequence. Certainly, the last book, *Revelation*, is more 'complex and experimental' than the first, *Timewyrm: Genesys* (1991), and more so than any of the preceding Timewyrm books. However, the pattern does not progress quite so evenly: the third book, *Timewyrm: Apocalypse* (1991), is comparable to the first and second, at least in terms of complexity and experimentality. Indeed, in many ways, *Timewyrm: Apocalypse* is a step back from *Timewyrm: Exodus*, the second book.

Once the *New Adventures* reached *Timewyrm: Revelation*, however, they seemed to realise that they had found their voice. The novel represented a tidemark in quality, a standard that every subsequent author had to aim for and hope to surpass. Nonetheless, fan opinion at the time and since[21] has consistently proclaimed Terrance Dicks' *Timewyrm: Exodus* the better novel. It's easy to see why: Dicks' novel is written by an established writer at the peak of his powers; Cornell's is an extremely talented young writer's first novel. Cornell happily admits that Dicks 'created the style of written *Who* in all its forms. One will always be playing one of his tunes when one is writing a *Doctor Who* book, and you can either fall back on that melody and expand on it, like I do, or rather jarringly attempt to escape it' (Cornell, 2004).

Neither book has much competition from the other entries in the Timewyrm series[22] but there is a subtle difference between them that explains why *Exodus*, the superior book, is deemed inferior in relation to the *New Adventures* as a whole. *Timewyrm: Exodus* is action adventure in the grand tradition of *Doctor Who*: the story is basically that Adolf Hitler would have died in obscurity if it wasn't for some manipulation in time, which the Doctor and Ace have to discover and then repair. The historical setting is brought to life vividly, and the characters complement the story perfectly: the Doctor is mysterious and yet ultimately right; Ace is idealistic and naïve but able to learn from the Doctor's wisdom, much as she was in the TV series; the Nazis are self-serving, evil or, in most cases, both; the real villain of the piece has a motive that stretches as far as revenge for revenge's sake and no further. It is, in short, the kind of story that the TV series would have done, if it possessed an unlimited budget and an audience devoid of very young children. It lived up to the blurb on the back of the books, 'stories too broad and too deep for the small screen', without attempting to think too much about what could be achieved with a prose *Doctor Who* story.

Timewyrm: Revelation was different – but then so was its author. Cornell was the only author of the Timewyrm books without a discernible *Doctor Who* pedigree (apart from fan fiction[23]), indeed without any publishing pedigree at all.[24] Peter Darvill-Evans had been keen to discover new writers with the *New Adventures*, for three very good reasons:

> [1] First-time authors are cheap – they don't have agents making unrealistic demands for advances. [2] Authors who are *Doctor Who* fans know and love the TV series, which always helps. They can – and did – talk to each other, co-operate on story lines, and so on. [3] First-time authors have very, very few opportunities – I was able, through the *New Adventures*, to give dozens of them a break. It was just an excellent thing to be able to do. (Darvill-Evans, 2004)

Darvill-Evans had let it be known to the fan press that Virgin were intending to produce the books specifically so that he would receive proposals from unknown writers. Throughout their lifetime, the *New Adventures* were keen to support and promote new talent, giving an opportunity to many first-time writers who have since become the lifeblood of the *Doctor Who* ranges. The *New Adventures* went to remarkable lengths to commission new writers, mainly because Peter Darvill-Evans wanted to give new authors opportunities and Rebecca Levene,[25] according to Darvill-Evans, 'had a genius for finding authors and developing stories' (Darvill-Evans, 2004). First-time *New Adventure* author Daniel Blythe made it clear how rare this was:

> There was a recession on, publishers were cutting back their lists – not to mention the fact that half my friends were leaving university without jobs [. . .] I'd been sending stuff to publishers since I was about 19 and getting the same thanks-but-no-thanks response – PD-E's open door policy was a beacon of light in the darkness [. . .] A publisher was actively *looking* for submissions for unknowns? Unheard-of! (Blythe, 2004)

If the *New Adventures* have a lasting legacy, it is that they have introduced so many new writers into the industry. Paul Cornell has gone on to write several scripts for television, including *Casualty*, and is now a writer on the new series of *Doctor Who*; Gareth Roberts worked on *Emmerdale* and *Brookside* and is currently writing his own TV sitcoms; Lance Parkin was part of the script team for *Emmerdale* and has written several TV tie-ins about the programme; Justin Richards is the current consultant to the BBC *Doctor Who* Books range, and is enjoying success with his own *Invisible Detective* series of novels; Daniel O'Mahony created the characters in the *Time Hunter* range of novellas for Telos Publishing. This is without considering those who had already begun making steps towards creative careers independent of *Doctor Who*, but couldn't resist the opportunity of contributing to such an interesting and exciting range. The most prominent examples include Matt Jones, who script edited *Queer as Folk* (1999–2000) and is writing for the second series of the relaunched *Doctor Who*, and Russell T. Davies, creator and writer of *Queer as Folk* as well as several other high-profile TV series – including, of course, the new series of *Doctor Who*. All of this is directly linked to Peter Darvill-Evans' original decision to commission Paul Cornell for *Timewyrm: Revelation*. According to another *New Adventures* discovery, Craig Hinton, 'seeing *him* being commissioned was the springboard for many of us to send off submissions; it showed us that writing a book wasn't some distant, unreachable dream, but something that might be possible for *us* to do. Paul was a living, breathing person that we knew' (Hinton, 2004).

But, for all of Darvill-Evans' talk of wanting 'to make a selling point of finding new talent' (Darvill-Evans in Howe, 2001: 11), Cornell would not have been published if *Revelation* had not been an effective conclusion to the Timewyrm sequence. The Timewyrm theme had only been a vague peg to hang each story on: the Timewyrm itself didn't manifest as a character until the closing moments of *Timewyrm: Genesys*,[26] and then (because of the medium of the Timewyrm infecting and getting trapped in other people) didn't really appear at all in *Timewyrm: Exodus* or *Timewyrm: Apocalypse*. It was important therefore that the final book featured the Timewyrm as a prominent threat. *Timewyrm: Revelation* did this, but in such a way as to add a new level of danger to the situation: the Timewyrm has taken over the Doctor's mind.

In many ways, *Revelation* is the epitome of fan-written *Doctor Who* books. Its roots are in a previously published fan fiction,[27] and right from the start it attempts to make clear that every *Doctor Who* adventure is part of a consistent universe: the prologue features the Doctor's mentor from 'Planet of the Spiders' (1974) and shows him existing in a Gallifreyan set-up akin to 'The Deadly Assassin' (1976). We also get fan fiction references (Ace's adulation of 'Johnny Chess', who is Keith Topping's fan fiction son of Barbara Wright and Ian Chesterton; little Alan Barnes being named as a character years before he became a *Doctor Who* writer).[28] But the quality of the prose and characterisation established *Revelation* as something different: a work written by somebody who had the talent to go on to be a respected writer in their own right.[29]

The main reason why *Timewyrm: Revelation* is clearly different from what had gone before isn't so much its willingness to interrogate the character of the Doctor, but the position it puts its readers in. Stories based on illusory landscapes had been done before in the TV series,[30] and so had stories that investigated the morality of the Doctor's actions.[31] Cornell's novel did both these things, but much more immediately – by setting the action firmly in the Doctor's head. In many ways, this is merely a progression from what had gone before: *Timewyrm: Revelation*'s true innovation was that it was the first *Doctor Who* story to address an adult audience.

According to Jac Raynor (date unknown) 'the target audience for *Doctor Who* books is young adults from fifteen years old and up' and as such the fiction tended to approach situations from a child's point of view. Frightening things might happen, but so long as the Doctor was there everything would turn out all right. In many ways, the most enduring Doctor and companion duo (Tom Baker's Fourth Doctor and Elisabeth Sladen's Sarah Jane Smith) played the roles as two children exploring a particularly interesting sandbox. The Target novelisations were aimed a step lower than this, on the whole presenting a simple version of a broadcast story that the average eight-year-old could understand. Peter Darvill-Evans remembers that he 'wanted the novels to appeal to adults – because I'm an adult, I suppose, and I don't read many books intended for kids' (Darvill-Evans, 2004), but even so the first three Timewyrm novels (from John Peel's teenaged boy's fantasy to Terrance Dicks' and Nigel Robinson's longer and more involved versions of what could have been at heart TV stories) still addressed this core teenaged audience. With Cornell's book, *Doctor Who* is suddenly speaking to an audience in its early twenties. Nowhere is this shift in focus more clear than in the novel's depiction of Chad Boyle.

For the first time, we are shown a story that is looking back on childhood, rather than existing in a safe and exciting version of childhood watched over by an eccentric uncle (the Doctor). More than that, we are shown a remembrance of a childhood that wasn't all that happy: Ace is the main viewpoint character for the reader, and it is through her that we are presented with a childhood where a bully (Chad Boyle) becomes the most important thing in her younger life, still having an impact on her adult life. The worst horror that Cornell's novel shows is the indignity of Ace being forcibly reverted to her childhood self, where Boyle still has influence over her, making her life a living horror.

Most interesting is chapter 9 of the novel, where Ace finds herself trapped back in a fictional representation of her teenage life, faced with the kind of traumas that are so important then but grow less so with age. The chapter is interwoven with an adult regret at the memories of things done when younger and less confident – the things ignored and never challenged that perhaps should have been. The chapter gives these regrets an adult resolution (they are changed so that the younger Ace does the things she would do as an adult) but the irony is that in terms of the story, Ace is merely reasserting her actual history, whereas for the author and the reader there is a very real sense of regret that their childhood actions couldn't also be amended. Ace did the right thing in her childhood, but the author and the reader are left with the memories of the times when they didn't.

The main battle in *Timewyrm: Revelation* isn't the Doctor against the Timewyrm, but Ace against her memories of Chad Boyle: a grown-up coming to terms with the fact that they were bullied as a child. In the end, Ace manages some kind of resolution (she forgives Boyle enough that she can see him as a child when she is an adult, and attempt to save him from the Timewyrm) but in many ways this doesn't matter – the important factor is that Ace is an adult looking back at being a child, instead of (as with *Doctor Who* previously) a child who appears to be an adult looking out with wonder at the universe. It is this subtle shift in emphasis that allows for the greater nuances of character and emotion[32] that are so typical of the Virgin *New Adventures*.

The lasting impact of the *New Adventures* isn't that they gave voice to a whole new generation of authors, nor is it that they placed human emotion and drama at the centre of the story or that they opened the floodgates for wave after wave of *Doctor Who* tie-in merchandise. It is, most simply, that for the first time – in a process that started with *Timewyrm: Revelation* – they addressed an adult audience. In doing that, they allowed for a greater level of maturity that gave rise to more complex and emotion-lead storytelling that is still a feature of *Doctor Who* today.

Notes

1   The Target imprint was created in 1973 by Universal-Tandem Publishing Co. Ltd and then sold in 1975 to Howard and Wyndham, who merged with their general publishing house W.H. Allen. By 1978, the Wyndham's identity had been phased out, and Target became the paperback identity for the company. In 1987, in return for a shareholding in W.H. Allen, Virgin Communications merged their Virgin Books imprint with W.H. Allen, with the Target books continuing until Virgin Communications acquired a controlling share in W.H. Allen and instigated a reorganisation that prompted some concern for the future of Doctor Who books. The resulting company was renamed Virgin Publishing, and the Target range continued with them until 1994, when the reprinting of the novelisations of TV stories ceased due to dwindling sales.

2   David Whitaker. *Doctor Who in an Exciting Adventure with the Daleks*. London: Frederick Muller, 1964.

3   Interestingly, this point has yet to be reached: failure to negotiate an agreement with the story's writers meant the TV episodes 'The Pirate Planet' (1978), 'City of Death' (1979), 'Resurrection of the Daleks' (1984) and 'Revelation of the Daleks' (1985) were not officially novelised (fan-produced novelisations exist). The 'lost episode' 'Shada' (1979) – which never completed filming due to industrial action – also awaits its official novelisation.

4   Tony Attwood's *Turlough and the Earthlink Dilemma* (1986) and Ian Marter's *Harry Sullivan's War* (1986).

5   Darvill-Evans acknowledges that this might not be the whole picture: later in the same interview he notes the necessary U-turn when the BBC took back the licence and Virgin had to continue the *New Adventures* without the Doctor.

6 These titles are *The Nightmare Fair* (1989) by Graham Williams, *Mission to Magnus* (1990) by Philip Martin and *The Ultimate Evil* (1989) by Wally K. Daly.

7 For example, Marc Platt's *Cat's Cradle: Time's Crucible* (1992) and *Lungbarrow* (1997) both presented a history and society for the Doctor's home planet of Gallifrey that – whilst not contradicting the TV series – was very different to and more in-depth than anything seen before.

8 *The Chase* (1989) and the two volume *The Daleks' Masterplan* (both 1989).

9 Terrance Dicks' Target novelisations are far too numerous to list: he is Target's most prolific author, having written the bulk of the Target novelisations. His first was *The Auton Invasion* a.k.a. 'Spearhead from Space' (1974) and his last *The Space Pirates* (1990), and in that period he managed to produce over sixty novelisations.

10 *The Sensorites* (1987), *The Time Meddler* (1987), *The Edge of Destruction* (1988) and *The Underwater Menace* (1988).

11 These included a scene with a glass Dalek, something that wouldn't appear on screen until 'Revelation of the Daleks' (1985).

12 According to Cornell (2004) 'those were works of prose also, doing the things which only prose can do'.

13 'The other' was the third member of the ruling Triumvirate of Gallifrey in the pre-history of Gallifrey who, unlike Rassilon and Omega, had been forgotten by history. The *New Adventures* hinted at a relationship between the Doctor and the other, which was finally revealed in Marc Platt's *Lungbarrow* (1997) – by which time the other had gained capitalisation (as The Other) and his own Gallifreyan holiday, Otherstide. The character was first thought of in production meetings between Andrew Cartmel (*Doctor Who* script editor 1987–9) and Ben Aaronovitch and Marc Platt (who were both writing for season twenty-six and were intended to write for season twenty-seven). The notes from these discussions were written up at the request of Peter Darvill-Evans when the *New Adventures* were being planned, and became the backbone of the range.

14 The final chapter of *The Curse of Fenric* (1990) shows an older Ace having left the Doctor and settled down in Paris in 1887, a fate that eventually awaited her – with one or two slight amendments – in Kate Orman's *Set Piece* (1995).

15 This isn't entirely surprising: Briggs created Ace in the TV story 'Dragonfire' (1987).

16 It should be noted that the Target books took a great deal of time to reach the levels of sales that they did – for example, Target's reprint of *Doctor Who in an Exciting Adventure with the Daleks* (1974) reached its 100,000 sales figure after seventeen years in print. The *New Adventures* managed their sales in six years.

17 Virgin suspected that something was afoot when BBC Books produced an in-house novelisation of the 1996 TV Movie, before Virgin's exclusive licence to produce new fiction had expired. There was discussion in the fan press of a possible court case, but in the end Virgin conceded defeat and the BBC took over the production of original *Doctor Who* fiction in 1997, a month after the Virgin licence expired.

18 Compare and contrast the deaths of companions in the TV series – Sara Kingdom and Katarina in 'The Daleks' Masterplan' (1965–6), and Adric in 'Earthshock'

(1982) – where the constraints of an action-drama TV series meant that there was no time for grieving. In both cases, the deaths were all but forgotten by the next story, whereas when Roz died, the event cast a shadow over every subsequent novel published. This caused some confusion when *So Vile A Sin* (1997) was delayed and was eventually published after *Lungbarrow* (1997).

19 *Damaged Goods* (1996) by Russell T. Davies. Davies was a long-term fan of the TV series, and had already made a name for himself in the world of television. His most notorious TV works – *Queer as Folk* (1999–2000) and *The Second Coming* (2002) – were still in his future when *Damaged Goods* was published. According to Paul Cornell, *Damaged Goods* was nearly 'made into a (Who-less) TV movie by Granada' (Cornell, 2004).

20 Paul continues that this is 'often devalued as "angst", as if actual drama is a distraction from . . . well, whatever else a TV show should be about, though I can't think what that might be' (Cornell, 2004). The common criticism levelled against the *New Adventures* is that they were primarily concerned with 'angst'. Ironically, this is also cited as one of the main reasons why their supporters like them.

21 *Timewyrm: Exodus* was voted the best Timewyrm novel with 34 per cent of the vote in the Doctor Who Appreciation Society's 1992 reader survey (*Celestial Toyroom*, September 1992). *Timewyrm: Revelation* came second, with 22 percent of the vote. The other Timewyrm books all came in around the 20 percent mark. Of the 610 surveys returned, just under two-thirds returned an opinion on the Virgin *New Adventures*. At the time of writing (20 September 2005), *Timewyrm: Exodus* has a vote of 81.6 per cent in the on-line rankings voted for by readers and located at www.physics.mun.ca/~sps/rank.html. *Timewyrm: Revelation* has a vote of 74.8 percent. The next book for the quartet to feature is *Timewyrm: Genesys* with 54.8 percent.

22 John Peel's *Timewyrm: Genesys* is an uncomplicated boys' own adventure that provoked some tabloid interest for having a topless teenage prostitute as a lead character. The author tries to deflect criticisms of needless titillation with a running theme from the Doctor of how unreasonable it is for a modern-day audience to judge a prehistoric society by modern standards. However, this is undermined when the Doctor's reaction to a princess refusing to bare her breasts to pass as a priestess is 'Don't let the fact that it might save all our lives influence you'. By comparison, *Timewyrm: Apocalypse* (1991) by Nigel Robinson was in a more traditional vein. However, as an action adventure story of time manipulation and universal peril, it suffered mainly from not being as well written as the preceding *Timewyrm: Exodus* (1991).

23 Paul Cornell started out writing fan fiction – indeed the story that eventually became *Timewyrm: Revelation* famously started life as a Fifth Doctor fan fiction called 'Total Eclipse' in a fanzine called *Queen Bat*. The influence of fan fiction on the *New Adventures* was pronounced, since many of the authors began as fans and then carried across some of their ideas. One of the most memorable ideas to come from the *New Adventures* (that the Seventh Doctor had sacrificed his sixth incarnation to bring himself about) came from a Paul Cornell fan fiction called 'The Ashes of Our Fathers' (1991), published in July by the Doctor

Who Appreciation Society's *Cosmic Masque* Issue XIV, before the publication of *Timewyrm: Revelation* in December.

24 When Paul Cornell submitted his proposal for *Timewyrm: Revelation* to Virgin, he had sold a text story and a comic strip script to Marvel UK's *Doctor Who Magazine*. He was also about to win a BBC scriptwriting competition and had written for Arnold Brown's Radio 4 comedy show – but these didn't play a part in Peter Darvill-Evans' decision to commission him since 'he didn't know about those at the time, because, madly, I didn't tell him!' (Cornell, 2004). By the time the novel was published, he had told somebody, as the credits were all listed on the author's cover blurb.

25 Rebecca Levene took over from Peter Darvill-Evans as editor of the *New Adventures* when his duties expanded.

26 And even then only because of a series of horrible miscalculations by the Doctor. John Peel is on record as saying, 'I had never liked the Seventh Doctor [. . .] and decided from the start that my interpretation of him would include him making some grave errors' (Peel in Howe, 2001: 10). Not only did this go against the portrayal of the Seventh Doctor as he evolved throughout the Virgin *New Adventures*, but in terms of the story of *Timewyrm: Genesys* it made for some very interesting characterisation: the Timewyrm was created because Ishtar had connected herself to a nuclear device that would explode if she was killed; when Ishtar was infected with a computer virus that would kill her, it became a race against time to ensure that this nuclear device didn't decimate prehistoric Mesopotamia; the Doctor, in these circumstances, took the nuclear device to the TARDIS and then connected a portion of Ishtar – a living computer virus – directly into the TARDIS' controls so that the nuclear device would think that she was still alive; then, and only then, did the Doctor defuse the nuclear device, in a matter of seconds. Not only was the Doctor surprised when Ishtar managed to take control of the TARDIS systems, but he didn't once consider that since he had managed to defuse the nuclear device so quickly – after he had wasted considerable time connecting Ishtar to the TARDIS (and hence creating this ultimate creature of destruction) – without it exploding, perhaps his technical expertise would have been better served in immediately defusing the bomb and letting Ishtar just be destroyed by the computer virus. It is quite clear that the Timewyrm was created because John Peel didn't like season twenty-six.

27 Paul Cornell. 'Total Eclipse'. *Queen Bat*, 1985.

28 An accusation often levelled at the *New Adventures* was that they were just fan fiction with an official logo. This is frankly nonsense – as discussed, Peter Darvill-Evans' main goal was to make a profit for Virgin by creating high-quality novels that might appeal to the casual science fiction fan, not to create a second tier of legitimacy for fan opinions and theories. However, it is aspects like this that gave rise to the claim. See Seavey (date unknown) for an interesting take on Cornell's output.

29 Since the publication of *Timewyrm: Revelation*, Paul Cornell has gone on to write for television and has had his own original science fiction novels published: *Something More* (2001) and *British Summertime* (2002).

30 'The Deadly Assassin' (1976).
31 'Remembrance of the Daleks' (1988).
32 Compare, for example, something as simple as the presentation of the Timewyrm across the first four *New Adventures*. In *Timewyrm: Genesys* she is wholly evil, killing people for minor indiscretions without a care, a typical monster; by *Timewyrm: Revelation* she is allowed a moment of sympathy as the Doctor is about to destroy her, with her human aspect admitting a fear of dying.

References

Aaronovitch, Ben. 1990. *Doctor Who: Remembrance of the Daleks*. London: Target Books.

Blythe, Daniel. 2004. 'Re: Where did the NA authors come from?' Message posted to 'Outpost Gallifrey: Doctor Who Books' forum, 23 September. www.gallifreyone. com/forum (accessed 19 September 2005).

Briggs, Ian. 1990. *Doctor Who: The Curse of Fenric*. London: Target Books.

Cornell, Paul. 2004. Interview with the author. 16 November.

Cornell, Paul. 1991. *Timewyrm: Revelation*. London: Virgin Publishing.

Darvill-Evans, Peter. 1992. 'Great forgotten bands of our time, number 1: bees make honey'. *Celestial Toyroom*, No. 182, April.

Darvill-Evans, Peter. 2004. Interview with the author. 29 November.

Dicks, Terrance. 1991. *Timewyrm: Exodus*. London: Virgin Publishing.

Hinton, Craig. 2004. 'Re: Where did the NA authors come from?' Message posted to 'Outpost Gallifrey: Doctor Who Books' forum, 22 September. www.gallifreyone. com/forum (accessed 19 September 2005).

Howe, David J. 2001. 'Tales from the fiction factory – chapter one: dancing in the dark'. *Doctor Who Magazine*, No. 305, pp. 6–11.

Michael, Matt. 2000. 'Revelation of the Doctor'. Review posted to 'The Doctor Who Ratings Guide', 10 August. www.pagefillers.com/dwrg/twrev.htm (accessed 19 September 2005).

On-Line Rankings. www.physics.mun.ca/~sps/rank.html (accessed 19 September 2005).

Peel, John. 1991. *Doctor Who – The New Adventures: Timewyrm: Genesys*. London: Virgin Publishing.

Raynor, Jac. Date unknown. 'Guidelines for writing BBC books'. www.bbc.co.uk/ cult/doctorwho/books/guidelines.shtml (accessed 19 September 2005).

Robinson, Nigel. 1991. *Doctor Who – The New Adventures: Timewyrm: Apocalypse*. London: Virgin Publishing.

Russell, Gary. 1990a. 'Off the shelf: *Remembrance of the Daleks*'. *Doctor Who Magazine*, No. 160, pp. 37–8.

Russell, Gary. 1990b. 'An open book: interview with Peter Darvill-Evans, W.H. Allen books editor'. *Doctor Who Magazine*, No. 167, pp. 48–50.

Russell, Gary. 1990c. 'Off the shelf: *The Curse of Fenric*'. *Doctor Who Magazine*, No. 168, pp. 20–1.

Seavey, John. Date unknown. 'Retrospectives: the authors of the Virgin era – part one'. Available online at www.gallifreyone.com/article.php?id=retro1 (accessed 19 September 2005).

Walker, Clive. 2002. 'A review'. Review posted to 'The Doctor Who Ratings Guide', 30 April. www.pagefillers.com/dwrg/twrev.htm (accessed 19 September 2005).

Whitaker, David. 1964. *Doctor Who in an Exciting Adventure with the Daleks*. London: Frederick Muller.

Chapter 17

Televisuality without television?
The Big Finish audios and discourses
of 'tele-centric' *Doctor Who*

Matt Hills

> The fact that *Doctor Who* ceased regular television production in 1989 has pro-
> foundly altered the forms taken by fan culture: it has removed an easy center and
> made more commonplace debates about [the] canonicity of the various products
> that have replaced it. So, in the case of *Doctor Who*, self-proclaimed fans – con-
> sumers – have become particularly involved in the production of more or less
> canonical texts. (McKee, 2004: 182)

This chapter will consider one of these post-original-TV series of 'more or less
canonical texts': the Big Finish audio adventures, produced by 'professionalised
fans' (Hills, 2002: 40) such as Gary Russell from 1999 onwards. Featuring
many of the original lead actors and actresses who appeared in TV *Doctor
Who*, these audio stories are sold on CD, being dramatisations (akin to radio
plays) rather than mere readings of text. As Gary Russell himself has commented: 'If *Star Trek* inspired people to become scientists and doctors, *Doctor
Who* inspired its fans to become media folk' (in Cook, 2003: 9).

I will argue here that fans' memories and discourses of 'golden age' *Doctor
Who* on television (Tulloch and Jenkins, 1995; Gregg, 2004; Hills, 2004) have
played a crucial role in framing the production and reception of the Big
Finish stories, made by fan producers for fan consumers, with the indus-
trially delimited format of the original TV series being preserved in certain
ways. However, in what follows, I will tend to discuss 'the Big Finish audios'
as if they can be taken to constitute a unit of analysis. It should be borne in
mind that given the diversity of Big Finish's writers/performers/production
teams, no such unity or homogeneity fully exists. The range covers many
different styles, tones and approaches to *Doctor Who*, from campy comedy
('The One Doctor' [2001]: see Roberts and Hickman, 2003: 67–70) through
to Gallifreyan space opera ('Neverland' [2002]), character-driven two-handers
('Scherzo' [2003]), formally complex experiments ('Flip Flop' [2003]), and
hard-hitting 'what-if' or counterfictional reworkings of the Doctor's character ('Full Fathom Five' [2003]). However, given my focus on the media-

specificity and media essentialism (or otherwise) of these adventures, I will tend to treat them, at least analytically and provisionally, as a unitary object of study.

Doctor Who's continued and still unfolding existence as a series of audio stories raises intriguing questions about the text's 'televisual' identity. Using and challenging John Thornton Caldwell's (1995) concept of 'televisuality', I will suggest that *discourses of televisuality* are more important than essentialist notions of media-specificity when analysing the Big Finish *Doctor Who* audios. That is, I am arguing that how these sonic adventures imitate structures and formats of televised *Who*, as well as how they utilise fan experiences and memories of *Who* on TV, are all more important to understanding and analysing these adventures than an essentialist notion of what audio 'has' to be or do, where it is assumed that it *has* to work essentially in certain ways. What is significant about these adventures, as an act of fan-producer 'textual conservationism' (Hills, 2002: 37–8), is the way that 'authentic', 'traditional' and 'televisual' (that is, tele-centric) *Doctor Who* is realised entirely without the technology of television. In other words, one thing Big Finish are (re)creating for their target market of fan-consumers is a specific *experience* of *Doctor Who*: the phenomenology (or 'fan-omenology': see Nightingale, 1996: 124) of consuming an episodic format, complete with cliffhangers and opening and closing theme music, as well as including faux *Radio Times* entries, up to and including release number 33 'Neverland', for each 'week's' episode. These entries very precisely follow the format and typeface from real *Radio Times* entries for the original television series. Such surrounding 'para-texts' (Genette, 1997) – official material circulating around the 'text' of the episodes, such as liner notes – constitute an elaborate, knowing game between fan-producers and consumers, a game which seeks to discursively contextualise the Big Finish audios as if they were part of the TV series. Although release 34, 'Spare Parts' (2002), doesn't include such inlay-card material, *Radio Times* episode guides were prepared for this story and then rejected (see Platt, 2003). The mocked-up *Radio Times* entry for part one of 'Sirens of Time' (1999), first in the BF range of audios, even includes a 'New Series' header, emulating the way that new seasons of *Doctor Who* on TV (1963–89) were marked out in *Radio Times*' publicity. Although efforts may be made to capture the spirit of certain seasons or Doctor–companion partnerships, the ageing of actors' voices partly works against this; rather than seeking to perfectly recreate certain periods of the show (as do many of the BBC's Missing Adventures novels), the audios seem instead to focus on recreating an *archetypal fan experience* or 'popular memory' (see Spigel and Jenkins, 1991) of the TV programme. Though it could be argued that simulated *Radio Times* entries are just as characteristic of radio programmes as television, such para-texts nevertheless work specifically, in this context, to cue fans' recollections of 'classic' *Doctor Who* on TV, and its accompanying promotion and publicity. In this sense, such practices remain firmly tele-centric.

There is certainly a type of 'textual conservationism' on show here, but it is not that of obsessive continuity, nor does it indicate an eternal sameness of characterisation. Quite to the contrary, Big Finish audios have developed new companions for various Doctors, such as Evelyn Smythe (Maggie Stables) who appears with Colin Baker's Sixth Doctor in a range of stories, and Charlotte Pollard (India Fisher) who accompanies Paul McGann's Eighth Doctor. The Big Finish audios have also sought to deliberately amend/revise the ways in which lead actors and their version of the Doctor were handled on TV:

> Is the Sixth Doctor's audio reign simply a chance to set right what was wrong on TV? Superficially, yes. He gets properly structured quartets of 25-minute episodes as all the other Doctors did. He features strongly in all his stories from the outset, rather than taking half the time to arrive at the action. He gets a full adventure with the Brigadier, which tellingly includes an author's sleeve note bemoaning that this Doctor 'never had a chance' to visit its archetypal *Doctor Who* setting [. . .] It's as if the Sixth Doctor has seen the advert for Claims Direct and called to get his compensation. (Owen, 2003a: 56)

But these variations on a theme have, nevertheless, sought to create moments that many fans wish could have happened on TV, such as the Sixth Doctor encountering the character of the Brigadier, thereby restoring a pattern that had held true since the era of Patrick Troughton's Second Doctor (and which Big Finish further continue by having the Brig appear in a 2001 Eighth Doctor story, 'Minuet in Hell'). The 'textual poaching' (Jenkins, 1992) of the Big Finish audios, i.e. their selection of certain textual meanings and their observation of certain 'traditions', thus frequently reflects the values and priorities of *Doctor Who*'s fan culture, while also being deliberately pro-vocative on occasion, for instance by bringing back monsters thought of as having been highly unsuccessful on TV (such as the Nimon in Paul Cornell and Caroline Symcox's 'Seasons of Fear' from 2002).

It is the conservation of fans' nostalgic memories of watching and follow-ing *Doctor Who* in its 'proper' four-part format – of excitedly awaiting the resolution to a cliffhanger, or of reading the *Radio Times* to try to glean story information – which many of the Big Finish audios playfully trade on. Operating in a radically different media environment or context to both the original TV series and the new 2005 incarnation starring Christopher Eccleston, Big Finish do not need to address a range of different audiences (cf. Gregg, 2004). They are free instead to address fan audiences first and foremost as established fans. Fan practices – ways of consuming or 'poaching' meaning from the original series (Jenkins, 1992; Bignell, 2004) – can thus be read back into the material production and presentation of these audio adventures. This amounts to more than saying that fans are represented in some of these stories (as in 'The Natural History of Fear' [2004], or 'Deadline' [2003]), something which the original TV series had already achieved in 'Greatest Show in the Galaxy' (1988–9). Beyond this, how fans are *communally and subculturally assumed to have read Doctor Who* (see Jenkins [1992] on fan reading practices), that is, the very distinctiveness of fan consumption, is attested to and amplified by the Big Finish range.

If these adventures can be described as tele-centric, then this is seemingly a matter of fan nostalgia, being a textualised marker of the desire to re-experience 'classic' *Doctor Who* as it was as an ongoing TV programme. The ironic 'as-if' televisuality of these audio stories suggests that where fan-subcultural memories and narratives of consuming *Doctor Who* are concerned, television culture (Fiske, 1987) can be faked, if you like, or commemorated/ memorialised without the presence of TV itself, becoming akin to what Alison Landsberg (1995: 176) has described as 'prosthetic memory'.

The significance of fan nostalgia is further evident in pieces written about the Big Finish audios for *Doctor Who Magazine*'s 'We Love *Doctor Who*' Special Edition (2003), which details and analyses results of the fortieth anniversary poll (in which some 2,800 fans took part: see also McKee, 2001). Jonathan Morris says of Rob Shearman's (2002) 'Chimes of Midnight' (voted best audio adventure):

> When I was about six, *Doctor Who* was scary. I didn't watch it from behind the sofa, because then I wouldn't have been able to see the television, but I do remember being terrified of the Virus, Kroll and the Stones of Blood. But, watching those stories now, they aren't remotely frightening. We all like to think that *Doctor Who* has the ability to send shivers down spines, but you're unlikely to find any stories that do that in your DVD collection. And that's why I love *The Chimes of Midnight* [. . .] Because it scared me [. . .] It was *Doctor Who* as I remembered it. *Doctor Who* as I wish it was. (Morris, 2003: 27)

In Morris's poetic phrasing, remembrance becomes something virtual or longed for, rather than simply a trace of the past. What this fan-writer is referring to is not *Doctor Who*'s continuity or televisuality *per se* (although story details are picked out, and the place of the TV is mentioned), but an experience of consuming/watching the TV series, an idealised experience that is phenomenologically (re)created by 'Chimes of Midnight'. Nicholas Briggs also begins his 'We Love *Doctor Who*' contribution, on Shearman's 'The Holy Terror' (2000), by referring to the matter of memory:

> What is it that makes a 'favourite thing'? Well, ideally it's because that thing is good, original or surprising. But often, the overriding reason is more to do with the memory of that first encounter. (Briggs, 2003: 28)

Perhaps a certain section of fandom is never going to get past the '*Doctor Who* only exists on TV' perspective. For media-essentialist fans, televisuality and being-on-telly are condensed into one seamless experience; the supposed 'essence' of *Who* is carried in its *tele*snaps, or perhaps in its non-VIDfired video and non-CGIed DVD releases. Thus, while fan debate may still rage over the relative merits of specific stories or eras, for many fans the 'telly' question tends to play like a trump card, defining *Who*ness beyond all other murky arenas of dispute (see Miles and Wood, 2004: 6). As Russell T. Davies puts it in his Foreword to *The New Audio Adventures: The Inside Story*, 'my head had forged that idiot equation, the dull $e = mc^2$ of fandom: canon = telly' (in Cook, 2003: 3).

But it needn't be this way, and it hasn't been for a range of writers and creators of a thing called, under licence, *Doctor Who*. Much has been made, by fans and critics, of the fact that *Doctor Who* outside the medium of television offers the possibility of transcending the TV show's occasionally all-too-risible limitations (see, for example, Wright, 1999). Big Finish may want to be true-to-*Who* as it was on TV, but regardless of this fact, the audios often produce a sense of scale and menace through their creation of 'epic' soundscapes (as in 'Sword of Orion' [2001]) that have rarely, if ever, been evident on screen. In the next section I want to explore the term 'televisuality' in more detail, before moving on to consider the ways in which various Big Finish audios have drawn on discourses of the televisual, as well as the ways in which their differences and distinctions from TV *Doctor Who* have occasionally been highlighted and played up.

Regenerating the televisual

John Thornton Caldwell developed the term 'televisuality' in his 1995 study of the same name, using it to explore how 1980s and 1990s American TV became style-conscious, using increasingly filmic and videographic aesthetics, as TV producers attempted to create 'event' TV along with deploying new notions of 'quality' TV which were tied into specific audience demographics. Shows like *24* (2001–) and *The Sopranos* (1999–) are a part of this legacy, playing with ideas of TV drama as having a filmic, in-your-face aesthetic style, and working hard to individuate their formats, while *Miami Vice* (1984–9) and *Twin Peaks* (1990–1) contributed to earlier waves of 'televisuality'. For Caldwell, televisuality occurs at a specific moment in television's history, being part of a drive to keep TV drama of the 1980s and 1990s distinctive and noticeable in the media marketplace. Being televisual therefore isn't the same thing as simply being on television: *Coronation Street* is on TV, but it isn't (usually or often) televisual; instead, we might say that it is typically an example of zero-degree style, and relatively anonymous direction, in which the 'reality' of the characters' predicaments is what we should focus on, if we appreciate soap operatic drama.

Caldwell's analysis of US televisuality may sound pretty alien to the worlds of *Doctor Who*, which were far from the hues of *Miami Vice* (perhaps bar the pink of 'The Happiness Patrol' [1988]) and generally beyond the Lynchian games of *Twin Peaks* (perhaps bar the watch-it-again-and-see-if-you-get-it, video-friendly narrative compression of 'Ghostlight' [1989]). Where 1980s US 'televisuality' was all self-conscious, artsy glitz, *Doctor Who* was, possibly excepting the enervation of season eighteen, rather more shabby.

So, can the notion of televisuality really offer anything other than an American yardstick against which to measure BBC *Doctor Who* production values, or a stick to beat the TV Movie with? Well, it does at least raise the question of TV drama's aesthetics, and of the television formats that help to shape and carry beloved narratives and characters. At one point in his capacious book-length study, John Thornton Caldwell alights on TV science fiction, noting that:

> It is worth considering [. . .] why many primetime televisual shows also became cult shows that attracted fan followings. *Beauty and the Beast*, *The X-Files*, *Quantum Leap*, *Star Trek* and *Max Headroom* all initiated fan activity not simply because they were visual, but because they also utilized self-contained and volatile narrative and fantasy worlds [. . .] Their preoccupation with alternative worlds [. . .] justified and allowed for extreme narrative and visual gambits [. . .] Like sci-fi, televisuality developed a system/genre of alternative worlds that tolerated and expected both visual flourishes – special effects, graphics, acute cinematography and editing – and narrative embellishments – time travel [etc.]. (Caldwell, 1995: 261)

According to this connection, science fiction is privileged in relation to televisuality, offering ways of closely realising the distinctive narrative pleasures of the televisual. Televisuality is 'like sci-fi', and seemingly not just in its technobabble. Whereas most naturalistic TV drama and soaps like *Coronation Street* lack any interest in 'alternative worlds', telefantasy seems closer to the televisual from the outset.

But if televisuality is so readily enmeshed with the science fictional (or with telefantasy), then we might suggest that *Doctor Who* was 'televisual' *avant la lettre*, and hence that televisuality was already lurking within BBC TV production at least from 1963 onwards, awaiting its ultimate US glorification. Extreme narrative and visual gambits: Dalekmania, anyone? Or Saturday night Zarbi and Zygons? Or the beautifully blank, Cocteau-derived mise-en-scène of 'Warriors' Gate' (1981). Self-reflexivity and pastiche . . . well, here, the names 'Douglas Adams' and 'Philip Hinchcliffe' might spring to mind. Thought of as televisuality, even the episode one cliffhanger to 'Dragonfire' (1987), and the same story's quotation from academic study *Doctor Who:*

The Unfolding Text (Tulloch and Alvarado, 1983) get their moments in the limelight.

If TV *Doctor Who* wasn't, after all, foreign to 'the televisual' – despite having been produced in the wrong country and at the wrong time to fit neatly into Caldwell's definition – then it follows that many of the pleasures of this series were, and are, pleasures of televisuality. Again, note that this isn't the same thing as saying that *Doctor Who* was good when it was on TV. *Doctor Who* was good, in part, because it was intrinsically televisual. And herein lay the post-1996 and pre-2005 fan dilemma: how were such pleasures to be found in new non-television *Who*? Could Big Finish cut it? If the fan battle was joined here, then this certainly wasn't about 'a bunch of grumpy old men, getting nostalgic about "glory days" that never really existed', as Stephen Searle argues way back in *Doctor Who Magazine* No. 294 (Searle, 2000: 7). This was more than a 'Golden Age' debate, with each generation of fans championing their favourite period of the programme. This was about something else: the very televisuality of *Doctor Who*. Because if televisuality isn't quite the same thing as 'being on telly', then it can be recreated (or challenged) in audio adventures. The show's evolving but ever-recognisable format, its aesthetic style, as well as how it was slotted into a TV-industry-led form that now barely exists (twenty-five-minute episodes complete with cliff-hanger): all can potentially be replayed and textually/discursively constructed outside the realms of television. The world's longest-running TV science fiction series doesn't need TV. It just needs to be 'televisual', whether or not it's actually on the telly.

This takes us into what has been termed the 'trad' and 'rad' debate. Trads want *Doctor Who* stories to be forever in twenty-five-minute-ish chunks, times three or four; they're not enamoured by attempts to pull in 'story arc' narrative structures gleaned from *The X-Files* (1993–2002) or later *Star Trek*s; and they tend to be dismissive of efforts to rework the *Who* format. Whether or not it's on TV, *Doctor Who*'s televisuality – part of the basic phenomenology/ essence of fans' experience of the show – has to be conserved. And, by and large, this aesthetic choice has been very much championed by the Big Finish audios. The anchoring of *Who* to a certain televisuality is undoubtedly a major part of what makes the Big Finish adventures seem satisfyingly *Doctor Who*-esque for their many fan-consumers. This movement towards seeking to recapture or recreate fans' memories of watching the original series has, furthermore, progressed across the Big Finish range. Initially, only the Ron Grainer/Delia Derbyshire theme music was used on releases, resulting in the rather jarring fan experience of hearing a non-synthesised rendering of the show's theme leading into a Peter Davison, Colin Baker or Sylvester McCoy story. However, from 'Bang-Bang-a-Boom!' (2002) onwards, the CDs used 'the apposite *Doctor Who* theme' (Cook, 2003: 176) for relevant Doctors, or even more specifically, to evoke and memorialise specific periods of a Doctor's tenure, such as the Dominic Glynn theme that occurs on 'Jubilee' (2003). 'Bang-Bang-a-Boom!' also goes so far as to feature mock pre-episode 'BBC 1-style continuity announcements' (Cook, 2003: 176), working (like inlaycard simulated *Radio Times* entries) to playfully recreate para-texts that characterised TV *Who*.

Audio adventures in space and time

If the Big Finish audios variously work to recreate fan memories of experiencing TV *Who*, drawing on discourses of televisuality and at the very least becoming tele-centric, then this still does not exhaust how they play with different media. A number of audio adventures strongly emphasise their lack of visuals by carrying out narrative conceits that would be difficult to sustain in filmed or televised versions. For example, shock twists at the end of 'Omega' (2003) episode three, or at the conclusion to 'Natural History of Fear', hinge on audiences making certain assumptions on the basis of what (or who) they are hearing. Nev Fountain has said of his script for 'Omega' that 'I realised I could do an "audio *Fight Club*"! As someone who writes a lot of radio, writing a story that could only work in the audio medium greatly appealed to me' (in Cook, 2003: 215).

Other Big Finish stories have made exaggerated use of sound design to construct meaning: 'Deadline' (2003) is particularly notable in this respect, where incidental music is repeated so that it becomes uncanny, stilted and mechanical-seeming, adding greatly to the surrealism of Rob Shearman's script, and capturing the story's blurring of fantasy and reality. Much earlier in the Big Finish range, in the third release, 'Whispers of Terror' (1999), the audio in 'audio adventures' was also being stressed. The writer of this story, Justin Richards, has suggested that '[i]f there's a single *Doctor Who* audio adventure that simply couldn't be done in another medium [. . .] no question, *Whispers of Terror* it is' (in Cook, 2003: 23). This tale features a sound creature and the Museum of Aural Antiquities, and makes repeated use of recorded, replayed and distorted sound in line with Richards's original notion to 'fully use (exploit?) the medium' (in Cook, 2003: 21).

Such a story may seem to radically contradict the notion that these audios are tele-centric in terms of seeking to recreate televisual and TV-industrial forms of the original series, but it is worth considering that even this story repeats the episodic form of the original TV series. Furthermore, as the third Big Finish release, 'Whispers of Terror' clearly serves notice that the audios can achieve effects that would not work as TV drama, but it nevertheless does so after two fairly traditional *Who* stories. 'The Sirens of Time' is a multi-Doctor story involving Gallifrey, and is perhaps only notable for its formal device of separating the Fifth, Sixth and Seventh Doctors for much of its running time, whilst 'Phantasmagoria' (1999) is a very traditional gothic tale, as well as self-consciously fitting into 'the age of the one-word title' (Gatiss in Cook, 2003: 20), the Davison era. Big Finish hence deliberately began with an 'event' story and a trad, tele-centric piece before opting to stress the possible scope of an audio adventure. In fact, I would suggest that Big Finish's output can be categorised into stories that are, in a sense, only incidentally audio adventures, and those that rely on the medium to work, with the former far outweighing the latter. This puts the likes of 'Whispers of Terror', 'Omega', 'Deadline', 'The Rapture' (2002) and 'Doctor Who and the Pirates' (2003) in the distinct minority, with 'Whispers' acting as a potential limit-case. And though it could be suggested that 'Whispers' et al. make the style of their (audio) presentation their subject matter – potentially re-enacting the very gesture which characterises 'televisuality' for Caldwell – this self-referential turn has been discursively positioned in surrounding texts as a way of establishing clear distance between 'classic' Doctor Who on TV, and audio Who.

Perhaps unsurprisingly, the Big Finish range has most consistently moved away from 'traditional' tele-centric Doctor Who in its Eighth Doctor adventures starring Paul McGann, beginning with 2001's 'Storm Warning'. After all, in a sense, these BF audios do not possess a sustained and televised 'era' to recapture, beyond relating to the one-off 1996 TV Movie. Unusually, they create new Who without referring back to a nostalgia-laden template, and without consistently citing an archetypal fan experience of watching Doctor Who. Although the McGann audios are arranged in 'seasons' – thereby imitating patterns of broadcast TV Who – they have taken on an increasingly 'epic' science fictional identity. As Dave Owen has observed:

> this [venture . . .] had the benefit of four years of collective expression of the Eighth Doctor's essence [e.g. in BBC Books – MH]. The Doctor Who creative community had somehow achieved a consensus of what this Doctor was like, and what he did and didn't do, that was slightly at odds with Philip Segal and Matthew Jacobs' vision for their film. (Owen, 2003b: 70)

This re-engineered McGann Doctor has appeared in dramas which don't so much play on televisual qualities, or refer to TV culture's para-texts, as draw on historically important radio plays like Orson Welles' (1938) 'War of the Worlds' (in Mark Gatiss's [2002] 'Invaders From Mars').

However, such exuberant, free-standing audio-dramas-about-audio-dramas have become subordinated to intricate story arcs requiring listeners to link scenes and details across McGann 'seasons', at least from the story 'Neverland' onwards (see Barnes, 2002: 219–22). In this case, Big Finish audios operate in the shadow of Eighth Doctor BBC Books, similarly attempting to 'reset' *Doctor Who*'s diegetic world by taking the Doctor out of his 'usual' universe (in 'Zagreus' [2003]), and restricting the narrative possibility of time travel (across the Divergent Universe arc running from 'Scherzo' through to 'The Next Life' [2004]). McGann's BF stories have partly moved away from *Doctor Who*'s televisuality in favour of presenting mythic science fiction on a grand scale; for example, 'The Next Life' intertextually recalls the likes of *The Matrix Reloaded* (2003) via its philosophical vision of a cyclically reset world.

While positioning the Eighth Doctor's adventures as mythic or 'serious' SF, this section of Big Finish's output still draws significantly on 'traditional' elements of the original TV series which were present/implied in the 1996 TV Movie (Moore and Stevens, 2003: 7): i.e. the Doctor's homeworld, Gallifrey, and its villainous ur-Time Lord, Rassilon. By doing so, Eighth Doctor audios have tended to reach a specialised target audience of established *Doctor Who* fans who are also fans of science fiction, replicating the way that the Eighth Doctor's television outing 'had precisely nothing to do with the "target audience" of the original series and everything to do with trying to generate an instant single-demographic following' among SF fans (Miles and Wood, 2004: 129). And yet the cliffhanger conclusion to 'The Next Life' seems slightly out of alignment with the SF epic preceding it, literally welcoming the character of the Eighth Doctor back to a more accessible *Who* – one open to a diverse audience of the kind possessed by the original series (see Tulloch and Alvarado, 1983) and hoped for by the 2005 production.

A powerful tension between neo- and retro- concepts of *Doctor Who*, between audio media-specificity and tele-centricity, also occurs across Big Finish's representations of the Doctor's infamous enemies, the Daleks, up to and including their appearance in 'The Juggernauts' (2005). They are initially used in a 'very old fashioned and traditional' way in the (2000) audio, 'The Genocide Machine' (Mike Tucker in Cook, 2003: 36), only appearing at the end of Part One of the story, as they did in many televised tales. Nicholas Briggs, responsible for sound design for 'The Genocide Machine', recounts the process behind the realisation of Dalek voices: 'Gary [Russell] and I spent a morning debating what the Daleks should sound like. We watched and listened to scenes from [original TV series] Dalek episodes, then rushed upstairs to make Alistair [Lock's] ring modulator achieve that effect' (in Cook, 2003: 38).

Here, it is not only the case that the story is structured in a traditional and tele-centric way; the producers also stress how the Dalek voices from the TV series act as a template and reference point for their sound design in order for an 'authentic' or canonical effect to be realised. Once again, fan-producer nostalgia shines through, as when the story's creator, Mike Tucker, observes that:

I was overwhelmed [by hearing it]. As a child, I used to record *Doctor Who* off air with an old mono cassette recorder and then listen to the episodes in my bedroom between seasons; listening to *The Genocide Machine* gave me the same cosy nostalgic feeling, albeit with better sound quality. (in Cook, 2003: 38)

It is not just that Big Finish's audio adventures draw on discourses of tele-visuality; the bleeding together of televisual and audio media via fan practices also works in the reverse direction, with Tucker-as-child-fan converting a TV programme into a sound recording for the purpose of textual conservation, and so as to re-experience the powerful affective relationship of *Doctor Who* fandom. Audio recording was a common practice among *Who* fans prior to VCR technology; as a young fan *sans* VCR, 'Warriors' Gate' was the first story that I audio-recorded, and the novelty of the fact that I was able to re-experience its soundtrack at will – nostalgically cueing memories of the televised story – may somewhat account for the high regard in which I still hold it.

It is only much later in the Big Finish range that Dalek voices are used in ways that expand and challenge the creatures' TV portrayals, with both 'Time of the Daleks' (2002) and 'Jubilee' delighting in the incongruity of having ring-modulated Dalek voices recite Shakespeare or mutter about 'scarpering' from the Doctor. Justin Richards, writer of 'Time of the Daleks', has offered an intriguing explanation of the story's genesis, suggesting that it is actually the audio 'equivalent' of TV story 'Evil of the Daleks' (1967), where the pepperpot menaces were shown 'completely out of context [. . .] roaming the candlelit corridors of a Victorian mansion'. Richards goes on:

I wanted the aural equivalent of that shock – of seeing Daleks out of place, where they shouldn't be. Of the ideas that I had, I decided that having them quote Shakespeare would be disconcerting without being silly. I did consider singing Daleks – but I guess I wasn't as brave as Rob Shearman! (Richards in Cook, 2003: 150)

Rather like Mike Tucker's discussion of 'The Genocide Machine', TV and audio media bleed together discursively here: 'Time of the Daleks' is represented both as a nostalgic, tele-centric recapturing of canonical TV *Who*, and simultaneously as the 'aural equivalent' of a strikingly incongruous visual image, thereby stressing the story's identity as an audio adventure. Similarly, the more recent Sixth Doctor audio 'The Juggernauts' combines retro, TV-based continuity – the reappearance of the Daleks' 1960s enemies, the 'Mechonoids' – with neo- and sonic incongruity; in this case the 'clean' and non-ring-modulated voice of actor Terry Molloy as a 'familiar' and yet 'alien'- (because more human-) sounding Davros.

It is easy to assume that what distinguishes the Big Finish audios from TV adventures is their lack of visuals, but I am arguing that the situation isn't at all as clear-cut as this. Although the audio stories usually lack moving images, a number of audio-only CD releases ('Real Time' [2002] and a re-worked 'Shada' [2003] featuring Paul McGann) were initially BBCi webcasts produced by Big Finish and accompanied by flash animations. Furthermore, the audio stories have accompanying images in the shape of cover designs – with Paul McGann 'seasons' being graphically distinguished from regular releases in a further tele-centric emulation of TV 'seasons' – as well as specially commissioned illustrations for *Doctor Who Magazine*. In a variety of ways, then, the audio adventures are never fully bounded as purely sound-based, challenging any absolute separation, or binary opposition, between sound-only and sound-and-(moving)-image *Doctor Who*.

Despite the common-sense notion that 'TV = visuals' and 'audio = sound-only' Piers Britton and Simon Barker have recently argued in their study *Reading Between Designs* that the importance of visual imagery and design has been greatly under-rated in analysis of the original *Doctor Who* TV series:

> There was a much greater underlying continuity in the costumes worn by the eight successive lead players [now disrupted by 2005's Ninth Doctor – MH] than is generally acknowledged [. . .] In the first place, the costumes all incor-porated some legacy from the Victorian age [. . . and] each of the Doctors wore a garment that was powerfully redolent of professional authority or the upper class: morning coats for the first two, a smoking jacket [. . .] for the third, and frock coats for all but one of the others. (Britton and Barker, 2003: 146–7)

By focusing on the construction of meaning through costume design, Britton and Barker restore the visual to a central place in TV studies, which has sometimes tended to analyse narrative structure etc. in a way that works to downplay the importance of TV's mise-en-scène. However, Britton and Barker's emphasis on the visual can also lead us to discern unusual absences in the imagery accompanying Big Finish releases. For example, given the importance of the Doctor's costume attested to in *Reading Between Designs*, it is striking that the Big Finish *Doctor Who Unbound* range – featuring new actors playing the character of the Doctor rather than those who have already appeared in 'canonical' TV *Who* – does not attempt to reimagine/re-engineer new costumes for its counterfictional versions of the Doctor. Instead, this range's CD covers are uniformly images of each actor's face superimposed over a 'time tunnel'-type effect. This results in new representations of the Doctor that have no visual reference point beyond the actor playing the part. As such, *Doctor Who Unbound* seems, rather unusually for Big Finish, to violate the norms and practices of *Doctor Who* fan culture and its tele-centricities, in which the Doctor's costume is taken to be a key part of his (or her) characterisation and identity.

In this discussion I have argued that the Big Finish range is typically charac-terised by a nostalgic attempt to recapture the format, and fan experiences, of the original TV series, meaning that the Doctor's audio adventures draw on discourses of televisuality and tend to be tele-centric. TV *Who* is a consistent reference point for the construction of these stories as 'authentic' or (more-or-less) 'canonical', with fan-producers hailing fan-consumers as fans, and hence seeking to replay, and knowingly play with, fan practices of *Who* watching: the enjoyment of episodes and cliffhangers, the use of para-texts in anticipation of a story, the reproduction of different eras' versions of the theme music, and so on. Despite this continual and knowing 'as-if' reactivation of TV *Who* and its own historical, TV-cultural para-texts, a number of audio adventures, either in their realisation of the Daleks, or via their specific use of sound design and production, have especially stressed the audio medium. This push towards media-specificity or media-essentialism occurs alongside, and in tension with, Big Finish's 'trad' position, being subordinated to the range's dominant tone and tenor of fan nostalgia and tele-centricity. Therefore, for fans to ignore or neglect these audio adventures because 'telly = canon' seems rather short-sighted. The Big Finish audios acknowledge that very fan equation, and go on to appropriate it in order to discursively construct their texts as 'televisual', albeit without television. With *Doctor Who* finally back on TV screens as of 26 March 2005, it will be interesting to see what, if any, impact this has on Big Finish's use of tele-centric narrative structures and para-texts linked to the show's original 1963–89 run. It may result in stories less directly aimed at an established *Doctor Who* and science fiction fanbase (as the conclusion to 'The Next Life' hinted). And it could perhaps also lead to a greater emphasis on audio media-specificity, with Big Finish's CDs seeking to differentiate themselves from the audio-visual spectacle of the new *Who*. In any case, the nostalgic, textually conservationist 'trad' fan-consumers of Big Finish's output may no longer be able to view 4 × 25 minutes, plus cliffhanger (a 1960s/1970s industry-delimited format) as the 'natural' shape of the TV series. In the radically changed media context of multi-channel, digital and non-terrestrial TV, what it means to be a 'tele-centric' and 'trad' fan of *Doctor Who* is, perhaps, in the process of undergoing a seismic shift. It's about time.

References

Barnes, Alan. 2002. 'Neverland'. *Doctor Who: The Audio Scripts*. Maidenhead: Big Finish, pp. 219–22.
Bignell, Jonathan. 2004. *An Introduction to Television Studies*. London: Routledge.
Briggs, Nicholas. 2003. 'The Holy Terror'. *Doctor Who Magazine Anniversary Special: We Love Doctor Who*, p. 28.
Britton, Piers D. and Simon J. Barker. 2003. *Reading Between Designs: Visual Imagery and the Generation of Meaning in The Avengers, The Prisoner and Doctor Who*. Austin: University of Texas Press.

Caldwell, John Thornton. 1995. *Televisuality: Style, Crisis and Authority in American Television*. New Brunswick, NJ: Rutgers University Press.

Cook, Benjamin. 2003. *The New Audio Adventures: The Inside Story*. Maidenhead: Big Finish.

Davies, Russell T. 2003. 'Foreword'. In Benjamin Cook. *The New Audio Adventures: The Inside Story*. Maidenhead: Big Finish, p. 3.

Fiske, John. 1987. *Television Culture*. London: Methuen.

Genette, Gerard. 1997. *Paratexts*. Cambridge: Cambridge University Press.

Gregg, Peter B. 2004. 'England looks to the future: the cultural forum model and *Doctor Who*'. *Journal of Popular Culture*, Vol. 37, No. 4, pp. 648–61.

Hills, Matt. 2002. *Fan Cultures*. London and New York: Routledge.

Hills, Matt. 2004. '*Doctor Who*'. In Glen Creeber (ed.). *Fifty Key TV Programmes*. London: Arnold, pp. 75–9.

Jenkins, Henry. 1992. *Textual Poachers*. London and New York: Routledge.

Landsberg, Alison. 1995. 'Prosthetic memory: *Total Recall* and *Blade Runner*'. In Mike Featherstone and Roger Burrows (eds). *Cyberspace Cyberbodies Cyberpunk: Cultures of Technological Embodiment*. London: Sage, pp. 175–89.

McKee, Alan. 2001. 'Which is the best *Doctor Who* story? A case study in value judgements outside the academy'. *Intensities: The Journal of Cult Media*. Issue 1. www.cult-media.com/issue1/Amckee.htm (accessed 20 September 2005).

McKee, Alan. 2004. 'How to tell the difference between production and consumption: a case study in *Doctor Who* fandom'. In Sara Gwenllian Jones and Roberta Pearson (eds). *Cult Television*. Minneapolis: University of Minnesota Press, pp. 167–85.

Miles, Lawrence and Tat Wood. 2004. *About Time 4*. New Orleans: Mad Norwegian Press.

Moore, Fiona and Alan Stevens. 2003. 'The past is an all-too-familiar country'. *In-Vision*. No. 109, pp. 6–8.

Morris, Jonathan. 2003. 'The Chimes of Midnight'. *Doctor Who Magazine Anniversary Special: We Love Doctor Who*, p. 27.

Nightingale, Virginia. 1996. *Studying Audiences: The Shock of the Real*. London and New York: Routledge.

Owen, Dave. 2003a. 'Further adventures: audios'. *Doctor Who Magazine Special Edition: The Complete Sixth Doctor*, pp. 56–8.

Owen, Dave. 2003b. 'Further adventures: audios'. *Doctor Who Magazine Special Edition: The Complete Eighth Doctor*, pp. 70–2.

Platt, Marc. 2003. 'Spare Parts'. *Doctor Who: The Audio Scripts – Volume Three*. Maidenhead: Big Finish, pp. 1–4.

Roberts, Gareth and Clayton Hickman. 2003. 'The One Doctor'. *Doctor Who: The Audio Scripts – Volume Two*. Maidenhead: Big Finish, pp. 67–70.

Searle, Stephen. 2000. 'Timelines: trad rad lad fad mad (etc)'. *Doctor Who Magazine*, No. 294, p. 7.

Spigel, Lynn and Henry Jenkins. 1991. 'Same bat channel, different bat times: mass culture and popular memory'. In Roberta E. Pearson and William Uricchio (eds). *The Many Lives of the Batman*. London: BFI Publishing, pp. 117–48.

Tulloch, John and Manuel Alvarado. 1983. *Doctor Who: The Unfolding Text*. London and Basingstoke: Macmillan.

Tulloch, John and Henry Jenkins. 1995. *Science Fiction Audiences: Watching Doctor Who and Star Trek*. London and New York: Routledge.

Wright, Peter. 1999. 'The shared world of *Doctor Who*: from the New Adventures to the Regeneration'. *Foundation: The International Review of Science Fiction*, No. 75, pp. 78–96.

Select discography

Doctor Who: 'The Sirens of Time' (1999) Produced by Gary Russell and Jason Haigh-Ellery. Directed by Nicholas Briggs. Written by Nicholas Briggs. Music by Nicholas Briggs. 126 mins (4 episodes). Big Finish.

Doctor Who: 'Phantasmagoria' (1999) Produced by Gary Russell and Jason Haigh-Ellery. Directed by Nicholas Briggs. Written by Mark Gatiss. Music by Alistair Lock. 89 mins (4 episodes). Big Finish.

Doctor Who: 'Whispers of Terror' (1999) Produced by Gary Russell and Jason Haigh-Ellery. Directed by Gary Russell. Written by Justin Richards. Music by Nicholas Briggs. 93 mins (4 episodes). Big Finish.

Doctor Who: 'The Genocide Machine' (2000) Produced by Gary Russell and Jason Haigh-Ellery. Directed by Nicholas Briggs. Written by Mike Tucker. Music by Nicholas Briggs. 115 mins (4 episodes). Big Finish.

Doctor Who: 'The Holy Terror' (2000) Produced by Gary Russell and Jason Haigh-Ellery. Directed by Nicholas Pegg. Written by Robert Shearman. Music by Russell Stone. 136 mins (4 episodes). Big Finish.

Doctor Who: 'Sword of Orion' (2001) Produced by Gary Russell and Jason Haigh-Ellery. Directed by Nicholas Briggs. Written by Nicholas Briggs. Music by Nicholas Briggs. 123 mins (4 episodes). Big Finish.

Doctor Who: 'Invaders from Mars' (2002) Produced by Gary Russell and Jason Haigh-Ellery. Directed and written by Mark Gatiss. Music by Alistair Lock. 96 mins (4 episodes). Big Finish.

Doctor Who: 'Chimes of Midnight' (2002) Produced by Gary Russell and Jason Haigh-Ellery. Directed by Barnaby Edwards. Written by Rob Shearman. Music by Russell Stone. 116 mins (4 episodes). Big Finish.

Doctor Who: 'Time of the Daleks' (2002) Produced by Gary Russell and Jason Haigh-Ellery. Directed by Nicholas Briggs. Written by Justin Richards. Music by Nicholas Briggs. 122 mins (4 episodes). Big Finish.

Doctor Who: 'Spare Parts' (2002) Produced by Gary Russell and Jason Haigh-Ellery. Directed by Gary Russell. Written by Marc Platt. Music by Russell Stone. 121 mins (4 episodes). Big Finish.

Doctor Who: 'Bang-Bang-a-Boom!' (2002) Produced by Gary Russell and Jason Haigh-Ellery. Directed by Nicholas Pegg. Written by Gareth Roberts and Clayton Hickman. Music by Andy Hardwick. 143 mins (4 episodes). Big Finish.

Doctor Who: 'Omega' (2003) Produced by Gary Russell and Jason Haigh-Ellery. Directed by Gary Russell. Written by Nev Fountain. Music by Russell Stone. 141 mins (4 episodes). Big Finish.

Doctor Who (Unbound): 'Deadline' (2003) Produced by Jason Haigh-Ellery and John Ainsworth. Directed by Nicholas Briggs. Written by Robert Shearman. Music by Nicholas Briggs. 61 mins. Big Finish.

Doctor Who: 'The Next Life' (2004) Produced by Gary Russell and Jason Haigh-Ellery. Directed by Gary Russell. Written by Alan Barnes and Gary Russell. Music by Andy Hardwick and Russell Stone. 220 mins. Big Finish.

Doctor Who: 'The Juggernauts' (2005) Produced by Gary Russell and Jason Haigh-Ellery. Directed by Gary Russell. Written by Scott Alan Woodard. Music by Steve Foxon. 120 mins (4 episodes). Big Finish.

Afterword
My adventures

Paul Magrs

My best friend moved away from our street. His dad worked with mine –
both were policemen. They kept in touch. My best friend's family hadn't
moved all that far away. Just across town. Darlington's suburbs, where the
tall houses turned into bungalows and the town itself gradually thinned
out into farmland; into gentle hills of churned-up mud and brilliant yellow
and green.

They thought a lot of themselves, living out by the countryside. I was 6,
but well aware of the ripples and currents of bragging and condescension all
that afternoon of our visit. (They had an avocado bathroom suite! A down-
stairs loo!) The purpose of our visiting was so we could see how settled in
they were, and to let us boys see each other again, because we'd been such
good friends, hadn't we? Back in that busy, noisy street in the middle of
town, where we still lived.

My friend's name was Tom. He had a younger, toddler brother, same as
I had. Tom was keen that we went to look at the den they had made in their
new back garden. We could see it from their kitchen window. The windows
(double-glazed! It was evidently a far more up-to-the-minute police house
than ours!) were all silvery and dripping with rain. It teemed down all that
Saturday afternoon. We stared out, waiting for a gap in the weather: ready to
dash out, to examine that clump of trees at the back. The heaped branches
and twigs; the sheets of cardboard; the bits of old carpet that Tom had
lumped together and called a den. I wasn't all that impressed by it.

I think we went out. I think we had a desultory poke around, looking at
the camp he had built. I think the skies opened and I think we got soaked.
And, of course, that didn't matter to us. Not to us. There's only so wet you
can get, isn't there? After that it doesn't count. And we loved getting soaked
and standing under all that dripping, shivering greenery: listening to the
bronchial roar of thunder approaching from the north.

'It's better than the den we used to have, isn't it? On the wasteground? It's better than the one before. Cause – look – this one is mine. It's in our garden. So it's all mine. It belongs to me.'

Tom was really showing off. He was really keen on having his den, and all his adventures, right in his own back yard.

Someone – my dad, his mam, my mam, his dad – one of the adults who'd grown bored of chatting with the others – had drifted to the window, and seen us standing there, dripping in the rain – clothes growing heavier and heavier – pudding-bowl hair plastered down to our skulls.

'What on earth are you doing out there?'

They couldn't believe it. They called us in. We'd catch our deaths, otherwise.

It was teatime. Cake and chocolate biscuits in silver wrappers, set out in geometric designs on plates and doillies. Petals of Kitkats, Blue Ribands and Penguins. (Tom's mam trying hard to impress her first Saturday teatime guests in her new house. Putting on – as we used to say – a good spread.) Bird's Eye trifle standing at the ready – chilling in the fridge. And, with clean towels rubbed through our hair, we were made to sit quiet on the intricately and verdantly patterned living-room carpet and watch the telly.

Doctor Who was coming back on. The start of a new series. It was that time of year again. We would have to be quiet and watch. Give the grown-ups some peace. This was what kids like us liked to watch, wasn't it? The grown-ups all started talking about watching this programme back when they were kids, when everything was black and white, when it was all very frightening and he was an old man then, but he was much younger now, wasn't he? With those boggling eyes and that mad scarf.

I could just about remember some of last year's adventures. They came from prehistory, from winter teatimes when I was 5. They came back in lurid, hallucinatory glimpses. Back then I'd been parked in front of the telly: Watch this! There's Daleks in it this week! And I remembered dank caverns dripping gold; brilliant white rooms in outer space; Daleks painted greeny blue with flashing eyes; that withered up man in the wheelchair shouting; the potato-faced troll with his head deflating like a burst football. I remembered my dad on a rare weekend home from police training courses, watching this with us, and him laughing aloud at the monster's squashed face – and all of us joining in with the laughter. Deflating the horror. Making it funny again.

I wasn't sure I wanted to watch this programme now.

But this was a visit. You had to be polite. You had to do what everyone else wanted to do. And this wasn't like visiting grandparents. You couldn't kick up a fuss. These were friends-of-the-family, near-strangers now in their new, big house in the suburbs with its avocado suite. You had to behave, and sit quietly on their junglelike, swirling green and brown carpet. You had to watch the tumbling blue of the time tunnel and remember that howling, thundery theme tune. You had to watch these monsters, that looked bloody and babylike, dripping with slime and baked bean juice – living under a lake and keeping dinosaurs as pets. Hissing angrily at each other and sucking out people's minds.

You had to watch it all, and it was fantastic.

And after that . . .

Every den you ever built had to be the monsters' secret base, or the villain's deadly lair. Or the interior of the Doctor's marvellous TARDIS, with its six-sided console and hatstand for slinging your hat and scarf onto.

And every game you ever played when you played out, no matter who you played with – they were always *Doctor Who*. The other kids were companions, villains, monsters. Your brother was always a robot dog.

And every story you ever wrote. That was always *Doctor Who*, as well. At home, unashamedly so. You turned out tales too broad, too deep, too ludicrous for the small screen. And these stories were so exciting you couldn't even bring yourself to finish them off. Those adventures went on and on and on. They were the adventures in which the Daleks and the Cybermen and the Zygons all invaded Gallifrey and Victorian London and prehistoric Earth, and they set about attacking the Silurians and Sea Devils and Dinosaurs and Time Lords and Sherlock Holmes and Queen Victoria and EVERYONE! And all the Marvel surperheroes and Planet of the Apes and Dracula somehow became involved. The Fantastic Four declared war on the Cybermen, and Galactus – much to the chagrin of Davros (who had teamed up with Dracula to breed vampire Daleks!) – was threatening to liquidate Skaro. On and on and on and on and on, and you were drawing all the pictures, too.

And all the stories you ever wrote at school, they were *Doctor Who*, too. When your class read *The Hobbit*, the Daleks invaded Middle-earth and that was the end of that. When you fell in love with *The Lion, the Witch and the Wardrobe*, the Master joined forces with the wicked queen of winter and the Doctor was called for by Aslan, and his various incarnations were sprinkled in time throughout Narnia's long centuries. And then your teachers were telling you to stop, stop, stop! They told your parents you were a mite obsessed. Well, quite a bit obsessed. In fact, far too obsessed. You had to be stopped. You couldn't have time machines and monsters in every story you wrote. You should try to make up stories for characters of your own. You shouldn't allow your own characters to simply escape from the confines of their lives by stepping aboard a battered blue police box and travelling elsewhere. Your characters should stay at home and learn about real life. It didn't do – it really didn't do at all – to be so obsessed with something as silly as *Doctor Who*.

The point of this essay isn't to suddenly go: How wrong they were! Hahahahaha!

I think the point of it might actually turn out to be . . . They were right! They should have stopped him! They should have stopped him watching it! And reading all the books again and again! And having posters on his walls! And talking Daleks and model Tom Bakers and Top Trumps cards and Weetabix collectible stand-up figures! And buying *Doctor Who Weekly* on its first day of publication! And begging begging begging for day trips to Blackpool to visit that subterranean, sepulchral holy of holies: the *Doctor Who* exhibition! Shabby old costumes and props standing in cupboards with multi-coloured lights flashing round them! Brilliant! Buying LOADS of merchandise and feeling dizzy and sick with candy floss and excitement. All of it, all of it, far too exciting! Thrilled with your own knowledge and expertise in the *Doctor Who* universe . . . and what a vocabulary it gave you . . . Capacious! Voluminous! Dimensionally transcendental! Neutron flow! Vortex! War of attrition! Serendipity!

Yes! Stop him now! Go back in time and prevent it ever happening! They were right! It was true!

He did ruin his life!

'The whole wide world doesn't revolve around *Doctor Who*, you know. You might think it does. But it doesn't. You should get out more. Broaden your horizons.'

Oh dear. I got this again and again. Mam would get exasperated with me. And with my brother, too. We were both obsessed.

The high point of it all – and the most exasperating period for everyone around us – was probably between 1980 and 1985.

In 1980 there was a collision of things that made sure that we became completely obsessed. First there was the start of *Doctor Who Weekly*, and then there was our discovery of the Target novelisations.

We bought both from Stevens – a narrow, rather dark newsagent in our town centre, the old, good type of newsagent that sold cheap toys and novelties and the more arcane kinds of sweets. The comic cost 12p and gave these alluring glimpses of the creatures and characters inhabiting the mass unconscious of the recent past: the Zarbi, the Yeti and the giant maggots with gnashing jaws. We had never seen these beings in – as it were – the flesh; but our parents had. They stirred up the old ancestral memories.

The novels, too, made available to us in lucid, concise prose all those adventures that occurred in the Doctor's life before we were even born. At that point Target novels cost 75p. It all started off when my brother discovered the recently published *Destiny of the Daleks* and determined to buy it for me for Christmas. He needed to borrow 15p from me in order to do so. (I think he actually wanted it for himself, as much as he wanted to buy it for me. But that's how it always was: we *shared* this stuff. That was important. *Doctor Who* was the region in time and space where sibling rivalry didn't exist.) Mark stood there, hiding the slim paperback behind his back: hand out, palm up, waiting for change.

After that: no stopping us. Each weekend we frequented W.H. Smith's in Darlington, Clarkes in Durham. And we discovered quite how many *Doctor Who* books there were. A tiny fraction, of course, of how many there now are, but at the time, it was a dizzying profusion of brightly coloured covers. We couldn't buy them all immediately, but we were making a good start – on building a collection (*Doctor Who* fans love having collections).

Newton Aycliffe town library helped, too. It was very modern and glass-walled. A tiny place, really. They seemed to have one whole wall of hardbacked W.H. Allen *Doctor Who* novelisations. Covered in stickybacked plastic, their spines opening with that satisfyingly fresh cracking noise. They were under the 'D' section in the library, making it the widest letter in the fiction alphabet – D for Dicks and *Doctor Who*. There were so many you needed never to read anything else, other than *Doctor Who*. You went back and reread favourites. Rather like kids do nowadays, with Harry Potter.

You read the Dalek stories first. Then the ones featuring other recognisable monsters (Ice Warriors, Cybermen, troll-faced Sontarans) and then you read the ones that seemed to have humanoid enemies and often, more complicated plots. Last of all you read the historical adventures. Only later, in the Eighties, would you turn to those, and fancy yourself a bit literary and intellectual for seeing the merit in these tales: the ones in which people dressed extravagantly, bellowed in archaic tongues and drew swords on each other.

The advent of the Fifth Doctor on TV kept us hooked, too. This was our Doctor. He could belong to us in a way that Tom Baker never did, though we wanted him to. Tom was doing that typical actor's trick – leaving a role we loved him for – turning his back on our love. He even looked massively depressed and hungover in his last few autumnal, then wintry stories . . . Tom was being an actor and an artist and looking for new challenges. He was doing what actors always do and 'returning to the stage'. A couple of years later we felt betrayed all over again by him, when he failed to return for 'The Five Doctors'. He was really rubbing our noses in it. He had left it all behind. He had learned to grow up. Why couldn't we? Tom had gone off to find art and life and fulfilment. There'd be no more messing about in police boxes, running up and down corridors and laughing in the faces of ludicrous space villains. He had outgrown all that stuff.

By the time Peter Davison was in, I was 12. He was playing it straight. A real character: a believable, bewildered hero, one that was occasionally miffed at a perplexing universe. As I say, he belonged to us. Even if his stories did seem bereft of some of the more thrillingly shlocky moments of *Doctor Who* madness. Even if some of his more SF-type stories didn't make a lot of sense . . . We still loved it all.

And we kept on loving it, tenaciously, throughout the Eighties, and then the Nineties, as things got pretty rocky and strange.

Tenacity is another quality the fans of *Doctor Who* always have.

But if I'm asked, these days, why I have written *Doctor Who* stories, novels, scripts, in amongst my more 'mainstream' efforts, my more 'literary' output, I end up saying that I write these things because I have always written them. I've always been right in the middle of *Doctor Who*: as viewer and reader and writer.

Another very good reason I give is that *Doctor Who* is the longest piece of continuous prose narrative featuring one ongoing character.

In the world. Ever.

And something like that . . . well, you've got to be involved in it, haven't you? As a writer, you've just got to stick your oar in.

I'm talking here not about the TV series, the audios, comic strips, anything else. Just words on the page. The fiction. The novels, beginnning with David Whitaker's deliriously wonderful John Wyndham/Edgar Rice Burroughs pastiche, *Doctor Who in an Exciting Adventure with the Daleks*, through the Targets, the Virgins, the BBC books, up to the very present day and beyond.

Seriously. The longest story in the world. Longer and more outrageously complex than any other story cycle in any culture. *Doctor Who* keeps the same lead character: the stories don't fritter off into arabesques like the 1001 nights, or into portmanteau form like *The Decameron*. The Doctor is always the Doctor, with a cumulative and capacious memory of all his adventures. All of this stuff has all happened to him: to all of him. His are regenerations – not reincarnations or reinventions. He is always he.

So, although Batman, Robin Hood or Sherlock Holmes might be said to rival him in volume of text and story, these are characters for whom the 'reset' button has been hit countless times. Those characters don't carry their baggage like the Doctor does.

As a kid one of the most alluring things about *Doctor Who* was the gaps. Bits of it were missing.

I was too young to have watched and read from the very beginning. There was always a glamorous, strange and grainy prehistory going on before. The Target books and *Doctor Who Weekly* let you know tantalising bits of what you had missed. And you were also aware that actual episodes were missing from the BBC archives. They'd trashed them! They'd burned and frittered away the only master copies! Those elusive spools of film had been sucked right through a gap in the Very Fabric of Time and Space!

So . . . this is important: *Doctor Who* is never complete.

It is about a lack. A need. A hunger.

And it is unending. There's that old cliché about the elasticity and infinitude of its format. Which is kind-of true, but it's truer that its consumers don't half enjoy repetition and recurrent patterns. Like the Arabian Nights. Arabesques of infinite variety. Fulfilment of the design being infinitely deferred. Stories opening out into other, further stories . . . The nights of prevarication and storytelling go on and on and on. Just as the Doctor always finds a new companion, a new incarnation, a new adventure to have.

But as we go on, the audience, the reader, the fan-consumer is always aware that we are *missing something*. We all always vaguely remember that there was an old Doctor. Now he's long gone. And there were others before him. They are in our memories like family members who died or who went abroad when we were small. And one day, maybe, they will come back . . .

Oooh, lacunae! Absences! Gaps! Let's get all Lacanian.

Or not. But I am sure that my sense, as a kid, of the endlessness of the *Doctor Who* narrative, and perceiving the gaps and holes in its fabric, were what set me off wanting to contribute to it. (This is why the ridiculously long multi-coloured scarf was a beautiful, perfect object for the Doctor to wear. It's a metaphor for the storyline itself.)

I think others have the same response. The show requires a response. It invites us to contribute. Somehow.

Some of the fans want to complete the narrative. They construct continuity guides and canons. They want to plug the gaps. The completist wants to collect, restore, arbitrate on hefty canonical debates. They catalogue things, rather like Time Lords.

No, my impulse is always to further complicate matters.

The idea of 'completism' terrifies me. What happens when it's all complete? What goes on then? Where do you go? It sounds a bit dull to me. (Remember when the Doctor eventually got to the Eye of Orion? His much-vaunted 'most peaceful place in the universe'? It was rubbish. It was boring and you could tell he was only pretending to enjoy it. It was wet and there was sheep shit everywhere.)

Is it just me? – I doubt it – thinking: This is the last time I'll write for *Doctor Who*. No more audios. No more stories. Doesn't matter who asks. And then I've pulled back and recanted and gone into it all over again. Why? Why can't you leave it alone?

If you want to write the last word – *your* last word – on *Doctor Who*, well, then it might as well be your last word on your own childhood.

So you are drawn back again and again. Timescooped. As last words go, they're inexhaustible.

It's actually very hard work writing *Doctor Who*. You don't want to let anyone down. You don't want to let yourself down. There's so much to say. You feel very complicated about it. You feel silly about it. And you still feel caught up in it. At least, in a universe of your own no one really cares if you bugger it all up.

There are various metaphors that persist, to do with the writing of fiction related to the 'Doctor Who Universe'. Often these metaphors evoke the toys and games of childhood. Authors refer to 'playing in the sandpit' or 'playing with someone else's Lego'. The gist of these metaphors – often used by authors in interviews, introductions to novels, or web-based discussion groups – is usually that the author is saying that it's a pleasure and an honour to be allowed and sanctioned to play with toys that don't really belong to them. With toys that they feel are the best in the world. They have actually been allowed to lay their hands on them . . . at last.

'At last! At LAAASSST!'

Like any deluded supervillain – any Mehendri Solon or Magnus Greel – with their devilish fulfilment in sight, the fan-turned-professional-writer of *Doctor Who* stories can hardly believe his or her luck.

The metaphors are infantilising precisely because of this. This is wish-fulfilment stuff. This is *taking part* in the *Doctor Who* universe.

It is literally true, of course, that the writer has been *permitted* to enter this universe. Or, in the case of fan fiction, not permitted, but perhaps tolerated. Permission is granted or witheld and is of import because we are talking about writing about copyrighted characters, situations and concepts. Characters and concepts that belong to someone else. They belong – legally and literally – to a grand corporation. In every other way, of course, they belong to a huge, global and transhistorical audience. And it is they who, through endless tale-spinning in one form or another, have kept the story going.

It is a very odd business, this stepping-into the *Doctor Who* universe in order to write. To give these characters adventures and to put words in their mouths. Words and deeds they didn't actually say or do first time around. (Do opera buffs dream about penning sequels to their faves? Do Dickensians busy about knocking off prequels or alternate universe versions of *Great Expectations*? Do Jane Austen freaks want to dwell in her world and invent more men and more balls and more frou-frou shenanigans? Ah yes, they do. They have done! Like the Holmesians, the Trekkers! Like any driven fans. Fans, it seems, like to produce. To respond. To get carried away and eventually turn professional.)

Doctor Who fans are notorious for knowing everything about the mythos, backstory, history, development and trivia to do with the show. Any serious discussion of the ongoing narrative of *Doctor Who* has, at some point, to get itself into laborious questions of canonicity, authenticity, apocrypha. If you watch and read *Doctor Who* you are already very used to the idea of alternate timelines, divergent realities, side-steps and missing adventures. Contrasting and contradictory narratives proliferate and abound – even from the start of the series. (Look at how 'An Unearthly Child' differs from its unbroadcast pilot, from the first Peter Cushing film, from the David Whitaker novelisation, from the Terrance Dicks novelisation.) Not even the ostensible 'beginning' is stable and fixed.

So . . . participants in this ongoing narrative have tacitly agreed that new, hitherto untold stories can 'take place' between already known tales. Rather than taking a well-earned break between dashing off after the end of the Key to Time saga, and arriving on the blasted surface of Skaro to meet the Daleks and Davros once more, the Fourth Doctor and Romana could actually have had a whole load more adventures. We just didn't get to see them at the time. Hurray!

A whole spate of other fandangos, débâcles and farragos might have occurred in that interstitial gap. And still could!

Maybe the winter of 1979 just went on and on and on . . . forever.

This came about partly as a result of the show's TV hiatus, between 1989 and 2005. Novels, stories, audios, comic strips and a TV Movie flooded in to fill those gaps. To fill any gap. But only because this stuff had already and always happened with *Doctor Who*. We were used to the proliferating canonicities and the variant versions. We all wanted a universe – surely? – where the Fourth Doctor could be having the TV adventure 'City of Death' and the marvellous comic strip story 'The Iron Legion' at *precisely the same time*. I know I did. And I didn't see it as a problem of quantum whatsits, or a continuity problem of theological proportions. I just saw it as fun! More stories! More adventures! Hurray!

It has become the job of the *Doctor Who* writer to weigh in there and to invent the missing hours, days, years. Those in the past, and those in the future.

Time is necessarily elastic to the *Doctor Who* writer. We have the TARDIS, naturally, and the whole panoply of time-travel technology and dimension-bending storytelling tropes available to us – in order to stretch time; to make it endless; to mash it up; to pull it apart. To do all kinds of mad stuff to it . . . simply in order to write our very own *Doctor Who* stories.

This is what we have been doing. For years, some of us!

And I used to tell myself very grand theories, to do with British SF and post-post New Wave SF, and magical realism and Queer Realism and all sorts of literary critical and theoretical nonsense . . . in order to justify messing around with this stuff. But maybe the answer and the real reason is that by playing with these tropes and this Lego, and by learning to stretch time and credibility and canonicity like this . . . we are all finding out how to revisit our childhoods. We are finding out how to travel in time.

Perhaps the answer is as easy as that.

Tom Baker said something along those lines in a recent interview. What's wrong with being a fan of anything, if it makes you happy and doesn't hurt anyone else? And it makes you happy because it reminds you – strongly and viscerally – of a time in the past when you were happy. Returning to it, again and again, obsessively, creatively – whatever it is – seems to make you happy still.

This whole essay seems to be as if in reply to the question: 'Why on earth do you want to write this Doctor Who stuff anyway?' At times, people have asked me this incredulously, as if involving myself in this universe was a way of deliberately sabotaging my literary reputation. (I've tried pointing out 'respectable' precedents: Kingsley Amis wrote James Bond! Doris Lessing wrote science fiction! Ah yes, comes the solemn, literary reply: but she wrote very serious science fiction. Nothing about gun-toting poodles.)

Anyway. My answer is, that if you were that kind of kid, in that particular time and country – Britain in the Seventies – you can't imagine not wanting to write *Doctor Who* stories in later life.

I found my 1982 diary in 1998. We were moving into our new house in Norwich; I had been lecturing at UEA for a year by then. For the first time I had my crates and crates of books together. For the first time I was reunited with all my very many capacious and voluminous diaries. 1982 was the earliest surviving record of what I was up to on this planet on a day-to-day, mundane basis. And guess what? My days at the age of 12 were much the same as when I was 28. I was writing my roman-à-clef in the morning, dealing with correspondence from publishers at lunchtime and writing my *Doctor Who* novel in the afternoon. At 12 and 28 and every year between! And since!

That afternoon in 1998, sitting on the chintz in our lovely new house, I didn't know whether to feel foolish or relieved and reassured. In the end, I found those continuities immensely satisfying and consoling. It made me feel like I was writing *Doctor Who* stories – at 12 and 28 – in order to make the world around me familiar and safer. I was writing in order to organise, reshape and reinvent my world and my imagination. 1998 was the year I finished writing my first published *Doctor Who* novel. *The Scarlet Empress* is such a long book – a romping, ridiculous, well-nigh plotless road movie. And I was writing it through a very disorienting year when I moved cities and jobs and there was a lot of drama and brou-haha amongst family and friends. It was a terrible time!

But writing *The Scarlet Empress* dragged me through it. Getting on the red double decker bus that was meandering through the perplexing deserts of

Hyspero. Trying to make magic and sorcery and outrageous camp work in a *Doctor Who* context. I was taking it all very personally, as I have – I hope – all the *Doctor Who* stuff I've done since.

I had never heard the delicious term 'fanwank' until I started looking at the reviews and discussions of *Doctor Who* books and audios on the Internet. I was delighted and amazed by the extent and the sophistication of the discussions, and I loved the term, which seemed, more often than not, to be levelled at the material produced for the marketplace by so-called 'professional fans' or, rather, 'fan-professionals'. 'Fanwank' sounded naughty and silly but, as I read on, deeper and deeper into the worldwide web, I started to gather that it was a phenomenon to be avoided – by both writer and discerning fan. Some writers were being routinely dismissed and even castigated for being 'too fanwanky'.

But what did it mean?

I had to find out.

It seemed to be part of my job. I'd unearthed a method of literary critique I felt sure was unknown to the mainstream. 'Fanwanking' or 'fanwankery' was something I needed to investigate, as part of the ongoing and wayward exploration of writing in all its forms that I seem to have devoted myself to. I love all forms of writing, but I especially love the fictional languages and forms that exist around us in our present day and age. It seems to me that fiction is everywhere: transmitted through airwaves and buzzing through cables underfoot; downloaded in stupendously huge text files; lent and borrowed from libraries in millions of cities . . . the print large and black on the yellowing pages; large enough to be read by myopic story junkies like me. Fiction is everywhere – cheaper, freer and less contaminated than either our water or air.

It is my job – as this writer/critic/reader/teacher thing I have made myself into – to pull and tease at these floating strands of fiction, and to ravel them up. I explore where they come from, and where they're going to. It's my role to become aware of and be fascinated by new mutations and innovations and departures. And so I love things like genre fiction, franchise fiction, spin-offs, fan fiction, slash fiction and even 'fanwankery'. These tales and texts seem to spread robustly like wild flowers between paving slabs, disrupting continuities and copyrights as they proliferate (just as, apparently, the common weed can crack pavements and tarmac in its humble tenacity). Fankwankery and slash fiction alike have a saucy, masturbatory association, if not function. I'm sure people really do get off on reading and writing this stuff. And that's an important part of it. That's about writing fiction itself. Fiction *is* saucy and sexy. Whether these readers/writers are getting off on a Dalek/Cyber War, or a Fifth Doctor/Turlough shag, I don't really care. To me, it all sounds wonderful. And naturally, as a teenager, I was writing precisely those stories.

Still I don't know why this 'fanwankery' is despised by the fans at large. Perhaps because it's infantile. The kind of things you *would* write when you were fifteen. Not now, though. Not now that we're so mature and grown up and different. (Ah, but are you sure you're not secretly *repressing* that desire to witness a Dalek/Cyber War? A Multi-Doc and old companion gangbang?)

Another reason people might despise this fiction that reveals the oddity of the fan-mass-unconscious is that it is sometimes gloriously badly written.

But I love bad writing. Like some people collect garage paintings, art brut, naïve art, outsider art, I can't help picking up prime examples of bad writing – both amateur and professional. I mean good old-fashioned, godawful, nasty, plain bad writing that doesn't even know how good it isn't. I love it.

I love the despised, the forgotten, the neglected. All of them touch my heart. Sometimes there's more truth in the bad faith of our poor art than in the heightened and often false consciousness of that which we consider our best. Old paperbacks tossed into cardboard boxes at car boot sales, or on shelves in old charity shops . . . they make me itch to buy them up. They're like puppies in the pet shop. Looking doomed and smelling of wood pulp, pee and abandonment. There I was this afternoon, in a basement book exchange off Piccadilly in Manchester – weighing up *A Bouquet of Barbed Wire*, *The Cylon Death Machine*, Alice Thomas Ellis's first novel and *Doctor Who and the Ribos Operation*. I had to gently talk myself out of blowing another whack of cash on another pile of tat.

As a writer and critic I am meant to – I am trained to – know the difference between what is good and bad. What is worthwhile and what isn't. What is usefully good and interesting, what is trashy and interesting, or just trashy and dull. It's a very nimble, sophisticated balance, I suppose, now that the Western Canon has been so successfully exploded. All we're left with is a rubble of old paperbacks – hurray!

I can always find something in the rubbish. Something worthwhile and adventurous, that makes me glad I saved this particular piece of writing from the brink.

Even the diabolical can be illuminating, is what I'm saying.

I feel much the same about my own writing. I find it all very hard work, but I gear myself up to do it by telling myself that it is an act of rescue. Of salvage and intervention. I tell myself: No one else will do this writing for you. Without you, it will never get done. And so, you are dooming these memories, ideas and images; you are damning these made-up adventures to nothingness, if you don't get them down on paper now.

They'll vanish! Into the Phantom Zone. Writing them down will make them real. At the least, it will give them the tiniest purchase on a chance of canonical existence . . .

It seems to me that Fanwank is the worst thing that the fan-consumers can think to call these latterday *Doctor Who* novels and audios. Because what they mean by that is: 'Just like something I could have written. Something like I'd have written when I was ten. As crappy and as self-indulgent as that. Of course, I'd never do that now. Oh, no. I'm much more grown-up and discerning than that now . . .'

Such self-hatred.

They want the pros to be better than that. To resist the need for fanwanking. To do it modestly and without overt-seeming relish or pleasure.

Ha! What's the point of writing modestly? Of writing without pleasure and relish?

It's a curious irony, I think, in a series with a rabble-rouser as a hero, and in a narrative about multiverses, alternities and possibilities, that the fans of this very show seem to want to close possibilities down. Sometimes it's as if the fans want reality dictated to them – definitively. Canonically. They want parameters setting and concretising around them. Maybe they want a stable universe after all . . .

And now?

I feel I need to apologise to all my friends, who have been dragged into *Doctor Who* world with me. When I was growing up they had to share my obsession for as long as our friendships lasted. I'll never forget the feeling of shame and betrayal from when I was thirteen, and Tom told me he'd grown out of *Doctor Who* at last. He took up body building and, as if to prove several points at once, ripped up all 120 of his Target novelisations in his back yard. In front of me! And some of them I didn't even have!

My poor brother has never left the *Doctor Who* universe behind. He was too young to know about it, when I first wandered in.

And my poor friends who couldn't really care less about *Doctor Who*, and how they have to be interested and pleased when I give them copies of my *Doctor Who* books. And then they have to read them and become weirdly expert in the whole thing. My family and friends are used to me going on as if all of it is real. Like it was when I was 10, 14, 21, 29 . . .

This is just what novelists do. To a novelist, it's all very real.

Sometimes I think I've found a way to believe it's all real forever. And to remember precisely what it's like to be a kid.

If that means getting patronised en route, so be it. It's even happened in recent years. When *Buffy* Studies became all the rage in the Academy. Even then *Doctor Who* could still be seen as a little bit freakish and odd by comparison.

But . . . no more!

I think we're at the start of *Doctor Who* Studies. And it really is about time.

I think it's to do with a freakish generation of talents growing up at the same time. Salutations to Russell T. Davies and the current cast and crew! You seem kind of respectable and legitimate!

I don't actually know if I have written what I set out to write.

But that's how I've always gone about this scribbling business. So yes, this essay is all shards and fragments. It consists of half-developed thoughts and mangled, discordant themes, with flashes of memories and ideas and inspirations crossing our meandering path here and there, seemingly at random.

Maybe it was *Doctor Who* itself that taught me to be wayward and brave like that. It seems important to brave out the sense of yourself. The untidy truth of yourself.

Maybe writing an essay *should* be like running through dark woods, batteries on your torch running out, fearful fiend treading hard behind you, screaming at the top of your voice . . .

I always liked it in stories when the Doctor created some kind of device: knocking together a load of disparate items – electronic circuitry and miscellaneous junk. They were always called 'unstable-looking lash-ups' in the books.

He created these machines – these lash-ups – to defy science and logic. He switched them on and they lit up and juddered and shook. They made an unholy racket and out shot blue sparks. But . . . in the very last instant they would go and do something *miraculous*.

Doctor Who taught you to disobey rules. To knock together devices that would be like artworks, like pieces of statuary, rather than usable machines. It taught you to brave out the stares. Taught you to be proud of seeming, looking, sounding eccentric. So – my writing career has been just like this. Writing just as me. Even in academic essays. It's important that my stories, essays, whatever, don't feel or sound or get shaped like anyone else's.

Well. There's next to no chance that that could happen. I've tried to shoehorn my work into other people's shapes in the past. It doesn't work. For some people it does. Not me.

So . . . this isn't a very tidy essay.

It's a lash-up. And here I come, running into the control room, skidding on the metallic floor in the last, fraught seconds of this adventure. As the countdown to deadly danger creeps closer to the end, here I come, with coat-tails and scarf ends flapping, dragging all my bits and pieces of tatty junk with me. I've got one huge armload of ideas and associations, and I'm ready to fling them all down, right here, in the madly fervent hope that these components will fall happily into the shape of something worthwhile. A device which – if it doesn't save the day and all our necks – will at least take us all somewhere else; somewhere unexpected, familiar, fun.

Select bibliography

Bentham, J. Jeremy. 1986. *Doctor Who: The Early Years*. London: W.H. Allen.

Bignell, Jonathan. 2005. 'Space for "quality": negotiating with the Daleks'. In Jonathan Bignell and Stephen Lacey (eds). *Popular Television Drama: Critical Perspectives*. Manchester: Manchester University Press.

Bignell, Jonathan and Andrew O'Day. 2004. *Terry Nation*. Manchester: Manchester University Press.

Bignell, Richard. 2001. *Doctor Who: On Location*. Richmond: Reynolds and Hearn.

Blum, Jonathan. 2001a. 'Where have all the monsters gone? Part 1: Dad's army'. *Doctor Who Magazine*, No. 308, pp. 6–11.

Blum, Jonathan. 2001b. 'Where have all the monsters gone? Part 2: Ironic legion'. *Doctor Who Magazine*, No. 309, pp. 26–30.

Britton, Piers D. 1999. 'Dress and fabric of the television series: the costume designer as author in *Doctor Who*'. *Journal of Design History*, Vol. 12, No. 4, pp. 345–56.

Britton, Piers D. and Simon J. Barker. 2003. *Reading Between Designs: Visual Imagery and the Generation of Meaning in The Avengers, The Prisoner and Doctor Who*. Austin: University of Texas Press.

Caldwell, Nick. 1999. 'A decolonising Doctor? British SF invasion narratives'. *M/C: A Journal of Media and Culture*, Vol. 2, No. 2. http://journal.media-culture.org.au/9903/who.php (accessed 19 March 2006).

Cartmel, Andrew. 2005. *Script Doctor: The Inside Story of Doctor Who 1986–89*. Richmond, Surrey: Reynolds and Hearn.

Chapman, James. 2006. *Inside the TARDIS: A Cultural History of Doctor Who*. London: I.B. Tauris.

Clapham, Mark, Eddie Robson and Jim Smith. 2005. *Who's Next: An Unofficial and Unauthorised Guide to Doctor Who*. London: Virgin Books.

Cook, Benjamin. 2003. *The New Audio Adventures: The Inside Story*. Maidenhead: Big Finish.

Cook, John R. 1999. 'Adapting telefantasy: the *Doctor Who and the Daleks* films'. In I.Q. Hunter (ed.). *British Science Fiction Cinema*. London: Routledge, pp. 113–27.

Cook, John R. and Peter Wright (eds). 2005. *British Science Fiction Television: A Hitchhiker's Guide*. London: I.B. Tauris.

Cooke, Lez. 2003. *British Television Drama: A History*. London: BFI, pp. 60–3, '*Doctor Who* and 1960s science fiction'.

Cornell, Paul (ed.). 1997. *License Denied: Rumblings from the Doctor Who Underground*. London: Virgin Publishing.

Cornell, Paul, Martin Day and Keith Topping. 1995. *Doctor Who: The Discontinuity Guide*. London: Virgin Publishing.

Couch, Steve, Tony Watkins and Peter S. Williams. 2005. *Back In Time: A Thinking Fan's Guide to Doctor Who*. Southampton: Damaris Publishing.

Cull, Nicholas J. 2001. 'Bigger on the inside: *Doctor Who* as British cultural history'. In Graham Roberts and Philip M. Taylor (eds). *The Historian, Television and Television History*. Luton: University of Luton Press, pp. 95–111.

Cull, Nicholas J. 2005. 'Tardis at the OK Corral: *Doctor Who* and the USA'. In John R. Cook and Peter Wright (eds). *British Science Fiction Television: A Hitchhiker's Guide*. London: I.B. Tauris, pp. 52–70.

Fiske, John. 1984. 'Popularity and ideology: a structuralist reading of *Dr. Who*'. In Willard D. Rowland, Jr and Bruce Watkins (eds). *Interpreting Television: Current Research Perspectives*. Beverly Hills, CA: Sage.

Fox, Kamal. 2004. 'Doctoring who? Aliens, invasion and immigration in the British popular imagination'. *Journal for the Arts, Sciences and Technology*, Vol. 2, No. 2, pp. 62–8.

Gillatt, Gary. 1998. *Doctor Who from A to Z: A Celebration of Thirty-Five Years of Adventures in Time and Space*. London: BBC Books.

Gregg, Peter B. 2004. 'England looks to the future: the cultural forum model and *Doctor Who*'. *Journal of Popular Culture*, Vol. 37, No. 4, pp. 648–61.

Herman, David. 2005. 'Smallscreen'. *Prospect*, No. 110, May. www.prospect-magazine.co.uk/pdffiles/6886.pdf (accessed 12 November 2005).

Hills, Matt. 2004. '*Doctor Who*.' In Glen Creeber (ed.). *Fifty Key Television Programmes*. London: Arnold, pp. 75–9.

Howe, David J., Mark Stammers and Stephen James Walker. 1992. *Doctor Who: The Sixties*. London: Virgin.

Howe, David J., Mark Stammers and Stephen James Walker. 1994. *Doctor Who: The Seventies*. London: Virgin.

Howe, David J., Stephen James Walker and Mark Stammers. 2005. *The Handbook: The Unofficial and Unauthorised Guide to the Production of Doctor Who*. Tolworth, Surrey: Telos.

Howe, David J. and Stephen James Walker. 2003. *The Television Companion: The Unofficial and Unauthorised Guide to Doctor Who*. Tolworth, Surrey: Telos.

Howe, David J. and Arnold T. Blumberg. 2004. *Howe's Transcendental Toybox-2003 Update Edition: The Unauthorised Guide to Doctor Who Collectibles*. Tolworth, Surrey: Telos.

Johnson, Catherine. 2005. *Telefantasy*. London: BFI.

Latourette, Debra Jane. 1990. 'Doctor Who meets Vladimir Propp: a comparative narrative analysis of myth/folktale and the television science fiction genre'. Unpub. Ph.D. dissertation, Northwestern University.

Layton, David. 1994. 'Closed circuits and monitored lines: television as power in *Doctor Who*'. *Extrapolation*, Vol. 35, No. 3, pp. 240–1.

Lofficier, Jean-Marc. 1997. *The Nth Doctor: An In-Depth Study of the Films that Almost Were*. London: Doctor Who Books.

Lyon, J. Shaun. 2005. *Back to the Vortex: The Unofficial and Unauthorised Guide to Doctor Who 2005*. Tolworth, Surrey: Telos.

Macdonald, Philip. 2002a. 'Too much too young?' *Doctor Who Magazine Special Edition: The Complete Fifth Doctor*, pp. 4–7.

Macdonald, Philip. 2002b. 'Seasons in the sun'. *Doctor Who Magazine Special Edition: The Complete Third Doctor*, pp. 5–8.

Macdonald, Philip. 2003a. 'Loving the alien'. *Doctor Who Magazine Special Edition: The Complete Sixth Doctor*, pp. 4–8.

Macdonald, Philip. 2003b. 'Don't look back in anger'. *Doctor Who Magazine Special Edition: The Complete Eighth Doctor*, pp. 5–9.

Macdonald, Philip. 2004a. 'Shapes of things'. *Doctor Who Magazine Special Edition: The Complete First Doctor*, pp. 5–9.

Macdonald, Philip. 2004b. 'Golden years'. *Doctor Who Magazine Special Edition: The Complete Fourth Doctor Volume One*, pp. 4–8.

Macdonald, Philip. 2004c. 'Games without frontiers'. *Doctor Who Magazine Special Edition: The Complete Fourth Doctor Volume Two*, pp. 4–9.

Macdonald, Philip. 2005. 'Sign "O" the times'. *Doctor Who Magazine Special Edition: The Complete Seventh Doctor*, pp. 4–9.

McKee, Alan. 2001. 'Which is the best *Doctor Who* story?: a case study in value judgements outside the academy'. *Intensities: The Journal of Cult Media*, No. 1, www.cult-media.com/issue1/Amckee.htm (accessed 17 September 2005).

McKee, Alan. 2004a. 'How to tell the difference between production and consumption: a case study in *Doctor Who* fandom'. In Sara Gwenllian Jones and Roberta Pearson (eds). *Cult Television*. Minneapolis: University of Minnesota Press, pp. 167–85.

McKee, Alan. 2004b. 'Is *Doctor Who* political?' *European Journal of Cultural Studies*, Vol. 7, No. 2, pp. 201–17.

Miles, Lawrence and Tat Wood. 2004a. *About Time 3*. New Orleans: Mad Norwegian Press.

Miles, Lawrence and Tat Wood. 2004b. *About Time 4*. New Orleans: Mad Norwegian Press.

Miles, Lawrence and Tat Wood. 2005. *About Time 5*. New Orleans: Mad Norwegian Press.

Miles, Lawrence and Tat Wood. 2006. *About Time 1*. New Orleans: Mad Norwegian Press.

Muir, John Kenneth. 1999. *A Critical History of Doctor Who on Television*. Jefferson, NC: McFarland.

Newman, Kim. 2005. *BFI TV Classics: Doctor Who*. London: BFI.

O'Mahony, Daniel. 2003a. 'The accidental tourist – Part 1: Trouble in mind'. *Doctor Who Magazine*, No. 333, pp. 12–17.

O'Mahony, Daniel. 2003b. 'The accidental tourist – Part 2: Curse of the cat people'. *Doctor Who Magazine*, No. 336, pp. 20–5.

O'Mahony, Daniel. 2004. 'The accidental tourist – Part 3: Kill Bill'. *Doctor Who Magazine*, No. 338, pp. 26–31.

Olivier, Gwendolyn Marie. 1987. 'A critical examination of the mythological and symbolic elements of two modern science fiction series: *Star Trek* and *Doctor Who*'. Unpub. Ph.D. dissertation, The Louisiana State University and Agricultural and Mechanical College.

Parkin, Lance. 2002. 'Postmodern revue?' *Doctor Who Magazine*, No. 323, pp. 10–16.

Pixley, Andrew. 2004a. 'Scheduled for success – Part 1: "Damned lies and statistics"'. *Doctor Who Magazine*, No. 338, pp. 20–5.

Pixley, Andrew. 2004b. 'Scheduled for success – Part 2: "Leader of the opposition"'. *Doctor Who Magazine*, No. 340, pp. 20–5.

Pixley, Andrew. 2004c. 'Scheduled for success – Part 3: "Clash of the titans"'. *Doctor Who Magazine*, No. 342, pp. 40–5.

Pixley, Andrew. 2004d. 'Scheduled for success – Part 4: "Today is Saturday – watch and smile"'. *Doctor Who Magazine*, No. 344, pp. 14–19.

Pixley, Andrew. 2004e. 'Scheduled for success – Part 5: "Too short a season"'. *Doctor Who Magazine*, No. 346, pp. 26–31.

Pixley, Andrew. 2004f. 'Scheduled for success – Part 6: "Whatever happened to the likely lad?"' *Doctor Who Magazine*, No. 348, pp. 20–5.

Richards, Justin. 2005. *Doctor Who: The Legend Continues*. London: BBC Books.

Rigelsford, Adrian. 1995. *Classic Who: The Hinchcliffe Years*. Boxtree: London.

Segal, Philip with Gary Russell. 2000. *Doctor Who: Regeneration*. London: Harper-Collins Entertainment.

Tulloch, John. 2000. 'Producing the national imaginary: *Doctor Who*, text and genre'. In Dudley Jones and Tony Watkins (eds). *A Necessary Fantasy? The Heroic Figure in Children's Popular Culture*. New York and London: Garland Publishing, Inc.

Tulloch, John and Manuel Alvarado. 1983. *Doctor Who: The Unfolding Text*. London and Basingstoke: Macmillan.

Tulloch, John and Henry Jenkins. 1995. *Science Fiction Audiences: Watching Doctor Who and Star Trek*. London and New York: Routledge.

Wright, Peter. 1999. 'The shared world of *Doctor Who*: from the New Adventures to the Regeneration'. *Foundation: The International Review of Science Fiction*, No. 75, pp. 78–96.

Select list of films and programmes

Alchemists of Sound (2004) Produced by John Warburton. Directed by Roger Pomphrey. Music by Dave Stewart (title music only). 60 mins. BBC 4.

The Avengers (1960–9) Produced by Albert Fennell and Brian Clemens. Directed by various. Written by various. Music by Laurie Johnson, et al. 161 × 50 mins. Associated British.

Behind the Sofa: Robert Holmes and Doctor Who (2003) Produced and directed by Richard Molesworth. Special documentary feature on 'The Two Doctors' DVD. BBC Worldwide.

Blake's 7 (1978–81) Produced by David Maloney and Vere Lorrimer. Directed by various. Written by Chris Boucher, Robert Holmes, Tanith Lee, Terry Nation, et al. Music by Dudley Simpson. 52 × 50 mins. BBC 1.

Culloden (1964) Produced, written and directed by Peter Watkins. 75 mins. BBC 1.

Dad's Army (1968–77) Produced by David Croft. Directed by David Croft, Harold Snoad, Bob Spiers and Robert Knights. Written by David Croft and Jimmy Perry. Music by Jimmy Perry and Derek Taverner. 77 × 30, 1 × 35, 1 × 40, 1 × 60 mins. BBC 1.

The Devil and Daniel Mouse (1978) Directed by Clive A. Smith. Written by Stephen Vincent Benet. Music by Bauhaus. 30 mins. Nelvana.

Doctor Who: 'An Unearthly Child' [also referred to as '100,000 BC'] (1963) Produced by Verity Lambert. Directed by Waris Hussein. Written by Anthony Coburn. Music by Norman Kay. 4 × 25 mins. BBC Television.

Doctor Who: 'The Daleks' [also referred to as 'The Mutants'] (1963–4) Produced by Verity Lambert. Directed by Christopher Barry and Richard Martin. Written by Terry Nation. Music by Tristram Cary. 7 × 25 mins. BBC Television.

Doctor Who: 'Marco Polo' (1964) Produced by Verity Lambert. Directed by Waris Hussein and John Crockett. Written by John Lucarotti. Music by Tristram Cary. 7 × 25 mins. BBC Television.

Doctor Who: 'The Keys of Marinus' (1964) Produced by Verity Lambert. Directed by John Gorrie. Written by Terry Nation. Music by Norman Kay. 6 × 25 mins. BBC 1.

Doctor Who: 'The Aztecs' (1964) Produced by Verity Lambert. Directed by John Crockett. Written by John Lucarotti. Music by Richard Rodney Bennett. 4 × 25 mins. BBC 1.

Doctor Who: 'The Reign of Terror' (1964) Produced by Verity Lambert. Directed by Henric Hirsch and (episode 3) John Gorrie (uncredited). Written by Dennis Spooner. Music by Stanley Myers. 6 × 25 minutes. BBC 1.

Doctor Who: 'The Dalek Invasion of Earth' (1964) Produced by Verity Lambert. Directed by Richard Martin. Written by Terry Nation. Music by Francis Chagrin. 6 × 25 mins. BBC 1.

Doctor Who: 'The Romans' (1965) Produced by Verity Lambert. Directed by Christopher Barry. Written by Dennis Spooner. Music by Raymond Jones. 4 × 25 mins. BBC 1.

Doctor Who: 'The Web Planet' (1965) Produced by Verity Lambert. Directed by Richard Martin. Written by Bill Strutton. Music – stock. 6 × 25 mins. BBC 1.

Doctor Who: 'The Crusade' (1965) Produced by Verity Lambert. Directed by Douglas Camfield. Written by David Whitaker. Music by Dudley Simpson. 4 × 25 mins. BBC 1.

Doctor Who: 'The Space Museum' (1965) Produced by Verity Lambert. Directed by Mervyn Pinfield. Written by Glyn Jones. 4 × 25 mins. BBC 1.

Doctor Who: 'The Chase' (1965) Produced by Verity Lambert. Directed by Richard Martin (with uncredited additional material by Douglas Camfield). Written by Terry Nation. Music by Dudley Simpson. 6 × 25 mins. BBC 1.

Doctor Who: 'The Time Meddler' (1965) Produced by Verity Lambert. Directed by Douglas Camfield. Written by Dennis Spooner. Music by Charles Botterill. 4 × 25 mins. BBC 1.

Doctor Who: 'The Myth Makers' (1965) Produced by John Wiles. Directed by Michael Leeston-Smith. Written by Donald Cotton. Music by Humphrey Searle. 4 × 25 mins. BBC 1.

Doctor Who: 'The Daleks' Master Plan' (1965–6) Produced by John Wiles. Directed by Douglas Camfield. Written by Terry Nation and Dennis Spooner. Music by Tristram Cary. 12 × 25 mins. BBC 1.

Doctor Who: 'The Massacre of St. Bartholomew's Eve' (1966) Produced by John Wiles. Directed by Paddy Russell. Written by John Lucarotti and Donald Tosh. 4 × 25 mins. BBC 1.

Doctor Who: 'The Ark' (1966) Produced by John Wiles. Directed by Michael Imison. Written by Paul Erickson and Lesley Scott. Music by Tristram Cary. 4 × 25 mins. BBC 1.

Doctor Who: 'The Gunfighters' (1966) Produced by Innes Lloyd. Directed by Rex Tucker. Written by Donald Cotton. Music by Tristram Cary. 4 × 25 mins. BBC 1.

Doctor Who: 'The War Machines' (1966) Produced by Innes Lloyd. Directed by Michael Ferguson. Written by Ian Stuart Black (from a story by Kit Pedler). Music by Raymond London. 4 × 25 mins. BBC 1.

Doctor Who: 'The Smugglers' (1966) Produced by Innes Lloyd. Directed by Julia Smith. Written by Brian Hayles. 4 × 25 mins. BBC 1.

Doctor Who: 'The Tenth Planet' (1966) Produced by Innes Lloyd. Directed by Derek Martinus. Written by Kit Pedler and Gerry Davis. 4 × 25 mins. BBC 1.

Doctor Who: 'The Power of the Daleks' (1966) Produced by Innes Lloyd. Directed by Christopher Barry. Written by David Whitaker. Music by Tristram Cary. 6 × 25 mins. BBC 1.

Doctor Who: 'The Highlanders' (1966) Produced by Innes Lloyd. Directed by Hugh David. Written by Elwyn Jones and Gerry Davis. 4 × 25 mins. BBC 1.

Doctor Who: 'The Evil of the Daleks' (1967) Produced by Innes Lloyd. Directed by Derek Martinus (Dalek fight in episode 7 directed by Timothy Combe). Written by David Whitaker. Music by Dudley Simpson. 7 × 25 mins. BBC 1.

Doctor Who: 'The Tomb of the Cybermen' (1967) Produced by Peter Bryant. Directed by Morris Barry. Written by Kit Pedler and Gerry Davis. 4 × 25 mins. BBC 1.

Doctor Who: 'The Web of Fear' (1968) Produced by Peter Bryant. Directed by Douglas Camfield. Written by Mervyn Haisman and Henry Lincoln. 6 × 25 mins. BBC 1.

Doctor Who: 'The Wheel in Space' (1968) Produced by Peter Bryant. Directed by Tristan de Vere Cole. Written by David Whitaker from a story by Kit Pedler. Special sound by Brian Hodgson and the BBC Radiophonic Workshop. 6 × 25 mins. BBC 1.

Doctor Who: 'The Dominators' (1968) Produced by Peter Bryant. Directed by Morris Barry. Written by Norman Ashby. Special sound by Brian Hodgson and the BBC Radiophonic Workshop. 5 × 25 mins. BBC 1.

Doctor Who: 'The Mind Robber' (1968) Produced by Peter Bryant. Directed by David Maloney. Written by Derrick Sherwin (episode one) and Peter Ling (episodes two to five). Music – stock. 5 × 25 mins. BBC 1.

Doctor Who: 'The Invasion' (1968) Produced by Peter Bryant. Directed by Douglas Camfield. Written by Derek Sherwin (from an outline by Kit Pedler). Music by Don Harper. 8 × 25 mins. BBC 1.

Doctor Who: 'The Krotons' (1968–9) Produced by Peter Bryant. Directed by David Maloney. Written by Robert Holmes. 4 × 25 mins. BBC 1.

Doctor Who: 'The Space Pirates' (1969) Produced by Peter Bryant. Directed by Michael Hart. Written by Robert Holmes. Music by Dudley Simpson. 6 × 25 mins. BBC 1.

Doctor Who: 'The War Games' (1969) Produced by Derrick Sherwin. Directed by David Maloney. Written by Malcolm Hulke and Terrance Dicks. Music by Dudley Simpson. 10 × 25 mins. BBC 1.

Doctor Who: 'Spearhead from Space' (1970) Produced by Derrick Sherwin. Directed by Derek Martinus. Written by Robert Holmes. Music by Dudley Simpson. 4 × 25 mins. BBC 1.

Doctor Who: 'The Dæmons' (1971) Produced by Barry Letts. Directed by Christopher Barry. Written by Guy Leopold (pseudonym for Robert Sloman and Barry Letts). Music by Dudley Simpson. 5 × 25 mins. BBC 1.

Doctor Who: 'Day of the Daleks' (1972) Produced by Barry Letts. Directed by Paul Bernard. Written by Louis Marks. Music by Dudley Simpson. 4 × 25 mins. BBC 1.

Doctor Who: 'The Sea Devils' (1972) Produced by Barry Letts. Directed by Michael Briant. Written by Malcolm Hulke. Music by Malcolm Clarke. 6 × 25 mins. BBC 1.

Doctor Who: 'The Time Monster' (1972) Produced by Barry Letts. Directed by Paul Bernard. Written by Robert Sloman and Barry Letts (uncredited). Music by Dudley Simpson. 6 × 25 mins. BBC 1.

Doctor Who: 'Carnival of Monsters' (1973) Produced and directed by Barry Letts. Written by Robert Holmes. Music by Dudley Simpson. 4 × 25 mins. BBC 1.

Doctor Who: 'Planet of the Daleks' (1973) Produced by Barry Letts. Directed by David Maloney. Written by Terry Nation. Music by Dudley Simpson. 6 × 25 mins. BBC 1.

Doctor Who: 'The Green Death' (1973) Produced by Barry Letts. Directed by Michael E. Briant. Written by Robert Sloman. Music by Dudley Simpson. 6 × 25 mins. BBC 1.

Doctor Who: 'The Time Warrior' (1973–4) Produced by Barry Letts. Directed by Alan Bromly. Written by Robert Holmes. 4 × 25 minutes. BBC 1.

Doctor Who: 'Death to the Daleks' (1974) Produced by Barry Letts. Directed by Michael Briant. Written by Terry Nation. Music by Carey Blyton (performed by the London Saxophone Quartet). 4 × 25 mins. BBC 1.

Doctor Who: 'The Ark in Space' (1975) Produced by Philip Hinchcliffe. Directed by Rodney Bennett. Written by Robert Holmes. Music by Dudley Simpson. 4 × 25 mins. BBC 1.

Doctor Who: 'The Sontaran Experiment' (1975) Produced by Philip Hinchcliffe. Directed by Rodney Bennett. Written by Bob Baker and Dave Martin. Music by Dudley Simpson. 2 × 25 mins. BBC 1.

Doctor Who: 'Genesis of the Daleks' (1975) Produced by Philip Hinchcliffe. Directed by David Maloney. Written by Terry Nation. Music by Dudley Simpson. 6 × 25 mins. BBC 1.

Doctor Who: 'Pyramids of Mars' (1975) Produced by Philip Hinchcliffe. Directed by Paddy Russell. Written by Stephen Harris (pseudonym for Robert Holmes and Lewis Greifer). Music by Dudley Simpson. 4 × 25 mins. BBC 1.

Doctor Who: 'The Deadly Assassin' (1976) Produced by Philip Hinchcliffe. Directed by David Maloney. Written by Robert Holmes. Music by Dudley Simpson. 4 × 25 mins. BBC 1.

Doctor Who: 'The Talons of Weng-Chiang' (1977) Produced by Philip Hinchcliffe. Directed by David Maloney. Written by Robert Holmes. Music by Dudley Simpson. 6 × 25 mins. BBC 1.

Doctor Who: 'Horror of Fang Rock' (1977) Produced by Graham Williams. Directed by Paddy Russell. Written by Terrance Dicks. Music by Dudley Simpson. 4 × 25 mins. BBC 1.

Doctor Who: 'Image of the Fendahl' (1977) Produced by Graham Williams. Directed by George Spenton-Foster. Written by Chris Boucher. Music by Dudley Simpson. 4 × 25 mins. BBC 1.

Doctor Who: 'The Sun Makers' (1977) Produced by Graham Williams. Directed by Pennant Roberts. Written by Robert Holmes. Music by Dudley Simpson. 4 × 25 mins. BBC 1.

Doctor Who: 'Underworld' (1978) Produced by Graham Williams. Directed by Norman Stewart. Written by Bob Baker and Dave Martin. Music by Dudley Simpson. 4 × 25 mins. BBC 1.

Doctor Who: 'The Ribos Operation' (1978) Produced by Graham Williams. Directed by George Spenton-Foster. Written by Robert Holmes. Music by Dudley Simpson. 4 × 25 mins. BBC 1.

Doctor Who: 'The Stones of Blood' (1978) Produced by Graham Williams. Directed by Darrol Blake. Written by David Fisher. Music by Dudley Simpson. 4 × 25 mins. BBC 1.

Doctor Who: 'The Androids of Tara' (1978) Produced by Graham Williams. Directed by Michael Hayes. Written by David Fisher. Music by Dudley Simpson. 4 × 25 minutes. BBC 1.

Doctor Who: 'The Power of Kroll' (1978–9) Produced by Graham Williams. Directed by Norman Stewart. Written by Robert Holmes. Music by Dudley Simpson. 4 × 25 mins. BBC 1.

Doctor Who: 'Destiny of the Daleks' (1979) Produced by Graham Williams. Directed by Ken Grieve. Written by Terry Nation. Music by Dudley Simpson. 4 × 25 mins. BBC 1.

Doctor Who: 'City of Death' (1979) Produced by Graham Williams. Directed by Michael Hayes. Written by David Agnew (pseudonym for Douglas Adams and Graham Williams). Music by Dudley Simpson. 4 × 25 mins. BBC 1.

Doctor Who: 'The Creature from the Pit' (1979) Produced by Graham Williams. Directed by Christopher Barry. Written by David Fisher. Music by Dudley Simpson. 4 × 25 mins. BBC 1.

Doctor Who: 'The Horns of Nimon' (1979–80) Produced by Graham Williams. Directed by Kenny McBain. Written by Anthony Read. Music by Dudley Simpson. 4 × 25 mins. BBC 1.

Doctor Who: 'The Leisure Hive' (1980) Produced by John Nathan-Turner. Directed by Lovett Bickford. Written by David Fisher. Music by Peter Howell. 4 × 25 mins. BBC 1.

Doctor Who: 'State of Decay' (1980) Produced by John Nathan-Turner. Directed by Peter Moffatt. Written by Terrance Dicks. Music by Paddy Kingsland. 4 × 25 mins. BBC 1.

Doctor Who: 'Warriors' Gate' (1981) Produced by John Nathan-Turner. Directed by Paul Joyce. Written by Steve Gallagher. Music by Peter Howell. 4 × 25 mins. BBC 1.

Doctor Who: 'Logopolis' (1981) Produced by John Nathan-Turner. Directed by Peter Grimwade. Written by Christopher H. Bidmead. Music by Paddy Kingsland. 4 × 25 mins. BBC 1.

Doctor Who: 'Castrovalva' (1982) Produced by John Nathan-Turner. Directed by Fiona Cumming. Written by Christopher H. Bidmead. Music by Paddy Kingsland. 4 × 25 mins. BBC 1.

Doctor Who: 'Kinda' (1982) Produced by John Nathan-Turner. Directed by Peter Grimwade. Written by Christopher Bailey. Music by Peter Howell. 4 × 25 mins. BBC 1.

Doctor Who: 'Black Orchid' (1982) Produced by John Nathan-Turner. Directed by Ron Jones. Written by Terence Dudley. Music by Roger Limb. 2 × 25 mins. BBC 1.

Doctor Who: 'Earthshock' (1982) Produced by John Nathan-Turner. Directed by Peter Grimwade. Written by Eric Saward. Music by Malcolm Clarke. 4 × 25 mins. BBC 1.

Doctor Who: 'Snakedance' (1983) Produced by John Nathan-Turner. Directed by Fiona Cumming. Written by Christopher Bailey. Music by Peter Howell. 4 × 25 mins. BBC 1.

Doctor Who: 'Resurrection of the Daleks' (1984) Produced by John Nathan-Turner. Directed by Matthew Robinson. Written by Eric Saward. Music by Malcolm Clarke. 2 × 45 mins. BBC 1.

Doctor Who: 'The Caves of Androzani' (1984) Produced by John Nathan-Tuner. Directed by Graeme Harper. Written by Robert Holmes. Music by Roger Limb. 4 × 25 mins. BBC 1.

Doctor Who: 'Vengeance on Varos' (1985) Produced by John Nathan-Turner. Directed by Ron Jones. Written by Philip Martin. Music by Jonathan Gibbs. 2 × 45 mins. BBC 1.

Doctor Who: 'The Two Doctors' (1985) Produced by John Nathan-Turner. Directed by Peter Moffatt. Written by Robert Holmes. Music by Peter Howell. 3 × 45 mins. BBC 1.

Doctor Who: 'Revelation of the Daleks' (1985) Produced by John Nathan-Turner. Directed by Graeme Harper. Written by Eric Saward. Music by Roger Limb. 2 × 45 mins. BBC 1.

Doctor Who: 'The Trial of a Time Lord' (1986) Produced by John Nathan-Turner. Directed by Nicholas Mallett, Ron Jones and Chris Clough. Written by Robert Holmes, Philip Martin, Pip and Jane Baker and (uncredited) Eric Saward. Music by Dominic Glynn, Richard Hartley, Malcolm Clarke. 13 × 25 mins plus 1 × 30 mins. BBC 1.

Doctor Who: 'Dragonfire' (1987) Produced by John Nathan-Turner. Directed by Chris Clough. Written by Ian Briggs. Music by Dominic Glynn. 3 × 25 mins. BBC 1.

Doctor Who: 'Remembrance of the Daleks' (1988) Produced by John Nathan-Turner. Directed by Andrew Morgan. Written by Ben Aaronovitch. Music by Keff McCulloch. 4 × 25 mins. BBC 1.

Doctor Who: 'The Happiness Patrol' (1988) Produced by John Nathan-Turner. Directed by Chris Clough. Written by Graeme Curry. Music by Dominic Glynn. 3 × 25 mins. BBC 1.

Doctor Who: 'Silver Nemesis' (1988) Produced by John Nathan-Turner. Directed by Chris Clough. Written by Kevin Clarke. Music by Keff McCulloch. 3 × 25 mins. BBC 1.

Doctor Who: 'The Greatest Show in the Galaxy' (1988–9) Produced by John Nathan-Turner. Directed by Alan Wareing. Written by Stephen Wyatt. Music by Mark Ayres. 4 × 25 mins. BBC 1.

Doctor Who: 'Battlefield' (1989) Produced by John Nathan-Turner. Directed by Michael Kerrigan. Written by Ben Aaronovitch. Music by Keff McCulloch. 4 × 25 mins. BBC 1.

Doctor Who: 'Ghost Light' (1989) Produced by John Nathan-Turner. Directed by Marc Platt. Written by Alan Wareing. Music by Mark Ayres. 4 × 25 mins. BBC 1.

Doctor Who: 'The Curse of Fenric' (1989) Produced by John Nathan-Turner. Directed by Nicholas Mallett. Written by Ian Briggs. Music by Mark Ayres. 4 × 25 mins. BBC 1.

Doctor Who: 'Survival' (1989) Produced by John Nathan-Turner. Directed by Alan Wareing. Written by Rona Munro. Music by Dominic Glynn. 3 × 25 mins. BBC 1.

Doctor Who: 'The TV Movie' (1996) Produced by Philip Segal and Peter Ware. Directed by Geoffrey Sax. Written by Matthew Jacobs. Music by John Debney. 84 mins. BBC Worldwide/Universal TV.

Doctor Who: 'Rose' (2005) Produced by Phil Collinson. Directed by Keith Boak. Written by Russell T. Davies. Music by Murray Gold. 45 mins. BBC Wales.

Doctor Who: 'Aliens of London' (2005) Produced by Phil Collinson. Directed by Keith Boak. Written by Russell T. Davies. Music by Murray Gold. 45 mins. BBC Wales.

Doctor Who: 'World War Three' (2005) Produced by Phil Collinson. Directed by Keith Boak. Written by Russell T. Davies. Music by Murray Gold. 45 mins. BBC Wales.

Doctor Who: 'The Long Game' (2005) Produced by Phil Collinson. Directed by Brian Grant. Written by Russell T. Davies. Music by Murray Gold. 45 mins. BBC Wales.

Doctor Who: 'The Christmas Invasion' (2005) Produced by Phil Collinson. Directed by James Hawes. Written by Russell T. Davies. Music by Murray Gold. 60 mins. BBC Wales.

Doctor Who: 'Doomsday' (2006) Produced by Phil Collinson. Directed by Graeme Harper. Written by Russell T. Davies. Music by Murray Gold. 45 mins. BBC Wales.

Dr. Strangelove or: How I Learned to Stop Worrying and Love the Bomb (1964) Produced by Stanley Kubrick. Directed by Stanley Kubrick. Written by Stanley Kubrick, Terry Southern and Peter George. Music by Laurie Johnson et al. 94 mins. Hawk Films Ltd.

Edward the Seventh (1975) Produced by Cecil Clarke. Directed by John Gorrie. Written by David Butler and John Gorrie. Music by Cyril Ornadel. 13 × 50 mins. ATV.

Fawlty Towers (1975, 1979) Produced by John Howard Davies and Douglas Argent. Directed by John Howard Davies and Bob Spiers. Written by John Cleese and Connie Booth. Music by Dennis Wilson. 12 × 30 mins. BBC 2.

The First Churchills (1969) Produced by Donald Wilson. Directed by David Giles. Written by Donald Wilson. 13 × 50 mins. BBC 1.

Forbidden Planet (1956) Produced by Nicholas Nayfack. Directed by Fred McLeod Wilcox. Written by Cyril Hume (based on a story by Irving Block and Allen Adler, itself based on a story by William Shakespeare). Music (credited as 'electronic tonalities') by Louis and Bebe Barron. 85 mins. MGM.

The Forgotten Faces (1960) Written and directed by Peter Watkins. 17 mins. Playcraft Film Unit.

The Forsyte Saga (1967) Produced by Donald Wilson. Directed by Donald Wilson and others. Adapted by Donald Wilson, Constance Cox, Anthony Steven and Vincent Tilsley from the novels by John Galsworthy. 26 × 50 mins. BBC 2.

The Four Seasons of Rosie Carr (1964) Written by Ted Willis. 4 × 50 mins. BBC 1.

Horror of Dracula (1958) Produced by Anthony Hinds. Directed by Terence Fisher. Written by Jimmy Sangster. Music by James Bernard. 82 mins. Hammer Pictures.

The Hound of the Baskervilles (1959) Produced by Anthony Hinds. Directed by Terence Fisher. Written by Peter Bryan. Music by James Bernard. 83 mins. Hammer Pictures.

The Hound of the Baskervilles (1982) Produced by Barry Letts. Directed by Peter Duguid. Written by Alexander Baron. Music by Carl Davis. 4 × 25 mins. BBC 1.

I, Claudius (1976) Produced by Martin Lisemore. Directed by Herbert Wise. Written by Jack Pulman. Music by Wilfrid Josephs. 13 × 50 mins. BBC 1.

The Illustrated Man (1969) Produced by Howard B. Kreitsek and Ted Mann. Directed by Jack Smight. Written by Ray Bradbury and Howard B. Kreitsek. Music by Jerry Goldsmith. 103 mins. SKM.

The Ladykillers (1955) Produced by Michael Balcon. Directed by Alexander Mackendrick. Written by William Rose. Music by Tristram Cary. 97 mins. Ealing Studios/Rank Organisation Film Productions.

Listen to Britain (1943) Produced by Ian Dalrymple. Directed and written by Humphrey Jennings and Stewart McCallister. 20 mins. Crown Film Unit.

Monty Python's Flying Circus (1969–74) Produced by John Howard Davies and Ian MacNaughton. Directed by John Howard Davies and Ian MacNaughton. Written by John Cleese, Graham Chapman, Terry Gilliam, Eric Idle, Terry Jones and Michael Palin. Music by Neil Innes. 45 × 30 mins. BBC 1 (seasons one to three) and BBC 2 (season four).

More Than Thirty Years in the TARDIS (1994) Produced and directed by Kevin Davies. Music by Mark Ayres. 87 mins. BBC Enterprises. BBC Video BBCV 5403.

Moulin Rouge (2001) Produced by Martin Brown, Baz Luhrmann and Fred Baron. Directed by Baz Luhrmann. Written by Baz Luhrmann and Craig Pearce. Music by Craig Armstrong, et al. 143 mins. 20th Century Fox.

The Nightmare Man (1981) Produced by Ron Craddock. Directed by Douglas Camfield. Written by Robert Holmes (from the novel *Child of the Vodyanoi* by David Wiltshire). Music by Robert Stewart. 4 × 30 mins. BBC 1.

Out of the Unknown: 'The Machine Stops' (1967) Directed by Philip Saville. Written by Kenneth Cavender and Clive Donner (story by E.M. Forster). Music and special sound by Brian Hodgson and the BBC Radiophonic Workshop. 60 mins. BBC 2.

Panorama (1953–) Edited by (inter alia) Jeremy Isaacs, Michael Peacock, Paul Fox, David Wheeler. BBC Television/BBC 1.

The Quatermass Experiment (1953) Produced and directed by Rudolph Cartier. Written by Nigel Kneale. Music by Gustav Holst (title music only). 6 × 30 mins. BBC Television.

Quartermass and the Pit (1958–9) Produced by Rudolf Cartier. Directed by Rudolph Cartier. Written by Nigel Kneale. Music by Trevor Duncan. 6 × 35 approx. mins. BBC Television.

Quick Before They Catch Us (1966) Produced by William Sterling. Directed by Derek Martinus, Morris Barry, Paddy Russell and James Cellan Jones. Written by George F. Kerr, Jack Trevor Story, Margot Bennett and John Gray. 20 × 25 mins. BBC 1.

The Seekers (1964) Written by Ken Taylor. 3 × 75 mins. BBC 2.

She (1965) Produced by Michael Carreras. Directed by Robert Day. Written by David T. Chandler. Music by James Bernard. 101 mins. Hammer Pictures.

The Singing Detective (1986) Produced by Kenith Trodd. Directed by Jon Amiel. Written by Dennis Potter. Music by various. 6 × 65 mins approx. BBC/ABC.

Solaris (1972) Produced by Viacheslav Tarasov. Directed by Andrei Tarkovsky. Written by Fridrikh Gorenshtein and Andrei Tarkovsky from a story by Stanislav Lem. Music by Edward Artemiev and J.S. Bach. 165 mins. Mosfilm/Unit Four/ Creative Unit of Writers and Cinema Workers.

Star Trek (1966–9) Produced by Gene Roddenberry, Gene L. Coon, et al. Directed by various. Written by various. Music by Alexander Courage et al. 79 × 45 mins. Desilu Productions.

Tonight (1957–65) Produced by Donald Baverstock. Directed by Alasdair Milne. Numerous × 40 mins. BBC Television.

Twelve Monkeys (1995) Produced by Charles Roven. Directed by Terry Gilliam. Written by David Peoples and Janet Peoples. Music by Paul Buckmaster. 124 mins. Atlas Entertainment/Classico/Universal Pictures.

Walking with Dinosaurs (1999) Produced and directed by Tim Haines and Jasper James. Music by Ben Bartlett. 6 × 30 mins. BBC/Discovery Channel/TV Asahi/ProSieben/France 5.

The War Game (1965; not transmitted by the BBC until 1985 although available for theatrical distribution from 1965 onwards) Produced, written and directed by Peter Watkins. 47 mins. BBC 1.

Whicker's World (1959, 1965–8) Produced by Donald Baverstock. Directed by Alan Whicker and Cyril Moorhead. Numerous × 30 mins (later 55 mins). BBC Television/BBC 1.

Zoo Quest (1954–64) Produced by David Attenborough. Directed by Charles Lagus. 12 × 25 mins. BBC Television.

Contributors

Jonathan Bignell is Professor of Television and Film at the University of Reading and Director of the Centre for Television Drama Studies. He is a series editor of Manchester University Press's 'Television Series' which includes his co-authored study *Terry Nation* (2004). He is the author of *Postmodern Media Culture* (2000) and *An Introduction to Television Studies* (2004), editor of *Writing and Cinema* (1999) and co-editor of *British Television Drama: Past, Present and Future* (2000) and *Popular Television Drama: Critical Perspectives* (2005).

David Butler lectures in Screen Studies at the University of Manchester. He is the author of *Jazz Noir: Listening to Music from Phantom Lady to The Last Seduction* (2002) and is active in practice-based research, collaborating most recently with the composer and jazz musician John Surman on *The Cairn* (2005).

Alec Charles has taught at universities in Britain, Japan and Estonia, where he served as Professor of Media and Head of Communications at Concordia International University, and also worked as a freelance journalist, commentator and screenwriter. He has been a writer and producer for BBC Radio 3, and has published numerous essays on film, television, journalism, culture and literature in Britain, Japan and the Baltic States. He is currently Senior Lecturer in Media at the University of Bedfordshire.

Kevin J. Donnelly teaches in the Department of Film, Theatre and Television at the University of Wales, Aberystwyth. Once a professional musician, his extensive publications on the relationship between music and the moving image include *Film Music: Critical Approaches* (2001) and *Pop Music in British Cinema* (2002).

Matt Hills lectures in Media and Cultural Studies in the Cardiff School of Journalism, Media and Cultural Studies. He is the author of *Fan Cultures* (2002), *The Pleasures of Horror* (2005) and *How To Do Things With Cultural Theory* (forthcoming). He has contributed work on fandom to books such as *The Television Studies Reader* (2004), *Horror Zone* (2005) and *Teen TV* (2004), as well as journals such as *American Behavioral Scientist* (2005) and *Spectator* (forthcoming).

Matthew Kilburn received his PhD, on eighteenth-century British history, from Oxford University in 1997 and has been research editor in eighteenth-century history at the *Oxford Dictionary of National Biography* since 1999. As well as writing and editing entries on royalty and aristocracy for the *ODNB*, he contributed entries on Terry Nation and Sydney Newman. He has also written on the use of the King Arthur figure in the eighteenth century, and has contributed to several *Doctor Who* fanzines.

Alan McKee won the *Doctor Who Magazine* short story competition (under 14 section) in 1984. His writing career never recovered and he has since failed to publish seven novels with Virgin's *New Adventures*. His heroes are Gary Gillatt and Russell T. Davies. He now runs the Television degree at Queensland University of Technology, Australia. He is the editor of *Beautiful Things in Popular Culture*.

Paul Magrs is Senior Lecturer in Creative Writing at Manchester Metropolitan University. He is the author of numerous novels, including *Marked for Life* (1996), *Modern Love* (2000), *Strange Boy* (2002) and *To the Devil: A Diva!* (2004) as well as several *Doctor Who* stories for BBC Books and Big Finish audio, creating the recurring character Iris Wildthyme in the process.

Fiona Moore is Lecturer in International Human Resource Management at Royal Holloway, University of London. An industrial anthropologist, her recent publications include *Transnational Business Cultures: Life and Work in a Multinational Corporation* and 'One of the Guys Who's One of the Gals: Men, Masculinity and Drag' (in *Changing Sex and Bending Gender*). With Alan Stevens, she has written *Liberation: The Unofficial and Unauthorised Guide to Blake's 7* (2003), as well as regular *Doctor Who* story reviews to *Celestial Toyroom*.

Andy Murray is a freelance writer and critic. He is a regular contributor to Manchester's *City Life* magazine, and the website www.kamera.co.uk. He programmes the annual 'Darkness Over Britain' screenings at Cornerhouse arts centre, is the biographer of Nigel Kneale, *Into the Unknown: The Fantastic Life of Nigel Kneale* (2006) and editor of the horror anthology *Phobic* (2006).

Louis Niebur is a musicologist at the University of Nevada, Reno, where he teaches courses on film, television and popular music. He received his PhD from the University of California, Los Angeles with a dissertation on the establishment of the BBC Radiophonic Workshop. His writings deal with such topics as electronic dance music, English football songs and gender issues in electronic music.

Daniel O'Mahony has an MA in Media Studies and is author of the *Doctor Who* novels *Falls the Shadow* (1994), *The Man in the Velvet Mask* (1996) and *The Cabinet of Light* (2003) as well as the audio drama *Storm Mine* (2004) for Magic Bullet's *Kaldor City* series and *Timeless Passages* (2006) for Big Finish. His first non-*Doctor Who* novel is due for publication in 2007.

Lance Parkin is the author of a number of novels and short stories. He was a storyline writer for *Emmerdale*, and has written and co-written a number of non-fiction books, including works on the writers Alan Moore and Philip Pullman. His *Doctor Who* novels and audio plays include *The Infinity Doctors* (1998), *The Gallifrey Chronicles* (2005) and *Davros* (2003).

Ian Potter is a freelance writer, having been curator of television at the National Museum of Photography, Film and Television for thirteen years. He is also a sound designer and occasional contributor to Radio 4's arts magazine *Front Row*. He has written five *Doctor Who* short stories for Big Finish Productions' *Doctor Who – Short Trips* range and has provided the sound design and post-production on three *Doctor Who* audio dramas for the same company.

David Rafer received his PhD from De Montfort University in 2003, specialising in myth and fantasy literature. His earliest memory of *Doctor Who* was 'The Power of the Daleks', from which he developed an enduring passion for science fiction. He is currently developing his doctoral thesis, 'Mythic Structures in the Works of C.S. Lewis', for publication as well as articles on Philip Reeve and J.R.R. Tolkien.

Dave Rolinson is Lecturer in Film Studies at the University of Hull. He is the author of *Alan Clarke* (2005) for Manchester University Press's 'Television Series' and has published articles on British film and television in various books and journals. Writing for such erudite fanzines as John Connors's *Top* and Colin Brockhurst's *Circus* started it all.

Dale Smith is an award-winning playwright and author of the BBC *Doctor Who* novel *Heritage* (2002). He once submitted a proposal for a sequel to Ian Briggs' 'The Curse of Fenric' (1990) to Virgin Publishing. He was so embarrassed by the politeness of Peter Darvill-Evans' response to such a terrible idea that he never dared submit a proposal again.

Alan Stevens has written for a number of telefantasy publications, including *TV Zone*, *Doctor Who Magazine* and *Celestial Toyroom*. He is the author, with Fiona Moore, of *Liberation: The Unofficial and Unauthorised Guide to Blake's 7* (2003). He has produced, directed and written various productions for audio, including Lawrence Miles' *Faction Paradox* series, as well as devising, with Chris Boucher, the *Doctor Who/Blake's 7* crossover series, *Kaldor City*, released through his own audio drama production company, Magic Bullet (kaldorcity.com).

Tat Wood is the co-author, with Lawrence Miles, of *About Time*, a multi-volume series of essays on *Doctor Who* published by Mad Norwegian Press throughout 2004, 2005 and 2006. He has written for *Film Review*, *TV Zone*, *Starburst*, *SFX*, *Dreamwatch*, *Doctor Who Magazine* and *X-pose*. Currently lecturing and tutoring, he is busy mentoring mature students from across the Commonwealth and the new Europe.

Index